The Ethical Emergency Manager:

Issues, Morality and Dilemmas

3rd Edition

David Etkin

Dedication

To my wife Deborah, my children Jonathan and Stephanie, my stepdaughter Heidi, and my grandchildren Ryan, Alice, and Alexandra. It is the loving relationships in my life that give it meaning and context.

Acknowledgments

Thank you to my valued colleagues who provided invaluable reviews and advice – Peter Timmerman, whose brilliant mind and lateral thinking makes every conversation with him a learning experience (and who wrote chapter twelve) and Mark Schwartz, who taught me so much about ethics. Special thanks to Catherine Kenny, who did an exemplary job editing this book.

Table of Contents

Chapter 3: Ethical Risk Assessment

Chapter 4: The Precautionary Principle

Chapter 5: Victim Blaming

Chapter 6: Duty to Respond

Chapter 7: Land Use Planning

Chapter 8: Humanitarianism

Chapter 9: Lifeboat Ethics and the Value of Life

Chapter 10: Special Topics

Chapter 11: Code of Ethics

Chapter 12: Eastern Perspectives on Ethics

Chapter 13: Concluding Thoughts

FOREWORD FOR THE ETHICAL EMERGENCY MANAGER

Emergency management professionals address the most diverse, complex risk portfolio of any field. Their risk portfolio focuses on risk to people, property, and the environment within interconnected and interdependent systems which are sensitive to small changes. It is their job, as a managerial function, to create a framework that can effectuate the necessary preparedness, mitigation, response, and recovery activities to reduce vulnerability to hazards and enable their constituents to cope with disaster. These professionals, whether they are working in a business, organization, community, state, or at the national level, must create expansive collaboration and coordination between a wide variety of partners and stakeholders in the public, private, and nonprofit sectors, as well as citizens. It is not an easy undertaking, but it is essential. Unmanaged risk can result in additional injury, death and destruction and can decimate regions, industries, and economies.

Yet, despite emergency management's expansive risk portfolio, the field has not yet been able to achieve the status of profession it has long sought. Such status is necessary to be able to set, maintain, and monitor expected levels of professional practice; control entry into the field; and, be recognized as the subject matter experts who are equipped to address the specialized body of knowledge that informs emergency management practice. The pursuit of emergency management professionalization is inextricably tied to the field's ability to understand, articulate, and be able to enforce ethical standards related to practice.

The responsibilities emergency management professionals have regarding safety, security, and operational resilience, clearly require the daily use of ethical thinking. Emergency management professionals must possess not only the required subject matter knowledge and expertise required to bear the responsibilities of practice, but also meet legal and ethical standards of care to their constituents, partners, stakeholders, and the field of emergency management. The weight of these duties has been carried for many decades by emergency management professionals who have aligned their practice with their own individual beliefs, employer expectations and standards, and sporadic guidance from within the emergency management community. Currently, there are no overarching ethical standards that guide emergency management practice. This needs to change, for the benefit of emergency management professionals and those they serve.

David Etkin has been furthering the discussion of emergency management ethics in the practitioner and academic community for many years. His tireless efforts focused on the importance, value, and challenges regarding the development of ethical standards for emergency management have resulted in ongoing initiatives that seek to advance this essential work. He continues his work in this arena with *The Ethical Emergency Manager*, which is destined to become a treatise in the development and examination of ethics in emergency management.

The Ethical Emergency Manager helps the reader understand not only the importance of ethics to emergency management practice, but also the myriad of ways in which ethical dilemmas may arise. Building from an overview of key ethical theories illustrated with practical examples that will resonate with the emergency management audience, *The Ethical Emergency Manager* takes the reader on a learning journey that is punctuated with opportunities for self-contextualization and engagement. The value of the book is as much in the pondering it prompts from the reader as it is in the content itself.

David's efforts to contextualize and sensitize emergency management scholars, educators, professionals, and students to the ethical dimensions of practice in *The Ethical Emergency Manager* will reap benefits for decades to come. These benefits will extend far beyond the readers of this book – they will accrue to the citizens, businesses, organizations, communities, and jurisdictions that these emergency management professionals serve. The challenge I present to each reader of this book is this: consider how you will use what you have learned from *The Ethical Emergency Manager* to enhance the practice of emergency management and advance professionalization efforts. David starts you on this journey, but it is yours to finish.

Carol L. Cwiak, J.D., Ph.D.
Department of Emergency Management
North Dakota State University

PREFACE

Welcome. Bienvenu. Bienvenido. أهلا بك. خوش آمدی. 欢迎.

ברוך הבא. स्वागत है. ようこそ. 환영. Желанный.

My experience is that most (though not all) people want to do the "right" thing. Certainly, the vast majority of emergency managers I have met are so inclined, with strong social justice leanings. But knowing what is the "right" thing to do can be challenging at times, either because a situation is murky or confusing, or because of an ethical dilemma where a choice must be made between two rights or between two wrongs. There are often no easy answers (or even any answers) that are singularly correct. But it is always possible for emergency managers to engage in ethical thinking, which provides a pathway to decision-making that creates greater levels of comfort and often arrives at better solutions.

> *"In civilized life, law floats in a sea of ethics."*
>
> Earl Warren, 1891-1974, 14th Chief Justice of the United States

When I began studying ethics about twelve years ago it gave me new insights; I only wish I had begun to read about this field earlier. It is my hope that this book will do for you what my studies have done for me, and be a doorway that helps you enter a world where you look at issues from a different perspective than you may have in the past—an ethical perspective. It may be that you are already there because of your natural curiosity or having been formally educated in the subject of ethical analysis, but many emergency managers have not had this exposure. I am writing this book for them, as well as for students studying in this field. Even for those who are inclined towards looking at the world from an ethical point of view, it is useful to be exposed to the many theories and studies that focus on this area. Ethics is fundamental to the theory and practice of emergency management, but its importance has not been sufficiently recognized within the profession.

Because of my strong interest in this field, I co-organized a webinar series and workshop on disaster ethics with Professor Olivier Rubin of the Copenhagen Centre for Disaster Research (postponed twice because of the COVID-19 pandemic), devoted a chapter to this topic in my textbook on disaster theory,[1] published several papers on ethics and emergency management,[2,3,4,5] and teach courses in disaster ethics at York University, Toronto, Canada. The graduate course is not a required course as is the undergraduate one on ethics, but those students who do enroll in it are passionate about the topic and often comment that it should be mandatory. If the field of emergency management is ever to become a recognized profession with governing bodies, then this will have to happen.

The main reason I wrote this book is because there was no text that specifically addressed the topic of emergency management ethics; thus, it fills a gap. It is also an important topic. I am hoping that you will not find this a dry, boring read. Many if not most academic books and textbooks are written in an impersonal and formal style that is not very engaging. Where possible, I have tried to avoid that approach and hope that you find this book both interesting and useful.

Everyone has their own set of values and biases that, if given the slightest opportunity, slant their analyses and judgements. In the interest of transparency (since my values and biases no doubt surface periodically in this book), I acknowledge mine as follows: I lean towards egalitarianism and communitarianism, and believe that a just society should care for those who cannot care for themselves. Thus, I lean to the political left, though I am an economic conservative and abhor debt. At the same time, I believe in personal responsibility for one's actions and am of the opinion that moral hazard should be avoided where possible. I am horrified by the damage our species is doing to the environment and fear the impacts of climate change and species extinction. Nevertheless, I have done my best to remain neutral as I wrote this book and hope that it is a useful tool for both students and practitioners of emergency management.

If you have any comments or feedback, please feel free to email me at etkin@yorku.ca.

Sincerely,

David Etkin

York University, Toronto, Canada

---

[1] Etkin, D. (2015). *Disaster theory: An interdisciplinary approach to concepts and causes*. Butterworth-Heinemann.

[2] Etkin, D. (2019). How risk assessments by emergency management organisations fall prey to narrow framing. *International Journal of Emergency Management*, *15*(1), 81-97.

[3] Feldmann-Jensen, S., Smith, S., Etkin, D., & Jensen, S. (2016). Toward a substantive dialogue: The case for an ethical framework in emergency management, Part 1. *Australasian Journal of Disaster and Trauma Studies, 20*(1), 45-47.

[4] Etkin, D., Feldmann-Jensen, S., Smith, S., & Jensen, S. (2016). Toward A substantive dialogue: The case for an ethical framework in emergency management, Part 2. *The Australasian Journal of Disaster and Trauma Studies, 20*(1), 49-53.

[5] Etkin, D. and Timmerman, P. (2013). Emergency management and ethics. *International Journal of Emergency Management, 9*(4), 277-297.

INTRODUCTION TO THE ETHICAL EMERGENCY MANAGER

"Look back, to slavery, to suffrage, to integration and one thing is clear. Fashions in bigotry come and go. The right thing lasts."
Anna Quindlen, New York Times, Jan. 31, 1993

"If no set of moral ideas were truer or better than any other, there would be no sense in preferring civilized morality to savage morality."
C.S. Lewis, "Mere Christianity"

"Believe me, Eugenie, the words 'vice' and 'virtue' supply us only with local meanings. There is no action, however bizarre you may picture it, that is truly criminal; or one that can really be called virtuous. Everything depends on our customs... What is considered a crime here is often a virtue a few hundred leagues away; and the virtues of another hemisphere might, quite conversely, be regarded as crimes among us."
Marquis de Sade, *Philosophy in the Boudoir*[1]

Figure I.1: Depiction of the Marquis de Sade[2]

I believe that almost everybody struggles with the question "What is the right thing to do?" at many times throughout their lives. Often these struggles relate to our personal lives, but they also emerge in a professional context where we have layers of duties and obligations prescribed by law, policy, and culture. The field of emergency management is no exception. Within the public sector the field exists to serve the common good of citizens, and within the humanitarian space it exists to aid victims of disasters. For this reason, at its most fundamental level, emergency management is an ethical and moral exercise.

How can one answer the question "What is the right thing to do?" Intelligent, well-informed, thoughtful people who want to do the "right thing" will often disagree in their responses to this question. The sources of these disagreements are many, and perhaps the most important takeaway from this book is that there is generally no one correct answer to this very important question. In that way, the study of ethics differs greatly from mathematics or physics, where finding the one correct answer to a problem is the ultimate goal.

An *Example*:

To illustrate some of the ethical and moral issues (note that I differentiate between the terms *ethical* and *moral* – more on that in Chapter 1) that must be faced within this field, consider the following scenario:

- You are the site commander where a building collapse has resulted in a number of deaths and several people (it is unclear exactly how many) being trapped under wreckage.
- Heavy Urban Search and Rescue (HUSAR) is on the way but delayed because of bad weather, mechanical problems, and distance.
- The situation is desperate for the trapped people and they have little time left if they are to survive. Temperatures are near freezing.
- The city engineer has told you that the situation is not safe and that if you send in rescue workers the probability is "moderate" that they may be caught in more collapses. You ask her what "moderate" means, but she is unclear in her answer. She emphasizes that her assessment is just a guess, since there has not been time or opportunity for a proper engineering analysis.
- The people in the community, especially the families of the trapped people, are demanding that you send in your rescue workers, and the premier of the province and the city mayor are both insisting that further rescue attempts be made. Your chief has said to you that as site commander the decision is yours, so you cannot defer the decision to another person.
- Fire rescue is willing to attempt to save the victims if you order it, but they are clearly reluctant, and their families (some of whom you have known for many years) are pleading with you not to send their spouses in because the risk is so high.

- A decision must be made immediately.
- There is a great deal of media coverage and you are at the centre of it.

My first reaction to this scenario is that I am thankful that I, as an academic, will never be placed in such a difficult situation (my worst conundrum is whether to fail or to pass a student who is doing poorly)! You, however, as site commander, must decide. What ethical considerations are relevant to your decision?

First, you must consider your duties and obligations (the difference between a *duty* and an *obligation* is discussed in Chapter 1).

- You have an obligation to keep your staff reasonably safe. The job is risky, a fact that they know and understand, but they have a right not to be put in unreasonably risky situations and this may be one of those times.
- You also have duties toward the victims, who have a right to be rescued, if possible.
- Which is stronger: the obligation or the duty?

Second, think about the implications for yourself. After all, what happens to you matters too!

- No matter your choice you will be pilloried by some, including the families of the victims if you don't attempt a rescue and the families of your staff if you do. Public opinion will certainly be aroused because of the media attention. Is this a no-win situation? Is one choice better than the other?
- Given that the premier of the province is demanding that you attempt a rescue, not doing so may be professional suicide. Are you willing to risk your career by not going in?
- Should career consequences to yourself be a factor in your decision?

Third, which approach serves the greater good?

- You know that not attempting a rescue means with certainty that a few will die. Those few may be saved if a rescue is attempted, but then you risk the lives of the rescue workers.
- The numbers might look something as follows: three deaths with 100% certainty versus six deaths with 50% probability. Those two calculations are mathematically equivalent.
- However, the exact numbers of people at risk and the 50% probability are guesses. You are faced with great uncertainty. Decisions are much easier when the probability of outcomes are well known. When they are not well known, doing a risk analysis and determining the greater good becomes deterministically impossible.

Fourth, consider the issue of character.

- You admire the virtues of courage, honesty, compassion and loyalty, and want to be the kind of leader who embodies them. What character traits would a virtuous person demonstrate in her decision-making process?
- Attempting the rescue would be courageous, but perhaps also foolhardy. Remember the charge of the Light Brigade?[i]
- It would also be courageous to resist pressure from others, especially political pressure. However, the presence of political pressure does not necessarily mean a particular course of action is wrong. Where is the boundary between fortitude and stubbornness?
- You feel compassion for the victims and their families, but also for the families of your staff.

Each of the above considerations is important, but the extent of that importance depends upon context. What if one of the trapped victims was a family member, a baby, or prime minister? Would that change how the above factors would be weighed? Suppose the victims were terrorists who had blown up the building? Is everybody's life of equal value or do some people deserve special consideration?

Ethical Analysis:

The purpose of an ethical analysis is to sort through these kinds of issues in a way that is transparent, explicit, and makes clear the values and reasoning used to arrive at decisions. Ethical analyses create clarity and provide narratives that explain the harm that is sometimes done to some as a result of having to make terribly difficult decisions.

The focus of ethical reasoning is often upon an individual, but it can also be on organizations or communities. Emergency managers work within institutions and for communities, and the degree to which they can engage with and apply an ethical framework will largely depend upon the support provided by those institutions and communities. It is for this reason that in Chapter 11 (A Code of Ethics for Emergency Managers), I emphasize that two codes are needed: one for individual emergency managers and another for emergency management organizations.

The values that emergency managers adopt and the principles that guide our decisions and actions reflect the complex society in which we work, and will vary according to many factors including culture, geography, religion and politics. There is no one universal doctrine for emergency managers, though there are common themes. Emergency management, everywhere, works to reduce human suffering, but how gender issues are addressed, for example, varies greatly according to culture. In some places, women's roles and rights are more restricted than in others, which impacts policies related to disaster risk reduction. One example of this happened in Saudi Arabia when religious police prevented

---

[i] The charge of the Light Brigade was a courageous charge of British calvary against Russian artillery on October 25, 1854, during the Crimean War. It was a disaster for the British. A poem written by Lord Alfred Tennyson praised the valor of the cavalry, in spite of the outcome.

schoolgirls from leaving a burning building because they were not wearing proper attire. They "stopped men who tried to help the girls and warned 'it is a sinful to approach them [sic].'"[3] Many of the girls perished.

There are some important fundamental ethical questions, such as "Is there an absolute morality or does morality only depend on culture?" These kinds of questions reside in the area of metaethics. A strong fundamentalist faith-based perspective would likely adopt the notion of absolute morality to a much greater extent than a more secular one. Abortion is a good example of this. The "right to life" perspective has strong religious support. Pope Pius XII said in a 1951 papal encyclical that

> Every human being, even the child in the womb, has the right to life *directly* from God and not from his parents, not from any society or human authority. Therefore, there is no man, no human authority, no science, no "indication" at all—whether it be medical, eugenic, social, economic, or moral—that may offer or give a valid judicial title for a *direct* deliberate disposal of an innocent human life.[4]

A more secular approach to this issue emphasizes the right of a women to control her body and reproduction.

Different kinds and levels of analysis can be done that are reflective of various ethical theories, some of which are mentioned in the scenario above. Examples include theories based upon duties, justice, the greater good, and virtues. Consider the issue of gun ownership in the United States. Arguments to restrict gun ownership generally address the greater good, arguing that fewer gun-related deaths would result from such a policy. Those in favor of gun ownership typically rely upon their right to own a gun according to the U.S. Constitution. This is, therefore, an ethical dilemma resulting from the use of two different ethical theories.

Ethical analysis can be very complicated and subject to varying perspectives.

Student Exercise:

- What can you say about the ethical perspectives of the authors of the three quotes at the beginning of this introduction?

- Do you agree with them? If so, why? If not, why?

Some ethical studies are descriptive, in that they describe the state of society. Others are normative and address the way things ought to be. Both are important and should be included in an ethical analysis, but differentiating between the two is crucial. Simply because something has been done historically is not an ethical argument that it ought to be done that way (though it may well be a legal argument). Though there is (hopefully) a strong connection between law/policy and ethics, a law or policy may be viewed as unjust by different cultures or generations. There are many examples of this, including apartheid, residential schools for First Nations children, and the internment of Japanese citizens during World War II.

This book is based upon the assumption that ethics is at the core of emergency management. One model illustrating this perspective is shown in Figure I.2. Knowledge, intelligence and technology are all powerful tools that help us accomplish our goals. Values and ethics point us in the right direction.

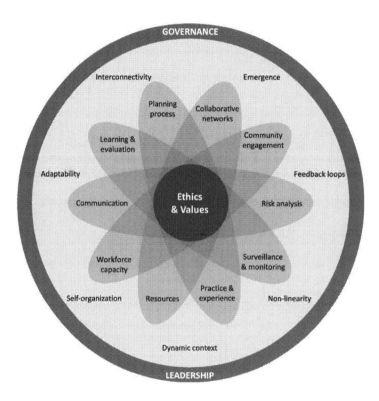

Figure I.2: Resilience Framework for Public Health Emergency Preparedness[5]

Overview of **The Ethical Emergency Manager:** The purpose of this book is to introduce students of emergency management and emergency management professionals to the topic of ethics as it applies to their profession. It assumes no prior formal exposure to ethical theory.

Chapter 1 overviews the main ethical theories that are relevant to emergency management. These include utilitarianism, deontological theory, virtue theory, environmentalism, social contract theory, paternalism and corporate social responsibility (which are not so much theories as moral stances), and care ethics. Each of these theories offers valuable perspectives, but by themselves are usually not adequate to deal with most of the ethical issues and dilemmas that societies face. Please keep in mind that although this is the longest chapter in the book it barely scratches the surface of these topics.

Chapter 2 addresses the moral development of individuals. We do not begin our life as developed moral beings. What are the stages people go through as they transition from children to adults and move towards greater moral sophistication? What does it mean to be a moral being? What moral traps restrict our ability to choose, and what are the characteristics of a moral leader?

Chapter 3 looks at how risk assessment can be approached from an ethical perspective. This is a serious issue in the field of risk assessment in general, and risk assessment by emergency management organizations specifically. Ethics is rarely, if ever, addressed in risk assessments, yet it underlies the assumptions and metrics used. How risk assessments are done in our profession must be expanded to include ethical considerations.

Chapter 4 discusses the precautionary principle. This is an important principle that must be in the toolbox of emergency managers. There are times when a risk assessment, by itself, is inadequate to address an issue and it must be augmented or replaced by a broader analysis that takes into account power structures, the rights of the vulnerable, and wherein lies the burden of proof.

Chapter 5 examines the trait of blaming victims for their suffering. Why do we do this, and when is it appropriate, helpful, or harmful? What disaster narratives incorporate blame, and why?

Chapter 6 reviews the literature on duty to respond and examines situations where it may or may not be morally justified. Though there have been very few significant examples of it occurring, surveys suggest that it could be a potential problem in some disaster scenarios. The current COVID-19 pandemic has shown that role abandonment has happened in some nursing homes for the elderly. Under what circumstances do people make this choice?

Chapter 7 looks at land use planning, one of the most important tools available to reduce exposure to hazard. It is especially important for riverine flooding. There is a tension between (a) paternalism, where the state determines the level of risk people can choose, and (b) libertarianism, which argues that individual rights trump the rights of the state to restrict how people live. To what degree should a society be paternalistic and prevent its citizens from living in high-risk zones?

Chapter 8 contrasts the old and the new humanitarianism, looking at the pros and cons of each approach. Should humanitarian organizations be politically neutral, or should they actively support social justice goals? What are the advantages and pitfalls of the two approaches? When humanitarianism is blended with other agendas such as politics or proselytization, how does that impact its morality?

Chapter 9 analyzes lifeboat ethic scenarios and the value of life. When resources are insufficient to save everybody, how do you decide to allocate them? Are all lives of equal value, or are some more valuable?

Chapter 10 examines a variety of issues within emergency management that have significant ethical implications including price gauging, disaster financial assistance, risk communication and pandemic planning.

Chapter 11 discusses the importance of codes of ethics and presents a Code of Ethics for emergency managers developed by a FEMA SIG ethics committee.

Chapter 12, written by Peter Timmerman, discusses how Eastern perspectives on ethics differs from that of the West.

Chapter 13 provides a few concluding thoughts.

Becoming an ethical professional is a process and a journey. This book is a starting point that I hope will provide a level of knowledge of ethics as it applies to emergency management that will allow you to begin that quest.

Endnotes:

[1] Sade, D. A. F. (2020). *Marquis de Sade quotable quote.* Goodreads.
https://www.goodreads.com/quotes/7621246-believe-me-eugenie-the-words-vice-and-virtue-supply-us
[2] Marquis de Sade, Wikipedia (n.d.). Depiction of the Marquis de Sade by H. Biberstein in L'Œuvre du marquis de Sade, Guillaume Apollinaire (Edit.), Bibliothèque des Curieux, Paris, 1912,
https://en.wikipedia.org/wiki/Marquis_de_Sade#/media/File:Sade-Biberstein.jpg

[3] BBC News. (2002, March 15). Saudi police 'stopped' fire rescue.
http://news.bbc.co.uk/2/hi/middle_east/1874471.stm
[4] Pius XII. (1951, October 29). *Address to midwives on the nature of their profession.* Papal encyclicals online.
https://www.papalencyclicals.net/pius12/p12midwives.htm
[5] Khan Y, O'Sullivan T, Brown A, Tracey S, Gibson J, Généreux M, et al. (2018). Public health emergency preparedness: a framework to promote resilience. *BMC Public Health,* 18(1):1344. Available from:
https://doi.org/10.1186/s12889-018-6250-7. Used with permission available from:
http://creativecommons.org/licenses/by/4.0/

CHAPTER 1: OVERVIEW OF ETHICAL THEORIES[i]

"A man without ethics is a wild beast loosed upon this world."
Albert Camus (1913-1960),
winner of the Nobel Prize in Literature
at the age of 44 in 1957.

Figure 1.1: Albert Camus[1]

Contents

---

[i] Adapted from Chapter 9 of Etkin, D. (2015). *Disaster theory: an interdisciplinary approach to concepts and causes.* Butterworth-Heinemann.

1.0 Introduction

The study of ethics is ancient and there are literally innumerable resources in print and on the web that discuss various ethical theories. (An excellent free online resource, though somewhat dense reading at times, is the *Stanford Encyclopedia of Philosophy*.[2]) Many of these resources delve much deeper into ethical theories than I have the opportunity to do in this introductory chapter. My goal for this chapter is simply to expose you to the basics of the main ethical theories that are appropriate to an ethical analysis for emergency management, which will be referred to in subsequent chapters.

In this chapter I focus on the following ethical theories and orientations:

- *Utilitarianism*, which refers to maximizing a utility such as happiness.
- *Deontological,* which refers to rule-based approaches addressing rights, duties and obligations.
- *Social Contract*, which is about the formal and informal agreements between citizens and the state.
- *Justice,* which is about people being treated fairly.
- *Virtue*, which emphasizes good character.
- *Environmental,* which addresses the value of the environment.
- *Corporate Social Responsibility*, which is about the duties of private sector corporations towards the public.
- *Paternalism,* which is based upon the use of power to help those for whom there is a duty of care.
- *Ethics of Care,* which emphasizes personal relationships and emotions.

Ethical analysis can be done at levels ranging from the individual (such as, should I respond to a disaster in my professional capacity even if my family needs me?), to the organizational (such as, how should we prioritize vulnerable groups in our response plans?), to the community and societal (such as, what are the duties of communities to their members or the government to victims who have put themselves at risk?). Framing a question or problem will suggest an appropriate scale, and this is important. There are times when individuals are blamed—it is common, for example, to blame operators for errors—when the problems that led to failure may be systemic. An example of this is the nuclear meltdown at Three Mile Island in 1979, where the company blamed the operators for the meltdown when there were other serious problems that were a function of plant design.[3]

It is important to state up front that the study of ethics is both fascinating and frustrating. Unlike mathematics, there is often (or even generally) no one right answer. This may be due to differing fundamental values, but can also result from the difficult issue of ethical dilemmas, where people must choose between two rights or between two wrongs. When faced with an ethical dilemma decisions are made that help some, but often exclude or harm others (perhaps through inaction). It is easy to justify helping, but difficult and painful to justify harming. These are the situations where having the knowledge and ability to construct and deconstruct ethical arguments becomes important.

Some basic terms that must be defined before we move forward with a discussion of ethical theories are:

Ethical Dilemma: An ethical dilemma requires making a choice between two rights (the greater good) or between two wrongs (the lesser evil). I had to deal with many ethical dilemmas while serving on a scholarship, bursary and awards committee for graduate students at York University. Particularly for bursaries, the committee members were faced with numerous heartbreaking stories of personal loss and challenges, but were only able to make awards to a select few. These few were able to continue their education; most of those who were not chosen either had to leave the university or face great hardship, and I expect that for many their lives were changed forever. It was, I have to say, a torturous process for us.

Egoism: Ethical dilemmas need to be distinguished from cases of moral temptation. Many people are tempted to do something wrong, perhaps because they benefit from it (such as stealing from others), but this is not an ethical dilemma; this is a choice between self-interest and morality, which is one aspect of egoism. There are two types of egoism. *Ethical egoism* is a normative theory about how people ought to behave. It argues that "we have no moral duty except to do what is best for ourselves" and that "each person ought to pursue his or her own self-interest exclusively."[4] By contrast, *psychological egoism* is a descriptive theory of human nature concerned with how people do behave, arguing that "people do, in fact, always pursue their own interests."[5]

Ethical egoism was made popular during the 1960s and '70s by Ayn Rand, author of *The Fountainhead* and *Atlas Shrugged*. I remember reading *The Fountainhead* as a teenager and being much influenced by it, though now I am far more skeptical of its philosophy of unbridled individualism. But where do the boundaries of self-interest lie? Does an adherence to ethical egoism mean that charity and sacrifice should be abandoned? That does not necessarily follow since human beings not only engage in competitive behaviors, but also cooperative ones, and a society where people help and support each other operates in the self-interest of all. We all engage in ethical egoism to a degree – but to what degree should people behave selfishly as opposed to altruistically?

Paternalism: This refers to those in positions of power making decisions for others in their care. This is not so much a theory as an orientation, but is fundamental to how states manage risk. Examples are the Children's Aid Society and restricting development in flood plains.

Ethical versus Moral: These words are often used interchangeably, but for the purposes of this book I use *ethical* to refer to perspectives or analyses based upon the ethical theories listed above, and *moral* to refer to specific standards of what is good and what is bad (or right and wrong). The former is process-oriented and provides a framework for analysis, while the latter is content-oriented and incorporates values. Two people might be ethically similar in that they have a preference for deontological ethical theory (see Chapter 1.2) in their arguments, but different in that they come to opposite conclusions because they disagree on their moral notions of rightness. An example would be abortion and the tension between the right to life of the unborn (i.e., pro-life) and a woman's reproductive rights (i.e., pro-choice).

Descriptive versus Normative: A descriptive ethical study is an empirical approach that examines how people and societies actually behave. A normative approach considers how they should behave according to aspirational moral standards. For example, a descriptive ethical study might conclude that many employees in some organization are corrupt because they take bribes. A normative approach might conclude that they should not accept bribes. Both areas of study are very important and complement each other. An ethical analysis should consider both descriptive and normative ethics. Obviously, difficulties arise when there is a significant gap between the two.

Meta-Ethics: Meta-ethics addresses more fundamental moral questions such as, "What is a moral value?" and "Are there objective truths?" It is about the status of morality, not about specific content. Aside from various ethical theories that must be explored, the following two meta-ethical issues are important to an ethical analysis.

(1) *Ethical Plurality:* When dealing with an ethical problem using just one theory is possible, but is a highly constraining approach that may lead to morally horrible outcomes when taken to the extreme. For example, maximizing happiness can lead to the destruction of the few in the pursuit of happiness for the many, if that goal is not constrained. A rules-based approach, such as telling the truth, could result in the disclosure of persecuted minorities during genocides. Courage is a virtue, but sometimes prudence may be a better choice when one is powerless. A blending of ethical theories in an analysis is called ethical plurality, and though not all agree with this approach it is the one that I am most comfortable with and support.

(2) *Universal Truths:* There is an ongoing debate regarding universal truths. One view is that there exists an absolute morality independent of culture, while the other view (called ethical or cultural relativism) argues that there is no such thing as absolute morality, but that rightness and wrongness depend upon context and cultural values. Some arguments for universal truths are based upon theology, the notion that knowledge of ultimate good flows from God. (There is an interesting sub-theme regarding whether God recognizes good or whether he creates it.) Other arguments are based upon naturalism, the notion that there are absolute truths that flow from nature itself. Discovering natural truths involves an analysis of human cultures and a search for commonalities.

> *"I not only believe in universal morality, but in more than one of them."*
>
> Gregory B. Sadler

Sometimes an issue is clearly not about right or wrong, but rather about personal preferences and cultural differences. Examples include one's taste in food or perception of beauty. Other issues prompt debates, such as acceptable types of clothing (or how much clothing is acceptable); while some argue that this issue is strictly cultural, others apply moral virtues to it (such as the wearing of hijab or going topless). As I write this chapter, an example of this is playing out in the Province of Quebec, Canada, where Bill 21 formally bans public servants such as teachers, police officers, and judges from wearing items like hijabs, turbans, kippas, and crucifixes in the course of their duties. The Bill also reinforces requirements for citizens to uncover their faces when accessing public services, such as municipal transit and the legal system. The Canadian Civil Liberties Association critiques this law as being unfair and disproportionately impacting marginalized people. Another example is murder, which is often considered a universal wrong.

Do you believe that there are universal truths?

- If so, what are they?

- Why are they universal?

One of the Ten Commandments is not to kill, yet most societies acknowledge that killing is acceptable in some circumstances, such as in war or self-defense.

Moral Status: Moral status refers to an entity (such as a person, animal or site of cultural significance) having its status matter in an ethical analysis. The greater the moral status (if indeed there are degrees of it), the more it will be a factor in decision-making. For example, if you believe that animals have moral rights, then these rights would play an important role when considering whether or not to convert a wildlife area for commercial use.

Moral Agent: A moral agent is a person who has the ability to engage in ethical thinking and can therefore be held accountable for his/her decisions. This is recognized in law in many societies. Some people such as children, those with cognitive disabilities, or the mentally ill may not be recognized as moral agents and therefore may not be held responsible for wrongdoing.[6]

Duties and Obligations: These words are often used interchangeably, but I differentiate between them in this book. Obligations exist because of an agreement, a contract, or because of a benefit received. For example, an employer is owed obligations because an employee is paid a salary and has an agreement of some sort with the employer. A marketing executive may have an obligation to convince people to smoke cigarettes or purchase a useless product, though this action would be considered immoral by many. Duties exist because of moral standards or because of a requirement under law. Examples include the duty to help a friend or family member, or the duty of care a parent has towards his or her children.

1.1 Utilitarianism

Utilitarianism has its roots in an area of ethical theory known as *consequentialism*, which focuses on consequences.[ii] Within utilitarianism what matters is how much good or how little bad results from actions. Broadly speaking, consequentialism is divided into two types: *rule consequentialism* and *act consequentialism*. The former is rigid and requires adhering to social rules that are expected to result in the best overall outcomes for society. Utilitarianism specifically addresses creating the greatest good. According to *rule utilitarians*,

> a) a specific action is morally justified if it conforms to a justified moral rule; and b) a moral rule is justified if its inclusion into our moral code would create more utility than other possible rules (or no rule at all).[7]

But since sometimes following rules results in sub-optimal outcomes (after all, no set of rules can be perfect), this approach will not create the greatest good in all situations. It is a very bureaucratic approach. Act consequentialism is much more flexible and means that an act is moral if it results in the best outcome, compared to all other acts. This requires an ability to define and measure goodness and to predict the future (both of which are clearly difficult to do, or to reach agreement upon). This approach gives great power to those who define the nature of goodness and how to measure it, and therefore creates the potential for bias and abuse. A strength of this theory is that it forces consideration of the consequences of actions. The most common form of act consequentialism is utilitarianism.

Punishing Innocents:

- In Canada and the U.S. (and elsewhere), the justice system will punish people for crimes based upon the principles of "preponderance or balance of evidence" in tort law and "beyond a reasonable doubt" in criminal law.[8] This means that some innocent people will inevitably be found guilty (since the police, judges and juries are imperfect) so that most guilty people are punished. There are documented cases of innocent people being found guilty of many crimes, including murder.[iii] Similarly, some guilty people will not be punished. Errors occur in both directions (these are called Type 1 and Type 2 errors).

- What percentage of innocent people would you be willing to send to jail to ensure that all guilty are punished?

- Explain the values and ethics of your decision.

[ii] One form of consequentialism similar to utilitarianism is hedonism; the former is about maximizing happiness, while the latter is about maximizing pleasure. Hedonism tends not to be part of emergency managers agendas (at least professionally).

[iii] Wikipedia has a long list of wrongful convictions at https://en.wikipedia.org/wiki/List_of_wrongful_convictions_in_the_United_States.

The father of modern utilitarian theory (Figure 1.2) was Jeremy Bentham (1748-1832). This theory proposes that actions are good if, on balance, they contribute to happiness and/or other moral goals or benefits. Utilitarianism is sometimes characterized by the notion of the greatest good for the greatest number, or the greatest net good for all those affected. This process can accept bad things happening to some people as long as the end justifies the means, though there should be limits on how much badness the few suffer. If unconstrained, application of the greatest good for the greatest number can be used to justify morally repugnant actions. An extreme example of this, using a financial cost-benefit analysis, might be to deny health care to people on social benefits.

"The happiness of individuals, of whom a community is composed, that is their pleasures and their security, is the end and the sole end which the legislator ought to have in view."

Jeremy Bentham

Figure 1.2: Jeremy Bentham[9]

This theory is based upon the maximization of some utility (happiness is one example), but if more than one goal exists then the approach must be one of optimization as opposed to maximization. Consider the two goals of money and happiness: maximizing one of those goals would probably diminish the other. Happiness depends largely upon personal relationships and research shows that after a certain point more money does little or nothing to increase happiness.[10] Optimizing the money-happiness system requires finding the "sweet spot" where you have enough money but are still able to devote time and resources towards other factors that make you happy.

Operating with multiple goals simultaneously in the field of emergency management (EM) is common. With limited resources, managers must choose between allocating resources towards the different EM pillars (mitigation, prevention, preparedness, response and recovery), and also have to choose which projects to support.

There are four basic questions in a utilitarian analysis:

- Who or what will be affected?
- What are the consequences?
- How to maximize (or optimize) utility (e.g. happiness)?
- How to minimize anti-utility (e.g. suffering)?

"Actions are right in proportion as they tend to promote happiness; wrong as they tend to produce the reverse of happiness. By happiness is intended pleasure and the absence of pain."

John Stuart Mill

Figure 1.3: John Stuart Mill[11]

Many social programs are based upon utilitarian goals where a harm (perhaps in the paying of more taxes) is done to many to create a benefit for a minority (such as building a library). An EM example is governmental disaster relief programs,[iv] though these programs may not be purely altruistic since taxpayers who contribute to them benefit from living in a more just and a healthier society, or because a common good is restored.

A common conundrum faced by utilitarians is agreeing upon what is good; different people or groups often view this in very different ways (examples are the value of life or health, the value of a forest, or the value of a political philosophy). A nature conservationist and a real estate developer are likely to have very different opinions about how to weigh the value of the natural environment as compared to a retail development. Another challenge, especially as it relates to the public good, is that foreseeing the future is very difficult, particularly in the complex and rapidly changing world in which we live. As a result, outcomes from different decisions made now cannot be easily evaluated or compared (especially if the problem being examined is a wicked problem[v, 12]). A high-profile example of such a debate is the

---

[iv] In Canada, for example, both the federal government and provincial governments have disaster relief programs.
[v] A wicked problem is a social or cultural problem that is difficult or impossible to solve for as many as four reasons: there is incomplete or contradictory knowledge, there are a large number of people and opinions involved, the problem involves large economic burden, and these problems interconnect with *other* problems. Horst Rittel was one of the first to formalize a theory of wicked problems. As noted by Jon Kolko, Rittel cites ten characteristics of wicked problems, as follows:

1. Wicked problems have no definitive formulation. The problem of poverty in Texas is grossly similar but discretely different from poverty in Nairobi, so no practical characteristics describe "poverty."

2. It's hard, maybe impossible, to measure or claim success with wicked problems because they bleed into one another, unlike the boundaries of traditional design problems that can be articulated or defined.

3. Solutions to wicked problems can be only good or bad, not true or false. There is no idealized end state to arrive at, and so approaches to wicked problems should be tractable ways to *improve* a situation rather than solve it.

4. There is no template to follow when tackling a wicked problem, although history may provide a guide. Teams that approach wicked problems must literally make things up as they go along.

5. There is always more than one explanation for a wicked problem, with the appropriateness of the explanation depending greatly on the individual perspective of the designer.

varying perspectives on the environmental and social impacts of climate change, and the need to reduce carbon emissions.[vi] This is also an important issue in the debate between the old and new humanitarianism (see Chapter 9).

The Trolley Dilemma

- Suppose there was a trolley heading towards five people on a track, but you had the ability to pull a switch so that it would hit only one person instead. Would you pull the switch? A utilitarian analysis would suggest that you should, since that would result in a net saving of four lives. On the other hand, do you have the right to condemn the single person on the top track to death?

- For those of you who pulled the switch, would you want a doctor to take the lungs, heart and kidneys from a healthy patient without consent, in order to save the lives of five other patients who need transplants in order to live?

- What is the difference, if any, between these two cases?

From an EM perspective, a utilitarian argument may support mitigation and prevention efforts for the purpose of creating efficiency. Most studies show very favorable cost-benefit ratios for mitigation

---

6. Every wicked problem is a symptom of another problem. The interconnected quality of socio-economic political systems illustrates how, for example, a change in education will cause new behavior in nutrition.

7. No mitigation strategy for a wicked problem has a definitive scientific test because humans invented wicked problems and science exists to understand natural phenomena.

8. Offering a "solution" to a wicked problem frequently is a "one shot" design effort because a significant intervention changes the design space enough to minimize the ability for trial and error.

9. Every wicked problem is unique.

10. Designers attempting to address a wicked problem must be fully responsible for their actions.

[vi] Issues around climate change are addressed in more detail in Chapter 3. Authoritative information on this topic can be obtained from a number of sources, including the Intergovernmental Panel on Climate Change (IPCC) website. Beware the many sites that provide biased and untrue information!

efforts[13] (although these efforts can also increase risk if they are badly done). Actions to prevent or mitigate disaster risk often require much smaller investments than the cost of response and recovery activities without such a priori actions, thereby contributing to efficiency and welfare maximization. However, from a political perspective investing in mitigation tends to be unattractive (except sometimes during a window of opportunity immediately after a disaster) because of the difficulty in convincing people that the needs of future disaster victims exceed needs in the present.

In *Ethical Land Use*, Timothy Beatley provides an in-depth discussion of utilitarian values as applied to land-use planning.[14] I found his book very useful and highly recommend reading it. Many land uses can create significant harm to society or the environment; examples include land and water pollution or an increase in flood risk. Beatley argues that land-use policy makers have the moral and ethical duty to prevent or minimize such harms, particularly if they are public harms. Post-disaster arguments to fund disaster risk reduction based upon a utilitarian framework assume that the marginal value of resources directed towards potential victims exceeds the value of those same resources directed elsewhere because of the acute needs involved, or because something is highly valuable (such as a critical industry or infrastructure).[15]

Various organizations promote the ethical use of floodplains in order to prevent flood disasters. The European Union Life-Environment Project proposes the "Wise Use of Floodplains," which puts ecology at the heart of integrated water management. This approach has ethical support from a utilitarian analysis, as well as from deontological and environmental ethics. The U.S. Association of State Floodplain Managers advocates for a "No Adverse Impact" approach, which is based upon the deontological principle (Chapter 1.2) that the actions of property owners should not adversely affect the rights of each other.[vii] Conservation Authorities in Ontario, Canada have been particularly good at restricting flood plain development in order to protect the public good.[16] Such is not always (or even normally) the case; significant development in flood risk areas frequently occurs in many parts of the world and is the primary cause of the increase of flood disasters.[17] Climate change may now also be playing a role and will almost certainly be an increasingly important factor in the future.

Public goods can be divided into those that are pure and those that are impure. A pure public good is equally available to all people; nobody is excluded and there is no rivalry (i.e., the resource is not scarce). An example where I live, in Toronto, Canada, is water. An impure public good is not equally available and there may be rivalry for its acquisition. An example is subsidized housing. One of the reasons why applied ethics during disasters is different than during "normal" times, is that during a disaster situation a pure public good can become impure. This is the motivation behind hoarding and

---

[vii] In the United States, the No Adverse Impact (NAI) floodplain management approach also supports the use of floodplains in such a way as to avoid flood damage. For more details visit the webpage of the Association of State Floodplain Managers at http://www.floods.org/index.asp?menuID=460.

the reason for triage, a situation when it is no longer possible for the medical community to meet the needs of all.

An ethical dilemma.[18]

You are a news reporter for CNN and also a medical doctor. You are covering the Haiti earthquake. There are reported threats of armed individuals in the area, and a makeshift medical tent has been abandoned by relief doctors. Security forces have also left. You can remain and attempt to keep the victims alive through the night or leave with the other doctors to safety.

- What is the nature of the ethical dilemma?

- What would you do?

This was the situation faced by Dr. Sanjay Gupta of CNN following the Haiti earthquake of 2010.[19] He chose to stay with the victims.

After analyzing issues related to limited resources, difficulties in preferential treatment of various groups, and incomplete preparedness, Naomi Zack argues that utilitarian ethics result in a best policy of "Fairly Save All Who Can Be Saved with the Best Preparation."[20] What is fair, of course, is subject to some debate. She proposes triage, random selection, or first-come first-served.

Utilitarian arguments are powerful when it comes to disaster ethics and should play an important role in disaster management. However, if unconstrained by ethical thinking related to rights, duties and obligations, these arguments can lead to morally repugnant actions, such as the abandonment of innocents or release of the guilty. One example of such a dilemma can occur during an evacuation; should criminals in prison (to whom society owes a duty of care) be released if there is a serious threat to their safety, though they may harm others if they do not remain in captivity?

1.2 Deontology or Duty-Based Ethics

"To be is to do."

"Do what is right, though the world may perish."

"Morality is not the doctrine of how we may make ourselves happy, but how we may make ourselves worthy of happiness."

Immanuel Kant

Figure 1.4: Immanuel Kant[21]

Deontology, an ethic based upon rights, obligations, and duties, argues that there are intrinsic goods and bads that are not situationally dependent, but that either should, or should not, be followed under any circumstances (thus avoiding an important weakness in utilitarian theory) no matter the outcome.

Immanual Kant, one of the founders of this theory, articulated the following imperatives in his attempt to ground ethical judgements through rational reflection:[22]

- *Universalizability:* Act only according to that maxim by which you can also will that it would become a universal law. (Should everybody do it, or would that be self-defeating?)

- *Reversibility (Golden Rule):* Do unto others as you would have them do unto you.[viii]

- *Respect (no exploitation):* Act in such a way that you always treat humanity, whether in your own person or in the person of any other, never simply as a means, but always at the same time as an end. (The end does not justify the means.)

In this theory, which applies to duties, obligations, and rights, morality is a function of the actions themselves and the intent/motive of those who are acting. The terms duties and obligations are often used interchangeably, but in this book I use the word *duty* to refer to that which is owed, but not specifically required by law or contract (such as the duty to help a friend), and *obligation* to refer to that which is owed and is required by law or a contract. Some duties can be considered as *perfect duties* (e.g., telling the truth) that should always be followed, and others as *imperfect duties* (e.g., the duty of self-improvement and the duty to aid others) that should be done as often as possible. For example, the duty to aid others is limited because of the needs of self-care and the impossibility of helping everybody in need. Some examples of duties are:

[viii] One problem with this rule relates to masochists. Do we want masochists in society to do to others as they would have others do unto them? For this reason, reversibility must be constrained by universalizability and respect.

- Voting,
- Donating blood,
- Tithing to the church (this might be considered an obligation), and
- Giving charity to those in need.

"Do unto others 20% better than you would expect them to do unto you, to correct for subjective error."

Dr. Linus Pauling, Nobel Prize Winner, 1954 and 1962.

Figure 1.5: Linus Pauling[23]

There are many lists of people's rights. The Universal Declaration of Human Rights, created by the United Nations in 1948, has 30 articles pertaining to rights and duties.[24] Two examples are: "Everyone has the right to life, liberty and security of person" and "Everyone has the right to a standard of living adequate for the health and well-being of himself and of his family... and the right to security in the event of... circumstances beyond his control."[25]

If followed absolutely, a deontological framework can be critiqued for not allowing gray areas. And one can argue that sometimes doing the "right thing" can result in horrible consequences (for example, choosing not to kill a terrorist about to explode a large bomb in a heavily populated area because killing is prohibited). In addition, social norms of determining what is right can be confusing, in part because of conflicting values, but also because of bias, since deciding on moral actions suffers from the influence of vested interests (as summarized by the saying, "the hat you wear depends upon the seat you sit in"). The philosopher John Rawls in his discussion of societal justice proposed a thought experiment using a "veil of ignorance" concerning our own interests in order to remove this sort of bias (see Chapter 1.3 for more on this topic).[26]

Along these lines Zack lists several values that are commonly accepted in western democratic society:

- "Human life has intrinsic worth.
- Everyone's life is equally valuable.
- Everyone has the same right to freedom from harm by others.
- Everyone is entitled to protection from harm by nonhuman forces."[27]

From these, a set of ethical principles follow:

- "We are obligated to care for ourselves and our dependents.
- We are obligated not to harm one another.
- We are obligated to care for strangers when it doesn't harm us to do so."[28]

- If you had to choose, would you allocate resources to very rich people who have suffered in a disaster, or to the homeless who are in much greater need?

- What is the ethical argument for your answer?

- What values is your argument based upon?

There are various implications of these principles for disaster ethics, depending upon the values espoused. One implication is reflected in the principle that preparing for emergencies begins with the individual, which is a common tenet in emergency preparedness in North America, where individuals are expected to be self-sufficient for 72 hours. Another implication is that various levels of government have duties and obligations towards their citizens related to emergencies through the functions of mitigation, prevention, preparedness, response, and recovery. The issue of whether policies and actions are mandated or voluntary is important. Libertarians, for example, hold liberty and property rights sacred and object to restrictions or costs imposed by government (though they may well consider charity a virtue). This became an issue during the U.S. presidential race of 2012 when Governor Mitt Romney criticized taxation to support disaster relief programs by saying it is immoral.[29] This has important consequences, such as for flood plain development. Libertarians do not like to be told that they cannot live in a flood plain. Communitarians accept such restrictions because of their dedication towards the common good.

Libertarians would also likely object to disaster assistance programs that transfer funds to victims, viewing it as a violation of the rights of non-victims. This critique is often perceived as harsh, and one could argue that not providing such aid violates the welfare rights of victims and principles of distributive justice.[30] Distributive justice addresses how wealth, opportunity, or welfare is distributed amongst the citizens of a community (e.g., equal to all, according to need, equal opportunity, etc.). Other preparedness actions such as purchasing family emergency response kits are clearly voluntary. It is difficult to decide upon the degree to which government should invest in or mandate risk reduction actions, but such decisions are important.

In western societies egalitarian values, based upon the belief that people are of equal moral worth and should have the same rights and opportunities, are widely accepted and can be considered a basis for disaster mitigation and relief programs. Dunfee and Strudel critique this approach, noting that equity issues might be applied to the distribution of resources or wealth, the distribution of welfare, or the distribution of opportunity.[31] The first approach is clearly fraught with difficulties, although in some countries social programs work to reduce the gap between the rich and poor. The second suffers from the problem that those who are worst off in society may not be disaster victims (in fact, disaster victims are often quite wealthy), and therefore it begs the question as to why resources should be diverted in that direction. Disaster assistance programs often favor the wealthy.[32]

In the public sphere, Canada and the U.S. have taken different approaches with respect to managing flood risk. Historically, the Canadian government has been far more paternalistic than the U.S. government which, unlike Canada, embraced a National Flood Insurance Program (NFIP). (However, as of 2019, discussions are underway between the Insurance Bureau of Canada and Public Safety Canada regarding a possible public-private partnership to address flood insurance.[33]) The net result of the NFIP might well have been to dramatically increase flood risk in the U.S. as compared to Canada.[34] One interesting study compared flooding in the summer of 1986 in Michigan and Ontario, and found that the difference in costs ($500 million in Michigan and less than $0.5 million in Ontario) was accounted for entirely by the greater degree of flood plain development in Michigan as a result of different governmental policies and regulations.[35]

The notions of intrinsic rights, wrongs, duties, and obligations have a long history in society and fill an important gap in utilitarian theory. Deontological theory underlies much of how society prepares for and responds to disasters. Different values can result in different sets of duties though, and inflexibility associated with some actions (such as stealing) can be an issue. For example, looting during a disaster in order to obtain basic goods such as food and water that are needed by your children would be considered acceptable by many, even though it is stealing. This issue received a great deal of media attention post-Hurricane Katrina.[36] General Honoré, the person ultimately brought in to coordinate the federal response, commented on this issue, saying, "It was way over-reported. People confused looting with people going into survival mode. It'll happen to you and I if we were just as isolated."[37] One variant of deontology is called "threshold deontology," which holds that beyond some threshold where consequences are extremely grave, acts that would otherwise be categorically forbidden become morally acceptable.[38] In other words, beyond some threshold deontology should be replaced by consequentialism.

In some countries social justice issues are strongly related to race. The worst victims of disaster are usually those without access to resources, wealth and power. Where race denies opportunities with respect to any of these factors, there are inevitable inequities at many levels – economic, health and social. One demonstration of this is that as of May, 2020 in the city of Chicago, though blacks make up 30% of the population, they account for 68% of the COVID-19 related fatalities.[39] Figure 1.6 compares demographic and COVID-19 fatality data in the U.S.). It is clear that Black populations suffer disproportionally compared to White. This is mostly, if not entirely, related to social determinants of health[40] such as access to health care, frequency of underlying medical conditions, lack of economic opportunities and living conditions.

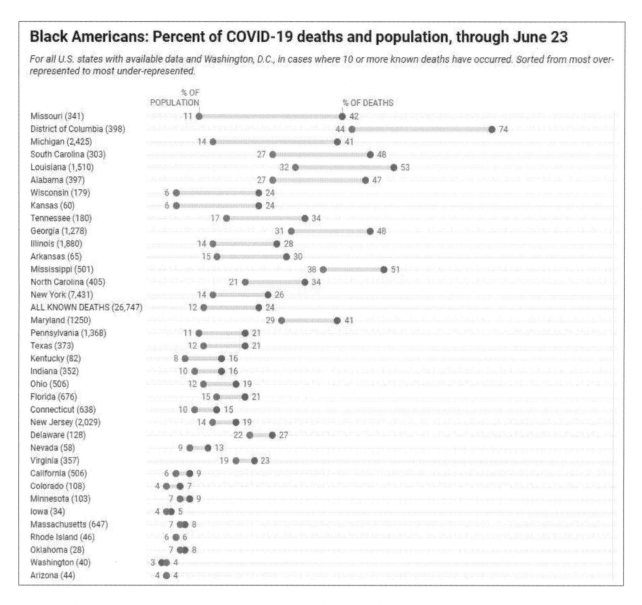

Black Americans: Percent of COVID-19 deaths and population, through June 23

For all U.S. states with available data and Washington, D.C., in cases where 10 or more known deaths have occurred. Sorted from most over-represented to most under-represented.

Figure 1.6: Black Americans: Percent of COVID-19 deaths and population[41]. In all states Blacks suffer disproportionally; in many states by huge margins.

Student Exercise:

- Make a list of several policies or programs under the categories of mitigation, preparedness, response and recovery, and comment on the obligations of individuals and government for each of them.

1.3 Social Contract Theory and Justice

"By me kings reign, and princes decree justice."

Proverbs 8:15-16

Social contract theory contrasts with the medieval belief that kings ruled through divine decree. It is based upon the notion that there is an agreement, implicit and explicit, between citizens and those who govern them, that specify rights, duties, obligations, freedoms, justice and liberties. In particular, citizens forego some rights and freedoms in order to live in a state that provides security and safety. It is then the responsibility of government to provide citizens with a society that is better than that which would have existed without such an agreement. John Locke, Thomas Hobbes, and John Rawls are important philosophers who have written on this topic. Fundamental to this theory is the question of "what is just?".

Notions of justice are eternal in human societies and discussions of it are recorded as far back as Aristotle and Plato in the western ethical tradition. For example, Aristotle is recorded as saying that "equals should be treated equally and unequals unequally", which is an expression of the notion of equity. Much earlier, The Code of Hammurabi[42] that was written between 1792 to 1750 B.C. is a set of 282 laws intended to create a just society, given the moral culture of the time. By todays' standards several of the laws would be viewed as draconian and unfair. As it related to the safety of buildings, the code specified the following:

- 228. If a builder builds a house for someone and completes it, he shall give him a fee of two shekels in money for each sar of surface.
- 229. If a builder builds a house for someone, and does not construct it properly, and the house which he built falls in and kills its owner, then that builder shall be put to death.
- 230. If it kills the son of the owner, the son of that builder shall be put to death.
- 231. If it kills a slave of the owner, then he shall pay slave for slave to the owner of the house.
- 232. If it ruins goods, he shall make compensation for all that has been ruined, and inasmuch as he did not construct properly this house which he built and it fell, he shall re-erect the house from his own means.
- 233. If a builder builds a house for someone, even though he has not yet completed it; if then the walls seem toppling, the builder must make the walls solid from his own means.

Justice is based upon giving people what they deserve, or their due. But how can that be decided? There are different approaches and criteria. It makes a difference what degree of control or agency a person has. Where there is no agency, for example, people are not held liable or are more entitled to compensation.

There are different kinds of justice, including retributive (punishing those who have done wrong), restorative (healing the wounds of victims and restoring offenders to law-abiding lives), compensatory (compensating victims for the harm done to them), procedural (having a just process that is transparent, unbiased, and gives a voice to all stakeholders), distributive (having a fair distribution of goods, wealth, power, etc.), and social (based upon the relationship between individuals and society, and addressing such issues as discrimination on the basis of race, gender, and religion).

An example of retributive justice are the penalties and fines given out to people who do not abide by public health measures during pandemics. This coercive enforcement approach is supported by the argument that it is needed in order to save more lives in society (a utilitarian argument), and that people have an obligation not to put others at risk and that others have a right not to be exposed to disease (deontological arguments). It does limit personal freedom however, and libertarians often object to it strenuously – hence the vigorous debate on this issue during COVID-19.

Examples of restorative justice are: (1) The Truth and Reconciliation processes held in South Africa after the end of apartheid (headed by Desmond Tutu when Nelson Mandela was president), and (2) The Truth and Reconciliation Committee of Canada, created to address discrimination and crimes committed against First Nations peoples by the Government of Canada. The latter came about as a result of the Indian Residential Schools Settlement Agreement, the largest class-action settlement in Canadian history.

An example of the application of distributive justice occurs during the allocation of disaster financial assistance to people and communities following a disaster. There are different approaches, such as providing equal amounts to all victims or giving greater amounts to those whose need is higher or who were impacted more severely. There is an important difference between equality and equity. Equality emphasizes giving the same to everybody, while equity emphasizes raising everybody to a similar level (the more needy get proportionally more). In disaster management, equity is generally accepted as a more important principle than equality.

From a procedural justice perspective, it is important how disaster financial assistance is allocated; the rules must be transparent, unbiased, accurate, representative, consistent, and fair. Where resources are allocated because of political favor or corruption then trust in governance is lost and the utility of the assistance will be reduced.

Social justice is important in vulnerability and capacity assessments. Where groups of people are discriminated against and have lesser access to resources, they are more vulnerable and inevitably suffer more in disasters. It is difficult to overemphasize the importance of social justice to how vulnerability is created; it includes issues of race, ethnicity, gender, class, and religion.

The stability of society depends upon people believing that they are being treated fairly or justly. And, as pointed out by Kant, human beings are equal in having the same dignity and being deserving as being treated as equals. Where decisions are arbitrary or subject to bias, their dignity is violated. John Rawls published *A Theory of Justice* in 1971 and posited the interesting notion of decision-making to achieve distributive justice behind a veil of ignorance to avoid bias or the influence of vested interests.[43] From this he developed "Two Principles of Justice," which determine how economic goods and civil liberties are distributed in society. The first principle maximizes the total amount of liberty, ensuring that they are granted to all (with the constraint that the liberties of people do not infringe upon the liberties of others), while the second principle allows inequalities, but requires that there be equal opportunity with the greatest benefit going to the least advantaged (with the proviso that some benefit is saved for future generations).

The notion of a social contract is fundamental to disaster management, both in planning and response. In *Famine Crimes*, Alex de Waal places social contracts at the center of his analysis, noting, "History is replete with successful methods of preventing famine."[44] Common to these methods are versions of a "political contract that impose political obligations on rulers. In the most effective anti-famine contracts, famine is a political scandal."[45] He also says that "An important step in that struggle is for those directly affected by famine to reclaim this moral ownership," referring to the tendency for humanitarian organizations to co-opt moral ownership of famines during the relief stage.[46] This is an argument against being overly paternalistic.

In western democracies such a contract does exist, both informally in the minds of citizens and formally through legislation and policy. The mission of FEMA in the United States, for example, is "to support our citizens and first responders to ensure that as a nation we work together to build, sustain, and improve our capability to prepare for, protect against, respond to, recover from, and mitigate all hazards."[47] Similarly, the mandate of Public Safety Canada is "to keep Canadians safe from a range of risks such as natural disasters, crime and terrorism."[48] Citizens, as part of the social contract, give up freedoms in exchange for the benefits that government can provide; thus, it follows that federal, state, provincial, and municipal governments have obligations to engage in disaster risk reduction activities. This is not to say that individuals do not have responsibilities as well; they do (for example, purchasing insurance if it is available). The issue of where individual obligations and duties end and collective ones begin is a complex problem that can only be resolved through social discourse. As society becomes increasingly dependent upon critical infrastructure far beyond the locus of control of any individual or small group, the obligations and duties of government become greater. Neoliberalism complicates this issue by advocating for the transfer of control of the economy to the private sector.

Social contracts are the basis for disaster risk reduction activities undertaken by different levels of government; yet, an unclear and worrisome region exists where government intervention may be deemed excessive by those whose rights are being constrained. Pre-disaster, this issue especially relates to land-use planning, building codes, and other forms of government regulation designed to reduce disaster risk. In the post-disaster state (response and recovery), the issue of when governments can adopt extraordinary powers to respond and when those powers should be rescinded is critical. This became an issue in Canada during the "Freedom Convoy" protests of 2022, when the federal government enacted emergency legislation to protect public safety[49]. Governments do have the responsibility to ensure they can continue to function (hence the emphasis on Continuity of Operations programs) in order to fulfill their side of the contract.

At times, however, such powers can become the new normal as rulers use a post-disaster period to bolster their power or restructure society to benefit elites. This is the basis of much of Naomi Klein's argument in in *The Shock Doctrine*.[50] An example of this, Jay Arena argues in his emotional article "A People's Reconstruction" in the magazine *Jacobin*, occurred during the reconstruction of New Orleans after Hurricane Katrina.[51] He quotes a real-estate entrepreneur saying, "We finally cleaned up public housing. We couldn't do it, but God could," and that

> authorities have not only demolished all of the city's remaining traditional public housing, but have also converted almost the entire public school system into charters, eliminated the teachers' collective bargaining agreement (which the U.S. Supreme Court has recently sanctioned by refusing to hear a court challenge), and have overseen the permanent closure — despite it receiving little flood damage — of the public hospital dedicated to serving the poor.[52]

Kevin Gotham also discusses the implementation of neoliberal policies in New Orleans, saying,

> With increasing frequency since the 1980s, government officials and agencies have applied privatization strategies at the federal, state, and city levels to a wide variety of services, from road maintenance to weapons development to human service provision. Over the last decade, prisons, public water supplies, public transportation, and military contracting have also become the targets of these strategies.[53]

He notes that these policies have been enacted in New Orleans post-Katrina with various negative consequences. For instance, he says, "Privatization is not a pragmatic or impartial response to governance problems or policy limitations; instead, it represents an assault on traditional relays of democratic accountability."[54] The conclusion of his article is available in the Appendix at the end of this Chapter. I have included it because it highlights the strong links between ethics and political philosophy.

Zack spends a good deal of time in her book *Ethics for Disaster* discussing the difference between security and safety, and the problems that arise when the two are conflated as security.[55] This issue developed in many western countries, and particularly in the U.S., after the terrorist attack of September 11, 2001. She argues that a diminishment of public safety occurs under such a situation "in favor of more dramatic police and military initiatives for security."[56] Other scholars of disaster studies such as James Mitchell have made similar arguments.[57]

Without trust, the social contract in western democracies cannot function well. Unfortunately, trust in politicians tends to be very weak in much of the world (See Figure 1.7, where they are ranked as least trustworthy). Different professions tend to have very different trust levels, as shown in Figures 1.7 and 1.8a, and these levels of trust have important implications with respect to governance and risk communication. In some countries levels of public trust in government have been decreasing (Figure 1.8b); in the U.S. for example, trust have decreased from over 70% in the 1950s to around 20% in 2015 .

Trust in professions varies by country; for example, high levels of trust in scientists range from 76% in Russia to 40% in Japan. A broad measure of the level of trust by civil society can be calculated by subtracting the levels of low trust (4-5) from the levels of high trust (1-2) (Figure 1.8).

Social contract theory does not conflict with utilitarianism or Kantian ethical theories; rather, these theories may be the basis for the type of contract that exists. As well, social contracts are not static but evolve with changes in environment and culture, and can be quite different depending upon the social philosophy of the political party currently in power.[ix, 58]

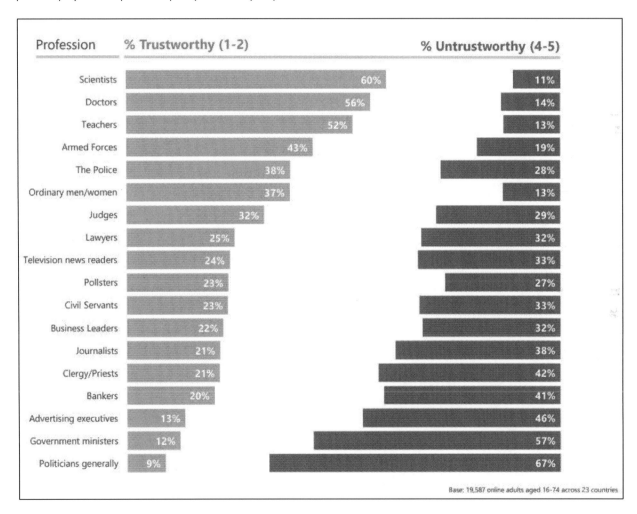

Figure 1.7: Global Trust by Profession (IPOX Survey). Caveat: 15 of the 23 countries surveyed online generate nationally representative samples in their countries (Argentina, Australia, Belgium, Canada,

---

[ix] For example, in 2008 the Myanmar government refused international aid in the wake of a typhoon disaster.

France, Germany, Great Britain, Hungary, Italy, Japan, Poland, South Korea, Spain, Sweden, and the United States).[59]

Student Exercise:

- From a risk perspective, the world is changing rapidly due to phenomena such as globalization, shifting political alliances, environmental destruction, species extinction, greater dependence upon critical infrastructure, etc. Old hazards are evolving and new hazards are emerging, exposure to many hazards is increasing, and vulnerabilities are changing.

- How should social contracts evolve to reflect these realities?

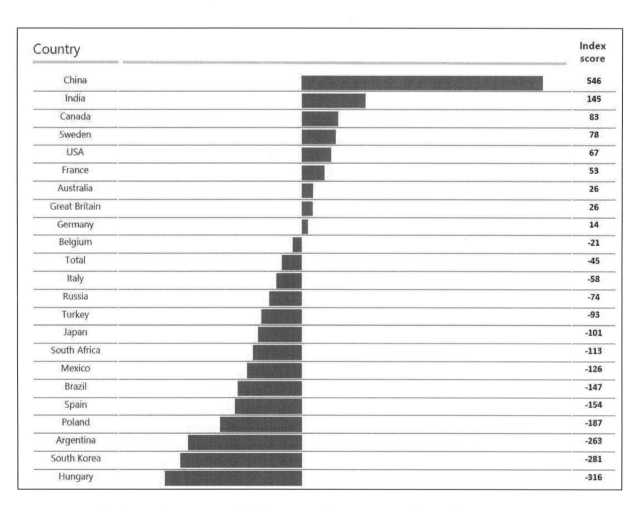

Country	Index score
China	546
India	145
Canada	83
Sweden	78
USA	67
France	53
Australia	26
Great Britain	26
Germany	14
Belgium	-21
Total	-45
Italy	-58
Russia	-74
Turkey	-93
Japan	-101
South Africa	-113
Mexico	-126
Brazil	-147
Spain	-154
Poland	-187
Argentina	-263
South Korea	-281
Hungary	-316

Figure 1.8a: Global Trust by Country. Global Trustworthiness Index = (Sum of high trust in all professions) - (Sum of low trust in all professions). (IPOX Survey). Caveat: 15 of the 23 countries surveyed online

generate nationally representative samples in their countries (Argentina, Australia, Belgium, Canada, France, Germany, Great Britain, Hungary, Italy, Japan, Poland, South Korea, Spain, Sweden, and the United States).[60]

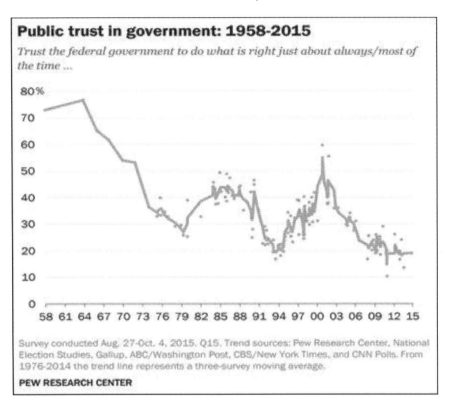

Figure 1.8b. Trends in public trust in the U.S.[61]

1.4 Paternalism

The degree to which personal liberties should be considered sacrosanct versus how far government should be allowed to restrict those liberties (i.e., developing in high risk zones) relates to the notion of paternalism. Paternalism acts to protect individuals from themselves. Such actions are accepted for children by their parents or the state, or for people who are clearly unable to make good decisions such as those who suffer from certain cognitive disabilities. But for others, to what degree is the state justified in making paternalistic decisions? Examples of state regulations on risk include rules for bike helmets, seat belts, and air bags; building codes and building inspectors; and conservation authorities limiting the ability of individuals or companies to build how and where they want.

Paternalism as a duty of government is one argument used in protecting homes in the urban-rural interface against wildfire. Those who wish to live in or near forests argue that they have the right to decide what risks they accept and should be allowed to do so. (For example, the FireSmart Canada Program makes homeowners responsible for deciding whether or not the principles should be adopted for themselves.[62]) This argument is imperfect, however, since there are larger social costs during wildfire response and many people are not fully aware of all the risks they are exposed to when making the decision to live in or near forests. Additionally there may be others, such as children, who do not knowingly or willingly undertake a risk. Furthermore, when disaster strikes, the harmful consequences are rarely only borne by those directly affected. Rather, they ripple outwards; once a risky development exists it affects future generations to whom we may owe duties and obligations.

Question to Ponder:

- Over time, what is considered a public good has changed. Society's dependence on critical infrastructure is much greater than it was in the past, and yet a large majority of critical infrastructure is owned by the private sector. Private companies do not have obligations to the public good the way that a democratic government does since their main duty is to their stockholders.

- How should the ethical obligations governments owe to their citizens take into account this shift of what is considered a public good?

Another justification for paternalism relates to the notions of bounded rationality and biases in risk perception.[63] It is simply not always possible for an individual to have access to the risk-related information they need to have, or to be able to process it even if they obtain it. Therefore, the need for experts to assess risk can be a justification for paternalism (an interesting aspect of risk theory called *risk homeostasis* is relevant to paternalism[64]). For all these reasons, a paternalistic attitude by the state may be justified. There is, of course, a downside to paternalism as well. People and communities are often better judges of the risks they face—at least in some ways—than outside experts who can become overconfident about solving problems in different areas. As well, allowing others to control risk management can create its own risks related to incompetence, indifference or corruption.[65]

1.5 Virtue Ethics[x]

"Courage is the most important of all the virtues, because without courage you can't practice any other virtue consistently. You can practice any virtue erratically, but nothing consistently without courage."

Maya Angelou, poet, writer, singer, and civil rights activist (1928-2014)

---

[x] This section was co-authored with Professor Peter Timmerman, York University.

"Heaven and hell suppose two distinct species of men, the good and the bad. But the greatest part of mankind float betwixt vice and virtue."

David Hume, philosopher (1711–1776)

"All virtue is summed up in dealing justly."

Aristotle, Greek philosopher (384–322 BC)

Virtue ethics emphasizes character—right being over right action. This form of ethics is different from utilitarianism and deontological theories in that it does not consider actions explicitly; rather, it considers what character traits and virtues a person should adopt, which in turn will help them to live a moral life and choose moral actions. Its founders go far back in time and include the Greek philosophers Plato and Aristotle. But what is a virtue? It may be considered a trait that results from good motivations and that contributes to the flourishing, happiness, or well-being of others (known as eudaimonia).

In terms of how we plan for and respond to disasters, there are many character traits of significance, including honesty, caring, compassion, generosity, empathy, impartiality, integrity (which refers to acting consistently according to one's stated values or principles), diligence, kindness, openness, reliability, resoluteness, respectfulness, sensitivity, tolerance, toughness, trustworthiness, and truthfulness.

Can a virtue sometimes be a fault? Aristotle discussed the importance of the *mean*, which lies between extremes of behaviors. For example, a right amount of courage may lie between being reckless and being cowardly, and good motivations may not always result in good outcomes; virtues are highly contextual. When I was younger I was a volunteer at a distress centre call line. Our trainers emphasized the importance of being sympathetic, but not too empathetic (i.e., feeling the pain of the caller). Too much empathy was self-destructive and resulted in burnout. According to Aristotle a moral person will act in accordance with reason as well as emotion. Those who are ruled by their appetites or passions will have difficulty recognizing or acting in reasonable ways.

Larkin and Arnold in their paper on ethics and emergency planning "espouse the notion that virtue-based ethics are more adaptable to the multiplicity of rapidly changing disaster circumstances than mere principles, rules and protocols, particularly since the scope, magnitude, and dynamics of a particular... challenge cannot be determined in advance."[66]

People will often identify virtues through positive and negative exemplars. These are our heroes and villains who we admire and strive to emulate, or despise and reject. Much of our arts are devoted to the portrayal of heroes and villains. I consider people such as Nelson Mandela, Albert Sweitzer, and Ghandi to be heroic exemplars.

Zack emphasizes the importance of integrity and diligence, noting, "In morally ambiguous extreme cases, we do well to rely on the character or virtues of those in positions to make decisions."[67] Personal networks and relationships are critical to effective disaster management, and unless there are trusting relationships in place, any process is likely to become dysfunctional. Co-workers and victims alike must have trust in the competence and character of those managing disasters.

Within the list of important character traits we should include how people view others in terms of their moral worth. The philosophy of Martin Buber provides an interesting and useful perspective on this issue.[68] According to Buber human beings may adopt two attitudes toward the world, *I-Thou* or *I-It*. Within an I-It relationship objects or beings are viewed by their functions. In the large and complex world we live in, this inevitably represents the majority of relationships. In an I-Thou relationship one engages in a mutual dialogue that goes beyond function and acknowledges the fundamental worth of the other. Unlike I-It relationships, I-Thou relationships are imbued with rights, duties, and moral worth. I believe, as suggested by Buber, that this disconnect takes form primarily as a lack of empathy.[xi]

Figure 1.9: Martin Buber[69]

This theme is also echoed in the works of others. For example, Thomas Homer Dixon, writing about challenges in dealing with future risk, says, "I believe this will be the central challenge – as ingenuity gaps widen the gulfs of wealth and power among us, we need imagination, metaphor and empathy more than ever, to help us remember each other's essential humanity."[70] At the core of empathy must be an acknowledgment of I-Thou relationships. Vanderberg makes this point as well, when he says, "[T]echnological and economic growth are guided primarily by performance values rather than by human and social values," and that it is critical to understand the larger social context and to ensure that technological and economic systems are compatible with it.[71]

In disaster management human beings are often treated as a means towards the greater good of the greater number—including themselves! In that sense, they are turned into objects/obstacles. A familiar example is when you are running to get somewhere, and someone is standing in your way; they have ceased for the moment to be a human being and are now a thing in your way. In an emergency people can very quickly be turned into obstacles to the greater good, and are thus transformed into an "It" as opposed to a "Thou." The most famous expression of this situation is to be found in Simone Weil's work on violence (see *War and the Iliad* by Simone Weil and Rachel Bespaloff).[72] Weil argues that part of the essence of violence is the turning of one's opponent into a thing (e.g., dead meat) as one inflicts violence. In order to get to one's goal, one must cut through the opposition. The goal is what matters; the dead or ruined that one creates as one drives towards that goal are merely collateral damage.

[xi] Buber believed that the expansion of a purely analytic, material view of existence was at heart an advocation of 'I-It' relations—even between human beings.

"'Do you feel no compunction, Socrates, at having followed a line of action which puts you in danger of the death penalty?'

"I might fairly reply to him, 'You are mistaken, my friend, if you think that a man who is worth anything ought to spend his time weighing up the prospects of life and death. He has only one thing to consider in performing any action—that is, whether he is acting rightly or wrongly, like a good man or a bad one.'"
— Socrates, *Apology*[73]

Figure 1.10: Socrates[74]

A bureaucracy or a dedicated force attempting to resolve an emergency or disaster situation can be all too prone to consider people as inconvenient things, even though saving people is what the activity is about. The experiences of Bradshaw and Slansky, two paramedics caught in New Orleans during Hurricane Katrina, reflect this as they observe the following about their treatment: "This official treatment was in sharp contrast to the warm, heart-felt reception given to us by the ordinary Texans. [...] Throughout, the official relief effort was callous, inept, and racist."[75]

Examples of I-It relationships resulting in disastrous outcomes in human terms abound. One classic case involves explosions of the Ford Pinto in the 1970s due to a defective fuel system design in which gas tanks often ruptured and exploded in crashes over 25 miles per hour. This may have cost the lives of between 500 and 900 people. The cost of repair was estimated to be larger than the cost of lawsuits from deaths, injuries, and car damages resulting from the explosions, and so Ford Motor Co. did not feel a recall was justified. The result of this decision was that many people were injured or killed unnecessarily. In fact, during the period of Ford's successful delaying tactics against Federal Motor Vehicle Safety Standard 301 between 1968 and 1972, 9,000 people were burned to death in all car accidents in the USA and over ten million new unsafe cars were sold.[76] A cost-benefit analysis like the one used by Ford placed people in the category of things. Another example of a disaster that resulted from categorizing people as things is the Johnstown flood of May 3, 1889, which resulted from the catastrophic failure of a dam developed by a group of rich speculators, who used it to create an exclusive resort.[77] The dam was inadequately maintained, primarily because the dam owners did not want to spend the money needed to do so, in spite of the risk to downstream communities. It was an instance of the elite abusing their power, with risk being transferred to other less powerful and less fortunate groups.

Both these examples illustrate a fundamental barrier to effective disaster management. When the institutions and people who construct risk are disconnected from those who bear its negative consequences, relationships become of an I-It kind, thus removing the issue of moral/ethical values from the risk management equation and reducing it to simple economics. As noted by Jonathan Glover, "It is more difficult to commit an atrocity against others if they have dignity and respect."[78]

"Real and fictional case studies in disasters seem to favor egalitarian or deontological moral principles over those of efficiency or a simple utilitarianism that saves the greatest number. In morally ambiguous extreme cases, we do well to rely on the character or virtues of those in positions to make decisions."

Naomi Zack, Ethics for Disaster

One expression of this humanistic approach has been the development of care ethics, a gendered ethic emerging from feminist philosophy that emphasizes the importance of feeling and sentiment in morality.[79] Caring ethics is distinguished from ethical behavior based upon duty by striving to maintain a caring attitude.[80]

The Parable of the Sadhu.[81] This article received the *Harvard Business Review*'s Ethics Prize in 1983.

- McCoy, a manager at Morgan Stanley, is fulfilling (at great expense) a life-long dream of climbing in the Himalayan mountains in Nepal. McCoy must decide whether to climb over the mountain pass or to give up on his dream and take care of a Sadhu (Indian holy man). McCoy decides to provide some aid, but then to leave the Sadhu with friend Stephen and continue his climb.

- Stephen, later said to McCoy, "How do you feel about contributing to the death of a fellow man?" "I wonder what the Sherpas would have done if the Sadhu had been a well-dressed Nepali, or what the Japanese would have done if the Sadhu had been a well-dressed Asian, or what you would have done… if the Sadhu had been a well-dressed Western woman?" McCoy replied "Where, in your opinion, is the limit of our responsibility in a situation like this?"

- This is a parable because it is a story that illustrates a moral issue. To what degree do we have a responsibility for others, and how much should we sacrifice for them?

- What is the difference between the Sadhu story and walking by a homeless person on a cold winter evening?

- What do you think McCoy ought to have done? What would you do?

There is one final note I would like to mention about virtues. Over the years I have often been asked to provide a reference for students applying for a job. Not once has an employer asked me about their marks or their adherence to a utilitarian or Kantian philosophy (even implicitly), but I have frequently been asked about their virtues and character flaws.

1.6 Ethics of Caring

"I feel the capacity to care is the thing which gives life its deepest significance."

Pablo Casals (1876-1973), one of the greatest cellists of all time.

The ethical frameworks discussed so far emphasize rationality, universality, and impartiality. Emotion from this perspective is viewed as a barrier that creates bias, prejudice, and diverts people from making good ethical decisions. These frameworks attempt to formulate general moral rules and assume that people are individual, empowered, rational agents capable of independent decision-making.

Beginning in the 1980s work by Carol Gilligan[82], Virginia Held[83] and Joan Tronto[84] argued for a different approach, one rooted in relationships, emotion, and responsibility, as opposed to individuality, rationality, and obligation. This approach—known as the ethics of caring or care ethics—argues that relational emotions such as caring and compassion are the basis of morality. It is closely tied to the feminist movement.

One can care about others, take care of others, be a caregiver, or receive care. Caring agents can be individuals, groups, institutions, or nations. Caring has the following elements:

> (1) attentiveness, a proclivity to become aware of need; (2) responsibility, a willingness to respond and take care of need; (3) competence, the skill of providing good and successful care; and (4) responsiveness, consideration of the position of others as they see it and recognition of the potential for abuse in care.[85]

It can be viewed as a value, a virtue, a disposition or a practice. Hence, a virtuous person will be one with a capacity to care and a disposition to do so. We value those who care for others, personally and professionally. For example, the nursing profession practices caring in their attitude towards patients.

According to Tronto,

> On the most general level we suggest caring be viewed as a species activity that includes everything we do to maintain, continue and repair our "world" so that we can live in it as well as possible. That world includes our bodies, ourselves and our environment, all of which we seek to interweave in a complex, life sustaining web.[86]

This approach reflects an ecological systems worldview and as such, advocates for a very different set of social relations than a worldview based upon homo-economicus, which views man as a perfectly rational creature that makes objective mathematically-based decisions to optimize economic outcomes.

As noted above, caring ethics focusses on specific relationships as opposed to generalized theories related to individual moral agents. It is often not perceived as an ethical theory per se, but rather an ethical orientation. It pays particular attention to issues of dependency, connectedness, reciprocity, and asymmetry, and begins with the observation that human beings are involved in caring relationships for most of their lives, beginning as children who require care to survive, but are unable to offer caring (hence the relationship is asymmetrical). Caring is not so much done because of an obligation (though at times that may be part of the rationale for our actions), but because of an emotional relationship that includes sets of responsibilities that are not contractual in the sense of Kantian duties and obligations. As an ethical approach it has received significant attention from helping professions such as nursing.

As opposed to traditional mainstream ethical theories that deal with universality, rationality, and impartiality, care ethics is particularist, passionate, and partialist:

- A *particularist* approach emphasizes morality as it applies to particular people and relationships. Context is critical. Care ethics does not seek universal moral laws or truths since individual circumstances differ so greatly that general rules are often not helpful.

- A *passionate* approach highlights the importance of emotion in moral judgements, such as kindness and altruism that result from empathy and sympathy, rather than dispassionate cognitive benevolence.

- A *partialist* approach sees relationships, as opposed to contractual obligations, as central to moral judgement. People should be treated differently depending upon social and emotional connections. Responsibilities beyond relationships are of lesser importance, though chains of caring extend networks beyond immediate relationships.

The underlying normative values in care ethics is the condemnation of hurting or exploiting others and a commitment to human flourishing. These values are similar to non-maleficence and beneficence in virtue ethics.[87] The main difference is that instead of being characteristics of a moral agent they are process-oriented.

A relationship can be caring but unjust (especially when there is an imbalance of power, such as a loving parent who is overly protective), or uncaring but just (such as in a business relationship). Recall earlier that we identified different types of justice including retributive, procedural, distributive, and social. Care ethics is most relevant to social justice issues.

Caring practices are not just between individuals, but are also present in chains of connections that ripple outward within sets of social institutions, structures, and relations. In many countries a degree of care for dependents has been removed from the individual and been given over to the state (e.g., old age homes) or privatized via the free market system by the hiring of caregivers (e.g., nannies). In such cases caring does not occur because of responsibility, but rather because of obligations such as contracts and job functions. As a result of privatization, care has therefore become transformed into something different since a free market economy is based upon profit maximization, which is quite different from humanistic social welfare values.

Insomuch as caring for those in need has been privatized and institutionalized within some societies, it has sometimes resulted in the exploitation of care workers that many have seen as unjust. It is the difference between neoliberal economies based upon the economic, the market and money, and a view of society based upon the moral, relationships and emotion. The term used to describe this is the *global care chain*, and it "is primarily concerned with the transfer of care labour and resources from poor to rich nations through the employment of women from poor countries in middle-class homes of the latter as caregivers."[88] Such migrant caregivers, because of economic needs, will frequently abandon their roles as carers at home to become paid carers of others. These neoliberal policies have been criticized for reinforcing and producing inequalities between the global north and south, and of therefore being a producer of social injustice. They are deeply rooted in societies that have traditionally economically valued male work in the public sphere, but not female work in the private sphere.

Kittay et al. argue that

> we have an obligation to the caregiver no less than the cared for. Caring is an asymmetrical relationship in which those who are cared for are frequently not in a position to reciprocate what is provided by the caregiver. Just reciprocal relations require that a third party provide for the caregiver what neither the cared for nor carer can provide for herself as she turns her attention to the cared for.[89]

There have been a number of criticisms of care ethics, outlined below.[90]

- *A slave morality*: A slave morality is rooted in self-sacrifice. This idea originated from Frederick Nietzsche who argued that oppressed peoples tend to develop moral theories that reaffirm subservient traits as virtues. There are times when self-sacrifice is considered appropriate (e.g. of a parent for a child), but it can also be viewed as overly harmful to the self and can reinforce harmful dependencies in a dysfunctional relationship. Caring does not necessarily require total subservience; doing so transforms a virtue into a flaw (as discussed by Aristotle).

- *Empirically flawed:* Some of the research on care ethics has been criticized for being based on samples that were too culturally narrow (for example, Gilligan's initial surveys that focused on homogeneous groups of women).

- *Theoretically indistinct*: Some arguments suggest that care ethics can be incorporated into other ethical theories (utilitarian, deontological and virtue theories) and is therefore not distinct.

- *Too limited in scope*: If care is a function of relationships, how does that affect caring towards the "distant other"? Can this approach be used to justify arbitrary favoritism and nepotism? How do issues of social justice fit into this perspective?

- *Overly simplifies relationships:* One critique of care ethics is that it simplifies and romanticizes caring relationships, and does not account for the variation and complexity that results from different cultural, social, and gender orientations.

- *Ambiguous*: Because care ethics avoids abstract generalizations and principles it is ambiguous and cannot offer concrete guidance.

How is care ethics relevant to emergency managers who work in public institutions? It provides a useful lens on the issue of role abandonment during disasters. As I write this in March 2020 we are in the midst of a pandemic, and many family physicians (including mine) are not seeing patients face-to-face because of fears of infecting their own family members. Care ethics supports such a decision, though from a utilitarian basis it is hard to support that approach. In terms of emergency planning, care ethics suggests avoiding blanket policy approaches that do not take into account how individuals relate to others, but would rather seek opportunities for flexible strategies.

1.7 Environmental Ethics

"Nature is not a place to visit, it is our home…"

Gary Snyder (1930-), poet

"What deep ecology directs us toward is neither an environmental ethic nor a minor reform of existing practices. It directs us to develop our own sense of self until it becomes Self, that is, until we realize through deepening ecological sensibilities that each of us forms a union with the natural world, and that protection of the natural world is protection of ourselves."

Alan Drengson (1934-), Canadian philosopher

"We are not outside the rest of nature and therefore cannot do with it as we please without changing ourselves … we are a part of the ecosphere just as intimately as we are a part of our own society …"

Arne Naess (1912-2009), Norwegian philosopher

A good place to begin a discussion on environmental ethics is to mention the writings of Aldo Leopold, specifically *A Sand County Almanac*[91] and "Land Ethic."[92] In these works Leopold preached environmental conservation, and the importance of caring about and taking action to save nature. He expanded the notion of community to include plants, animals, soil and water (the land). It is a deeply ecological vision of life on earth and he had an important impact on environmental ethics.

Another important historical publication is *Silent Spring* by Rachel Carson.[93] Warning of the devastating impact of chemicals such as DDT and the loss of birds (hence the name of the book), she questioned the impact of science on the environment and was influential in creating the environmental movement.

Recent trends validate her vision, including one study in 2019 that found that "bird populations have continued to plummet in the past five decades, dropping by nearly three billion across North America—an overall decline of 29 percent from 1970."[94]

Figure 1.11: Rachel Carson[95]

For a good summary of environmental ethics as it relates to land use planning I recommend reading Chapter 7 (Ethical Duties to the Environment) of *Ethical Land Use: Principles of Policy and Planning* by Timothy Beatley.[96] Beatley argues for a biocentric or deep ecology approach to environmental ethics, which believes that people owe duties to non-human life because there exists an intrinsic worth that is not related to human beings. A more homocentric or shallow ecology approach focuses on the worth of the environment to people, acknowledging the degree to which we depend upon it. Traditionally, environmental ethics has played a weak role in the field of EM, but it is becoming much stronger for two reasons. The first is an increasing recognition of the role that the degradation of natural systems plays in exacerbating natural hazards. Examples include the protection provided by mangrove swamps and wetlands to storm surges and tsunamis (case studies would include New Orleans and Hurricane Katrina, and the 2004 tsunami in Indonesia), and the effect of deforestation on landslides and floods—Haiti is one example. The second is a growing awareness and disenchantment with the extreme level of impact the human species is having on the rest of the natural world. This awareness affects many people at a visceral level since they are appalled at the massive loss of natural systems. This overuse of the environment is setting the stage for future catastrophes.[xii]

Student Research Project:

- Compare the effect of deforestation in Haiti to that of the Dominican Republic, in terms of flooding and landslide risk.

- In your research, explore the social and political root causes of the different environment paths taken by the two countries.

---

xii The case of Easter Island is often used as a metaphor for how current rates of environmental degradation might result in a global collapse of ecosystems. It is a small scale example of a closed environmental system where people overused the natural environment to the point of collapse.

How the human species is altering the earth can be viewed in terms of planetary boundaries, a model developed by the Stockholm Resilience Centre[97]. Of the processes that regulate the stability and resilience of the Earth system they estimate that five of them exceed a safe operating space (Figure 1.12).

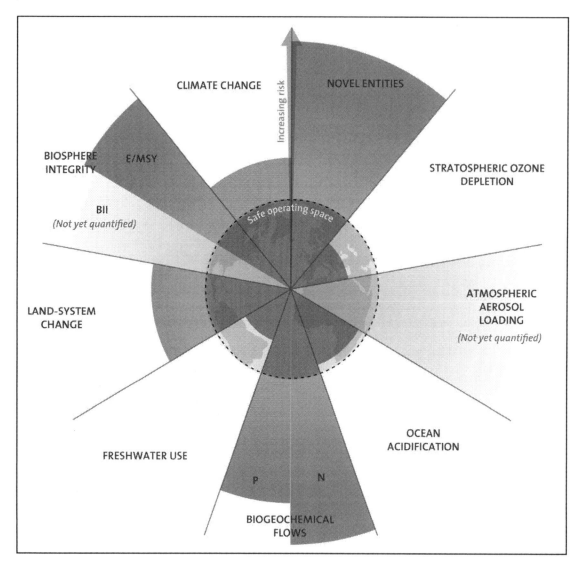

Figure 1.12. Nine processes that regulate the stability and resilience of the Earth system. The areas inside the dotted circle indicate safe operating spaces. Those spaces are exceeded in five processes, pointing to the urgency of global sustainability.

Although it was not true to a significant degree before the industrial revolution, economic development and population growth can now only occur along with the destruction of the natural environment. This is discussed in the *Millennium Ecosystem Assessment*, which notes,

> Many people have benefited over the last century from the conversion of natural ecosystems to human-dominated ecosystems and from the exploitation of biodiversity. At the same time, however, these gains have been achieved at growing

costs in the form of losses in biodiversity, degradation of many ecosystem services, and the exacerbation of poverty for other groups of people.[98]

Figures 1.13a and 1.13b illustrate the impact of economic and population growth on human welfare and on other species.

According to Nadeau, non-renewable resources aside, it would take two additional earths to support the world's current population if developing nations were to develop to the same level as the United States.[99] Economic systems rooted in exponential growth, which are embedded within a finite resource supply, must eventually reach limits to growth. This has the potential to be a catastrophic experience if it is not managed by humanity but is instead imposed upon us by nature. In *Limits to Growth: The 30 Year Update*, Meadows, Randers, and Meadows note,

> In every realistic scenario, we found that these limits force an end to physical growth [...] sometime during the twenty first century. [...] In our scenarios the expansion of population and physical capital gradually forces humanity to divert more and more capital to cope with the problems arising from a combination of constraints. Eventually so much capital is diverted to solving these problems that it becomes impossible to sustain further growth in industrial output. When industry declines, society can no longer sustain greater and greater output in the other economic sectors: food, services and other consumption. When those sectors quit growing, population growth also ceases.[100]

This theme has been explored in numerous books and papers, including *Limits to Growth*, *Our Final Hour*,[101] *The Gaia Hypothesis*,[102] *Right Relationship: Building a Whole Earth Economy*,[103] and others. In *Collapse*, Jared Diamond identified environmental problems as one of the five factors that result in a society failing.[104, xiii] Daly and Cobb, in their support of ecological economics, say that "we human beings are being led to a dead end – all too literally. We are living by an ideology of death and accordingly we are destroying our own humanity and killing the planet."[105] The importance of a resilient ecology was the first of six principles of sustainable hazards mitigation proposed by Mileti—that "human activities in a particular locale should not reduce the carrying capacity of the ecosystem for any of its inhabitants."[106]

The future is uncertain, but the risk is great. Environmental ethics must be part of an integrated framework to manage this risk.

[xiii] The other four factors are climate change, hostile neighbors, trade partners, and the society's response to the other four challenges.

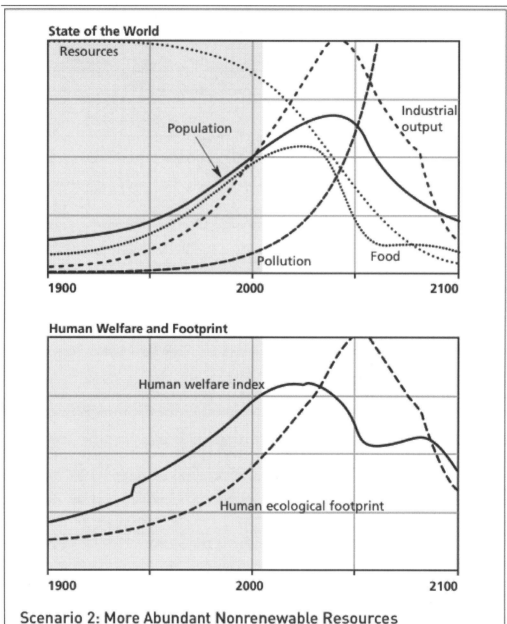

Scenario 2: More Abundant Nonrenewable Resources

This table postulates that advances in resource extraction technologies are capable of postponing the onset of increasing extraction costs. Industry can grow 20 years longer. Population peaks at 8 billion in 2040, at much higher consumption levels. But pollution levels soar (outside the graph!), depressing land yields and requiring huge investments in agricultural recovery. The population finally declines because of food shortages and negative health effects from pollution.

Figure 1.12: One model projection from the Club of Rome[107]

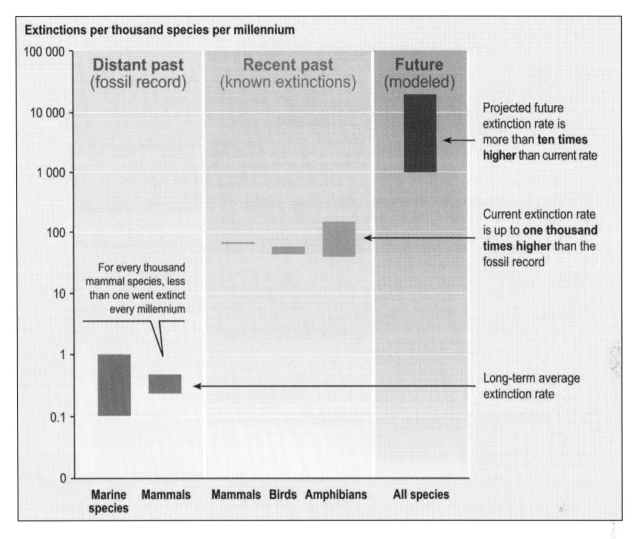

Figure 1.13: Species Extinction Rates[108]

One interesting route to sustainability relates to environmental ethics. In *The Environmental Endgame: Mainstream Economics, Ecological Disaster and Human Survival*, Nadeau suggests that the most probable pathway is through the development of a global environmental ethic, akin to a religious movement.[109] There is empirical evidence for this adaptation strategy. Studies have found that "pre-scientific societies can and do adopt conservation practices on the basis of their experience; practices that in the past were implemented through the medium of religious beliefs."[110] Nadeau's argument emphasizes the importance of embracing environmental ethics as part of a global ethos. Daly and Cobb echo this by noting that in their judgment, changes at a deep religious level are needed to avoid the trap of ad hoc and insufficient responses to crisis.[111] Brown and Garver[112] and Parfit[113] also talk about a spiritual awakening and the moral responsibility we have to future generations as part of the solution to the environmental crisis.

In *Respect for Nature: A Theory of Environmental Ethics*, Paul Taylor outlines several rules and principles of environmentally ethical behavior, as follows:

Rules:
- "The rule of non-maleficence: a duty not to harm creatures in the natural environment: particularly those that do not harm human beings."
- "The rule of noninterference: the duty to refrain from denying freedom to organisms and a general hands-off stance for ecosystems and organisms."
- "The rule of fidelity: retractions to deceiving or betraying wild creatures."
- "The rule of restitutive (or compensatory) justice: requirements to restore or compensate for previous injustices done to organisms and ecosystems."[114]

Principles:
- "Self-defence: individuals can protect themselves."
- "Proportionality: in conflicts between humans and other species, non-basic human interests cannot justify overriding a basic interest of other species."
- "Minimum wrong: people must choose alternatives which do the least damage to the natural world and harm or destroy the fewest number of organisms."
- "Distributive justice: where conflicting interests are all basic, fair shares are equal shares, and certain adjustments are required to ensure all species are treated fairly."
- "Restitutive justice: compensation is required for injustices done in the past; the greater the harm done, the greater is the compensation required."[115]

Student Exercise:

- Give one example for each of the above principles.

The rules of the environmental game are changing, and as students of disasters and citizens of our planet we need to give serious consideration to the ethical issues that underlie the choices made by society. If, indeed, we are in an environmental end-game (and it is my belief that we are), then the decisions humanity makes now will largely determine future catastrophes. Sadly, important social and political paradigms reject or minimize the inclusion of environmental ethics in society. It is common for interests vested in economic development to see environmental concerns as contrary to their purposes. In North America, legislation put to Parliament by the Conservative Government of Canada under former Prime Minister Stephen Harper rolled back decades of environmental progress,[xiv] and the environmental policies within the Trump administration are decidedly anti-environment (for example, withdrawing from the Paris Agreement, and weakening the Environmental Protection Agency—its budget in 2018 was the smallest since it was formed in 1970).[116] Similarly, but to a greater degree, the environment has suffered greatly in the name of economic development in many developing countries such as China and Brazil. For example, the president of Brazil in 2019, Jair Bolsonaro, has enacted policies leading to high deforestation rates of the Amazon forest.[117] As of 2010, one study ranked the 12 countries with the worst absolute composite environmental impact as Brazil, U.S.A., China, Indonesia, Japan, Mexico, India, Russia, Australia, Peru, Argentina, and Canada.[118] As long as environmental protection is perceived as being a barrier to economic growth, the future will be bleak from an environmental perspective.

1.8 Business Ethics or Corporate Social Responsibility (CSR)[xv]

"Business has a responsibility beyond its basic responsibility to its shareholders; a responsibility to a broader constituency that includes its key stakeholders: customers, employee, NGOs, government - the people of the communities in which it operates."

Courtney Pratt, Former CEO, Toronto Hydro

"We know that the profitable growth of our company depends on the economic, environmental, and social sustainability of our communities across the world. And we know it is in our best interests to contribute to the sustainability of those communities."

Travis Engen, CEO, Alcan

"It takes 20 years to build a reputation and five minutes to ruin it."

Warren Buffet, investor, business tycoon, and philanthropist

[xiv] For example, the omnibus budget legislation by Prime Minster Harper provides changes to the *Navigation Protection Act*, the *Fisheries Act,* and the *Environmental Assessment Act* that weaken environmental assessments and allows development with fewer constraints. As well, the Hazardous Materials Information Review Commission was eliminated, with its authority transferred to the Minister of Health; thus what was previously a civil service function is now political.

[xv] My thanks to Professor Mark Schwartz for much of the material in this chapter, which was taken from his course slides for DEMS 6070: Disaster Ethics.

Corporate social responsibility (CSR) is about the private sector, and the ethics and morals of corporations. In the past several decades discussions around CSR have become increasingly prevalent and important. Professor Mark Schwartz, a colleague of mine at York University (for more on this subject, I recommend reading his book *Corporate Social Responsibility: An Ethical Approach*[119]) raises the following questions in the introduction to his book:

- "What should a firm's responsibilities be toward society?
  - Should firms merely maximize profit while obeying the law, or do firms possess additional ethical, or even philanthropic (i.e., charitable), obligations toward society?
- What are the key arguments supporting a narrower (i.e., profit-based) approach to CSR, as opposed to a broader (i.e., beyond profit) approach?"[120]

These are important questions, especially since most of the critical infrastructure in many countries belongs to the private sector; in the United States and Canada it is over 85%.[121, 122] As well, much, if not most, of the risk people are exposed to is created by corporations (examples of such risks that resulted in disasters are the Bhopal disaster, Three Mile Island, The Love Canal, and the BP Horizon oil spill—a complete list would fill this chapter). Corporations are, therefore, critical stakeholders in disaster risk reduction. I also argue that as the world becomes more complex and interconnected, and as neoliberal policies become more accepted in many countries, CSR will become an increasingly important topic. Citizens depend upon critical infrastructure and the goods produced by corporations for their health and welfare and therefore critical infrastructure should be considered, in part, public goods. What are the ethical implications of private sector companies owning public goods, in terms of the obligations of companies and the government that regulates them? Trends towards privatization, as well as our increasing dependence on the systems that support us, make this issue increasingly important.

Student Exercise:

- Consider the questions posed by Mark Schwartz above, for the case of a hydro-electric company that is privately owned and supplying the only source of power to an isolated community.

Two definitions on CSR are:

- "The idea of social responsibility supposes that the corporation has not only economic and legal obligations, but also certain responsibilities which extend beyond these obligations."[123]
- "Social responsibility is the obligation of decision makers to take actions which protect and improve the welfare of society as a whole along with their own interests."[124]

CSR therefore focuses on the notion that corporations have obligations beyond creating profit. This is supported by three notions: (1) that all citizens are stakeholders and therefore a company has a moral obligation towards them, as well as to shareholders, (2) that because corporations are citizens of society the social contract requires reciprocity, and (3) that with power comes responsibility. These obligations integrate social, environmental, and governance issues into the practice of business.

A CSR framework consists of three intersecting domains, the economic, the legal and the ethical (Figure 1.14). A CSR approach is viable in the region where the three domains overlap, where the law is obeyed, where moral behavior is the norm, and when business is profitable.

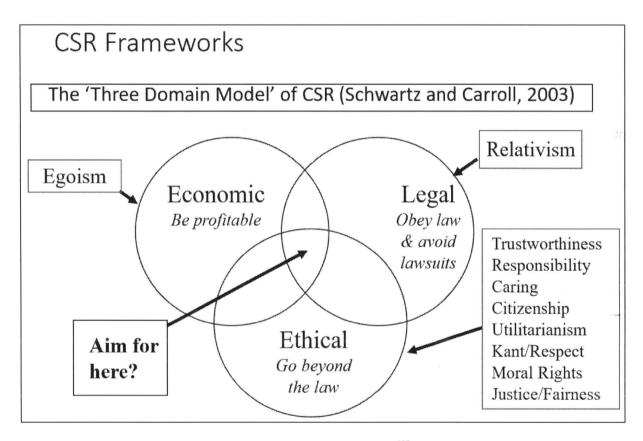

Figure 1.14: CSR Framework[125]

CSR in Practice: River Blindness.[126]

Source: World Bank. (2014). *Forty years later: The extraordinary river blindness partnership sets its sights on new goals.*
- "River blindness is a terrible disease that causes severe discomfort and eventual blindness among infected people. Known in the medical world as onchocerciasis, the disease has been steadily beaten back in Africa thanks to 40 years of coordinated efforts to defeat it.

- Trials of ivermectin (Mectizan) in the 1980s showed it could be used to prevent river blindness. In 1988, Mr. Roy Vagelos, former CEO of Merck & Co., and one of the team of scientists who developed the drug, promised to donate as much Mectizan to control river blindness in Africa as would ever be needed.

- Looking back on 40 years of partnership, World Bank Group President Jim Yong Kim noted that back in the day when there were scant resources for global health, this decision to donate ivermectin for as long as was needed in Africa was a "game changing intervention" by Merck and all other partners.

- Ms. Geralyn Ritter, Senior Vice President, Global Public Policy and Corporate Responsibility, Merck & Co. reaffirmed Vagelos's 1988 commitment to donate Mectizan free of cost for as long as needed, as much as needed, and wherever needed: "Twenty-seven years later, we are doing just that."[xvi, 127]

Is a corporation a moral agent? Arguments for "yes" include laws that define corporations as artificial persons, that corporations can act and form intended objectives, and that people hold corporations morally accountable. Arguments for "no" include that though corporations are made up of people, they do not feel or act alone, that only human beings can be morally blamed, and that corporations are really like machines. One well-known supporter of the "yes" camp is the Nobel Prize winner Milton Friedman (who was much criticized in Naomi Klein's book *The Shock Doctrine*). Friedman argues that managers are agents of shareholders, spend shareholders' money, and impose taxes; that companies pursuing profits leads to social utility maximization; that policy decisions are better left to government; that shareholders or managers can still give charity; and that firms can engage in "socially responsible" activity but only if it leads to maximizing profits.[128]

An example of a company that embraces CSR is The Body Shop, which believes that the "rules of the society" or the "rules of the game" have changed (i.e., societal expectations for firms), that corporations are citizens of society and must consider all stakeholders, that shareholders' desires often go beyond the bottom line, that shareholders have moral obligations towards society, that managers often make decisions under uncertainty, that corporations have the power and ability to make a positive moral difference, and that government is not always sufficient or willing to solve social problems.[129]

[xvi] Tax write-offs can be important incentives for such donations, as noted by Hernando, Colwell, and Wright:

> Our best estimate of the direct cost to Merck of the ivermectin tablets donated during 2005–2011 is around US$ 600 million, well below the stated value of US$ 3.8 billion. Our calculation of tax write-offs reduces the net cost to around US$ 180 million in that period. Indirect market benefits and effects on goodwill further enhanced the compatibility of Merck's donation programme with the company's profit-maximising objective. The case offers lessons for effective management of collaborations with public and non-profit organisations.

There are also examples of companies that focus solely on corporate profit, sometimes to the extent that safety is compromised and disasters result. The train derailment at Lac-Mégantic, Quebec, Canada is one such event. This disaster resulted from decades of neoliberal policies and deregulation on the part of the Canadian government – one example of the result of such deregulation is demonstrated by the comment that it was "great for its bottom line, the rail industry has met this spectacular surge in demand, for the most part, using tank cars that were not built for carrying hazardous materials."[130]

1.9 Example of an Ethical Dilemma: Temporary Settlement Versus Permanent Housing

Esra Bektas discusses the ethical dilemma faced by government after an earthquake in Turkey devastated the city of Duzce in 1999.[131] There was an urgent need for shelter; at the same time, providing shelter in the short term created negative long-term impacts in the city, such as increasing informal settlements and slum areas. Experience has shown that most temporary housing settlements exist far beyond their expected life and can become permanent in everything but name. This is a specific example of the Samaritan's dilemma, which is about the possible adverse effects of altruism by sabotaging positive adaptive behavior.[132] A psychologist might call this enabling. It is important to remember that altruism also has positive effects (which, of course, is why we do it) by providing tools for disaster victims to recover and become productive and self-supporting.

Figure 1.15: Damage from the Duzce earthquake[133]

The provision of short-term aid can save lives and alleviate suffering for victims immediately after a disaster and satisfies a Kantian ethical imperative of helping those in need. Providing shelter for those who have lost their homes in a disaster can be viewed as an intrinsic good and is supported by Article 25 of the UN Universal Declaration of Human Rights.[xvii, 134] There can be no doubt as to the needs of the great majority of disaster victims; consider the words of Mrs. Roseline Ogwe, a widow with three children who lives in Nigeria and suffered through a flood disaster:

> *"I lived in an old house left for us by my father and that house has been washed away; the little money I realised from the sales of my cassava and cocoyam had been spent here in the camp because the aid is not regular."*

Another widow, Mrs. Ellami Philip, said she and her six-year-old grandson managed to escape from being trapped by floodwaters in her town of Abua through the help of some youths who ferried them across to safety.

> *"I did not have any time to harvest the little crops I have in the farm; everything has been washed away. I have not gone back to see what has happened to my house, box of clothes and other belongings."*

> *"I am seeing an entirely different lifestyle here but my worry is what happens after now. We will not stay in this camp forever, how do we start again?"* she asked.[135]

Needs can be overwhelming, as can be the scale of disaster. The following description from the Food and Agricultural Organization of the UN (FAO)[136] about humanitarian crises in the Horn of Africa is an example:

> The Horn of Africa is one of the most food-insecure regions in the world. In the region as a whole, more than 40 percent of people are undernourished, and in Eritrea and Somalia the proportion rises to 70 percent. The seven countries of the region - Djibouti, Ethiopia, Eritrea, Kenya, Somalia, the Sudan and Uganda - have a combined population of 160 million people, 70 million of whom live in areas prone to extreme food shortages. Over the past 30 years, these countries, which are all members of the Intergovernmental Authority on Development (IGAD), have been threatened by famine at least once in each decade.

> Even in normal years, the IGAD countries do not have enough food to meet their peoples' needs. In four of them - Eritrea, Ethiopia, Kenya and Somalia - the average per capita dietary energy supply (DES) is now substantially less than the minimum requirement; in Somalia in 1996, for example, it was 26 percent less. This has a devastating effect on children, in particular, who face life-long physical and cognitive

---

[xvii] The Universal Declaration of Human Rights states,
> Everyone has the right to a standard of living adequate for the health and well-being of himself and of his family, including food, clothing, housing and medical care and necessary social services, and the right to security in the event of unemployment, sickness, disability, widowhood, old age or other lack of livelihood in circumstances beyond his control.

disabilities. In Ethiopia, two-thirds of children are stunted; in Somalia, 20 percent of children die before their fifth birthday. The nutritional status of women, who are the main farmers and carers of families, is also a grave concern.

Food insecurity combined with political unrest and ethnic violence have led to the establishment of long-term refugee camps, such as the ones at Dadaab, Kenya, where many Somalian refugees fled following the civil war in the 1990s. These camps often become permanent settlements as opposed to temporary shelters, creating an ongoing complex humanitarian crisis.

Figure 1.16: A Mass Grave for Children in Dadaab.[137]

It has also been shown, however, that aid (depending upon how the aid is delivered) can increase vulnerability by creating cultures of dependency through the creation of disincentives to autonomy and sustainable development. The anticipation of charity and aid can "crowd out" preventative actions by local governments and peoples. This argument underlies much of the critique by Alex de Waal of famine relief in Africa.[138] He argues that long-term international relief efforts have undermined the political processes of governments in Africa, which have abdicated responsibility for preventing famine in favor of foreign experts who tend to adopt technological solutions that do not address underlying social causes.

From the Samaritan's point of view, (s)he must commit to help, which provides an opportunity for both passive and active exploitation by recipients, whether they be individuals or governments. This is an example of moral hazard (where a person engages in risky behavior because she or he knows aid is available). In an extreme case this can be catastrophic for a recipient country, since it can lead to a spiral of disempowerment and dependency. Unless the capacity and commitment of the Samaritan is endless, the outcome may ultimately be harmful. It is always a question of degree, however, and in this sense the Samaritan's dilemma is a poor representation of the true choices faced by donors. The Good Samaritan cannot ignore victims but can make decisions regarding how much aid to provide, and in what form. This is what Buchanan calls strategic courage.[139]

Kantian ethics suggest that short-term aid must be provided, otherwise potential donors are allowing death and suffering when they have the ability to prevent or mitigate them. In this case the ethical question is not whether aid should be provided, but rather the degree and type of aid. Utilitarian ethics suggest that some aid should be withheld in order to force adaptive responses on the part of recipient nations and peoples, which leads to a greater good – eventually. Of course, none of us can predict the future precisely, and it may well be that withholding aid would create more harm than its provision. Some level of capacity and resilience must be present in the affected nation and population for the withholding of aid to be a reasonable ethical strategy. A corollary of the utilitarian position might mandate supporting the development of local capacities. One risk of the utilitarian argument is the withholding of aid for the supposed good of the victims, but which may really serve selfish ends of potential donors.

Of course, real life situations are generally not black and white. As noted previously, much depends on how aid is delivered. Aid that supports local development is helpful, whereas aid that increases debt, harms local industry, is not culturally appropriate, or serves as a mechanism to increase the wealth of companies from donor countries is probably not helpful and may even be harmful. In practice this issue can be largely addressed not by the reduction of aid, but rather by the rethinking of strategies and the creation of more effective aid programs. Such strategies should incorporate procedural ethics by using a transparent and fair system of decision making that involves recipients in deciding their fates. A paternalistic approach is more likely to fall into the trap this dilemma addresses.

The Parable of The Blind Men and The Elephant.[140]

There is an ancient parable about six blind men trying to understand the nature of an elephant.

- The first blind man reached out and touched the side of the elephant. "How smooth! An elephant is like a wall."

- The second blind man reached out and touched the trunk of the elephant. "How round! An elephant is like a snake."

- The third blind man reached out and touched the tusk of the elephant. "How sharp! An elephant is like a spear."

Figure 1.17: Parable of the six blind men and the elephant.[141]

- The fourth blind man reached out and touched the leg of the elephant. "How tall! An elephant is like a tree."

- The fifth blind man reached out and touched the ear of the elephant. "How wide! An elephant is like a fan."

- The sixth blind man reached out and touched the tail of the elephant. "How thin! An elephant is like a rope."

They were all correct, and they were all wrong. Without context we perceive partial truths without understanding their limitations.

Can you think of a time in your life where you believed a partial truth was the whole truth, which resulted in a bad decision?

1.10   The Context of Emergency Management

Ethical decision making requires a knowledge of context. Without context we are like one of the blind men reaching out to touch the elephant and believing that their partial truth encompasses the whole. I suggest that the context of emergency management includes the following:

Context #1: The Formal Social Contract (obligations)

- The formal legislation and policy environment of EM vary by state, province and country, but is the first context that must be understood. These determine the primary obligations of emergency mangers within the public sector. The International Federation of Red Cross and Red Crescent Societies (IFRC) provides a set of disaster law tools at https://media.ifrc.org/ifrc/what-we-do/disaster-law/, and Kristian Cedervall Lauta has a chapter, "Disasters and Responsibility. Normative Issues for Law Following Disasters," in an edited volume, *Disasters: Core Concepts and Ethical Theories*, which is available for free from Amazon.[142] Another source of material is the American Society of International Law (https://www.asil.org/community/disaster-law).

Context #2: Culture and Duties

- Cultural values (hopefully reflected in the first context) comprise the second context. Much of the normative social contract exists informally, but is powerful in terms of how emergency management organizations need to relate to citizens. One source on this topic is a report, entitled "Culture and Risk: Understanding the Sociocultural Settings that Influence Risk from

Natural Hazards," which is a synthesis of a global e-conference focused on enhancing understanding of the connection between social and cultural factors and risks from natural hazards (https://www.preventionweb.net/files/11039_icimodculture1.pdf).

Context #3: Bounded Rationality

- The best disaster management plan is (to the extent possible) not to let a disaster happen in the first place. There have been many studies demonstrating the positive benefits of investing in mitigation and prevention as compared to response and recovery, yet the resources devoted to mitigation and prevention are relatively small. Because people are imperfect (we have limited knowledge, resources, time and abilities, and many emotional and cognitive biases), we make imperfect/irrational decisions, both as individuals and organizationally. Emergency planning must be evidence-based and take into account our decision-making limitations.

Context #4: Disasters are a Fat-Tailed Problem

- A utilitarian ethical analysis involves estimating consequences in order to determine the greater good. Many social metrics (such as student grades or mean monthly temperature) follow normal (bell-curved) distributions, which have statistical distributions that have narrow tails. This means that the cumulative impact of rare events is relatively unimportant compared to those near the mean. By contrast, disaster data sets typically have fat tails, which mean that rare events are much more important to a risk analysis. The ethics of rare events differ from more frequent, smaller ones for several reasons, including: (1) there may be insufficient resources to meet needs due to the scale of the event, which creates the need for outside aid, (2) there are likely a larger numbers of victims, including people and organizations who would typically be involved in response and recovery, and (3) the threats may be existential to a community. A larger systemic failure brings into question the duties and obligations of government and corporations that own public goods. These greatly affect the moral landscape including how to value life and property, duty to respond, and the degree to which "normal" behaviors should be adhered to. For a useful description of this issue see *Adapting to Extreme Events: Managing Fat Tails* by Carolyn Kousky and Roger Cooke (https://media.rff.org/documents/RFF-IB-10-12.pdf).

Context #5: Emergency Management Functions within a (Near?) Zero-Sum Game Environment

- In a zero-sum game when one wins by an amount "x," another loses by the same amount "x." Much of the creation of risk revolves around this issue, as some create risk for others in the pursuit of power and wealth. One example would be the dumping of toxic wastes by a company. Dumping reduces costs to the company, but results in health hazards to those that live nearby. The zero-sum game model applies particularly to environmental issues since, unlike centuries ago when natural resources were effectively infinite, economic and population growth happens at the expense of ecosystems. One metric related to this is Earth Overshoot Day, which is the date that humanity has exhausted the biological resources our planet can renew for the year (Figure 1.18). This also applies to response and recovery decisions that must be made where insufficient resources exist to meet needs. Budgets are limited, and resources applied to emergency management are not available for other social programs such as health care and education.

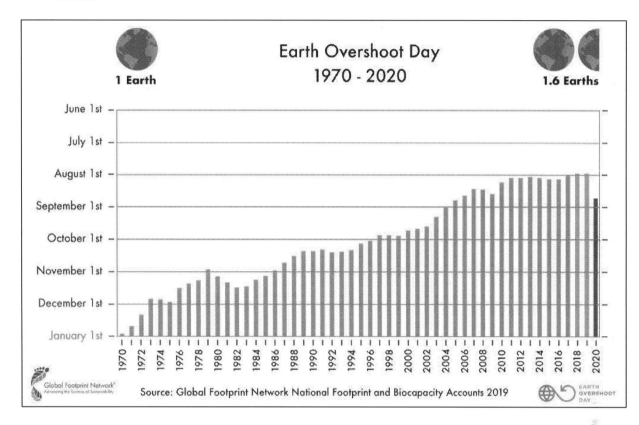

Figure 1.18: Ecological Overshoot as Measured by Earth Overshoot Day[143]

Context #6: The World is Changing Rapidly

- Population growth, urbanization, immigration, technology, geopolitics, and climate change are all factors that are changing our world in important ways, affecting hazards, exposure, and vulnerability. In this environment history can be a poor predictor of the future, and in the long term it is possible that some of these threats may be existential to our way of life.[144] Increasingly, the threats people face are a function of externalities beyond the control of local communities and governments. This creates moral duties for national governments and the international community and is the reason for the creation of governmental departments such as the Environmental Protection Agency. This has implications for political philosophy in that it supports arguments for increased governmental oversight over the private sector, in opposition to neoliberal philosophies.

- During non-emergency times people have a mixed level of duties and obligations towards oneself, one's family, community, etc. However, during emergencies and disasters, friends, family, neighbors, and fellow citizens are in greater need than during "normal" times, and therefore there are increased duties and obligations towards them. Of course, if one is also a victim there may not be a capacity to help others, but where capacity exists there is a different ethical standard that should be recognized.

Broadening an understanding of context is the first step in an ethical analysis.

1.11   Conclusion

Ethics is an enormously complicated topic that has been insufficiently addressed within the field of emergency management. There are a number of ethical theories that are applicable to this field, including utilitarianism, deontology, virtue ethics, environmentalism, corporate social responsibility, and theories of justice. The notion that there is a single ethical theory that can be used is rejected in favor of ethical plurality. Ethics are relevant to all phases of the emergency management cycle.

There is often, or even generally, no one right answer to an ethical dilemma, but an ethical approach to decision making can always be taken. Such an approach will usually lead to better outcomes that can be justified by the decision makers.

During emergencies and disasters, contexts are different than in non-emergency times and, as a result, ethical decision-making follows different paths. One example is making difficult decisions about who should gain access to resources in times of scarcity. At times, this can be a matter of life and death. As the profession of emergency management increasingly uses ethical thinking, it will become more relevant and its actions more defensible.

Appendix 1.1: Privatization and Post-Katrina Rebuilding in New Orleans

The impact of neoliberal policies and privatization on disaster risk is massive. A very good paper by Gotham (2012)[145] discusses this issue within the context of post-Katrina New Orleans, and I have copied his conclusion below since it presents the case so much better than I could.

Conclusion from Gotham (2012):

Recovery from large-scale urban disasters exposes national as well as local political dynamics, and reveals long-term political trends and policy priorities. Privatization, outsourcing, and contracting out are the latest policy trends affecting the formulation and implementation of disaster policy at the local, state, and federal levels. These policy trends are a major component of the neoliberalization of government policy that combines a commitment to the extension of markets and the logic of competitiveness with a profound antipathy to public sector planning and collectivist strategies. Yet privatization trends are not the outcome of intentional, concerted, or comprehensive planning processes. Rather, the post-9/11 approach to emergency management policy has entailed a series of ad-hoc, piecemeal, and uncoordinated policy actions that have had two major outcomes. First, funding for federal emergency management policies and services has been reduced and implementation has been devolved downwards to states and localities. Second, federal policies stressing privatization have become the modus operandi of FEMA and other agencies responsible for disaster mitigation, response, and rebuilding. These trends are consistent with the policies and decisions of other federal agencies, such as the Army Corps of Engineers and the Environmental Protection Agency (EPA), who have increasingly shifted from providing resources and services to purchasing and arranging them. These agencies now find themselves managing contracts amongst a labyrinth of complex networks that stretch from the federal government into state and local governments and the private sector.

As this paper illustrates, privatization is altering the face of social provision to disaster-devastated communities. Private firms have long been involved in delivering disaster aid to governments and communities. What is new is the increased reliance and dependence on large, multi-national corporations to implement emergency management policy, a development federal officials have supported and nurtured through neoliberalized policies and socio-legal regulations. Much like homeland security policy, large corporations are now key players in an expanding arena of emergency management: privately-delivered disaster aid and recovery resources. Recent post-Katrina policy reforms emphasizing greater community-level participation, increased reliance on public-private partnerships, and proactive federal leadership do not break with or challenge long-term policy trends stressing privatization. Rather, privatization has increased the amount of public dollars being funneled through government service contracts to private firms in charge of delivering disaster aid and services. More and more, the pace and trajectory of recovery and rebuilding in cities affected by disasters will depend on government decisions about how to allocate public service contracts. These decisions will greatly impact the local availability of key disaster services like housing, food, infrastructure rebuilding, and so on.

Interestingly, privatization does not involve the withdrawal or downsizing of government. Rather, privatization depends on the creation of new modes of expanded state intervention in the form of rules, laws, and policies to stimulate private investment and compensate for the failures and negative consequences of private sector action. Privatization is associated with an expansion of the state, because state policies and statutes provide the socio-legal regulations to create and enforce market transactions between the public and private sectors. Layers of bureaucracy are needed to promote and regulate private-sector actions. In addition, privatization necessitates state action to manage the inevitable problems and negative consequences of privatization. In response to the problems with city contracts with DRC and MWH, the New Orleans city government has created an Office of Inspector General (OIG), a new layer of public bureaucracy, to evaluate and oversee the privatization of disaster services that has occurred since the Hurricane Katrina disaster.

Finally, this article reveals the fundamental incompatibility of privatization logics and democratic governance. Over the last two decades, scholars and policy analysts have debated whether privatization means providing services without producing them, transferring public services to the private sector, abandoning public responsibility to the private sector, or a combination of all three strategies. As we have seen with the case of Hurricane Katrina and emergency management policy, privatization is a larger component of the neoliberalization of government that entails various forms of deregulation and dismantling of government programs and the corresponding liberation of markets and the private sector from public regulation and democratic oversight. Privatization is not a neutral policy adjustment, but instead reflects and reinforces relations of domination and subordination through the redistribution of public resources to the private sector. The tyranny of the bottom line and the single-minded pursuit of profit organize and motivate the decision-making actions of private sector firms and their web of contractors and subcontractors.

The idea that disaster victims have a democratic right to aid and recovery resources as members and citizens of a sovereign nation-state is antithetic to private sector logics and management. The point is that privatization undermines national sovereignty, since there is no reason for having a state in the first place if it cannot protect and aid citizens affected by a disaster. By transferring emergency management functions to the private sector, privatization undermines the meanings and definitions of citizenship, since private firms engage disaster victims as fragmented clients whose claim and access to resources depends on their ability to pay. In doing so, privatization contradicts the values of a democratic public sector while creating new institutional relays through which elite business interests can commandeer public resources and directly shape the content and implementation of policy.

1.12   Endnotes

[1] United Press International. (1957). [Albert Camus, Nobel prize winner, half-length portrait, seated at desk, facing left, smoking cigarette]. [Photograph]. *Library of Congress.* http://loc.gov/pictures/resource/cph.3c08028/

[2] Stanford University. (2020). *Stanford encyclopedia of philosophy.* https://plato.stanford.edu

[3] Perrow, C. (2011). *Normal accidents: Living with high risk technologies.* Princeton University Press.

[4] Rachels, J. (2012). Ethical egoism. In R. Shafer-Landau (Ed.), *Ethical theory: An anthology* (pp. 193-199). Wiley-Blackwell.

[5] Rachels, J. (2012). Ethical egoism. In R. Shafer-Landau (Ed.), *Ethical theory: An anthology* (pp. 193-199). Wiley-Blackwell.

[6] Justia. (2020). *Insanity.* https://www.justia.com/criminal/defenses/insanity/

[7] Nathanson, S. (n.d.). *Act and rule utilitarianism.* Internet Encyclopedia of Philosophy. https://www.iep.utm.edu/util-a-r/

[8] Judicial Education Centre (May 29, 2020). *Overview of Torts,* University of New Mexico, http://jec.unm.edu/education/online-training/torts-tutorial

[9] Pickersgill, H. W. (1829). [Jeremy Bentham]. [Oil on canvas]. *Wikipedia.* https://en.wikipedia.org/wiki/Jeremy_Bentham#/media/File:Jeremy_Bentham_by_Henry_William_Pickersgill_detail.jpg

[10] Mogilner, C. (2010). The pursuit of happiness: Time, money, and social connection. *Psychological Science, 21*(9), 1348-1354.

[11] London Stereoscopic Company & Hulton Archive. (ca. 1870). [John Stuart Mill]. [Photograph]. *Wikipedia.* https://en.wikipedia.org/wiki/John_Stuart_Mill#/media/File:John_Stuart_Mill_by_London_Stereoscopic_Company_,_c1870.jpg

[12] Kolko, J. (2012, March 6) *Wicked problems: Problems worth solving.* Stanford social innovation review. https://ssir.org/books/excerpts/entry/wicked_problems_problems_worth_solving

[13] Shreve, C. M., & Kelman, I. (2014). Does mitigation save? Reviewing cost-benefit analyses of disaster risk reduction. *International Journal of Disaster Risk Reduction, 10*(Part A), 213-235.

[14] Beatley, T. (1994). *Ethical land use: Principles of policy and planning.* John Hopkins University Press.

[15] Dunfee, T. W., & Strudler, A. (2000). Moral dimensions of risk transfer and reduction strategies. In A. Kreimer & M. Arnold (Eds.), *Managing disaster risk in emerging economies.* World Bank.

[16] Brown, D. W., Moin, S. M. A., & Nicolson, M. L. (1997). A comparison of flooding in Michigan and Ontario: 'Soft' data to support 'soft' water management approaches. *Canadian Water Resources Journal, 22*(2), 125-139.

[17] UNISDR, C. (2015). *The human cost of natural disasters: A global perspective.* The Centre for Research on the Epidemiology of Disasters (CRED).

[18] Schwartz, M. (2017). [Lecture notes on ethical dilemmas]. *DEMS 6070: Disaster Ethics.* York University.

[19] [nakarandosa]. (2010, Jan. 19). *A long night for Doctor Sanjay Gupta in Haiti* [Video]. YouTube. https://www.youtube.com/watch?v=axMRkTBC688

[20] Zack, N. (2009). *Ethics for disaster.* Rowman & Littlefield Publishers Inc.

[21] Unidentified Painter (circa 1790). Immanuel Kant, Prussian philosopher, Wikipedia, https://en.wikipedia.org/wiki/Immanuel_Kant#/media/File:Immanuel_Kant_(painted_portrait).jpg

[22] Kant, I., & Schneewind, J. B. (2002). *Groundwork for the Metaphysics of Morals.* Yale University Press.

[23] (1941). [Linus Pauling at the California Institute of Technology]. [Photograph]. *The Big T: California Institute of Technology Yearbook.* https://commons.wikimedia.org/wiki/File:Linus_Pauling_1941.png

[24] United Nations. (1948). *Universal declaration of human rights.* http://www.un.org/en/documents/udhr/index.shtml

[25] United Nations. (1948). *Universal declaration of human rights.* http://www.un.org/en/documents/udhr/index.shtml

[26] Rawls, J. (2009). *A theory of justice.* Harvard University Press.

[27] Zack, N. (2009). *Ethics for disaster.* Rowman & Littlefield Publishers Inc.

[28] Zack, N. (2009). *Ethics for disaster.* Rowman & Littlefield Publishers Inc.

[29] Blodget, B. (2012, Oct. 30). *Mitt Romney: It's 'immoral' to borrow money for disaster relief. Business Insider.* http://www.businessinsider.com/romney-disaster-relief-immoral-2012-10

[30] Dunfee, T. W., & Strudler, A. (2000). Moral dimensions of risk transfer and reduction strategies. In A. Kreimer & M. Arnold (Eds.), *Managing disaster risk in emerging economies*. World Bank.

[31] Dunfee, T. W., & Strudler, A. (2000). Moral dimensions of risk transfer and reduction strategies. In A. Kreimer & M. Arnold (Eds.), *Managing disaster risk in emerging economies*. World Bank.

[32] Hersher, R. and Benincasa, R. (2019). How Federal Disaster Money Favors The Rich, March 5, 2019, NPR, https://www.npr.org/2019/03/05/688786177/how-federal-disaster-money-favors-the-rich

[33] Insurance Bureau of Canada. (2019). *Options for managing the flood costs of Canada's highest risk residential properties.* http://www.ibc.ca/on/resources/media-centre/media-releases/options-for-managing-the-flood-costs-of-canada%E2%80%99s-highest-risk-residential-properties

[34] Burby, R. J. (2001). Flood insurance and floodplain management: The US experience. *Global Environmental Change Part B: Environmental Hazards, 3*(3), 111-122.

[35] Brown, D. W., Moin, S. M. A., & Nicolson, M. L. (1997). A comparison of flooding in Michigan and Ontario: 'Soft' data to support 'soft' water management approaches. *Canadian Water Resources Journal, 22*(2), 125-139.

[36] Tierney, K., Bevc, C., & Kuligowski, E. (2006). Metaphors matter: Disaster myths, media frames, and their consequences in Hurricane Katrina. *The Annals of the American Academy of Political and Social Science, 604*, 57-81.

[37] Guarino, M. (2015, August 16). *Misleading reports of lawlessness after Katrina worsened crisis, officials say.* The Guardian. https://www.theguardian.com/us-news/2015/aug/16/hurricane-katrina-new-orleans-looting-violence-misleading-reports.

[38] Hurd, H. M. (2002). Liberty in law. *Law and Philosophy 21*(4-5) 385–465.

[39] Maqbool, A. (2020). Coronavirus: why has the virus hit African Americans so hard?. *BBC News.*

[40] Adler, N. E., Glymour, M. M., & Fielding, J. (2016). Addressing social determinants of health and health inequalities. *Jama, 316*(16), 1641-1642.

[41] APM RESEARCH LAB STAFF (2020). The Color of Coronavirus: Covid-19 Deaths By Race And Ethnicity In The U.S., Accessed June 21, 2020, https://www.apmresearchlab.org/covid/deaths-by-race

[42] McNeil, D. G. (1967). The code of Hammurabi. *ABAJ, 53*, 444.

[43] Rawls, J. (2009). *A theory of justice*. Harvard University Press.

[44] De Waal, A. (1997). *Famine crimes: Politics & the disaster relief industry in Africa*. Indiana University Press.

[45] De Waal, A. (1997). *Famine crimes: Politics & the disaster relief industry in Africa*. Indiana University Press.

[46] De Waal, A. (1997). *Famine crimes: Politics & the disaster relief industry in Africa*. Indiana University Press.

[47] Federal Emergency Management Agency (FEMA). (2019). *About the agency.* http://www.fema.gov/about-fema

[48] Public Safety Canada. (2019). *About Public Safety Canada.* https://www.publicsafety.gc.ca/cnt/bt/index-eng.aspx

[49] Aiello, R. (2022). National inquiry called into Trudeau's use of Emergencies Act to end 'Freedom Convoy', CTV News, https://www.ctvnews.ca/politics/national-inquiry-called-into-trudeau-s-use-of-emergencies-act-to-end-freedom-convoy-1.5874628.

[50] Klein, N. (2007). *The shock doctrine. The rise of disaster capitalism*. Vintage Canada.

[51] Arena, J. (2015, August 28). *A people's reconstruction.* Jacobin. https://www.jacobinmag.com/2015/08/katrina-ten-year-anniversary-public-housing-charter-schools/

[52] Arena, J. (2015, August 28). *A people's reconstruction.* Jacobin. https://www.jacobinmag.com/2015/08/katrina-ten-year-anniversary-public-housing-charter-schools/

[53] Gotham, K. F. (2012). Disaster, Inc.: Privatization and post-Katrina rebuilding in New Orleans. *Perspectives on Politics, 10*(3), 633-646.

[54] Gotham, K. F. (2012). Disaster, Inc.: Privatization and post-Katrina rebuilding in New Orleans. *Perspectives on Politics, 10*(3), 633-646.

[55] Mitchell, J. K. (2003). The fox and the hedgehog: Myopia about homeland security in U.S. policies on terrorism. *Terrorism and Disaster: New Threats, New Ideas, 11*, 53-72.

[56] Zack, N. (2009). *Ethics for disaster*. Rowman & Littlefield Publishers Inc.

[57] Mitchell, J. (2003). The fox and the hedgehog: Myopia about homeland vulnerability in U.S. policies on terrorism. *Terrorism and Disaster: New Threats, New Ideas – Research in Social Problems and Public Policy, 11*: 53-72.

[58] Suwanvanichkij, V., Mahn, M., Maung, C., Daniels, B., Murakami, N., Wirtz, A., & Beyrer, C. (2009). *After the storm: Voices from the Delta*. The Center for Public Health and Human Rights and the Emergency Assistance Team

(Burma).https://www.jhsph.edu/research/centers-and-institutes/center-for-public-health-and-human-rights/_pdf/AfterTheStorm_Fullreport_2ndEd_May09.pdf

[59] Ipsos. (2019). *Global trust in professions: Who do global citizens trust?* https://www.ipsos.com/sites/default/files/ct/news/documents/2019-09/global-trust-in-professions-trust-worthiness-index-2019.pdf

[60] Ipsos. (2019). *Global trust in professions: Who do global citizens trust?* https://www.ipsos.com/sites/default/files/ct/news/documents/2019-09/global-trust-in-professions-trust-worthiness-index-2019.pdf

[61] Doherty, C., Kiley, J., Tyson, A., & Jameson, B. (2015). Beyond distrust: How Americans view their government. *Pew Research Center*. https://www.pewresearch.org/politics/2015/11/23/1-trust-in-government-1958-2015/.

[62] FireSmart Canada. (2020). *FireSmart Canada.* https://www.firesmartcanada.ca/

[63] Kahneman, D. (2003). A perspective on judgment and choice: Mapping bounded rationality. *American Psychologist, 58*(9), 697–720.

[64] Wilde, G. J. S. (1994). *Target risk: Dealing with the danger of death, disease and damage in everyday decisions.* Castor & Columba.

[65] HBR IdeaCast. (2019, April 16). *Avoiding the expertise trap* [Audio podcast]. Harvard Business Review. https://hbr.org/podcast/2019/04/avoiding-the-expertise-trap

[66] Larkin, G. L., & Arnold, J. (2003). Ethical considerations in emergency planning, preparedness, and response to acts of terrorism. *Prehospital and Disaster Medicine, 18*(3), 170-178.

[67] Zack, N. (2009). *Ethics for disaster.* Rowman & Littlefield Publishers Inc.

[68] Buber, M. (1958). *I and Thou* (R. G. Smith, Trans.). Charles Scribner's Sons.

[69] Martin Buber in Palestine/Israel (May 29, 2020). The David B. Keidan Collection of Digital Images from the Central Zionist Archives. https://en.wikipedia.org/wiki/Martin_Buber#/media/File:Martin_Buber_portrait.jpg

[70] Homer-Dixon, T. (1995). *The ingenuity gap: Facing the economic, environmental and other challenges of an increasingly complex and unpredictable future.* Knopf.

[71] Vanderburg, W. H. (2000). *The labyrinth of technology: A preventive technology and economic strategy as a way out.* University of Toronto Press.

[72] Weil, S., & Bespaloff, R. (2005). *War and the Iliad.* NYRB Classics.

[73] Plato. (ca. 399 BCE). *Apology.* https://www.goodreads.com/work/quotes/1692879

[74] (n.d.). [Bust of Socrates. Marble, Roman copy after a Greek original from the 4th century BC]. [Photograph of marble bust]. *Vatican Museums.* https://commons.wikimedia.org/wiki/File:Socrates_Pio-Clementino_Inv314.jpg

[75] Bradshaw, L., & Slonsky, L. B. (2005). *The real heroes and sheroes of New Orleans.* SocialistWorker.org. http://socialistworker.org/2005-2/556/556_04_RealHeroes.shtml

[76] Birsch, D., & Fielder, J. H. (1994). *The Ford Pinto case: A study in applied ethics, business and technology.* State University of New York Press.

[77] McCullough, D. (1968). *The Johnstown flood.* Simon & Schuster.

[78] Glover, J. (2000). *Humanity: A moral history of the twentieth century.* Yale University Press.

[79] Noddings, N. (2013). *Caring: A relational approach to ethics and moral education.* University of California Press.

[80] Boss, J. A. (1999). *Analyzing moral issues.* Mayfield Publishing Company.

[81] McCoy, B. H. (1997). *The parable of Sadhu. Harvard* Business Review. https://hbr.org/1997/05/the-parable-of-the-sadhu

[82] Gilligan, C. (1982). *In a different voice: Psychological theory and women's development.* Harvard University Press.

[83] Held, V. (2006). *The ethics of care: Personal, political, and global.* Oxford University Press.

[84] Tronto, J. (1993). *Moral boundaries: A political argument for an ethic of care.* Routledge.

[85] Tronto, J. (1993). *Moral boundaries: A political argument for an ethic of care.* Routledge.

[86] Tronto, J. C., & Fisher, B. (1990). Towards a feminist theory of caring. In E. K. Abel & M. Nelson (Eds.), *Circles of care: Work and identity in women's lives.* State University of New York Press.

[87] Pettersen, T. (2011). The ethics of care: Normative structures and empirical implications. *Health Care Analysis, 19*(1), 51-64.

[88] Nguyen, M. T. N., Zavoretti, R., & Tronto, J. (2017). Beyond the global care chain: Boundaries, institutions and ethics of care. *Ethics and Social Welfare, 11*(3), 199–212.

[89] Kittay, E. F., Jennings, B., & Wasunna, A. A. (2005). Dependency, difference and the global ethic of longterm care. *Journal of Political Philosophy, 13*(4), 443-469.

[90] Sander-Staudt, M. (n.d.) *Care Ethics.* Internet Encyclopedia of Philosophy. https://www.iep.utm.edu/care-eth/.

[91] Leopold, A. (1989). *A Sand County almanac, and sketches here and there*. Oxford University Press.

[92] Leopold, A. (2014). The land ethic. In F. O. Ndubisi (Ed.), *The ecological design and planning reader* (pp. 108-121). Island Press.

[93] Carson, R. (2002). *Silent spring.* Houghton Mifflin Company.

[94] Daley, J. (2019, Sept. 19). *Silent skies: Billions of North American birds have vanished.* Scientific American. https://www.scientificamerican.com/article/silent-skies-billions-of-north-american-birds-have-vanished/

[95] (2020). *The life and legacy of Rachel Carson.* https://www.rachelcarson.org/

[96] Beatley, T. (1994). *Ethical land use: Principles of policy and planning*. John Hopkins University Press.

[97] Persson, L., Carney Almroth, B. M., Collins, C. D., Cornell, S., de Wit, C. A., Diamond, M. L., ... & Hauschild, M. Z. (2022). Outside the Safe Operating Space of the Planetary Boundary for Novel Entities. *Environmental science & technology.* https://pubs.acs.org/doi/pdf/10.1021/acs.est.1c04158

[98] Duraiappah, A. K, Naeem, S., Agardy, T., Ash, N. J., Cooper H. D., Diaz, S., Faith, D. P., Mace, G., McNeely, J. A., Mooney, H. A., Oteng-Yeboah, A. A., Pereira, H. M., Polasky, S., Prip, C., Reid, W. V., Samper, C., Schei, P. J., Scholes, R., Schutyser, F., & Jaarsveld, A. V. (2005). *Ecosystems and human well-being: Biodiversity synthesis; A report of the Millennium Ecosystem Assessment*. World Resources Institute.

[99] Nadeau, R. L. (2006). *The environmental endgame: Mainstream economics, ecological disaster and human survival*. Rutgers University Press.

[100] Meadows, D., Randers, J., & Meadows, D. (2004). *Limits to growth: The 30-year update*. Chelsea Green Publishing.

[101] Rees, M. (2003). *Our final hour: A scientist's warning: How terror, error, and environmental disaster threaten humankind's future in this century—on earth and beyond*. Basic Books.

[102] Lovelock, J. E., & Cayley, D. (1995). *The GAIA hypothesis*. CBC RadioWorks.

[103] Brown, P. G., & Garver, G. (2009). *Right relationship: Building a whole earth economy*. Berrett-Koehler Publishers.

[104] Diamond, J. (2005). *Collapse: How societies choose to fail or succeed*. Penguin Books.

[105] Daly, H. E., Cobb, Jr., J.B., & Cobb, J. B. (1994). *For the common good: Redirecting the economy toward community, the environment, and a sustainable future*. Beacon Press.

[106] Mileti, D. S. (1999). *Disasters by design: A reassessment of natural hazards in the United States*. Joseph Henry Press.

[107] Meadows, D., Randers, J., & Meadows, D. (2004). *Limits to growth: The 30-year update*. Chelsea Green Publishing.

[108] Duraiappah, A. K, Naeem, S., Agardy, T., Ash, N. J., Cooper H. D., Diaz, S., Faith, D. P., Mace, G., McNeely, J. A., Mooney, H. A., Oteng-Yeboah, A. A., Pereira, H. M., Polasky, S., Prip, C., Reid, W. V., Samper, C., Schei, P. J., Scholes, R., Schutyser, F., & Jaarsveld, A. V. (2005). *Ecosystems and human well-being: Biodiversity synthesis; A report of the Millennium Ecosystem Assessment*. World Resources Institute.

[109] Nadeau, R. L. (2006). *The environmental endgame: Mainstream economics, ecological disaster and human survival*. Rutgers University Press.

[110] Gadgil, M., Hemam, N. S., & Reddy, B. M. (1998). People, refugia and resilience. In F. Berkes F. & C. Folke (Eds.), *Linking social and ecological systems: Management practices and social mechanisms for building resilience* (pp. 30-47). Cambridge University Press.

[111] Daly, H. E., Cobb, Jr., J.B., & Cobb, J. B. (1994). *For the common good: Redirecting the economy toward community, the environment, and a sustainable future*. Beacon Press.

[112] Brown, P. G., & Garver, G. (2009). *Right relationship: Building a whole earth economy*. Berrett-Koehler Publishers.

[113] Parfit, D. (1987). *Reasons and persons*. Oxford University Press.

[114] Taylor, P. W. (2011). *Respect for nature: A theory of environmental ethics*. Princeton University Press.

[115] Taylor, P. W. (2011). *Respect for nature: A theory of environmental ethics*. Princeton University Press.

[116] Aisch, G., & Parlapiano, A. (2017, March 16). *Trump's budget cuts some agencies to their lowest levels in decades.* New York Times. https://www.nytimes.com/interactive/2017/03/16/us/politics/trump-budget-cuts.html

[117] Borunda, A. (2019, August 29). *See how much of the Amazon is burning, how it compares to other years.* National Geographic. https://www.nationalgeographic.com/environment/2019/08/amazon-fires-cause-deforestation-graphic-map/

[118] Bradshaw, C. J. A., Giam, X., & Sodhi N. S. (2010). Evaluating the relative environmental impact of countries. *PLoS One*, 5(5): e10440 DOI: 10.1371/journal.pone.0010440

[119] Schwartz, M. S. (2011). *Corporate social responsibility: An ethical approach.* Broadview Press.

[120] Schwartz, M. S. (2011). *Corporate social responsibility: An ethical approach.* Broadview Press.

[121] Public Safety and Emergency Preparedness Canada. (2004). *Government of Canada position paper on a national strategy for critical infrastructure protection.* http://www.acpa-ports.net/advocacy/pdfs/nscip_e.pdf

[122] U.S. Government Accountability Office. (2006). *Critical infrastructure protection: Progress coordinating government and private sector efforts varies by sectors' characteristics.* https://www.gao.gov/assets/260/252603.pdf

[123] McGuire, J. W. (1963). *Business and society.* McGuire-Hill.

[124] Davis, K., & Blomstrom, R. L. (1975). *Business and society: Environment and responsibility.* McGraw-Hill.

[125] Schwartz, M. S., & Carroll, A. B. (2003). Corporate social responsibility: A three-domain approach. *Business ethics quarterly*, 13(4), 503-530.

[126] World Bank. (2014). *Forty years later: The extraordinary river blindness partnership sets its sights on new goals.* https://www.worldbank.org/en/news/feature/2014/07/03/forty-years-later-the-extraordinary-river-blindness-partnership-sets-its-sights-on-new-goals

[127] Hernando, Y., Colwell, K., & Wright, B. D. (2016). Doing well while fighting river blindness: The alignment of a corporate drug donation programme with responsibilities to shareholders. *Tropical Medicine & International Health*, 21(10), 1304-1310.

[128] Schwartz, M. S. (2011). *Corporate social responsibility: An ethical approach.* Broadview Press.

[129] Schwartz, M. S. (2011). *Corporate social responsibility: An ethical approach.* Broadview Press.

[130] Campbell, B. (2013). *The Lac-Mégantic disaster: Where does the buck stop?* Canadian Centre for Policy Alternatives. https://www.policyalternatives.ca/publications/reports/lac-mégantic-disaster

[131] Bektaş, E. (2005). *A post-disaster dilemma: Temporary settlements in Düzce City, Turkey.* Post-disaster reconstruction: Meeting stakeholder interests. http://www.grif.umontreal.ca/pages/bektas_esra.pdf

[132] Buchanan, J. M. (1975). The Samaritan's dilemma. In E. S. Phelps (Ed.), *Altruism, morality and economic theory.* (pp. 71-86). Russell Sage Foundation.

[133] Bilham, R. (1999). *Collapsed building in Duzce,* Wikimedia Commons, the free media repository, https://commons.wikimedia.org/wiki/File:Duzce_1999_earthquake_damage_Bilham_885.jpg

[134] United Nations. (1948). *Universal declaration of human rights.* http://www.un.org/en/documents/udhr/index.shtml

[135] Ikey, A. (2012, November 14). *What next for flood victims after relief camps?* The Nation. https://thenationonlineng.net/what-next-for-flood-victims-after-relief-camps/ Retrieved May 29, 2020

[136] FAO (n.d.). Food insecurity in the Horn of Africa, http://www.fao.org/3/x8530e/x8530e02.htm Retrieved May 30, 2020

[137] Hall, A. (2011). [A mass grave for children in Dadaab]. [Photograph]. *Oxfam East Africa.* Https://en.wikipedia.org/wiki/File:Oxfam_East_Africa_-_A_mass_grave_for_children_in_Dadaab.jpg

[138] De Waal, A. (1997). *Famine crimes: Politics & the disaster relief industry in Africa.* Indiana University Press.

[139] Buchanan, J. M. (1977). *Freedom in constitutional contract: Perspectives of a political economist.* Texas A&M University Press.

[140] Quigley, L. F. (1974). *The blind men and the elephant.* Scribner/Miller-Brody.

[141] (1907). [Blind men and an elephant]. [Illustration]. *D.C. Heath and Company.* https://en.wikipedia.org/wiki/Blind_men_and_an_elephant#/media/File:Blind_men_and_elephant4.jpg

[142] O'Mathúna, D., Dranseika, V., & Gordijn, B. (Eds.) (2018). *Disasters: Core concepts and ethical theories.* Springer.

[143] Global Footprint Network (2019). Earth Overshoot Day 2019 is July 29th, the earliest ever, https://www.footprintnetwork.org/2019/06/26/press-release-june-2019-earth-overshoot-day/

[144] Rees, M. (2003). *Our final hour: A scientist's warning: How terror, error, and environmental disaster threaten humankind's future in this century—on earth and beyond.* Basic Books.

[145] Gotham, K. (2012). Disaster, Inc.: Privatization and Post-Katrina Rebuilding in New Orleans. *Perspectives on Politics, 10(3), 633-646*. Retrieved January 29, 2020, from www.jstor.org/stable/23260183

CHAPTER 2: MORAL DEVELOPMENT

"Those are my principles. If you don't like them, I have others."

Groucho Marx

Figure 2.1: Groucho Marks (1890-1977), comedian, actor and writer.[1]

Contents

2.1 Introduction

A person might be a technical expert on the subject of ethics and yet, according to some, have bad morals. There is a huge difference between subject matter expertise and character. Having a knowledge of ethical theory, however, is a great help in understanding how to relate to the world in an ethical way. This book will help you with that, but whether or not you behave ethically is a personal decision and your personal level of moral development will largely determine your decisions and actions.

For that reason, I have devoted the second chapter of this book to the topic of moral development. In this chapter you will be exposed to the dominant theories and have an opportunity to rate your own level of moral development. It is extraordinarily difficult to be objective and honest when doing self-assessments, but they are opportunities to become more self-aware—an essential ingredient of personal growth.

2.2 An Exercise That May Surprise You

I would like to begin this chapter by asking you a question. What factors do you think determine whether or not people agree to donate their organs following their death? Write your top three choices in the box below:

Factors that determine organ donation:

1. _____

2. _____

3. _____

Take a moment and think about why you made these choices. What does this say about your character or about how you view people and what motivates their decision making? Document your thoughts below:

Response:

_____

_____

_____

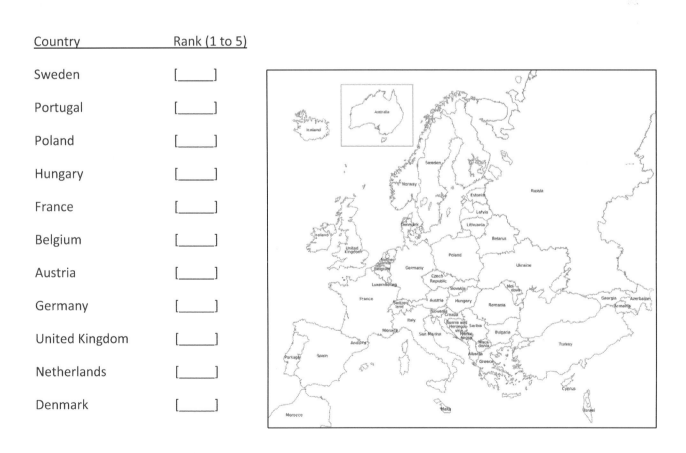

Now, given what you know about the following countries, rank them according to what you believe their consent rates for organ donation would be. Use the categories of (1) 81-100%, (2) 61-80%, (3) 41-60%, (4) 21-40%, and (5) 0-20%. The answer is in Figure 2.3 on the following page, but please do not look at it until you have completed your assessment.

Estimations for rates of organ donations:

Country	Rank (1 to 5)
Sweden	[_____]
Portugal	[_____]
Poland	[_____]
Hungary	[_____]
France	[_____]
Belgium	[_____]
Austria	[_____]
Germany	[_____]
United Kingdom	[_____]
Netherlands	[_____]
Denmark	[_____]

Figure 2.2: Europe

You may find the data in Figure 2.3 surprising; I certainly did! Firstly, I did not expect there to be such a pronounced gap between sets of countries and secondly, I thought the grouping would be different (more aligned with cultural similarities). Consider Table 2.1, which ranks the countries by moral freedom, which my intuition tells me should be related to organ donation. Countries that are starred (*) have low organ donation consent rates, while countries highlighted with no star have high consent rates. There is no correlation between consent rates and rankings of moral freedom.

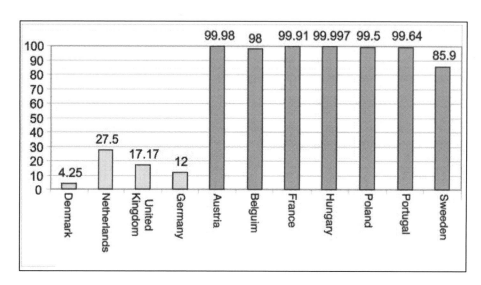

Figure 2.3: Percentage consent rates by country for organ donation. The four leftmost bars represent explicit consent (people must opt-in). The seven rightmost bars represent presumed consent (people must opt-out).[2]

COUNTRY	RANK	SCORE	COUNTRY	RANK	SCORE
The Netherlands*	1	91	France	21	68
Portugal	2	87	Sweden	25	66
Germany*	6	83	Hungary	30	65
Belgium	11	79	United Kingdom*	36	61
Austria	14	72	Poland	54	53
Denmark*	16	71			

Table 2.1: Ranking of Countries by Moral Freedom. Countries flagged with a "*" have low organ consent rates, while countries not flagged have high consent rates.[3]

Where did I go wrong in my initial assessment? The answer is that I had framed the issue incorrectly. I thought it was primarily one of morals, but that is not the case.

The four countries with low consent rates on the left of Figure 2.3 require their citizens to explicitly consent to become organ donors (i.e., check a box authorizing it), while the seven countries on the right assume consent (i.e., check a box if you do *not* want to be an organ donor). It turns out that the most important factor related to whether or not people choose to donate organs is the tendency to emphasize acts of omission over acts of commission (it is somehow easier just not to check a box, in situations where people are conflicted).

Re-Examining Your Answers:

- Look back on the choices you made on the previous page. How did you do? Would you change your answers, given the data in Figure 2.3?

There are two reasons I went through this exercise with you.

- The first is to demonstrate the importance of framing. Depending upon how choices are framed, people will make radically different decisions (if you want to learn more about this topic, search out literature on prospect theory[i]). Politicians and marketing executives know this well and use it effectively to their advantage (and to your disadvantage). Problem framing is an important tool in what has been referred to as *manufactured consent*—the idea that public consent is created by powerful elites through the use of slanted news media, advertising, and propaganda (both subtle and explicit).[4] If you think that you are independent in terms of many of the decisions you make in your life, you are probably mistaken! You and I have been, and are being, manipulated in ways that we are totally unaware of—and this manipulation is becoming both deeper and more widespread within society because of the power of the internet and social media.

- The second reason I include this exercise is to illustrate that there can be a significant gap between why we think people make some decisions, and the reality of decision-making processes. What we think of as an ethical issue may be processed by others as something entirely different.

---

[i] Daniel Kahneman, a psychologist, won the 2002 Nobel Memorial Prize in Economics for his work on prospect theory.

2.3 What is a Moral Person?

What constitutes a moral person or a moral community are questions of timeless importance. There are several ways of looking at this including the use of ethical reasoning (utilitarian, deontological, environmental, justice, etc.), or character traits (virtue theory and ethics of caring).

One procedural approach is justice-based; a moral person simply follows the ethical rules of society—the laws and unwritten cultural norms that guide our behavior. There are times, however, when using this approach is challenging because (a) rules can be unclear or contradict each other, (b) following rules does not work well when faced with an ethical dilemma, and (c) at times laws or rules may be unjust or repugnant, such as occurred in Nazi Germany.

Rules-Based Approach:

- Describe a situation you have been involved in where a rules-based approach worked well, and a situation where it did not work well.

A second procedural approach is that a moral person explicitly engages in ethical or moral thinking. This requires consideration of any assumptions and values that are relevant to the decision, and a decision-making process that balances various ethical considerations before arriving at a final evaluation. Keep in mind that there is not always a "correct" answer. Two people might both engage in ethical thinking and come to very different decisions if they have differing information, values, or worldviews. This is one of the great challenges of practical ethics; there is generally not just one correct answer that is beyond dispute.

Diverging Ethics:

- Describe a situation where two emergency managers, both using ethical/moral thinking, might arrive at different conclusions.

A third approach goes to the issue of character. The field of ethics that specifically addresses this is called virtue ethics (Chapter 1.5). Examples of virtues are benevolence, courage, empathy, integrity, self-control, fairness, generosity, truthfulness, and honesty. It is possible that having and exercising virtuous traits will not always have good outcomes and/or may break the rules of society; from this perspective, other moral theories such as utilitarianism (Chapter 1.1) and deontological ethics (Chapter 1.2) might view actions based upon virtuous behavior as immoral, though a virtue ethicist would disagree.

These three approaches (following rules, engaging in ethical thinking, and being virtuous or caring) need not be mutually exclusive. It is possible to incorporate all of them when addressing an ethical issue, but balancing different factors is often very difficult and greatly depends upon the specific context of a situation. Blending a mix of ethical approaches is called ethical plurality, as opposed to relying upon a single approach that can be very restrictive.

Self-Rate Your Stage of Moral Development:

- On a scale of 1 to 10, where 1 represents a total lack of morality (not necessarily an evil person, but one without a moral compass) and 10 represents angelic behavior, how would you rate your level of moral development?

- My level of morality is _____ on a scale of 1 to 10.

p.s. If you **are** evil, go ahead and give yourself a negative score.

There is some interesting research that shows that most people have a positive self-bias in terms of how they rate themselves; in other words, most people are not as good or moral as they view themselves to be, when judged by a more objective assessment. Ford and Richardson[5] in a review paper note that "there are a number of studies [...] that all report that respondents saw themselves as more ethical than their peers, supervisors or other people they knew."

With respect to acts of omission, when you think about all that you might have done but didn't (such as acts of charity), does that change your assessment of yourself? How do others view you? Generally, people are more judgmental about acts of commission than of omission, with the exception of special duties of care, such as those parents have towards their children. There is an assumption about intent for acts of commission that are absent or unclear for acts of omission.

Self-Rating and Bias:	

- To what degree do you think you are objective, when viewing yourself? Think about the following categories, in terms of your actions:

  a) Acts of Commission
     - What have I done that was moral or immoral?

  b) Acts of Omission
     - What could I have done that was moral or immoral, but that I did not do?
     - Should you get credit for immoral acts not committed?

My friend and colleague Professor Mark Schwartz suggests the use of three intuitive tests to decide if an act is moral or not. They are:

(1) the Pillow Test (would your decision allow you to sleep?)

(2) the Child Test (what would you tell your child to do?), and

(3) the Newspaper Test (would you want your decision to be in the public view?).

2.4 Stages of Moral Development

This section considers the stages of moral development. Generally, theories of moral development can be based upon some combination of the following: (1) a behaviorist approach (such as described by B. F. Skinner) that emphasizes learning rules of acceptable behavior, (2) a psychoanalytic approach (pioneered by Sigmund Freud) that considers the conflict between our instinctual drives and social norms, and (3) a cognitive approach that is based upon logic and reasoning.

The groundwork for much of the research on this topic was laid by Jean Piaget's work on cognitive development in the 1930s.[6] Building on his work, Lawrence Kohlberg studied moral development in the 1950s and '60s and proposed a theory of moral development that underlies much our current understanding of this topic.[7, 8]

2.4.1 Kohlberg's Stages of Moral Development

Kohlberg's theory is based upon the following three sequential and hierarchical levels of moral development.[9]

Level 1 – Preconventional Level

In this level people use the same reasoning process no matter what the situation. Within this level there are two stages. In the first stage (the punishment-and-obedience orientation) how good or bad an action is depends upon the outcomes of punishment or reward, and the action is characterized by obedience to authority. Stage 2 (the instrumental-relativist orientation) is based upon satisfying one's own needs and sometimes the needs of others. Actions are transactional and based upon reciprocity, not loyalty, gratitude, or justice.

Level 2 – Conventional Level

In this level people have evolved to value the expectations of their family and community, which is perceived as being valuable in and of itself. There is an emphasis on conforming and maintaining the social order. In stage 3 (the interpersonal concordance, or good boy-nice girl orientation) good behavior helps or pleases others and conforms to stereotypical images of "right" behavior. Stage 4 (the law and order orientation) emphasizes authority, rules and maintaining the social order. One is moral by doing one's duty and respecting authority.

Level 3 - Postconventional, Autonomous, or Principled Level

In this level people have moved beyond strict obedience and are able to critically evaluate which values and principles are worthy and meaningful depending upon context. In stage 5 (the social-contract, legalistic orientation) people consider normative rights and standards, but also exhibit an awareness of the relativism of personal values and agreed upon processes for decision making. The law is certainly respected, but there can be consideration that a law may be unjust and in need of revision. The final stage, stage 6 (the universal-ethical-principle orientation) incorporates abstract thought and ethical principles chosen by an individual based upon justice, reciprocity, and equity/equality. The viewpoints of others are considered, and universal principles are used to base judgements of what is moral or not.

Kohlberg used stories to assess a person's level of moral development. One of these stories concerns a man called Heinz who lived somewhere in Europe. The scenario is as follows:

> Heinz's wife was dying from cancer. Doctors said a new drug might save her. The drug had been discovered by a local chemist and Heinz tried desperately to buy some, but the chemist was charging ten times the money it cost to make the drug, and this was much more than the Heinz could afford.
>
> Heinz could only raise half the money, even after help from family and friends. He explained to the chemist that his wife was dying and asked if he could have the drug cheaper or pay the rest of the money later.

The chemist refused, saying that he had discovered the drug and was going to make money from it. The husband was desperate to save his wife, so later that night he broke into the chemist's office and stole the drug..[10]

Which of the following scenarios would you choose for Heinz?

1. Heinz should not steal the drug because he would be put to prison for his crime.
2. Heinz should steal the drug because he would feel gratified and happier.
3. Heinz should steal the drug because he's a good husband and it is expected of him to do so by his wife.
4. Heinz should steal the drug, but be incarcerated because he broke the law.
5. Heinz should steal the drug because saving a life is more important than breaking the law.
6. Heinz should steal the drug, but not be incarcerated because the law would be unjust in this situation.

If you chose Answer 1: You are probably at the pre-conventional level of moral development (stage 1) because you focus on the direct consequences of your actions on yourself (punishment).

If you chose Answer 2: You are probably at the pre-conventional level of moral development (stage 2) because you focus on what you believe benefits yourself.

If you chose Answer 3: You are probably at the conventional level of moral development (stage 3) because you try to live up to expectations of your social role and judge the morality of the action by focusing on relationships.

If you chose Answer 4: You are probably at the conventional level of moral development (stage 4) because you feel that it is morally wrong to violate laws, which should be obeyed.

If you chose Answer 5: You are probably at the post-conventional level of moral development (stage 5) because you believe that laws are social contracts that should not be rigid in the face of moral dilemmas.

If you chose Answer 6: You are probably at the post-conventional level of moral development (stage 6) because you are focused on universal human rights. You feel that justice demands that all individuals deserve access to the drug regardless of their wealth.

If you did not do well in the Heinz Dilemma, there are two possibilities: (a) your level of moral development may be less than you hoped, or (b) the test is flawed and your moral development is just fine. With respect to (b), critiques of Kohlberg primarily focus on gender and cultural issues—that he only included white males in his research, and that it may not apply to other cultures. For example, one study of Korean children found that there were cultural limitations to his model and that "it was not possible to match some of the responses from the Korean children to Kohlberg's manual," particularly related to emotional reasoning and the concept of *chung* (which refers to the boundary between individuals that is dimmed, creating a sense of one-ness, same-ness, affection, comfort, and acceptance).[11] From a gendered perspective, women are noted to have a greater orientation than do men towards the well-being and care of others and for harmonious relationships.[12] The justice and equity-based approach used by Kohlberg does not adequately capture this orientation.

2.4.2 Gilligan's Theory of Moral Development

"The moral imperative that emerges repeatedly in interviews with women is an injunction to care, a responsibility to discern and alleviate the "real and recognizable trouble" of this world."

Carol Gilligan

Carol Gilligan further developed the work of Kohlberg, incorporating a gender-based approach that emphasized caring, as well as the justice approach used by Kohlberg.[13] Her perspective is considered to be feminist one, since it highlights how society devalued women's voices compared to men. Her work was initially published in her book "In a Different Voice" and emphasizes the existence of different moral voices. In her words, "One voice speaks of connection, not hurting, care, and response ;and one speaks of equality, reciprocity, justice, and rights . . . The pattern of predominance, although not gender specific, was gender related . . ."[14]

Gilligan was concerned that Kohlberg's research was primarily based upon an analysis of white males and did not sufficiently address the complex and interdependent relationships between people. One of her concerns was that while boys tended to score mostly at level 4 in Kohlberg's scale, girls scored at level 3. Why was this so? Were boys more moral than girls? She thought not and observed that while males prioritize an "ethics of justice", females prioritize an "ethics of care".

Her theory has three levels, with two transitional periods between the levels.

Level 1 - Pre-Conventional/Orientation to Individual Survival

- The goal is individual survival. Others are of peripheral importance.
- Adherence to ethical egoism. Being selfish (such as is a young child).

Transition 1

- Moving from selfishness to responsibility for others.

Level 2 - Conventional/Goodness as Self-Sacrifice

- The world is based on reliance on others, and they must be considered as well as the self.
- Morality has social and relational contexts (e.g. wife or mother).

Transition 2

- From only thinking of others, to also seeing the self as a person.

Level 3 - Post-Conventional/The Morality of Nonviolence

- Principle of nonviolence
- Do not hurt others or self (principled morality).

The different stages of Gilligan's moral development depend upon an evolving sense of self. The Preconventional Level is the most selfish, recognizing only the needs of the self; at the Conventional Level, the needs of the self are minimized while the needs of others are given greater priority; finally, at the Postconventional Level, the needs of the self and others are both taken into consideration in a contextual way. Fundamental to this process are feelings of connection and responsibility toward others.

Gilligan's theory has been critiqued for not recognizing the diversity of voices that women have, and that their attitudes might largely reflect the cultural expectations that society has of women and men, as opposed to innate gender differences.[15]

2.4.3 Rest's Three Schemas

James Rest further developed Kohlberg's approach based upon data from the Defining Issues test, which uses schema theory and a Likert scale to give quantitative rankings to six moral dilemmas.[16, 17, 18] Schemas are "conceptions of institutions and role-systems in society."[19] Rest also emphasizes cognition and the personal construction of issues like rights, duties, justice, social order, and reciprocity. However, he does not approach the issue as being a derivative of foundational principles, but rather about community approaches to shared moral values. As explained by Rest[20] the three schema are:

(1) The Personal Interest Schema

"Individuals using the Personal Interest schema analyse what each stakeholder in a moral dilemma has to gain and lose as if they did not have to worry about organizing co-operation on a society-wide basis. The Personal Interest schema justifies a decision as morally right by appealing to the personal stake an actor has in the consequences of an action."

(2) The Maintaining Norms Schema

The Maintaining Norms schema has the following elements:

> "(a) The perceived need for generally accepted social norms to govern a collective,
> (b) The necessity that the norms apply society-wide, to all people in a society,
> (c) The need for the norms to be clear, uniform, and categorical (that there is "the rule of law"),
> (d) Norms are seen as establishing a reciprocity (each citizen obeys the law, expecting that others will also obey), and
> (e) The establishment of hierarchical role structures, of chains of command, of authority and duty."

(3) The Post-Conventional Schema

Unlike Kohlberg this schema does not adhere to a specific moral philosophy. It incorporates four elements:

> (a) The primacy of moral criteria,
>
> (b) The appeal to an ideal,
>
> (c) Shareable ideals, and
>
> (d) Full reciprocity.

2.4.4 Comparison of the Three Theories of Moral Development

Olivia Stankey[21] summarizes the differences in the three theories as follows (Table 2.2):

	Kohlberg's Theory of Moral Development	Gilligan's Theory of Women's Moral Development	Rest's Neo-Kohlbergian Approach
Timeline	• Original Theory • Built on Piaget's and Rawls Research • One of the First to Study Moral Development of Adolescents and College Students	• Built Off Kohlberg's Research • Argued that Women's Moral Development did not fit within current Moral Development Theories	• Built Off Kohlberg's Research • Viewed the Moral Development Framework more broadly than Kohlberg

Progression	• Hard Stage Model
	  ○ 6 Stages
	  ○ Must finish one stage to move onto another one
	• Three Criteria
	  ○ Structure Criterion
	  ○ Sequence Criterion
	  ○ Hierarchy Criterion
	• Justice Orientation
		• Three Levels and Two Transition Periods
		• Focused on Connection to Others
		• Care Orientation
		  ○ Relationships with others must carry equal weight with self-care when making moral decisions
			• More Fluid Stages
			  ○ May use or show forward movement in several stages at the same time
			• Three Schema
			  ○ Personal Interest Schema
			  ○ Maintaining Norms Schema
			  ○ Post-Conventional Schema

Population Studied	• Studied White Men	• Studied Women	• Studied White Men (assumed)
Scope of Application	• Men Only	• Women Only	• Most Likely Men

Contributions	• Looked at psychology + moral philosophy when forming his Moral Development Theory
	• Added vast knowledge to the study of Moral Development
		• One of the first to recognize and document two different moral orientations: care and justice
		• Linked Moral Development and Student Affairs more specifically – long standing relationship
			• Created an Objective Measure of Moral Development – Defining Issues Test (DIT)
			• Stressed that Moral Behavior had three additional components
			  ○ Moral Sensitivity
			  ○ Moral Motivation

Table 2.2 Comparison of three theories of moral development

2.5 Moral Foundations Theory

What are the moral foundations of our society, or perhaps even our species? Haidt and Joseph, using a survey of virtues from various cultures and anthropological taxonomies of morality, devised the following list:

The Five Moral Foundations of Society:

- Harm – protecting people from harm, caring, nurturing and empathy.
- Fairness – justice, reciprocity and altruism.
- Ingroup Loyalty – patriotism and self-sacrifice for the group.
- Authority – obedience and respect for authority.
- Purity/Sanctity – divine law, sanctity, the evolution of disgust. [22, 23]

Their approach is based upon cognitive/evolutionary arguments and is descriptive as opposed to normative (which means that it describes things as they are, as opposed to how they should be). [24] It is important to keep in mind the distinction between descriptive and normative as you engage in ethical thinking. Of course, we need to understand how society behaves, but we must not lose sight of how things should be, which (unfortunately) is often not very close to reality.

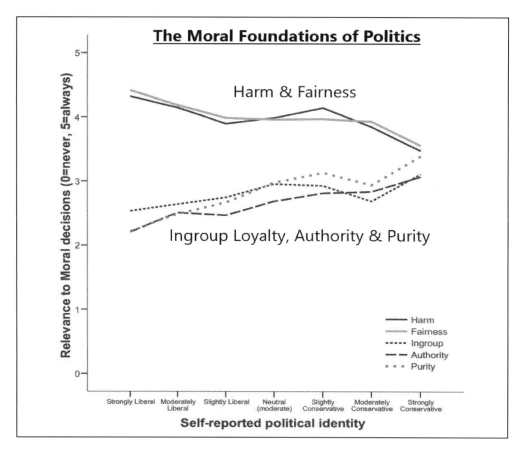

Figure 2.4: Relevance of moral foundations across political identity. [25]

Interestingly, Haidt and Joseph found that self-reported political identity has predictive value in terms of how much weight is given to these moral foundations (Figure 2.4).

Though the political left and political right often perceive the other as being less moral, the implication of this research is that the groups emphasize different moral foundations.[26] Those in the political right place much more emphasis on authority, purity, and in-group loyalty than those on the left, who emphasize harm and fairness to a much larger degree.

But, are the different emphases between the left and the right an issue of morality? Kugler argues that the conservative emphasis on ingroup loyalty, obedience to authority, and purity is a function of their orientation towards authoritarianism and social dominance (both of which are highly correlated with various forms of discrimination and intergroup hostility) and are amoral or even immoral.[27] As usual in an ethical discussion, the debate continues.

Exercise in Self-Reflection:

We do not always behave in moral ways, even according to our own judgments. There are a number of rationalizations that people use for immoral behaviors including.[28] Can you think of a time when you used one or more of these rationalizations to justify your actions?

- If it's necessary, it's ethical.
- If it's legal, it's ethical.
- We've always done it this way.
- Everyone else is doing it.
- It's a dumb rule.
- It's ethical as long as it doesn't hurt anyone.
- It's ethical if I don't gain personally.
- I've got it coming; they owe me.
- I'm doing it for my family.
- It's for a good cause.
- This is a business decision; ethics has nothing to do with it.
- I can't do anyone any good if I lose my job.
- Ethics is a luxury I can't afford right now.
- It's not my problem.
- Sometimes you have to take shortcuts to survive.

2.6 Case Study: Whistleblowing in the U.N. by Anders Kompass

Loyalty is a virtue, but what do you do when loyalty to an organization requires actions, or non-actions such as silence, that you believe are immoral? This is an ethical dilemma that sometimes results in "whistleblowing," an action that can greatly benefit some, but can also result in retaliation to the whistleblower.[1,ii,29]

In June of 2016 the *New Humanitarian* published a story of sexual abuse by U.N. peacekeepers in Central African Republic.[30] The report was made public by Anders Kompass, field operations director at the Office of the United Nations High Commissioner for Human Rights, because the U.N. failed to stop the abuse.

"The complete impunity for those who have been found to have, in various degrees, abused their authority, together with the unwillingness of the hierarchy to express any regrets for the way they acted towards me sadly confirms that lack of accountability is entrenched in the United Nations," Kompass told the New Humanitarian. "This makes it impossible for me to continue working there."[31]

Anders Kompass

Anders Kompass.[32]

The report indicates that

> [i]nstead of investigating those allegedly responsible for what proved to be an even wider crime – including the involvement of its peacekeepers – the UN's Office for Internal Oversight Services launched an internal investigation into Kompass' conduct. Accusing the former Swedish diplomat of leaking, it condemned his "misconduct", suspended him from his job, humiliatingly marched him out of his office, and demanded his resignation.[33]

Kompass commented that

> Sadly, we seem to be witnessing more and more UN staff less concerned with abiding by the ethical standards of the international civil service than with doing whatever is most convenient – or least likely to cause problems – for themselves or for member states.[34]

"[T]hose who take an ethical but unpopular stance, including by reporting the misconduct of others, have learned that the pain of disclosure and retaliation far exceeds any benefit."[35]

[ii] According to one study of whistleblowers, 90% lost their jobs or were demoted, 27% faced lawsuits, 25% got into difficulties with alcohol, 17% lost their homes, 15% were divorced, 10% attempted suicide, and 8% went bankrupt.

Mr. Kompass demonstrated a high level of moral development. His choice was between (a) following institutional rules and loyalty to senior officials in the organization he worked for, which he did not do (it could be argued, however, that he was demonstrating loyalty to the ethical principles of the U.N., which clearly considers sexual abuse by its employees to be unacceptable), and (b) protecting children from abuse and accepting retribution towards himself from those senior officials. His choice was ethical on several levels. Firstly, it served the greater good (a utilitarian approach). Secondly, by most moral standards it was the right thing to do (a rights-based or deontological approach). Thirdly, he was being virtuous (his public statements demonstrated courage and honesty, and his concern for the children showed empathy and compassion).

This is an extreme case, but there are numerous examples of people and institutions in government, the private sector, and the non-profit sector that have been corrupt or have acted with malfeasance. Often it can be difficult to balance loyalty issues versus other ethical considerations, and one should keep in mind that speaking against one's employer generally is very bad for one's career and personal life (Figure 2.5).

One must be careful to examine motives, those of others and those of yourself. Whistleblowing can be motivated by the best possible moral intentions, but striking out against an organization can also result from less lofty reasons, such as a hurt ego or the desire for revenge. Any ethical analysis must be inward-looking, as well as outward-looking.

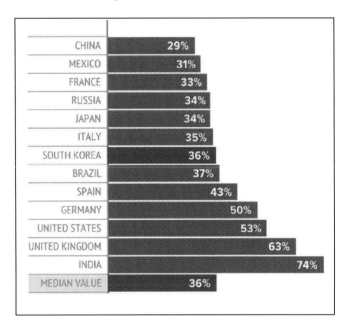

Figure 2.5: Retaliation rate against reporters of ethical misconduct (private sector). Retaliation rates were higher in the public sector for all countries except for Germany and South Korea.[36]

Moral Courage:

- What level of ethical misconduct on the part of your employer would it take for you to risk retaliation (and possibly your livelihood)?

Research shows that there is only a weak to moderate correlation between ethical reasoning (a cognitive analytical process) and moral action (which depends upon virtuous character traits).[37] We don't always do the right thing, even when we know what it is. It is likely that emotion plays an

Is it possible to be a moral person if your actions are not aligned with your values?

important role, as opposed to just reasoning. The impetus to act depends upon what level of responsibility we feel, our moral identity of self (willpower, integrity, and moral desire) and our tendency to be self-consistent. Many people (including myself) are inclined towards particular kinds of morality (such as helping the vulnerable or conserving the environment), but often do not sufficiently act upon it.

2.7 The Milgram Experiment: Obedience to Authority

In the early 1960s an important experiment was conducted by Professor Stanley Milgram from Harvard University. The purpose of the research was to investigate how people respond to instructions from a person in authority, when those instructions are clearly harmful; the context was humanitarian crimes committed during World War II in Nazi Germany.[38],[39] Milgram measured the willingness of people to perform harmful acts on others (in the form if electric shocks of increasing voltage) when instructed to do so by an authority figure, as part of a scientific research study.

Milgram found (using subjects from the U.S.) that

> [o]rdinary people, simply doing their jobs, and without any particular hostility on their part, can become agents in a terrible destructive process. Moreover, even when the destructive effects of their work become patently clear, and they are asked to carry out actions incompatible with fundamental standards of morality, relatively few people have the resources needed to resist authority.[40]

The reason behind this is that

> [t]he essence in obedience consists in the fact that a person comes to view himself as an instrument for carrying out another person's wishes and he therefore no longer regards himself as responsible for his actions.[41]

Any person working in an institution where there is a chain of command can be in this kind of situation, where we become instruments in carrying out the wishes of others or of an organizational agenda. When those agendas are judged to be immoral, how we should act in these types of situations may be one of the great ethical challenges of modern times.

2.8 Moral Traps

Why do people make decisions that harm others? Some people may simply be evil and not care or enjoy the feeling of causing harm. Others might knowingly or unknowingly do wrong to achieve a goal or benefit, either for personal gain or ideology. At other times there may be a desire or intention to behave morally but situational factors make such decisions or actions, difficult or impossible.

A trap is a situation from which it is difficult or impossible to escape and is generally associated with harm or unpleasant situations. In a moral trap harm is done to others and possibly to oneself. One kind of moral trap involves being caught in an ethical dilemma, where no matter the choice made harm is done, either through action or inaction. This kind of trap does not involve loss of agency, so I differentiate this kind of trap from those where agency is limited or absent.

Loss of agency can result from (a) external factors that are imposed by society in general (such as systemic forces like racial injustice or poverty), people with power and/or influence over you (such as an employer or family member) or (b) from internal factors (such as belief systems, biases, or cognitive limitations). Where agency exists, a moral trap may either (1) restrict a person from perceiving alternate moral choices, or (2) not allow them to make an alternate moral choice.

It may not always be clear whether loss of agency is internal or external. Research shows that there is a cognitive bias people have to "conclude that other people make mistakes because they are bad people whereas we make mistakes because we are trapped in a difficult situation".[42] This is called the fundamental attribution error.

Moral traps can therefore be categorized into 5 basic types:

1. Moral Trap type "A". Ethical dilemma. Agency exists but the agent is forced into a choice that causes harm to some because there are no other options.
2. Moral Trap type "B1". Lack of agency due to external factors that create moral blindness.
3. Moral Trop type "B2". Lack of agency due to external factors that restrict choice.
4. Moral Trap type "C1". Lack of agency due to internal factors that create moral blindness.
5. Moral Trap type "C2". Lack of agency due to internal factors that restrict choice.

How important are intentions as compared to situational context? "The psychology evidence is overwhelming that the situational dominates the dispositional; in other words, under the right conditions, good people can be induced, seduced, and initiated into behaving in evil ways".[43] One list of psychological moral traps listed below is as follows [44]:

1. Obedience to Authority (Moral Trap type "A"). Obey those in positions of power. The Milgram experiment (Chapter 2.7) is a good example of this.
2. Conformity Bias (Moral Trap type "C2"). We all have a need to feel accepted by our "tribe". Conforming to the normative values of those in our community is an important part of socialization, but there are times when those values are immoral. "In a famous experiment, psychologist Solomon Asch found that when asked to tell which of three lines was the same length as a fourth line, subjects had no difficulty unless they were placed in an experimental condition in the presence of six of the experimenter's confederates who gave obviously wrong answers. Almost all subjects then found it very difficult to give the obviously correct answer in contradiction to total strangers' erroneous answers."
3. Incrementalism (Moral Trap type "C1"). This is the "slippery slope" argument, where one small but bad decision leads to others.
4. Groupthink (Moral Trap types "B1" and "C1"). This refers to the tendency of members of a cohesive group to avoid introducing stress into their unanimity by suppressing dissent and characterizing potential critics as "just not getting it".[45] Groups under the sway of groupthink tend to assume that their goals are ethical and to avoid questioning the morality of their own behavior. Moral doubts are assuaged by group concurrence. Feelings of guilt are rationalized by thinking "we are a good and wise group."
5. Overoptimism (Moral Trap type "C2"). "Many people have a tendency toward optimism that is so strong it can lead to irrational beliefs and injurious decisions."
6. Overconfidence (Moral Trap type "C2"). "Students, psychologists, CIA agents, engineers, stock analysts, financial analysts, investment bankers, investors, and many other categories of people have been studied and shown to tend toward irrational confidence in the accuracy of their decisions." "Importantly, people's overconfidence in their own decision making extends to their ethical judgments. People tend to believe … that they are more honest and fair-minded than both their competitors and their peers"
7. Self-Serving Bias (Moral Trap type "C2"). This bias "inclines decision makers to gather information, process information, and even remember information in such a manner as to advance their perceived self-interest and to support their preexisting views." This tendency is also discussed in a paper on moral traps by Lin, Zlatev and Miller[46] who note that "people's desire to see themselves as moral disposes them to make attributions that enhance or protect their moral self-image. When approached with a prosocial request, people are inclined to attribute their own noncompliance to external factors, while attributing their own compliance to internal factors."
8. Framing (Moral Trap type "B1" and "C1"). This issue relates to prospect theory, the tendency of people's risk preferences to depend upon whether something is framed as a benefit or a loss.[47] For example, there is a purchase preference for potato chips that are 95% fat free, as compared to ones that are 5% fat, though they have the same fat content. With respect to ethical decisions, this would affect decision making if it were framed as lives saved versus lives lost.
9. Sunk Costs (Moral Trap type "C1"). This is about being committed to a course of action, even if it is a bad one, because of an earlier decision. It can result in an escalation of commitment. For example, "Consider how Nick Leeson kept irrationally doubling up his bets as he sank Barings Bank. He intentionally continued on a course of trading that destroyed the institution, although he clearly did not intend any such result and was, in fact, trying desperately (if irrationally) to avoid injuring the bank".[48]

10. The Tangible, the Close, and the Near Term (generally Moral Trap types "C1" and "C2"). There are a number of heuristics or intuitive rules of thumb that people use in decision making that bias their perspectives.[49]

For further discussion on these traps refer to Prentice, R. A. (2007). Ethical decision making: More needed than good intentions. *Financial Analysts Journal*, *63*(6), 17-30.

Hoyk and Hersey published a book called "The Ethical Executive: Avoiding the Traps of the Unethical Workplace"[50], where they categorize traps using the three primary criteria of:

- Primary Traps – traps that are predominantly external stimuli that impel us to move in a certain direction, without regard for our ethics.
- Defensive Traps – traps that are attempts to find easy ways to reverse course after the transgression has occurred.
- Personality Traps – traps that are based upon our various personality traits that make us more vulnerable to doing something wrong

They then list 45 sub-traps, each of which can also be categorized using the above schemes:

PRIMARY TRAPS

- Trap I: Obedience to Authority
- Trap 2: Small Steps
- Sidestepping Responsibility
  - Trap 3: Indirect Responsibility
  - Trap 4: Faceless Victims
  - Trap 5: Lost in the Group
- Trap 6: Competition
- Self-Interest
  - Trap 7: Tyranny of Goals
  - Trap 8: Money
  - Trap 9: Conflicts of Interest
- Trap 10: Conflicts of Loyalty
- Trap 11 & I2: Conformity Pressure
- Trap 13: "Don't Make Waves"
- Trap 14: Self-Enhancement
- Trap 15: Time Pressure
- Trap 16: Decision Schemas
- Trap 17: Enacting a Role
- Trap 18: Power
- Trap 19: Justification
- Trap 20: Obligation

DEFENSIVE TRAPS

- Annihilation of Guilt
  - Trap 21: Anger
  - Trap 22: Going Numb
  - Trap 23: Alcohol
  - Trap 24: Desensitization
- Minimizing
  - Trap 25: Reduction Words
  - Trap 26: Renaming
  - Traps 27 and 28: Advantageous Comparison and Zooming Out
  - Trap 29: "Everybody Does It"
  - Trap 30: "We Won't Get Caught"
  - Trap 3I: "We Didn't Hurt Them That Bad"
  - Trap 32: Self-Serving Bias
  - Trap 33: Addiction
  - Trap 34: Coworker Reactions
  - Trap 35: Established Impressions
  - Trap 36: Contempt for the Victim
  - Trap 37: Doing Is Believing

PERSONALITY TRAPS

- Trap 38: Psychopathy
- Traps 39 and 40: Poverty and Neglect
- Trap 4I: Low Self-Esteem

- Trap 42: Authoritarianism
- Trap 43: Social Dominance Orientation
- Trap 44: Need for Closure
- Trap 45: Empathy

Anybody can get caught in a moral trap. Sometimes it is inescapable, either because it is a dilemma with no good outcome, it is forced upon us, or because it is not perceived. But many moral traps can be mitigated or avoided by creating an awareness of how our worldviews, biases and decision-making shortcuts can affect our moral decision-making.

2.9 Moral Leadership

Leadership quotes[51]:

1. A leader is best when people barely know he exists, when his work is done, his aim fulfilled, they will say: we did it ourselves. —Lao Tzu
2. Where there is no vision, the people perish. —Proverbs 29:18
3. I must follow the people. Am I not their leader? —Benjamin Disraeli
4. A leader is a dealer in hope. —Napoleon Bonaparte
5. Effective leadership is not about making speeches or being liked; leadership is defined by results not attributes. —Peter Drucker
6. When I give a minister an order, I leave it to him to find the means to carry it out. —Napoleon Bonaparte
7. Outstanding leaders go out of their way to boost the self-esteem of their personnel. If people believe in themselves, it's amazing what they can accomplish. —Sam Walton
8. No man will make a great leader who wants to do it all himself, or to get all the credit for doing it. —Andrew Carnegie
9. Never tell people how to do things. Tell them what to do and they will surprise you with their ingenuity. —General George Patton
10. Do what you feel in your heart to be right–for you'll be criticized anyway. —Eleanor Roosevelt
11. If one is lucky, a solitary fantasy can totally transform one million realities. —Maya Angelou
12. In matters of style, swim with the current; in matters of principle, stand like a rock. —Thomas Jefferson
13. It is better to lead from behind and to put others in front, especially when you celebrate victory when nice things occur. You take the front line when there is danger. Then people will appreciate your leadership. —Nelson Mandela
14. Leadership cannot just go along to get along. Leadership must meet the moral challenge of the day. —Jesse Jackson
15. No man is good enough to govern another man without that other's consent. —Abraham Lincoln
16. There are three essentials to leadership: humility, clarity and courage. —Fuchan Yuan
17. The supreme quality of leadership is integrity. –Dwight Eisenhower
18. You don't lead by hitting people over the head—that's assault, not leadership. –Dwight Eisenhower

2.9.1 Leadership

There is a long history of literature on leadership, going back to ancient times. For an historical review of leadership perspectives, I recommend reading Ronald, B. (2014). Comprehensive leadership review-literature, theories and research. *Advances in Management*, 7(5), 52 (available online at researchgate.net).

Leaders are people in positions of power and/or influence that may be formal or informal. Some leaders obtain their power as a result of hiring or promotion within institutional settings, such as a director or CEO. Other leaders are political having been voted into power, while some (who can be very powerful) result from an individual's charisma, expertise, and the respect and/or love, or fear, they get from others. They can be governors, prime ministers, cardinals, poets, musicians, prophets, or cultural icons. They may be saints or sinners, competent or inept, benign or toxic, involved or disengaged. But who they are, and what they say and do (or don't say and don't do) has a compelling impact on those within their sphere of influence.

It is beyond the scope of this section to comprehensively discuss leadership theory, but a very brief overview is given below to provide context to section 2.9.2 on moral leadership. To begin, it is important to note that an effective leadership style is highly contextual and depends upon culture, objectives, and the capacities/personalities of those being led. Leadership is closely coupled with followership – if nobody is following there is no leadership, and it is therefore power that is either granted or coerced. This is the basis of social contract theory, where citizens abdicate rights to the state in return for a better life than they would otherwise have. Leadership-followership is an interactive dynamic. There is no one right or best style of leadership, but there are styles that are more (or less) appropriate and effective in different kinds of situations, to achieve different sorts of goals. It is a good idea for leaders to have a variety of tools in their toolbox, to best fit different contexts.

Generally, modern perspectives on leadership categorizes leadership styles into three main types: (1) directive, (2) transactional, and (3) transformational.[52] Note that these styles are not mutually exclusive; a leader might incorporate a mixture of them.

(1) Directive Leadership: This style of leadership addresses the degree to which followers are involved in decision-making. It can be autocratic (which may or may not be benevolent), consultative, participative, consensus building, or laissez-faire (i.e. hands off, which is really a lack of direction). One example of autocratic directive leadership is Gunnery Sergeant Hartman in the 1987 film Full Metal Jacket. More democratic styles emphasize being consultative, participative or consensus building. A consultative approach engages followers so that they can be heard, but their voices can be disregarded. Some consultative approaches are merely done for show, to give the appearance of engagement. A truly participative approach gives a degree of decision-making authority to others, while consensus building gives a strong voice to all.

(2) Transactional Leadership: As implied by the name, this style of leadership involves exchanges between leaders and followers, where each receives a benefit in return for providing something of value to the other. It has sometimes been characterized as managership as opposed to leadership. Transactional leadership does not try to alter followers' attitudes, values, or create vision. It is not concerned with the development or growth of followers, except to the degree that a quid-pro-quo exists. It tends to be short term and tactical.

An example of a corrupt transactional leader is Gordon Gekko (played by Michael Douglas), a wealthy, unscrupulous corporate raider in the 1987 movie Wall Street. An example of a lopsided transactional approach is evident in an interview President Donald Trump gave Business Insider; "It's give-and-take" ... "But it's gotta be mostly take. Because you can't give. You gotta mostly take."[53] Transactional leadership can also reward good behavior; examples would be a bonus or award for meeting worthy goals. For example, at York University where I teach, professors who are highly rated by their students receive a non-monetary teaching award. Additionally, if professors meet a minimum level of publication, they are given a course release. These are both examples of a transaction between the university and its faculty that benefits both parties (and students).

Transformational Leadership: This style of leadership focuses on empowering followers by stimulating and creating changes in values and attitudes. It emphasizes the importance of vision and mission. This style has more commonly been associated with ethical leadership than the other styles. Examples of transformation leaders include Jesus, Ghandi, Hitler, Jim Jones[54], and Nelson Mandela. Depending on their vision and how they try to achieve it the results can be the creation of a better world, or calamity.

The theoretical perspectives held by transactional leaders tend to have in common the following:

- influencing followers by establishing a vision for a better future,
- inspiring followers as opposed to controlling them,
- leading by example through role modeling,
- contributing to subordinates' intellectual stimulation,
- enhancing meaningfulness of goals and behaviours,
- fulfilling followers' self-actualization needs,
- empowering followers through intrinsic motivation,
- exhibiting confidence in subordinates' ability to attain higher levels of achievement, and
- enhancing collective identity.[55]

There are other categorizations of leadership styles as well. For example, a paper in Harvard Business Review[56] uses the following schema (which is basically a restructuring of the above styles. See Figures 2.6):

1. The coercive style. This "Do what I say" approach can be very effective in a turnaround situation, an emergency response, or when working with problem employees. But in most situations, coercive leadership inhibits an organization's flexibility and dampens employees' motivation.

2. The authoritative style. An authoritative leader takes a "Come with me" approach but gives people the freedom to choose their own means of achieving it. This style works especially well when a business is adrift. It is less effective when a leader is working with an experienced team of experts.

3. The affiliative style. The hallmark of the affiliative leader is a "People come first" attitude. This style is particularly useful for building team harmony or increasing morale. But its exclusive focus on praise can allow poor performance to go uncorrected. Also, affiliative leaders rarely offer advice, which often leaves employees in a quandary.

4. The democratic style. This style's impact on organizational climate is not as high as you might imagine. By giving workers a voice in decisions, democratic leaders build organizational flexibility and responsibility and help generate fresh ideas. But sometimes the price is endless meetings and confused employees who feel leaderless.

5. The pacesetting style. A leader who sets high performance standards and exemplifies them himself has a very positive impact on employees who are self-motivated and highly competent. But other employees tend to feel overwhelmed by such a leader's demands for excellence—and to resent his tendency to take over a situation.

6. The coaching style. This style focuses more on personal development than on immediate work-related tasks. It works well when employees are already aware of their weaknesses and want to improve, but not when they are resistant to changing their ways.

The Six Leadership Styles at a Glance

		Coercive	Authoritative
Our research found that leaders use six styles, each springing from different components of emotional intelligence. Here is a summary of the styles, their origin, when they work best, and their impact on an organization's climate and thus its performance.	The leader's modus operandi	Demands immediate compliance	Mobilizes people toward a vision
	The style in a phrase	"Do what I tell you."	"Come with me."
	Underlying emotional intelligence competencies	Drive to achieve, initiative, self-control	Self-confidence, empathy, change catalyst
	When the style works best	In a crisis, to kick start a turnaround, or with problem employees	When changes require a new vision, or when a clear direction is needed
	Overall impact on climate	Negative	Most strongly positive

Figure 2.6a: Summary of Six Leadership Styles

Affiliative	Democratic	Pacesetting	Coaching
Creates harmony and builds emotional bonds	Forges consensus through participation	Sets high standards for performance	Develops people for the future
"People come first."	"What do you think?"	"Do as I do, now."	"Try this."
Empathy, building relationships, communication	Collaboration, team leadership, communication	Conscientiousness, drive to achieve, initiative	Developing others, empathy, self-awareness
To heal rifts in a team or to motivate people during stressful circumstances	To build buy-in or consensus, or to get input from valuable employees	To get quick results from a highly motivated and competent team	To help an employee improve performance or develop long-term strengths
Positive	Positive	Negative	Positive

Figure 2.6b: Summary of Six Leadership Styles[57]

Niccolo Machiavelli, a 16th century Italian diplomat, philosopher, politician, historian and writer had much to say about leadership. He lived in a time when city states and religious institutions were frequently at war with each other, and this context informed his world view. In his book "The Prince"[58] he offers the following advice to rulers:

- "it is much safer to be feared than loved because …love is preserved by the link of obligation which, owing to the baseness of men, is broken at every opportunity for their advantage; but fear preserves you by a dread of punishment which never fails."
- "…he who seeks to deceive will always find someone who will allow himself to be deceived."
- "Since love and fear can hardly exist together, if we must choose between them, it is far safer to be feared than loved".

Figure 2.7. Portrait of Machiavelli by Santi di Tito. Source: Wikipedia

- "Any man who tries to be good all the time is bound to come to ruin among the great number who are not good. Hence a prince who wants to keep his authority must learn how not to be good, and use that knowledge, or refrain from using it, as necessity requires."
- "Men ought either to be well treated or crushed, because they can avenge themselves of lighter injuries, of more serious ones they cannot; therefore the injury that is to be done to a man ought to be of such a kind that one does not stand in fear of revenge."[59]

His approach is very utilitarian, using people as a means to an end, and fits best into the directive and transactional styles. According to Galie and Bopst[60] "The Prince" is "the best known, if not the most influential essay in the history of political philosophy" and continue to have a strong influence of leadership philosophies today.

Though one style may be more prone for moral considerations than another, to a great degree whether or not leadership is moral depends upon the character, intentions and actions of a leader. Authentic leadership and spiritual leadership (Tables 2.3a&b) are two other types of leadership that emphasize morality, specifically character and spirituality. Avolio et al.[61] defined authentic leaders as "those individuals who are deeply aware of how they think and behave and are perceived by others as being aware of their own and others' values/moral perspective, knowledge, and strength; aware of the context in which they operate; and who are confident, hopeful, optimistic, resilient, and high on moral character." Spiritual leaders encourage workplace engagement such that people experience meaning in life; this then promotes followers' growth and development.[62] Fry[63] argues "that spiritual leadership theory is not only inclusive of other major extant motivation-based theories of leadership, but that it is also more conceptually distinct, parsimonious, and less conceptually confounded. And, by incorporating calling and membership as two key follower needs for spiritual survival, spiritual leadership theory is inclusive of the religious- and ethics and values-based approaches to leadership" and identifies a number of qualities of spiritual leadership (Table 2.3a). To accomplish this leaders must first "create a vision wherein organization members experience a sense of calling in that their life has meaning and makes a difference", and second "establish a social/organizational culture based on altruistic love whereby leaders and followers have genuine care, concern, and appreciation for both self and others, thereby producing a sense of membership and feel understood and appreciated."[64]

Vision	Altruistic love	Hope/faith
Broad appeal to key stakeholders	Forgiveness	Endurance
Defines the destination and journey	Kindness	Perseverance
Reflects high ideals	Integrity	Do what it takes
Encourages hope/faith	Empathy/compassion	Stretch goals
Establishes a standard of excellence	Honesty	Expectation of reward/victory
	Patience	
	Courage	
	Trust/loyalty	
	Humility	

Table 2.3a Qualities of spiritual leadership

Similarities with and differences between ethical, spiritual, authentic and transformational theories of leadership		
	Similarities with ethical leadership	Differences from ethical leadership
Authentic leadership	Key similarities: – Concern for others (Altruism) – Ethical decision-making – Integrity – Role modeling	Key differences: – Ethical leaders emphasize moral management (more transactional) and "other" awareness – Authentic leaders emphasize authenticity and self-awareness
Spiritual leadership	Key similarities: – Concern for others (Altruism) – Integrity – Role modeling	Key differences: – Ethical leaders emphasize moral management – Spiritual leaders emphasize visioning, hope/faith; work as vocation
Transformational leadership	Key similarities: – Concern for others (Altruism) – Ethical decision-making – Integrity – Role modeling	Key differences: – Ethical leaders emphasize ethical standards, and moral management (more transactional) – Transformational leaders emphasize vision, values, and intellectual stimulation

Table 2.3b Similarities and differences between three theories of leadership

2.9.2 Moral Leadership

By definition, leaders are in positions of power and/or influence and therefore how they use that power and influence has important moral consequences. The ethical theories discussed in Chapter 1 provide a useful background for understanding moral leadership. Virtue theory speaks to the character of a leader. To what extent do leaders embody various virtues? Which virtues are most important? Consequentialism is relevant to achieving institutional or other goals, which may justify the use of means that may negatively affect followers, society or the environment. Deontological approaches emphasize using moral means to achieve worthy ends. Procedural ethics will consider what processes are used. But, are they just and fair? Moral leadership is a balancing act, as is any other ethical decision-making process.

The notion of power distance is an important one. Power distance is one of five cultural dimensions hypothesized by Hofstede[65], these being (1) individualism versus collectivism, (2) high versus low power distance, (3) masculinity versus femininity, (4) strong versus weak uncertainty avoidance, and (5) long-term versus short-term

Comparison of the dimensions of ethical leadership addressed by the ethical leadership measure to the conceptual dimensions identified in the literature	
Conceptual dimensions of ethical leadership	Scale dimensions of ethical leadership
Character and Integrity	*Character/Integrity* • Trust • Sincere • Just • Honest
Community/ People-Orientation	*Altruism* • Generous • Fraternal • Compassionate • Modest *Collective Motivation* • Communicative • Confidence Building • Group Orientation • Motive Arouser • Team Building
Motivating Encouraging and Empowering	*Collective Motivation Encouragement* • Encouraging • Morale Booster
Ethical Awareness	Not addressed
Managing Ethical Accountability	Not addressed

Table 2.4. Dimensions of ethical leadership from a cross-cultural survey of western societies

orientation.[66] He defines power distance as "the extent to which the members of a society accept that power in institutions and organizations is distributed unequally". Cultures with low power distances are more egalitarian and tend to be "more communicative and perceived as more approachable than managers from higher power distance countries." This would facilitate treating followers not as a means to an end but as people with rights to whom obligations are owed.

A cross-cultural survey of western societies by Resick et al[67] found that four aspects of ethical leadership were significant in terms or moral leadership: (1) Character/Integrity, (2) Altruism, (3) Collective Motivation, and (4) Encouragement. These four conceptual dimensions were correlated with a number of attributes (scale dimensions) in their literature review, as shown in Table 2.4.

To what degree does moral leadership affect followers? Research suggests that there are positive outcomes including higher levels of job satisfaction, trust in leadership, and lower levels of counterproductive work behaviors. From a moral leadership perspective, if followers perceive a leader as being concerned and caring about them, they will feel an obligation to reciprocate by supporting the leader.

Research into the effectiveness of leadership has focused on (1) social learning theory, which addresses how people learn cultural norms of conduct through their own experiences and by observing others, and (2) social exchange theory, which suggests that many social relationships are based upon reciprocity and perceived obligations.[68] Social learning theory is situational, whereas social exchange theory is based upon individual relationships. Actual behaviors are moderated by a number of factors including ethical context, moral intensity, self-monitoring, need for power, inhibition, moral reasoning, and moral utilization.[69]

In a review of ethical leadership, Mihelič et al identify the following characteristics:

1) The conduct of ethical leaders serves as role-modelling behaviour for followers.
2) Ethical leaders communicate and justify their actions to followers (i.e. they make ethics salient in their social environment).
3) Ethical leaders want to continually behave according to ethics, therefore they set ethical standards in the company and reward ethical conduct on the part of employees as well as punish unethical behaviour.
4) Ethical leaders incorporate ethical dimension in decision-making processes, consider the ethical consequences of their decisions, and try to make fair choices.

Table 2. 5 summarizes differences between ethical and unethical leaders. Mihelič et al also observe that "… we more frequently find effective and unethical or ineffective and ethical leaders", and that "leaders who demonstrated increased ethical leadership were no more likely to be viewed as promotable in the short-run in comparison with those who displayed less ethical behavior."[70]

The Ethical Leader	The Unethical Leader
Is humble	Is arrogant and self-serving
Is concerned for the greater good	Excessively promotes self-interest
Is honest and straightforward	Practices deception
Fulfils commitments	Breaches agreements
Strives for fairness	Deals unfairly
Takes responsibility	Shifts blame to others
Shows respect for each individual	Diminishes others' dignity
Encourages and develops others	Neglects follower development
Serves others	Withholds help and support
Shows courage to stand up for what is right	Lacks courage to confront unjust acts

Table 2.5 Comparison of ethical and unethical leader characteristics[71]

According the Blanchard and Peale[72] there are five virtues needed by ethical leaders, these being pride, patience, prudence, persistence, and perspective. Aristotle might comment, though, that too much pride would be a character flaw.

Brown and Treviño[73] use the following model (Figure 2.8) to understand ethical leadership. They describe ethical leaders as honest, trustworthy, fair, principled and caring about people and the broader society. They behave ethically both professionally and personally.

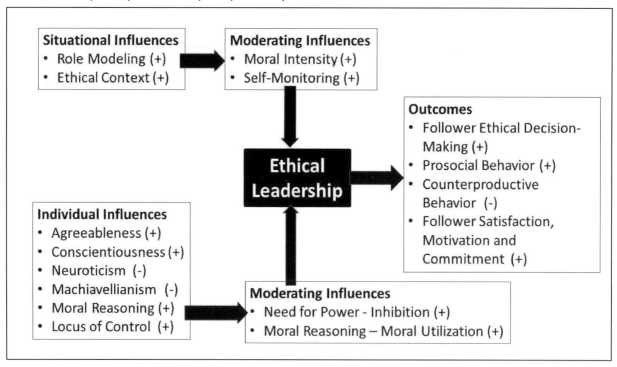

Figure 2.8. A model for ethical leadership. (+) indicates a positive correlation, and (-) a negative one.

Of the Five Factor typology of personality[74] they suggest that the first three influences in the bottom left hand box are most relevant to ethical leadership: (1) agreeableness (describing someone who is altruistic, trusting, kind and cooperative), (2) conscientiousness (dependable, responsible, dutiful, determined), and (3) neuroticism (anxious, hostile, impulsive, stressed) . Brown et al.[75] developed a 10-point ethical leadership scale[iii] that measure aspects of ethical leadership including trustworthiness, fairness, demonstrating concern for employees, setting ethical standards and disciplining those who violate these standards, and modeling ethical behavior to employees (Table 2.6).

Proposed relationships between ethical leadership and important correlates		
Construct	Predictions	Findings
Discriminant validity: personal characteristics		
Age	0	0
Gender	0	0
Perceived similarity w/supervisor	0	0
Discriminant validity: respondent beliefs		
Philosophies of human nature-cynicism	0	0
Philosophies of human nature-trust	0	+
Social desirability	0	0
Nomological validity: leadership styles and characteristics		
Idealized influence	+	+
Consideration	+	+
Interactional fairness	+	+
Affective trust	+	+
Abusive supervision	−	−
Leader honesty	+	+
Nomological validity: follower attitudes and contextual performance		
Satisfaction with leader	+	+
Leader effectiveness	+	+
Extra effort (job dedication)	+	+
Willingness to report problems	+	+

Note. +, positive relationship hypothesized; −, negative relationship hypothesized; 0, no relationship hypothesized.

Table 2.6 Correlates of ethical leadership

Other scales have also been developed to better understand and evaluate ethical leadership; one example is available online through the Institute for Ethical Leadership (http://www.ethicalleadership.com/EthicalLeadershipScales.html).

Ethical leadership varies from highly moral to toxic. Toxic leaders tend to be abusive and destructive, and are associated with psychological distress (i.e. anxiety and depression), emotional harm (i.e. emotional exhaustion, fear and social isolation) and physical health problems (i.e. chronic fatigue and insomnia in their followers. Common coping strategies by followers include "assertively challenging the leader, seeking social support, ruminating, taking leave and leaving the organization."[76] The impact on followers ethical behaviors by toxic leaders can be devastating. In one study of individuals confronted by toxic leadership it was found that "the majority of organizational members are unable to translate their moral beliefs and judgment into real moral action in the workplace."[77] To act morally when under the influence of a toxic leader requires great moral courage.

[iii] Brown et al define ethical leadership as the "demonstration of normatively appropriate conduct through personal actions and interpersonal relationships, and the promotion of such conduct to followers through two-way communication, reinforcement, and decision-making."

Ganu[78] proposes that the ability to take moral actions is dependent upon three main characteristics:

- Moral identity
    - Caring, fairness, dependable, honesty, compassion.
- Moral confidence
    - Based on a level of confidence to carry out ethical responsibilities in the workplace. It can be measured by positive responses to such statements as:
        - "I am able to confront others who behave unethically in my workplace"
        - "I have confidence in my ability to readily see the moral/ethical implications in the challenges i face"
        - "I am able to work with others to settle moral/ethical disputes"
        - "I am able to take decisive action when addressing a moral/ethical decision"
        - "I have confidence in my ability to determine what needs to be done when i face moral/ethical dilemmas."
- Moral courage
    - "...the fortitude to convert moral intentions into actions despite pressures from either inside or outside of the organization to do otherwise"[79].
    - Measured by a willingness to speak out and by positive responses to such statements as:
        - "Do you confront your peers if they commit an unethical act?"
        - "Do you confront your supervisor if he/she commits an unethical act?"
        - "Do you go against the group's decision whenever it violates your ethical standards?"

In a study based upon this model over 70% of respondents indicated that they would prefer to keep silent or do nothing when confronted by ethical issues, mainly because of fears of negative consequences to themselves (Table 2.7).

Aronson[80] departs from the traditional view that moral leadership is largely dependent upon leadership style, and suggests that it is the character of the leader that is most important. He says that *"The essential determining factor as to whether the leadership behaviours are ethical or not is the level of moral development or altruism of the leader."* The leadership style will then be molded to suit the moral attributes of the leader. For example, a charismatic and transformational leader (the style most often associated with moral leadership) can be toxic and destructive (for example, as mentioned earlier, Hitler or Jim Jones). A transactional style could reinforce either ethical or immoral behavior, depending upon the transactions chosen. Aronson developed a three-dimensional ethical leadership model that depends upon a leader's moral development (Figures 2.9).

Factors That Impede Employees' Moral Action	
Reasons for inaction	*Rank*
Fear (of victimization, threats, intimidation)	1
Protect relationships	2
Protect job or position or the future	3
Nothing will be done—Speaking up is a waste of time	4
Nothing will be done—Speaking up is a waste of time = Majority rules	5
Do not have a "voice" or the power to change things	6
It is someone else's job to correct such, not me—It is not my job	7
No established systems to deal with such situations	8
Unethical organizational culture	9
African culture—"don't oppose the 'elder'"	10

Table 2.7 Factors that impede moral action

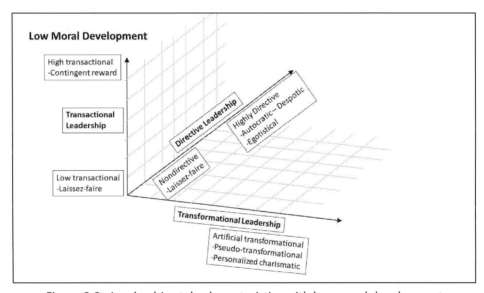

Figure 2.9a Leadership style characteristics with low moral development

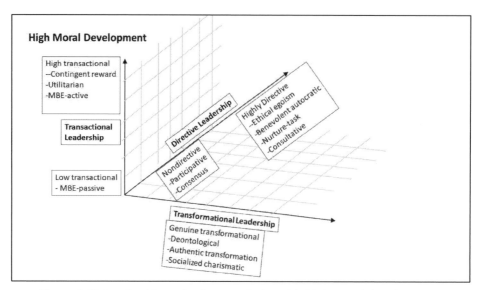

Figure 2.9b Leadership style characteristics with high moral development

The concept of moral leadership and followership is becoming increasingly recognized as an important aspect of organizational culture. Depending upon the character of leaders and their style of leadership it can elevate or diminish, create or destroy, engage or exclude. It is a crucial aspect of institutions in our society in general, and greatly determines how well the people who work in them live and function.

2.10 Conclusion

Emergency management is underlain by a social and humanist agenda, that being the reduction of harm to people. Emergency managers, therefore, work and act within a moral framework. This moral framework depends upon many factors such as culture, religion, legislation, policy, and the informal social contract that exists between citizens and their governments.

The degree to which we can be effective as emergency managers depends upon how mature we are as moral beings. Not everyone will agree upon a precise definition of what a moral being is, but we can all do the following:

- Be aware that our moral identity should form a significant part of our self-image,
- Include moral reasoning as an important aspect of our decision-making,
- Pay attention to our moral emotions, and
- Act upon our moral reasoning.

Moral perfection does not exist, but as noted by T. S. Eliot, *"The journey, not the destination, matters..."*

Figure 2.10. T.S. Eliot in 1934 by Lady Ottoline Morrell.[81]

2.9 Endnotes

[1] Source: Wikipedia, https://en.wikipedia.org/wiki/Groucho_Marx#/media/File:Groucho_Marx_-_portrait.jpg

[2] Johnson, E. J., & Goldstein, D. G. (2004). Defaults and donation decisions. *Transplantation, 78*(12), 1713-1716.

[3] Kohl, A., & Pina, J. (2016). *World index of moral freedom 2016: How free is your country from state-imposed moral constraints?* The Foundation for the Advancement of Liberty/Fundación Para el Avance de la Libertad. http://www.fundalib.org/wp-content/uploads/2016/04/World-Index-of-Moral-Freedom-web.pdf

[4] Chomsky, N., & Herman, E. S. (2003). *Manufacturing consent: The political economy of the mass media*. Random House.

[5] Ford, R. C., & Richardson, W. D. (1994). Ethical decision making: A review of the empirical literature. *Journal of Business Ethics, 13*(3), 205-221.

[6] Piaget, J. (1952). *The origins of intelligence in children* (M. Cook, Trans.). International Universities Press.

[7] Kohlberg, L. (1981). *Essays on moral development, volume one: The philosophy of moral development: Moral stages and the idea of justice*. Harper & Row.

[8] Kohlberg, L. (1984). *Essays on moral development, volume two: The psychology of moral development*. Harper & Row.

[9] Kohlberg, L., & Hersh, R. H. (1977). Moral development: A review of the theory. *Theory into Practice, 16*(2), 53-59.

[10] McLeod, S. (2013). *Kohlberg's stages of moral development.* Simply psychology. https://www.simplypsychology.org/kohlberg.html

[11] Baek, H. J. (2002). A comparative study of moral development of Korean and British children. *Journal of Moral Education, 31*(4), 373-391.

[12] Gilligan, C., & Attanucci, J. (1988). Two moral orientations: gender differences and similarities. *Merrill-Palmer Quarterly, 34*, 223–237.

[13] Gilligan, C. (1993). *In a different voice: Psychological theory and women's development*. Harvard University Press.

[14] Gilligan, C. (1988). ''Remapping the Moral Domain :New Images of Self in Relationship'', in C. Gilligan, J. V. Ward and J. Mclean Taylor (eds*), Mapping the Moral Domain*. pp. 3 – 19. (Center for the Study of Gender, Education and Human Development, Harvard University Press, 1988).

[15] Schlozman, K. L., Burns, N., Verba, S., & Donahue, J. (1995). Gender and citizen participation: Is there a different voice?. *American Journal of Political Science*, 267-293.

[16] Rest, J. R., Narvaez, D., Thoma, S. J., & Bebeau, M. J. (2000). A neo-Kohlbergian approach to morality research. *Journal of Moral Education, 29*(4), 381-395.

[17] Rest, J. R. (1979). *Development in judging moral issues*. University of Minnesota Press.

[18] University of Alabama. (2019). *About the Defining Issues Test.* Center for the Study of Ethical Development. https://ethicaldevelopment.ua.edu/about-the-dit.html

[19] Rest, J. R., Narvaez, D., Thoma, S. J., & Bebeau, M. J. (2000). A neo-Kohlbergian approach to morality research. *Journal of moral education, 29*(4), 381-395.

[20] Rest, J. R., Narvaez, D., Thoma, S. J., & Bebeau, M. J. (2000). A neo-Kohlbergian approach to morality research. *Journal of moral education, 29*(4), 381-395.

[21] Stankey, O. (2018). *An overview of the 3 main moral development theories.* Northwest Association of College & University Housing Officers. http://nwacuho.org/2018/01/overview-3-main-moral-development-theories/

[22] Haidt, J., & Joseph, C. (2004). Intuitive ethics: How innately prepared intuitions generate culturally variable virtues. *Daedalus: Special Issue on Human Nature, 133*(4), 55–66.

[23] ADAM FRIENDED. (2017, April 13). *Where does morality come from? | Moral foundations theory, Jonathan Haidt* [Video]. YouTube. https://www.youtube.com/watch?v=vxcgPFrmbng&t=93s

[24] Hear the Reasons. (2013, December 5). *Jonathan Haidt - The rationalist delusion in moral psychology* [Video]. YouTube. https://www.youtube.com/watch?v=kl1wQswRVaU&t=10s

[25] Graham, J., Haidt, J., & Nosek, B. A. (2009). Liberals and conservatives rely on different sets of moral foundations. *Journal of Personality and Social Psychology, 96*(5), 1029-1046.

[26] Haidt, J. (2008, March). *The moral roots of liberals and conservatives.* TED2008. https://www.ted.com/talks/jonathan_haidt_the_moral_roots_of_liberals_and_conservatives?language=en

[27] Kugler, M., Jost, J. T., & Noorbaloochi, S. (2014). Another look at moral foundations theory: Do authoritarianism and social dominance orientation explain liberal-conservative differences in "moral" intuitions? *Social Justice Research, 27*(4), 413-431.

[28] Schwartz, M. (2007). [Lecture notes]. *DEMS 6070: Disaster Ethics.* York University.

[29] Marcum, T. M., & Young, J. (2019). Blowing the Whistle in the Digital Age: Are You Really Anonymous: The Perils and Pitfalls of Anonymity in Whistleblowing Law. *DePaul Bus. & Comm. LJ, 17*, 1.

[30] Anyadike, O. (2016). *Exclusive: Top UN whistleblower resigns, citing impunity and lack of accountability.* The new humanitarian. http://www.thenewhumanitarian.org/news/2016/06/07/exclusive-top-un-whistleblower-resigns-citing-impunity-and-lack-accountability

[31] Anyadike, O. (2016). *Exclusive: Top UN whistleblower resigns, citing impunity and lack of accountability.* The new humanitarian. http://www.thenewhumanitarian.org/news/2016/06/07/exclusive-top-un-whistleblower-resigns-citing-impunity-and-lack-accountability

[32] Sierra, O. (2015). [Anders Kompass] [Photograph]. *Foreign policy.* https://foreignpolicy.com/2015/06/12/prince-zeid-u-n-high-commissioner-human-rights-africa-sexual-misconduct-france-u-n-whistle-blower/

[33] Anyadike, O. (2016). *Exclusive: Top UN whistleblower resigns, citing impunity and lack of accountability.* The new humanitarian. http://www.thenewhumanitarian.org/news/2016/06/07/exclusive-top-un-whistleblower-resigns-citing-impunity-and-lack-accountability

[34] Anyadike, O. (2016). *Exclusive: Top UN whistleblower resigns, citing impunity and lack of accountability.* The new humanitarian. http://www.thenewhumanitarian.org/news/2016/06/07/exclusive-top-un-whistleblower-resigns-citing-impunity-and-lack-accountability

[35] Kompass, A. (2016). *EXCLUSIVE: The ethical failure – Why I resigned from the UN.* The New Humanitarian. https://www.thenewhumanitarian.org/opinion/2016/06/17/exclusive-ethical-failure-why-i-resigned-un

[36] Ethics & Compliance Initiative. (2016). *Global business ethics survey 2016: Measuring risk and promoting workplace integrity.* https://www.ethics.org/knowledge-center/2016-global-business-ethics-survey/

[37] Shao, R., Aquino, K., & Freeman, D. (2008). Beyond moral reasoning: A review of moral identity research and its implications for business ethics. *Business Ethics Quarterly, 18*(4), 513-540.

[38] Milgram, S. (1963). Behavioral study of obedience. *The Journal of Abnormal and Social Psychology, 67*(4), 371-378.

[39] Milgram, S. (1965). Some conditions of obedience and disobedience in authority. *Human Relations, 18*(1), 57-76.

[40] Milgram, S., & Gudehus, C. (1978). *Obedience to authority.* Ziff-Davis Publishing Company.

[41] Milgram, S., & Gudehus, C. (1978). *Obedience to authority.* Ziff-Davis Publishing Company.

[42] Prentice, R. A. (2007). Ethical decision making: More needed than good intentions. *Financial Analysts Journal, 63*(6), 17-30.

[43] Prentice, R. A. (2007). Ethical decision making: More needed than good intentions. *Financial Analysts Journal, 63*(6), 17-30.

[44] Prentice, R. A. (2007). Ethical decision making: More needed than good intentions. *Financial Analysts Journal, 63*(6), 17-30

[45] Sims, Ronald R. 1992. "Linking Groupthink to Unethical Behavior in Organizations." Journal of Business Ethics, vol. 11, no. 9 (September):651–662.

[46] Stephanie C. Lin, Julian J. Zlatev, Dale T. Miller, Journal of Experimental Social Psychology, Volume 70, 2017, Pages 198-203, ISSN 0022-1031, https://doi.org/10.1016/j.jesp.2016.11.004.

[47] Tversky, Amos, and Daniel Kahneman. 1981. "The Framing of Decisions and the Psychology of Choice." *Science*, vol. 211, no. 4481 (30 January):453–458.

[48] Leeson, Nicholas. 1996. *Rogue Trader.* Boston, MA: Little Brown.

[49] Gigerenzer, G., & Gaissmaier, W. (2011). Heuristic decision making. *Annual review of psychology, 62*, 451-482.

[50] Hoyk, R. and Hersey, H. (2008). The Ethical Executive: Avoiding the traps of the unethical workplace, Stanford Business Books

[51] Kruze, K. (2012). 100 Best Quotes on Leadership, https://www.forbes.com/sites/kevinkruse/2012/10/16/quotes-on-leadership/?sh=21e78fd82feb

[52] Ronald, B. (2014). Comprehensive leadership review-literature, theories and research. *Advances in Management, 7*(5), 52.

[53] *Donald Trump explains the give-and-take of deal-making like only he can*, Colin Campbell Nov 19, 2015, 12:01 PM, https://www.businessinsider.com/donald-trump-deals-2015-11

[54] Moore, R., & McGehee III, F. (1989). New Religious Movements, Mass Suicide, and Peoples Temple. *Scholarly Perspectives on a Tragedy.*

[55] Aronson, E. (2001). Integrating leadership styles and ethical perspectives. *Canadian Journal of Administrative Sciences/Revue Canadienne des Sciences de l'Administration, 18*(4), 244-256

[56] Goleman, D. (2017). *Leadership that gets results (Harvard business review classics).* Harvard Business Press

[57] Goleman, D. (2017). *Leadership that gets results (Harvard business review classics).* Harvard Business Press

[58] Machiavelli, N. (1995). The Prince [1513]. *The Prince and other Political Writings, ed. S. Milner.*

[59] Source: https://www.goodreads.com/work/quotes/1335445-de-principatibus-il-principe

[60] Galie, P. J., & Bopst, C. (2006). Machiavelli & modern business: Realist thought in contemporary corporate leadership manuals. *Journal of Business Ethics, 65*(3), 235-250.

[61] Avolio, B., Gardner, W., Walumbwa, F., & May, D. (2004). Unlocking the mask: A look at the process by which authentic leaders impact follower attitudes and behaviors. *Leadership Quarterly, 15*(6), 801-823. In Klenke, K. (2007). Authentic leadership: A self, leader, and spiritual identity perspective. *International journal of leadership studies, 3*(1), 68-97.

[62] Wang, M., Guo, T., Ni, Y., Shang, S., & Tang, Z. (2019). The effect of spiritual leadership on employee effectiveness: An intrinsic motivation perspective. *Frontiers in psychology, 9*, 2627.

[63] Fry, L. W. (2003). Toward a theory of spiritual leadership. *The leadership quarterly, 14*(6), 693-727.

[64] Fry, L. W. (2003). Toward a theory of spiritual leadership. *The leadership quarterly, 14*(6), 693-727.

[65] Offermann, L. R. and P. S. Hellmann: 1997, _Culture's Consequences for Leadership Behavior: National Values in Action, *Journal of Cross-Cultural Psychology* 28, 342–351.

[66] Hofstede, G., (2001), *Culture's Consequences: Comparing Values, Behaviours, Institutions and Organisations across Nations*, Thousand Oaks, CA.

[67] "Resick, C. J., Hanges, P. J., Dickson, M. W., & Mitchelson, J. K. (2006). A Cross-Cultural Examination of The Endorsement of Ethical Leadership. *Journal of Business Ethics*, 63(4), 345-359"

[68] Bedi, A., Alpaslan, C. M., & Green, S. (2016). A meta-analytic review of ethical leadership outcomes and moderators. *Journal of Business Ethics, 139*(3), 517-536.

[69] Brown, M. E., & Trevin~o, L. K. (2006). Ethical leadership: A review and future directions. *Leadership Quarterly*, 17, 595–616.

[70] Rubin, R. S., Dierdorff, E. C., & Brown, M. E. (2010). Do Ethical Leaders Get Ahead? Exploring Ethical Leadership and Promotability. *Business Ethics Quarterly, 20*(2), 215-236.

[71] Zanderer, D. G. (1992). Integrity: An essential Executive quality. *Business Forum,* Fall, 12-16

[72] Blanchard, K. H., & Peale, N. V. (1996). *The power of ethical management*: Ballantine Books.

[73] Brown, M. E., & Treviño, L. K. (2006). Ethical Leadership: A Review and Future Directions. *The Leadership Quarterly*, 17(6), 595-616

[74] Holland, J. L. (1992). *Making vocational choices: A theory of vocational personalities and work environments* (2nd ed.). Odessa, FL: Psychological Assessment Resources.

[75] Brown, M. E., Treviño, L. K., & Harrison, D. A. (2005). Ethical leadership: A social learning perspective for construct development and testing. *Organizational behavior and human decision processes*, 97(2), 117-134.

[76] Webster, V., Brough, P., & Daly, K. (2016). Fight, Flight or Freeze: Common Responses for Follower Coping with Toxic Leadership. *Stress and Health,* 32(4), 346-354.

[77] Ganu, J. (2018). Moral Courage: The Essence of Ethical Leadership and Followership. *Journal of Applied Christian Leadership*, *12*(2), 42-53.

[78] Ganu, J. (2018). Moral Courage: The Essence of Ethical Leadership and Followership. *Journal of Applied Christian Leadership*, *12*(2), 42-53.

[79] May, D. r., Chan, A. Y., Hodges, t. D., & Avolio, B. J. (2003). Developing the moral component of authentic leadership. *Organizational Dynamics, 32,* 247–260.

[80] Aronson, E. (2001). Integrating leadership styles and ethical perspectives. *Canadian Journal of Administrative Sciences/Revue Canadienne des Sciences de l'Administration*, 18(4), 244-256.

[81] Morrell, O. (1934). [Eliot in 1934] [Photograph]. *Wikipedia.*
https://en.wikipedia.org/wiki/T._S._Eliot#/media/File:Thomas_Stearns_Eliot_by_Lady_Ottoline_Morrell_(1934).jpg

CHAPTER 3: ETHICAL RISK ASSESSMENT

"Whoever controls the definition of risk controls the rational solution to the problem at hand."

Paul Slovic

Contents

3.1 Introduction

Emergency management requires a knowledge of the threat environment, which is based upon a risk assessment (RA) process. Fundamentally, this is a process that bounds the world according to groups and then, when possible, quantifies them using various metrics. The terms "risk analysis" and "risk assessment" are often used interchangeably, and include the elements of risk identification, estimations of consequences (through consideration of hazard probability and severity, exposure, and vulnerability), communication with stakeholders, and approaches to prevent or mitigate impacts. Examples of groups are natural hazards, infrastructure in flood plains, and single-parent households. What groups are chosen will have an important impact on the outcome of a risk assessment. RA is essentially consequentialist, focusing on optimizing a system by minimizing losses or maximizing gains. One essential and common tool for RA is cost-benefit analysis, but when used issues related to rights and obligations, who loses and who benefits, and duties of care tend to get lost in the process.

Knowing your risks and ranking them in terms of importance is a basis for the "rational"[i] allocation of resources. (In the next chapter on the precautionary principle, I discuss situations for which conventional risk assessment methodologies do not work well.) For this reason, all emergency management organizations are required to do risk assessments.[ii, 1] However, risk assessment is a very difficult and complicated exercise if done thoroughly and robustly. This is especially true for comparing different risks and creating a risk ranking, which suffers from serious methodological problems that make the process problematic. One of the most glaring problems with the practice of risk assessment within the emergency management community is that ethical issues are notable by their absence.

Although science is an essential component of risk assessment, RA is much broader than that. This is partly because there are gaps and uncertainties that make scientific assessment difficult for some hazards. Some technical issues that can impact RA are:

- Making generalizations from small data samples.
- Assuming that high concentration exposures over short periods of time are equivalent to low concentration exposures over long periods of time.
- Making conclusions from animal studies regarding human health.
- Assuming single causes when there are multiple complex interactions.
- Paying insufficient attention to uncertainties.

---

[i] I put the word "rational" in quotation marks because the process is underlain by values that, although often unstated, determine choices of methodologies and metrics that ultimately determine outcomes.

[iii] For example, the CSA Z1600 standard requires the following:

> The entity shall conduct a risk assessment […] The risk assessment shall include evaluating the likelihood of a hazard or combination of hazards occurring, taking into account factors such as threat analysis, frequency, history, trends, and probability. […] The risk assessment shall include data on the impact of the risk event on the entity and on people, property, and the environment.

- Excluding the more vulnerable from an impact analysis.

"...all the things they told us couldn't happen happened."

—Mike Williams, Chief Electronic Technician on the oil rig Deepwater Horizon platform (2010)

Figure 3.1: Platform supply vessels battle the blazing remnants of the offshore oil rig Deepwater Horizon[2]

In addition to technical issues, there are choices that must be made based upon values and subjective judgements. One of the factors that makes RA difficult is that there are intangibles at play that require qualitative judgments that are based upon personal and cultural values. Examples are valuing nature (Chapter 1.7), the value of life (Chapter 10), and the value of culturally important places.

There are many sources available to assist with risk assessment methodologies and metrics, but this chapter will not address all aspects of that topic. It will, however, consider the importance of including an ethical component in a risk analysis, and the kind of thinking that is needed to accomplish that goal.

3.2 How Important is Ethics to a Risk Assessment?

In a study I did on risk assessments done by 50 U.S. states, nine Canadian provinces, ten nations, and several non-governmental organizations, I found that none of them included an ethical analysis.[3] This is in spite of the fact that values and ethical perspectives underlie the methodologies and metrics used within these assessments. I see this as a shocking gap in how risk assessment is conducted! It is not a problem just related to emergency management, but is widespread throughout most professions that engage in RA. This is an example of how common practice can be very different from best practice.

Where lives are lost and there is also economic damage, how should those two losses be compared or combined? Can a lost life be meaningfully assigned an economic value, and if so, what are the assumptions and values that lead to such a calculation? To what extent does it matter whose life is affected or lost? (See Chapter 9 for more on this topic.)

Consider, for example, the metric of total economic loss versus economic loss as a percentage of wealth. The former will emphasize the wealthy while marginalizing the poor. Loss as a percentage of wealth gives greater emphasis to those who are not wealthy and results in a very different ranking of who and what is at risk than does a total loss metric (see example in Table 3.1 for an example).

All the risk assessments reviewed in my study use total economic impacts and therefore emphasize and reinforce existing wealth and power structures. Why was (and is) this choice made by risk assessors?

If using fatalities, should total fatalities be used as a metric or fatalities as a percentage of community population? Are all lives of equal value, or should some (such as children) be given greater weight because they have lost more potential years of life or because society has a greater duty of care towards them? These are important questions that should be addressed in any risk assessment.

The issue of normalization (calculating losses as a percentage) gets more complicated when one considers how a metric should be normalized. For example, Hurricane Katrina, one of the United States' worst natural disasters, primarily impacted the southeastern U.S. When normalizing economic impact, should it be done relative to the entire U.S. or just the areas physically affected by the storm? Louisiana, the hardest hit state, contributes only 0.6% to the U.S. national GDP, so the storm impact will appear very different when normalized at a state level as opposed to a national level.[4] There is no right answer to this question; the most useful answer is contextual and depends upon the purpose of the risk assessment. Every list of disaster data and every risk assessment is underlain by values that should be acknowledged.

Disaster	Total Cost in Millions	Cost as % of GDP	Total Deaths	Deaths Per Million
2011 Japanese Tsunami	$235,000	3.6%	15,770	157
2010 Haiti Earthquake	$14,000	121.2%	230,000	22,945
Ratio Japanese Tsunami / Haiti Earthquake	16.8	0.02	0.1	0.01
Ratio Haiti Earthquake / Japanese Tsunami	0.1	44	14.6	171

Table 3.1: Comparison of the 2011 Japanese Tsunami and the 2010 Haiti Earthquake. Note how the tsunami was a much greater disaster based upon total economic impact, while the earthquake was much worse in terms of cost as a percentage of GDP.[5, 6, 7]

Similarly, methodologies, such as how a cost-benefit is calculated or whose expert opinions are included, create biases. Sometimes, if empirical data is not available, cost-benefit analyses must be based upon surveys of what people think something is worth. Should people be asked what they would pay to keep something, or what they would accept for its elimination? Depending upon which approach is chosen, very different results ensue. To illustrate this point, consider the potential loss of a loved family member. Many people would pay everything they have (a finite number—let's choose $200,000 as an example) to save their life, but would not accept $100,000,000 (or perhaps even an infinite amount of money) for them to lose their life; two very different outcomes for a cost-benefit calculation! Valuing life is an enormously difficult problem, and is further discussed in Chapter 9. Though the choice of methodology and metric largely determines the outcome of a risk assessment, it is often given insufficient (if any) attention in RA design, and even less in published RA documents.

Values and Assumptions:

- Any risk assessment that does not explicitly state the values and assumptions that underlie it allows assessors to evade critical examination of their own biases and assumptions (note the quote by Paul Slovic at the beginning of this chapter and Section 3.4 below).

Figure 3.2 below is a typical illustration of the emergency management risk framework. Note that like the CSA Z1600 standard it is absent any explicit ethical consideration. This is also true of the internationally accepted ISO risk management standard[8]. Figure 3.3, a First Nations model for pandemic planning, is quite different, incorporating community bonding and relations, collective and individual rights, as well as the spiritual and social realms. This model represents a very different worldview than the ISO and CSA models presented above or the four-phased approach to EM (Figure 3.2).

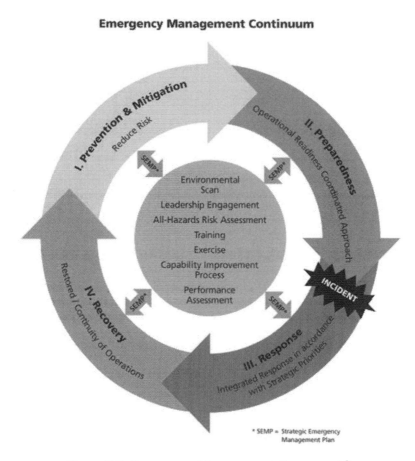

Figure 3.2: Emergency Management Framework[9]

There is a large literature on decision-making as it relates to risk, and also a large literature on ethical analysis, but a very small one that incorporates both approaches. As others have, I argue that they are two sides of the same coin. For example, Hansson notes that decision theory is intended to find a best means to an end, but once that end is determined the means are viewed as value-free and driven solely by rationality, without the requirement for value-based input.[10] However, what those ends should be lies not in the realm of risk assessment, but in social values and ethical reasoning. And given that disaster risk reduction is rarely a pure public good[iii], since goods (such as funds provided for mitigation or recovery) are not provided to all equally (and can also result in harms, such as discussed by Naomi Klein in *The Shock Doctrine*[11]), decisions regarding who benefits and who pays/suffers become an

---

[iii] A public good is one that is equally available to all and where use by one individual does not reduce availability for others.

essential component of decision-making. This frequently occurs within a context of scarce resources and competing agendas, which makes decision-making of greater ethical complexity.

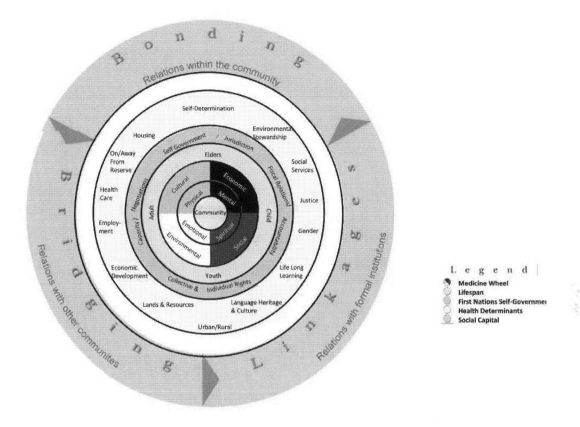

Figure 3.3: First Nations Wheel[12]

There are several ways in which the ethics-risk divide has expressed itself. Ethical theory emphasizes issues of justice and fairness, and who creates and bears the brunt of risks, while risk assessment emphasizes degrees of risk with little or no reference to justice or fairness issues. In risk assessment, risk is often defined to be a function of *probability x consequence* or *hazard x exposure x vulnerability*, which is the basis of many risk equations and the risk matrix model commonly used in emergency management risk analyses. By contrast, ethical analyses include discussions of how different ethical theories and values create alternate pathways of decision-making (see list of questions in Section 3.3), which cannot be adequately considered within a framework solely based upon probability and consequence.[13]

Two Sides of the Same Coin:

- Decision-making theory and ethical analysis are two sides of the same coin. Both need to be used by emergency managers when they do a risk assessment.

3.3 Incorporating Ethical Thinking Into a Risk Analysis

Much of descriptive ethical decision-making theory is based upon a framework that includes the following four components:

- Identifying the ethical nature of an issue;
- Making an ethical judgement;
- Establishing ethical intent; and
- Engaging in ethical action.[14]

According to Hermansson and Hansson, questions that should be addressed within ethical decision-making include:

1. "To what extent do the risk-exposed benefit from the risk exposure?
2. Is the distribution of risks and benefits fair?
3. Can the distribution of risks and benefits be made less unfair by redistribution or by compensation?
4. To what extent is the risk exposure decided by those who run the risk?
5. Do the risk-exposed have access to all relevant information about the risk?
6. Are there risk-exposed persons who cannot be informed or included in the decision process?
7. Does the decision-maker benefit from other people's exposure?"[15]

To these the following questions can be added:

1. Who is doing the risk analysis, and for what purpose?
2. What risks are being included / excluded, and why?
   a. How are future generations being factored into the assessment?
   b. How is the environment being factored into the assessment?
3. How is risk being defined, and what are the implications of this definition?
   a. How would an alternate definition of risk alter outcomes?
4. How does the risk analysis reflect power interests and divisions of wealth?
5. Are there groups of people who are owed special duties of care, such as wards of the state, children, or the especially vulnerable?
   a. How are their interests being recognized?
   b. Are their voices part of the decision-making process?
6. Is the precautionary principle (Chapter 4) recognized as part of the decision-making process?
7. What data gaps exist between what one would want to measure, and what can be measured?
   a. What are the implications of these gaps?
8. What are the assumptions and values that underlie the methodology being used?

a. How would alternate methodologies change the risk assessment?

9. What are the assumptions and values that underlie the metrics being used?

a. How would alternate metrics change the risk assessment?

There are ethical perspectives that largely avoid the issue of risk assessment; for example, virtue ethics emphasizes character and focuses on how people should behave if they are to embody various virtues, such as courage, honesty, and benevolence. Risk assessment is a utilitarian tool. But not all decisions that people make are based on risk, nor should they be. Sometimes people do something simply because they believe it is the right thing to do, or because to do otherwise would be sinful or vile.

The process of ethical decision-making is summarized in Figure 3.4.

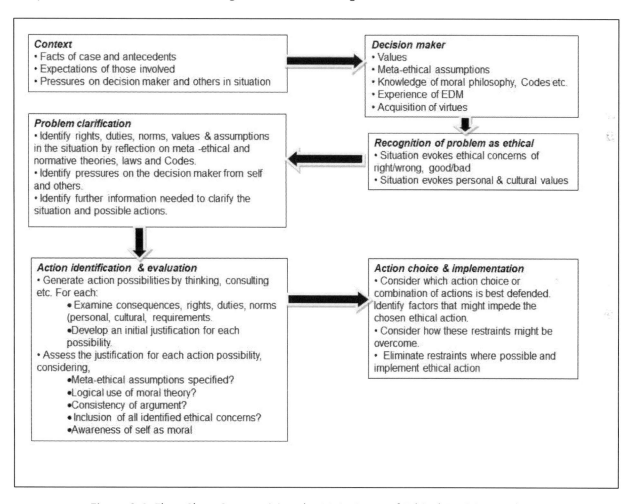

Figure 3.4: Flow Chart Summarizing the Main Steps of Ethical Decision-Making

If a Hazard Identification and Risk Assessment (HIRA) approach is being used in an emergency management risk assessment then it would fit into the fifth box, "Action Identification and Evaluation." Particular attention needs to be paid to the metrics used in the consequences axis, as discussed in Section 3.1.

3.4 Case Study: Risk Assessment by Det Norske Veritas for Trans Mountain Pipeline

Consider the risk assessment methodology used by Det Norske Veritas (DNV) in their report to Trans Mountain Pipeline ULC (TM), in support of TM's application to the National Energy Board of Canada for a certificate of public convenience and necessity in respect of the Trans Mountain Pipeline system and the expansion project.[16]

The purpose of this risk assessment was to evaluate risks related to tanker spills off the west coast of Canada. As can be seen from Figure 3.5 and Table 3.2, Segments 3 and 4 were eliminated for consideration because the probability of an accident was estimated as being too low. Segment 2 was also excluded, though this was not explicitly mentioned in Table 3.2. These three areas, however, are adjacent to the City of Vancouver and other important communities and ecological coastal areas! Though the probability of a spill may be relatively low in these areas, this should not be the basis for exclusion from a risk assessment, since risk is a function of both probability and consequences. This is a critical methodological error in the analysis that I interpret as being made solely for the purpose of biasing the risk assessment in favor of Trans Mountain Pipeline. It cannot be justified on methodological or ethical grounds.

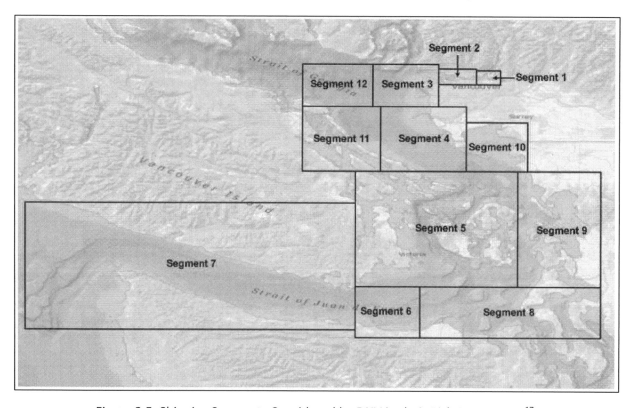

Figure 3.5: Shipping Segments Considered by DNV in their Risk Assessment[17]

| B | 3 | English Bay | Possible collision with ships at anchor in English Bay and traffic from Fraser river is low probability | Not considered as viable spill location due to relatively low frequency for an accidental oil cargo spill |
| C | 4 | Roberts Bank | Possible collision with crossing traffic from Fraser river and other crossing traffic is low probability | Not considered as viable spill location due to relatively low frequency for an accidental oil cargo spill |

Table 3.2: Rationale for Excluding Segments 3 and 4 of Figure 3.5. Segment 2 is absent from the table.[18]

Another issue that is problematic with this risk assessment is the interpretation of the phrase "credible worst-case scenario" used by DNV. This phraseology is included in the TERMPOL standards, but is not precisely defined.[19] It is hard to argue with the phrase, since including an event that is not credible is unreasonable by definition, but this language also creates a great deal of "wiggle room" for any risk analyst. DNV made the assumption that a spill of greater than 16% of tanker capacity exceeded this threshold (i.e., was not credible), and therefore any spills of greater than 16% were excluded from the risk assessment. There have certainly been significant decreases of spill volumes over the past several decades, but this is still an optimistic assumption that tilts the results of the risk assessment favorably towards Trans Mountain Pipeline. Residents of the Greater Vancouver Area (GVA) would likely be interested in a more inclusive analysis.

An ethical analysis by DNV would have addressed who is at risk, which would include the residents of the GVA and allow room for their voices in deciding what areas should be eliminated (or not). Their risk assessment, however, has the appearance of being biased towards the special interests of Trans Mountain, the company for whom the report was done, and therefore it seems unlikely that an ethical analysis would have served their purpose.

3.5 The Role of Emotion

Much of Western thought on ethics has approached it from a rationalist perspective, emphasizing the importance of logic and our "thinking" selves. But like recent research in the area of risk, ethics literature is now also discussing the importance of our "emotional" selves. For example, Zhong and Liljenquist found that moral transgressions literally make people feel dirty.[20] The feeling of disgust, which from an evolutionary perspective helped people to avoid eating dangerous food, is now a human response to cultural and moral wrongness.[21] This is not only felt by people, but can be seen in facial expressions and measured in physiological activations.

Zhong and Liljenquist point out the importance of using our logical, cognitive minds in conjunction with our affective, emotional selves when making moral judgements. Restricting judgements to only the rational process can result in dangerous outcomes, such as the rationalization of eugenics used by Hitler to justify his campaigns of extermination in Germany in the late 1930s and early 1940s.[iv] Similarly, relying only on emotions can lead to terrible outcomes; just because something "feels" right in the moment, does not make it so. Such feelings can be used to justify revenge killings and other acts that violate social norms. For that reason, modern societies have trended towards taking rights away from individuals and giving powers of justice to the state, to create an overall safer and more just society. It is part of our social contract that we repress taking justice into our own hands, in the belief that when it is handled by the state the greater good is served.

Barnes and Thagard discuss the importance of emotional processes in decision-making, noting that rational and emotional processes function together.[22] Emotion plays a critical role in ethical arguments and moral judgements relating to caring, compassion and empathy. More fundamentally, there are neurological studies that link the cognitive and emotional centers of the brain via neural connections.[23] In one case study a subject without these connections was "trapped in a never-ending cost-benefit analysis of numerous and conflicting options."[24]

3.6 Factors That Affect Ethical Decision Making

Risk analysis is an important component of decision-making and is subject to the same biases and influences that affect other aspects of this field. The choices that people make depend upon many internal and external factors, including their individual characteristics and background, as well as contextual and cultural factors. Ford and Richardson in a review of various factors that affect ethical decision-making summarized the state of the literature as follows:

Individual Factors:
- *Nationality, sex and age.* "Personal attributes are related to an individual's ethical beliefs and decision-making behavior in some studies but not in others."[25] Figures 3.6 and 3.7 illustrate how different countries have varying ethical cultural norms.
- *Education and Employment.* "In some instances, type and years of education and type and years of employment are related to an individual's ethical beliefs and decision-making behavior. However, in other situations, ethical beliefs and decision making are independent of education and employment."[26] There are few studies on this issue, and at times they contradict each other, so it is difficult to draw conclusions.
- *Personality, Belief and Values.* "Some personality traits of the decision maker are related to his/her ethical beliefs and behavior. Interestingly, the trait which would have the strongest predicted theoretical relationship (i.e. Machiavellianism) to ethical beliefs and decision making has been verified in the empirical work."[27]

[iv] In *Mein Kampf*, Hitler states that the purity of the German gene pool must stay pure, at any cost, including forced sterilizations of genetically inferior people and the genocide of non-Aryan races.

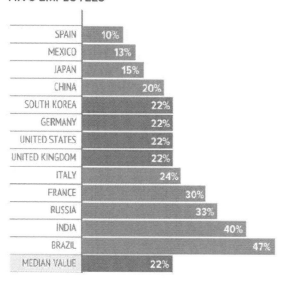

IN MOST GBES COUNTRIES, PRESSURE TO COMPROMISE STANDARDS IS FELT BY MORE THAN 1 IN 5 EMPLOYEES

Country	%
SPAIN	10%
MEXICO	13%
JAPAN	15%
CHINA	20%
SOUTH KOREA	22%
GERMANY	22%
UNITED STATES	22%
UNITED KINGDOM	22%
ITALY	24%
FRANCE	30%
RUSSIA	33%
INDIA	40%
BRAZIL	47%
MEDIAN VALUE	22%

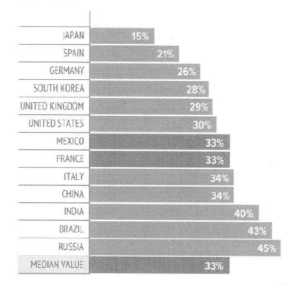

MISCONDUCT IS OBSERVED BY LARGE NUMBERS OF EMPLOYEES ACROSS GBES COUNTRIES

Country	%
JAPAN	15%
SPAIN	21%
GERMANY	26%
SOUTH KOREA	28%
UNITED KINGDOM	29%
UNITED STATES	30%
MEXICO	33%
FRANCE	33%
ITALY	34%
CHINA	34%
INDIA	40%
BRAZIL	43%
RUSSIA	45%
MEDIAN VALUE	33%

Figure 3.6: Percentage of employees in the private sector who feel pressure to compromise their ethical standards (left) or who observe ethical misconduct (right). Median rates in the public sector were 3% points higher than in the private sector.[28]

RATES OF BRIBERY AND CORRUPTION-RELATED MISCONDUCT VARY GREATLY ACROSS GBES COUNTRIES IN ALL SECTORS

Country	%
JAPAN	6%
FRANCE	10%
SPAIN	10%
ITALY	13%
UNITED KINGDOM	15%
RUSSIA	16%
UNITED STATES	16%
MEXICO	19%
BRAZIL	19%
SOUTH KOREA	21%
GERMANY	23%
CHINA	27%
INDIA	30%
MEDIAN VALUE	16%

Figure 3.7: Bribery and corruption rates in various countries (private sector). Mean rates in the public sector are 1% higher.[29]

Situational Factors:

- *Peers.* "The direct influence of the person's peers increases as the intensity and frequency of contact with that person's peers increases. People see themselves as more ethical than their peers, co-workers, and supervisors in their ethical beliefs and decision-making behavior." [30] The tendency for people to see themselves as more ethical than others is part of a broad positive self-bias that most people have, where they view themselves in a positive light. People tend to attribute their successes to their own efforts, but failures to outside forces. Self-bias becomes most extreme for narcissistic individuals.

- *Top Management.* "An individual's ethical beliefs and decision-making behavior will increasingly become congruent with top management's beliefs as defined through their words and actions as rewards provided for compliance congruency are increased." [31]

- *Codes of Conduct.* "The existence of corporate codes of conduct will positively increase an individual's ethical beliefs and decision behavior. The existence of corporate codes and top management's use of rewards and sanctions for code adherence and violations will increase ethical beliefs and decision making more than the existence of codes." [32]

Organizational Factors:

- *Culture.* "The more ethical the climate and culture of an organization is, the more ethical an individual's ethical beliefs and decision behavior will be. The strength of this influence may be moderated by the structure and design of some organizations." [33]

- *Size.* "As the size of an organization increases, individual ethical beliefs and decision-making behavior decreases." [34] This is of concern, given that organizational size has tended to increase in modern society.

- *Level.* "As an employee's level in the organization increases, that employee's ethical beliefs and decision-making behavior decreases." [35]

Industry Factors:

- *Industry Ethical Standards.* "Industry ethical standards are not related to an individual's ethical beliefs and decision-making behavior." [v, 36, 37]

An Exercise in Self-Awareness:

How have the following factors influenced moral decisions that you have made? To what degree have those influences been positive or negative?

- Your religion _____
- Your education_____
- Your personality_____
- Your peer group_____

---

[v] In the private sector, a majority of bribery involves management (23 percent top managers, 32 percent middle managers).

- Policy environment _____
- Corporate culture _____
- Senior/middle management _____
- Your job _____

3.7 Ethical Risk Versus Moral Hazard

Ethical risk refers to the potential consequences of bad behavior by people or organizations. Though not commonly present in EM HIRAs (reputational risk is sometimes present), corruption, malfeasance or poor ethical decision-making can expose people and organizations to reputational loss and/or legal suits. One example of this occurred in the pharmaceutical industry when "Turing Pharmaceuticals of New York bought the drug (*Daraprim*) from Impax Laboratories [...] for $55 million and raised the price from $13.50 a tablet to $750.00."[38] This resulted in one article calling the CEO of Turing the "most hated man in America" and "made him a pariah among patients-rights groups, politicians and hundreds of Twitter users."[39] The decision to raise the price of Daraprim was legal, but perhaps not moral, depending upon what values you have. Interestingly, but perhaps not surprising to many, he was later convicted and received a 7-year prison sentence for defrauding investors in his hedge funds and conspiring to manipulate the stock of Retrophin Inc.[40] To what extent should a company simply work to maximize profits? Does the private sector have any duties to the general public (Chapter 1.7 on Corporate Social Responsibility)?

There is evidence to support the notion that increased attention to ethical risk will benefit both society and institutions; for example, a study of Italian Credit Unions note that "[a]ll the ethical restrictions are necessary to reconcile the entity's interests (or utility) with those of society and are not detrimental for the purposes of the entity, but rather they are factors favouring consolidation and lasting prosperity."[41]

The 2008 economic meltdown was to a large extent a result of ethical risk. The banking industry in the U.S. supported by federal government policies, in the pursuit of short-term profits, allowed homeowners to obtain high risk mortgages. Though their actions were legal, many considered them to be unethical and bank reputations suffered as a result.

The importance of ethics is recognized by many organizations and governments. Without institutional support of ethical behavior and a formal culture that supports it, it is hard to avoid ethical risk. For example, the third report on corporate governance in South Africa includes as a principle that "[t]he board should ensure that the company's ethics are managed effectively," specifically, the board should ensure that:

"1.3.1. it builds and sustains an ethical corporate culture in the company;

1.3.2. it determines the ethical standards which should be clearly articulated and ensures that the company takes measures to achieve adherence to them in all aspects of the business;

1.3.3. adherence to ethical standards is measured;

1.3.4. internal and external ethics performance is aligned around the same ethical standards;

1.3.5. ethical risks and opportunities are incorporated in the risk management process;

1.3.6. a code of conduct and ethics-related policies are implemented;

1.3.7. compliance with the code of conduct is integrated in the operations of the company; and

1.3.8. the company's ethics performance should be assessed, monitored, reported and disclosed."[42]

Moral hazard is a phrase that is commonly used, but is very different from ethical risk, though it sounds similar. Moral hazard refers to the offloading of risk onto others, while engaging in risky behavior. It may be undesirable from some perspectives, but is not necessarily immoral. One example of this would be a willingness to live in a flood zone, with the knowledge that flood damage will be reimbursed by social programs and insurance with the costs being shared by those who do not live in flood zones. One of the principles of insurance is that risks are equitably distributed amongst subscribers. Where this principle fails, then moral hazard ensues.

When risk is socialized—Medicare is one example—there is always the problem of moral hazard, as some people will inevitably take advantage of the socialization process to benefit themselves at the expense of others. A libertarian might ask, "Why should I pay for the bad behavior of others?" This is a valid point. But many become victims through no fault of their own due to bad luck, heredity or situation (how can one blame a child for being a victim?), and most modern societies accept that some level of societal responsibility is valid in order to care for their fellow citizens. This is the basis of disaster relief programs and is discussed further in Chapter 8 on disaster financial assistance.

3.8 Conclusion

Ethics is fundamental to risk assessment, but is often not explicitly part of risk assessment methodologies or the metrics that are chosen to represent risk. This is especially true within the emergency management community. There is a large literature on ethical decision making, and the process of incorporating it into risk assessment is outlined earlier in this chapter, specifically illustrated in Figure 3.4. This process must recognize the importance of emotion and biases, which are present in all of us.

3.9 Endnotes

[1] Canadian Standards Association. (2014). Z1600-14-Emergency and continuity management program. https://webstore.ansi.org/standards/csa/csaz16002014

[2] (2010). [Deepwater Horizon fire] [Photograph]. *US Coast Guard.* https://en.wikipedia.org/wiki/Deepwater_Horizon_explosion#/media/File:Deepwater_Horizon_offshore_drilling_unit_on_fire_2010.jpg

[3] Etkin, D. (2019). How risk assessments by emergency management organisations fall prey to narrow framing. *International Journal of Emergency Management*, 15(1), 81-97.

[4] Chantrill, C. (2017). *Which state has the highest GDP?* US government spending. http://www.usgovernmentspending.com/gdp_by_state

[5] World Bank Open Data) https://data.worldbank.org/

[6] Nakahara, S., & Ichikawa, M. (2013). Mortality in the 2011 tsunami in Japan. *Journal of epidemiology*, JE20120114.

[7] Inter-American Development Bank (2010). *Haiti reconstruction cost may near $14 billion*, IDB study shows. https://www.iadb.org/en/news/webstories/2010-02-16/haiti-earthquake-reconstruction-could-hit-14-billion--idb%2C6528.html

[8] International Standards Organization (2018). *ISO 31000:2018(en) Risk management — Guidelines* https://www.iso.org/obp/ui#iso:std:iso:31000:ed-2:v1:en

[9] Public Safety Canada (2010). Emergency Management Planning Guide 2010–2011, https://www.publicsafety.gc.ca/cnt/rsrcs/pblctns/mrgnc-mngmnt-pnnng/index-en.aspx

[10] Hansson, S. O. (2010). The harmful influence of decision theory on ethics. *Ethical Theory and Moral Practice*, 13(5), 585-593.

[11] Klein, N. (2007). *The shock doctrine. The rise of disaster capitalism*. Vintage Canada.

[12] Assembly of First Nations. (2007). *A first nations wholistic approach to pandemic planning: A lesson for emergency planning*. 64.26.129.156/cmslib/general/pan-planning20078310219.pdf Retrieved June, 2014.

[13] Hermansson, H., & Hansson, S. O. (2007). A three-party model tool for ethical risk analysis. *Risk Management*, 9(3), 129-144.

[14] Rest, J. R. (1986). *Moral development: Advances in research and theory*. Praeger.

[15] Hermansson, H., & Hansson, S. O. (2007). A three-party model tool for ethical risk analysis. *Risk Management*, 9(3), 129-144.

[16] Det Norske Veritas. (2013). *TERMPOL 3.15 general risk analysis and intended methods of reducing risks: Trans mountain expansion project.* http://transmountain.s3.amazonaws.com/application/V8C_TR_8C_12_To_S08_TERMPOL_RPTS.pdf

[17] Det Norske Veritas. (2013). Figure 15 – Study area and segments defined in MARCs. In *TERMPOL 3.15 general risk analysis and intended methods of reducing risks: Trans mountain expansion project* (p. 32). http://transmountain.s3.amazonaws.com/application/V8C_TR_8C_12_To_S08_TERMPOL_RPTS.pdf

[18] Det Norske Veritas. (2013). Table 31 – Oil spill locations. In *TERMPOL 3.15 general risk analysis and intended methods of reducing risks: Trans mountain expansion project* (p. 76). http://transmountain.s3.amazonaws.com/application/V8C_TR_8C_12_To_S08_TERMPOL_RPTS.pdf

[19] Government of Canada. (2019). *TERMPOL review process – 2019 edition – TP 743 E.* Transport Canada. https://www.tc.gc.ca/eng/marinesafety/termpol-review-process-2019-edition-tp743e.html

[20] Zhong, C. B. (2011). The ethical dangers of deliberative decision making. *Administrative Science Quarterly*, 56(1), 1-25.

[21] Rozin P., Haidt J., & McCauley C. R. (1993). Disgust. In M. Lewis & J. M. Haviland (Eds.), *Handbook of emotions* (pp. 575–594). Guilford Press.

[22] Barnes, A., & Thagard, P. (1996). Emotional decisions. In *Proceedings of the 18th annual conference of the cognitive science society* (pp. 426-429). University of California San Diego. http://cogsci.uwaterloo.ca/Articles/Pages/Emot.Decis.html

[23] Pessoa, L. (2017). A network model of the emotional brain. *Trends in Cognitive Sciences*, 21(5), 357-371.

[24] Barnes, A., & Thagard, P. (1996). Emotional decisions. In *Proceedings of the 18th annual conference of the cognitive science society* (pp. 426-429). University of California San Diego. http://cogsci.uwaterloo.ca/Articles/Pages/Emot.Decis.html

[25] Ford, R. C., & Richardson, W. D. (1994). Ethical decision making: A review of the empirical literature. *Journal of Business Ethics*, *13*(3), 205-221.

[26] Ford, R. C., & Richardson, W. D. (1994). Ethical decision making: A review of the empirical literature. *Journal of Business Ethics*, *13*(3), 205-221.

[27] Ford, R. C., & Richardson, W. D. (1994). Ethical decision making: A review of the empirical literature. *Journal of Business Ethics*, *13*(3), 205-221.

[28] Ethics & Compliance Initiative. (2016). *Global business ethics survey 2016: Measuring risk and promoting workplace integrity.* https://www.ethics.org/knowledge-center/2016-global-business-ethics-survey/

[29] Ethics & Compliance Initiative. (2016). *Global business ethics survey 2016: Measuring risk and promoting workplace integrity.* https://www.ethics.org/knowledge-center/2016-global-business-ethics-survey/

[30] Campbell, K. W., & Sedikides, C. (1999). Self-threat magnifies the self-serving bias: A meta-analytic integration. *Review of General Psychology, 3*(1), 23–43.

[31] Ford, R. C., & Richardson, W. D. (1994). Ethical decision making: A review of the empirical literature. *Journal of Business Ethics*, *13*(3), 205-221.

[32] Ford, R. C., & Richardson, W. D. (1994). Ethical decision making: A review of the empirical literature. *Journal of Business Ethics*, *13*(3), 205-221.

[33] Ford, R. C., & Richardson, W. D. (1994). Ethical decision making: A review of the empirical literature. *Journal of Business Ethics*, *13*(3), 205-221.

[34] Ford, R. C., & Richardson, W. D. (1994). Ethical decision making: A review of the empirical literature. *Journal of Business Ethics*, *13*(3), 205-221.

[35] Ford, R. C., & Richardson, W. D. (1994). Ethical decision making: A review of the empirical literature. *Journal of Business Ethics*, *13*(3), 205-221.

[36] Ethics & Compliance Initiative. (2016). *Global business ethics survey 2016: Measuring risk and promoting workplace integrity.* https://www.ethics.org/knowledge-center/2016-global-business-ethics-survey/

[37] Ford, R. C., & Richardson, W. D. (1994). Ethical decision making: A review of the empirical literature. *Journal of Business Ethics*, *13*(3), 205-221.

[38] Zaslow, A. (2015, September 21). *Drug that fights complications of AIDS and cancer goes from $13.50 to $750.* NBC News. https://www.nbcnews.com/business/business-news/drug-fights-complications-aids-cancer-goes-13-50-750-n431211

[39] Thomas, Z., & Swift, T. (2017, August 4). *Who is Martin Shkreli - 'the most hated man in America'?* BBC News. https://www.bbc.com/news/world-us-canada-34331761

[40] Stempel, J. (2019, July 18). *'Pharma bro' Martin Shkreli to stay behind bars, loses appeal of conviction.* Reuters. https://www.reuters.com/article/us-usa-crime-shkreli/martin-shkreli-loses-appeal-of-conviction-sentence-idUSKCN1UD1ZW

[41] Caldarelli, A., Fiondella, C., Maffei, M., Spanò, R., & Zagaria, C. (2012). Ethics in risk management practices: Insights from the Italian mutual credit co-operative banks. *Journal of Co-Operative Accounting and Reporting*, 1(1), 5-18.

[42] Rossouw, G. J., Van der Watt, A., & Rossouw, D. M. (2002). Corporate governance in South Africa. *Journal of Business Ethics*, *37*(3), 289-302.

CHAPTER 4: THE PRECAUTIONARY PRINCIPLE

"It is better to be safe than sorry." (Sometimes)
Cultural Proverb

Contents

4.1 Introduction

The beasts of the field and forest had a Lion as their king. He was neither wrathful, cruel, nor tyrannical, but just and gentle as a king could be. During his reign he made a royal proclamation for a general assembly of all the birds and beasts, and drew up conditions for a universal league,

in which the Wolf and the Lamb, the Panther and the Kid, the Tiger and the Stag, the Dog and the Hare, should live together in perfect peace and amity. The Hare said, "Oh, how I have longed to see this day, in which the weak shall take their place with impunity by the side of the strong." And after the Hare said this, he ran for his life.

Aesop, *The Kingdom of the Lion*[1]

Figure 4.1: The Lion King[2]

Sometimes people accept a large risk because it is the right thing to do (such as risking one's life to save the lives of others). But there are many cautionary tales in our culture about the folly of some and the wisdom of others. The fable of the lion and the hare (above) is one of them. Sometimes it makes good sense to take a risk, especially if the potential benefit is large and the downside is small. At other times it does not make good sense and such a choice can be ruinous (e.g., the hare getting eaten by a dog is ruinous from the hare's point of view, if not the dog's). It is part of the job of an emergency manager to know the difference, and this chapter is mainly about the latter scenario.

Chapter 3 discussed ethical risk assessment. I have often heard it said that emergency management begins with the risk assessment process, but part of the risk assessment process needs to be a consideration of the underlying values and ethics that drive us, and the nature of the threats we face. The precautionary principle (PP) is relevant to both these issues.

There are some situations for which risk assessment (RA) is the wrong tool to use. Conducting an RA requires a good knowledge of probability and consequences, which is not always available. If the consequences of an event are trivial then how one manages it is of little import. But sometimes consequences can be catastrophic and lead to ruin. In these cases, an alternate approach must be considered. This is especially true for hazards where the chain of cause and effect is unclear, or when there is high scientific uncertainty. If effects are irreversible then the precautionary principle becomes even more important. Examples of threats where use of the PP are potentially justified include genetically modified foods, toxic chemicals, nuclear waste, and climate change.

One way of looking at the PP is that it is a reversal of the principle "innocent until proven guilty," to "guilty until proven innocent." It determines who has power and who is powerless, but it is only valid under specific conditions, described below.

There are various definitions of the precautionary principle; generally, it requires that where there is the potential for serious or irreversible harm to the ecosystem or human health, anticipatory measures should be taken to prevent such harm; furthermore, uncertainty as to the likelihood or extent of the harm should not result in the postponement of cost-effective measures to avoid it.

4.2 Conditions Required for Using the Precautionary Principle

To illustrate conditions under which the PP could be used, consider the following question:

What do these hazards have in common?

- Cigarette smoking;
- Asbestos;
- Synthetic chemicals resulting in endocrine disruption;
- Loss of biodiversity;
- Disposal of nuclear waste;
- Climate change from emission of greenhouse gases;

Answer: At some point in time:

- There was credible evidence or reasonable arguments that each could result in significant harm;
- There was a high degree of uncertainty and no credible way to deterministically assess risk;
- Causal chains were unclear;
- Probabilities were not well known;
- Outcomes were uncertain;
- Cost-benefit analyses were problematic;
- Each had both proponents and opponents; and
- Outcomes were irreversible.

Each of these issues had or has the potential to result in great harm, but using the decision-making principle that a risk requires scientific proof before addressing it results in these threats not being adequately addressed. Sometimes, being reactive does not work well; by the time you can prove that you are in trouble it is too late. Fundamental to this issue is predictability. To what extent are we able to predict the future, and how does ethics factor into that uncertainty?

The PP is partially utilitarian, in that it addresses scenarios that have the potential for great harm with the intent of eliminating or mitigating consequences. But it also addresses the rights of potential victims not to be exposed to risk, which is deontological. For example, society generates power from nuclear energy, which benefits all (though some more than others), but those who live near nuclear waste dumping sites (now and in the distant future) bear the brunt of the radiation risk. What ethics should prevail, and to what extent do we owe moral duties to future generations who will be exposed to radiation?[3]

Goldstein discusses the importance of the PP to public health, illustrating how it would have prevented significant harm if applied to the issues of (1) the addition of methyl tert-butyl ether (MTBE) to gasoline in the United States to decrease air pollution, (2) the drilling of tube wells in Bangladesh to avoid surface water microbial contamination, and (3) village-wide parenteral antischistosomiasis therapy in Egypt.[4] Goldstein notes that as of 2001 the decision-making process was not improving, saying that

> [p]erhaps most distressing is that US environmental authorities appeared to have learned little from the MTBE debacle. Oxygenated fuels continue to be required by [the Environmental Protection Agency], resulting in the replacement of MTBE by compounds such as tertiary amyl methyl ether, for which [there was] even less toxicological and environmental information.[5]

An example of how risk assessment does not deal well with a rare high-consequence event:

Within the EM profession the standard way of assessing risk is using the equation Risk = Probability x Consequences. Consider two communities, "Onward" and "Woops."

- Community "Onward": Average fatality rate = 1%/year. Every year 1% die.

- Community "Woops": Average fatality rate = 1%/year. Zero% fatalities for 99 years and 100% fatalities in the 100th year.

- Both communities have the same average risk over the 100-year time period, which is the way risk is usually calculated in EM HIRAs. But the end result is that "Onward" is sustainable while "Woops" is extinct at the end of the 100-year time period.

- When there is potential for ruin, standard RA methodologies must be augmented by broad interpretations of risk and use of the PP.

A traditional RA approach should be augmented or replaced by the PP when the following conditions are met:

- Significant scientific uncertainty exists around causations, probability, and magnitude;

- The threat is credible, even if not scientifically proven;
- Potential harm is not acceptable on moral grounds; and
- Interventions are required now, in order to prevent future harm (i.e., a wait and see approach will fail because the process is irreversible).

Consider Table 4.1 (an adaptation of Pascal's Wager[i]) for a potentially ruinous threat. In conditions of insufficient knowledge and/or high uncertainty, we do not know which column is true and generally have no ability to influence it. The columns indicate whether or not there is a causal link, such as for smoking and cancer. These links are determined by nature and the laws of physics. The rows represent decisions made to try to prevent harmful outcomes, and we can choose to do nothing or to take preventative action. Both rows have the potential for either a positive or a negative outcome, but on balance the top row (prevent action) is far less harmful since ruin is avoided.

		Causal Link (Nature)	
		No Causal Link Therefore Prevention Fails	**Causal Link Exists Therefore Prevention Succeeds**
Blaise Pascal[6]			
Decisions (People)	**Prevention**	Type 2 Error. Opportunity cost.	Ruin avoided.
	No Action Taken	Development or success.	Type 1 Error. Ruin occurs.

Table 4.1: A Modified Version of Pascal's Wager, for a Potentially Ruinous Event

Of course, Table 4.1 represents a simplified version of many issues, whereas there are usually "shades of grey" as opposed to just two choices, and there may be options besides prevention or no action. But it does illustrate the point that sometimes precautions are the best choice (even if an outcome is less serious than ruin). It makes sense to avoid ruin if possible, even at a cost. That is why I and many others have home and life insurance; though the future is uncertain, the costs of a disaster are potentially ruinous, while the costs of insurance are manageable. However, like most other ethical issues, using the PP is a complicated process. Rarely are issues "black and white" and those who advocate for use of the PP must make their case. It is not simply enough to invoke the PP (that would be a ridiculous situation that would lead to paralysis); there must be robust arguments to support its application.

It must be noted that there has been criticism of the PP from a number of sources (see below for an example). The main criticisms are that the principle is extreme, inflexible, anti-science, anti-growth, and anti-technology.[7]

---

[i] Pascal was a French mathematician who argued that it is more rational to believe in God than not to, since the outcomes of making a wrong decision are so much worse if God exists, than if (s)he doesn't.

An example where application of the PP is not valid (alien attack):	An example of where application of the PP is valid (cigarette smoking):

Figure 4.2: Interior illustration to H. G. Wells' novel *The War of the Worlds* from reprinting in *Amazing Stories*, August 1927.[10]	Figure 4.3: Tobacco ad in 1900 targeting women.[11]

These criticisms are only valid if the PP is being improperly invoked. Any tool, including RA or a hammer, can be used well or used badly. There can certainly be opportunity costs and tradeoffs that may have to be made when using the PP, but the benefits of having it in our toolbox of risk management strategies is significant. The world will never be completely safe and the PP cannot make it so. But it can help us to better understand our options and to protect us from certain kinds of risks.

4.3 Applying the Precautionary Principle

If a contextual analysis suggests that the PP is an appropriate approach in dealing with a threat, then there are several strategic principles that should be followed when applying it.

Strategic Principles:

- *Proportionality*. Prevention and mitigation strategies are proportional to the level of potential harm.
- *Transparency*. The process of decision-making is transparent, including explicit statements of assumptions and values.
- *Stakeholder engagement*. Those who have a stake in the issue have a voice in the decision-making process.
- *Openness*. Nothing is hidden or secret.
- *Consider alternative pathways*. Are there other ways of achieving goals.
- *Responsibility.* The burden of proof lies with those that are responsible for the potential harm to demonstrate that the threat does not exist or falls below a level of acceptable risk.
- *Re-evaluation.* Re-evaluate as new data or knowledge becomes available.

When engaging in a PP analysis the following steps should be taken:

- Identify the possible risk and characterize the problem (quantification is not necessary).
- Identify what is known and what is not known about the risk.
- Perform an ethical analysis.
- Consider reframing the problem and describe what needs to be done to address it.
- Assess alternatives.
- Determine the course of action.
- Monitor and follow up.[12]

Student Exercise:

- Apply the PP to the issue of vaping, or some other threat that you find of interest.
    - Is a traditional RA method sufficient, or should it be augmented or replaced by the PP?

4.4 Case Study: Asbestos – How Use of the Precautionary Principle Could Have Helped

We now know that asbestos causes a disease called mesothelioma, as well as lung cancer, ovarian cancer, laryngeal cancer, pleural plaques, pleural effusions, pleuritis, diffuse pleural thickening, and atelectasis. These diseases do not manifest themselves quickly after exposure but are very serious. Once mesothelioma develops it is usually fatal within a one-year period. According to the website Asbestos.com:

- Asbestos has been banned in more than 60 countries, but not in the U.S.
- Asbestos exposure is the No. 1 cause of work-related deaths in the world.
- Approximately 90,000 people die from asbestos-related diseases globally each year.
- An estimated 125 million people worldwide remain at risk of occupational exposure to asbestos.
- About 1.3 million U.S. workers in construction and general industry are at risk of exposure today.
- While there has been a fall in asbestos production throughout the world, certain countries — including the U.S. — have significantly increased importation of asbestos. Asbestos lobbying organizations play a major role in keeping asbestos trade alive.[13]

Asbestos began to be mined in 1879 and reports of its danger began in 1898. The product became widely used, and peaks in mesothelioma in countries occurred about 50 to 60 years following peak asbestos imports. Table 4.2 shows a summary timeline of events related to evidence of its harmful effects.

Figure 4.4: Asbestos mining 1876, in Quebec[14]

Asbestos and the Precautionary Principle:

Use of the precautionary principle in dealing with asbestos use could have saved numerous deaths and great suffering. Relying upon "proof" based upon a risk analysis resulted in decision-making paralysis.

Date(s)	Event(s)
1898	UK Factory Inspector Lucy Deane warns of harmful and 'evil' effects of asbestos dust
1906	French factory report of 50 deaths in female asbestos textile workers and recommendation for controls
1911	'Reasonable grounds' for suspicion, from experiments on rats, that asbestos dust is harmful
1911 and 1917	UK Factory Department finds insufficient evidence to justify further actions
1930	UK 'Merewether Report' finds 66 % of long-term workers in Rochdale factory with asbestosis
1931	UK Asbestos Regulations specify dust control in manufacturing only and compensation for asbestosis, but this is poorly implemented
1935– 1949	Lung cancer cases reported in asbestos manufacturing workers
1955	Research by Richard Doll (UK) establishes high lung cancer risk in Rochdale asbestos workers
1959– 1964	Mesothelioma cancer identified in workers, neighborhood 'bystanders' and the public in South Africa, the United Kingdom, and the United States, amongst others
1998– 1999	EU and France ban all forms of asbestos 2000–2001 WTO upholds EU/French bans against Canadian appeal

Table 4.2: Timeline of asbestos risk, adapted from the World Commission on the Ethics of Scientific Knowledge and Technology [15]

The lack of proof of harm early on meant that no action was taken to reduce asbestos exposure for many years, though there was significant anecdotal and statistical evidence of its harmful impacts. Of course, hindsight provides a current level of clarity not present in the past, but an approach not so firmly rooted in requiring scientific proof could have saved many lives.

For more case studies about the PP see deFur and Kaszuba, who summarize its use for the North Sea; Bovine growth hormone; the International Join Commission; Lake Pontchartrain; Striped Bass in the Chesapeake Bay; the Charles River, Massachusetts; and the Y2K Bug.[16]

4.5 Main Formulations of the Precautionary Principle

Two descriptions of the PP are:

Weak Formulation: Rio Declaration

- *Principle 15 of the Rio Declaration*:
    In order to protect the environment, the precautionary approach shall be widely applied by States according to their capabilities. Where there are threats of serious or irreversible damage, lack of full scientific certainty shall not be used as a reason for postponing cost-effective measures to prevent environmental degradation.[17]
- Does not shift the burden of proof to proponents.

Strong Formulation: Wingspread Statement

- *Wingspread Statement (Appendix A).* "When an activity raises threats of harm to human health or the environment, precautionary measures should be taken even if some cause-and-effect relationships are not fully established scientifically."[18]
- Shifts the burden of proof to the proponents.

Note that the weak formulation uses the phrase "cost-effective", which is not present in the strong formulation. The Rio Declaration is considered a weak formulation since it does not require proponents to apply the PP. The Wingspread Statement is considered a strong statement since it requires compliance. Both approaches are present in many policy declarations.

The issue of burden of proof is an interesting one. Consider smoking cigarettes as an example. The tobacco industry said to critics that they should prove that smoking is harmful to health. Though that proof now exists, there was a time when it did not, though there was credible evidence that it was so. Critics of smoking asked the tobacco industry to prove that it was safe as a condition for its advertising claims. Depending upon where the burden of proof lies, the decision making path bifurcates.

4.6 Legislative Examples of the Precautionary Principle

Beginning with the Rio Declaration in 1992, variations of the PP have been adopted by governmental and other organizations. The Government of Canada has a policy document on this issue, *A Framework for the Application of Precaution in Science-Based Decision Making About Risk.*[19] One example of its application is that "Canada's environmental policy is guided by the precautionary principle [...] as required by the Federal Sustainable Development Act which states that the Minister of Environment must 'develop a Federal Sustainable Development Strategy based on the precautionary principle.'"[20]

A brief on the PP within the Canadian legal system is available from the Environmental Law Centre at the University of Victoria and a Canadian Public Health Framework has also been developed. [21, 22] Two useful international resources are available from UNESCO and the World Health Organization. [23, 24]

Legislation in Canada that incorporates the PP:

- Canadian Environmental Protection Act (1999)
- Pest Control Products Act (2002)
- Canada Marine Conservation Areas Act (2002)
- Canada Consumer Product Safety Act (2010)
- Preamble to the Canadian Environmental Protection Act (1999)
- Oceans Act (1996)

- Species at Risk Act (2002)

International Agreements that incorporates the PP:

- Rio Declaration on Environment and Development (1992)
- United Nations Framework Convention on Climate Change (1994)
- World Trade Organization's (WTO) Agreement on Sanitary and Phytosanitary Measures (1994)
- Biosafety Protocol, Montreal (2000)

Case Law related to the PP:

- Appendix 4.3 shows the results of some cases in law where the PP has been argued with varying results.

4.7 Conducting a Precautionary Principle Analysis

When doing an analysis where the PP may be an appropriate approach the following questions need to be answered:

- What is meant by harm and how should it be measured?
- How much harm is sufficient to trigger the PP?
- What level of uncertainty is required to trigger the PP?
- What counts as a precautionary measure?
- Do measures to limit the effect count, or only measures to prevent causation?

It seems likely that the PP will become increasingly important in the future. As a society we are accelerating the creation of risks that are complex, poorly understood, and that have catastrophic potential. These trends are happening in a world that is changing rapidly due to climate change, population growth, urbanization, ecological devastation, and technological development. Since standard risk assessment methodologies are poorly equipped to deal with these kinds of risks, the precautionary principle is an essential approach that must be used in order to minimize the potential for catastrophe or ruin.

The kind of problems I am especially referring to are called "wicked problems." These problems are described as being ill-defined because the rules change over time, uncertainties are large, the problems are loosely constructed and there is no clear solution or stopping rule.[25] Complex strongly coupled systems[ii, 26] have these characteristics, and this is why ecosystem and social system related problems tend to be wicked.[27]

[ii] These are the kind of systems that Charles Perrow addresses in normal accident theory.

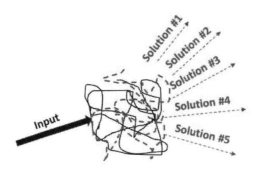

Figure 4.5: A wicked problem: Messy with multiple possible outcomes

Climate Change and the Precautionary Principle:

One of the issues that emergency managers are increasingly paying attention to is climate change. It is an issue well suited to the application of the PP, though the potential short-term costs of mitigation and prevention have created many opponents to dealing with it. Every 5 years a United Nations body, the Intergovernmental Panel on Climate Change (IPCC), publishes a scientific assessment of the academic literature summarizing what is known about this issue. Their reports can be downloaded from https://www.ipcc.ch/.

There are two sides to managing climate change risk. The first relates to reducing the forces that cause it, which is primarily the reduction of greenhouse gas emissions such as carbon dioxide that results from the burning of fossil fuels. The second side is adaptation: what decisions should be made now so that we are more resilient to the future detrimental effects of climate change, given that past emissions have made warming climate inevitable (though the amount and rate are uncertain)?

One ethical conundrum is that actions taken to reduce greenhouse gas emissions at local levels have a trivial impact on the problem, which is global. A utilitarian analysis might conclude that local emission reductions do not make sense if they are viewed as being detrimental to the local economy. (Of course, if everybody takes this approach the problem will not be addressed; this is a "tragedy of the commons" issue.) A deontological approach might conclude that reducing emissions locally is the right thing to do, even if it makes little difference globally.

Decisions relating to adaptation are different; they make sense from a utilitarian argument as long as future generations are being considered. A selfish (or egoist) perspective might not acknowledge the lives or rights of those who might be harmed in the future, but that is generally considered to be an immoral position. It is a good argument to say that we have a duty to our descendants since we have power over their circumstances, and they are currently powerless. The great difficulty is in deciding how to adapt. Some adaptations are win-win since there are many co-benefits. Examples are better housing insulation and greening cities; it is hard to see the downside of such actions. Other adaptations such as preparing for more frequent floods by installing larger storm drainage pipes have a cost associated with them (and it is unclear how flood frequency will change at local levels[iii]). It is virtually impossible to do a robust cost-benefit analysis for future local flood risk, which makes it very difficult to decide upon an appropriate level of investment.

Many governmental organizations are addressing the climate change problem. For example, the city where I live, Toronto, Canada has created a network of organizations to address this issue. There are many non-governmental organizations that also are working to mitigate the climate change problem. In spite of these efforts global emissions continue to rise, and the global forces of development make it seem unlikely that greenhouse gas emissions will decline in the near future. Stephen Gardiner wrote a compelling book, *A Perfect Moral Storm: Climate Change, Intergenerational Ethics and the Problem of Moral Corruption*, on the moral conundrums related to climate change that is well worth reading if this topic is of interest to you.[28]

4.8 The Ethical Basis of the Precautionary Principle

A PP argument is sometimes based upon the greater good, which is a utilitarian or consequentialist argument (see Chapter 1.2). In situations where few benefit and many are harmed (such as in the case of a popular commercial product that harms people like lead in gasoline) the greater good is clearly served by prevention. The asbestos example discussed above is a good example of this.

There will also be situations where this may not be the case, where a harm is created for the few in order to benefit the many (or perhaps a different few). John Rawls addressed this issue (Chapter 1.3) by arguing that the least advantaged in society should benefit the most, but there are clearly situations (such as the location of a dump) where some people will be disadvantaged in order to serve the common good.[29] Rarely, though, are those disadvantaged groups the wealthy and powerful.

More fundamentally, the PP has a strong rights-based component. Generally, people have the right not to be harmed by others as they pursue their self-interest. This is an ethic based upon duties, rights and obligations (or deontological ethics – see Chapter 1.3). For example, in the U.N. Universal Declaration of Human Rights, it states, "Everyone has the right to life, liberty and security of person."[30] Duties and obligations then accrue to governments to ensure these rights because of the social contract they have with their citizens. Some of these duties and obligations relate to the prevention of harm from various hazards, which is where the emergency management profession comes in. It is our job to assist governments with upholding their end of the social contract they have with their citizens.

The PP is often used in environmental arguments. Sometimes these arguments are based upon the need human beings have for the natural environment as a resource, but they can also be based upon a

---

[iii] One of the great difficulties related to adapting to climate change is that confidence in climate changes at local levels is much smaller that at larger scales. Scientific assessments may have a relatively high degree of confidence about global temperature changes, but uncertainty increases as scale decreases.

recognition of the rights of non-human species not to be unnecessarily harmed by people. The field of ethics that addresses this issue is called environmental ethics and is discussed in chapter 1.7.

4.9 Conclusion

The precautionary principle is an important approach that should be used when a risk analysis approach is insufficient. Its use is embedded in domestic and international law, but should only be applied when certain conditions are met, which have been discussed above. It is sometimes criticized for a variety of reasons, but those critiques do not stand up to a detailed analysis. Without the use of the PP, severe threats—possibly existential at times—are difficult to address.

Appendix 4.1: Wingspread Statement on the Precautionary Principle

The release and use of toxic substances, the exploitation of resources, and physical alterations of the environment have had substantial unintended consequences affecting human health and the environment. Some of these concerns are high rates of learning deficiencies, asthma, cancer, birth defects and species extinctions; along with global climate change, stratospheric ozone depletion and worldwide contamination with toxic substances and nuclear materials.

We believe existing environmental regulations and other decisions, particularly those based on risk assessment, have failed to protect adequately human health and the environment - the larger system of which humans are but a part.

We believe there is compelling evidence that damage to humans and the worldwide environment is of such magnitude and seriousness that new principles for conducting human activities are necessary.

While we realize that human activities may involve hazards, people must proceed more carefully than has been the case in recent history. Corporations, government entities, organizations, communities, scientists and other individuals must adopt a precautionary approach to all human endeavors.

Therefore, it is necessary to implement the Precautionary Principle: When an activity raises threats of harm to human health or the environment, precautionary measures should be taken even if some cause and effect relationships are not fully established scientifically.

In this context the proponent of an activity, rather than the public, should bear the burden of proof.

The process of applying the Precautionary Principle must be open, informed and democratic and must include potentially affected parties. It must also involve an examination of the full range of alternatives, including no action.

--Racine, WI, January 20, 1998[31]

Appendix 4.2:   Letter to the U.S. Chamber of Commerce

Dear Sir,

I just read the text on your web page related to the precautionary principle (https://www.uschamber.com/precautionary-principle).

The problem you worry about is not a problem related to the precautionary principle. That is just a tool, like risk assessment. It can be used well or used badly, like any other tool.

I support your statement about sound and robust risk analyses – they are fundamental to our policy decisions. I am totally opposed to badly done risk analyses (which are all to common, unfortunately). Yes, there are radical environmentalists who may not act rationally, but there are also corporations who have knowingly harmed the public in the pursuit of profit.

Similarly, the precautionary tool when used well is an important aspect of risk management. There are times when it is better to be safe than sorry (which is why I buy home and life insurance), just as there are times when it makes sense to take risks because the rewards are great and the downside is manageable. To advocate for the elimination of the precautionary principle exposes society to a set of risks that have potentially horrible outcomes. Do we really want more thalidomide babies?

I would ask that you alter your position to emphasize the need for use of the precautionary principle only in appropriate cases where the conditions for its use have been met, these being:

- Credible evidence or reasonable arguments that significant harm could occur
- A high degree of uncertainty and no credible way to deterministically assess risk
- Causal chains are unclear
- Probabilities not well known
- Outcomes uncertain
- Cost-benefit analysis could not be done
- Outcomes are irreversible

Sincerely,

David Etkin

Professor David Etkin
Disaster & Emergency Management
York University, Toronto, Ontario Canada

Appendix 4.3: Examples of Legal Decisions Related to the Precautionary Principle

Example 1: EU Regulatory and Court Decisions

Table IV. Strength of Application of the Precautionary Principle: Examples of EU Regulatory Decisions and Court Judgments					
Case	Subject(s) of Protection	Severity of Potential Harm	Conditions for Precautionary Action: Standard of Proof	Nature of Regulatory Action	Strength of Application
United Kingdom v. Commission: C-180/96 (BSE)	Human health	Severe	Relatively low-to-moderate	Product ban upheld; hazard considered "sufficiently severe," despite uncertainty about the causal link	Moderate-to-strong
Commission Decision 1999/832/EC (Netherlands, creosote)	Environment/ human health	Severe-to-moderate	High	Product ban upheld; "credible evidence" of a threat of harm, where local circumstances warrant precautionary action	Weak-to-moderate
Commission Decision 2003/653/EC (Austria, GMOs)	Environment/ human health	Moderate-to-low	High	Product ban rejected; insufficient evidence around a "local or geographic-specific" risk of potentially "dangerous effects"	Weak
Council Decision 2009/121/EC (antimicrobials)	Human health/ environment	Low	High	Product ban rejected; lack of sufficient evidence around "likelihood of occurrence and severity of consequences"	Weak
Commission v. Denmark: C-192/01 (fruit juice)	Human health	Low	High	Product ban rejected; insufficient scientific data to substantiate "real" threat to public health	Weak
Germany v. Commission: C-512/99 (mineral wool)	Human health/ consumer safety	Low	High	Reclassification of carcinogenic potential of product rejected; lack of a definitive scientific position on potential for harm	Weak
Commission v. Kingdom of the Netherlands C-41/02 (breakfast cereal)	Human health	Low	High	Product ban rejected; insufficient scientific data to substantiate "real" threat to public health	Weak

Table 4.3: EU Regulatory and Court Decisions Regarding Use of the Precautionary Principle[32]

Example 2: Pesticide Ban in Quebec

As noted by Alan Hahn of Dragun Corporation, an environmental consultant agency,

> The second case involved the use of pesticides in a town in Quebec (*Canada Lt´ee [Spraytech, Soci´et´ d'arrosage] v Town of Hudson*). Quebec law allows towns to enact bylaws to regulate *toxic materials.* In ruling in favour of the pesticide ban, the Supreme Court of Canada acknowledged that the town had not proven the pesticides were toxic and, nevertheless, allowed the ban. This ruling stated, in part: *The interpretation of By-*

law 270 set out here respects international law's 'precautionary principle.' In the context of the precautionary principle's tenets, concerns about pesticides fit well under their rubric of preventive action.[33]

Example 3: Aquaculture in British Columbia

Siskinds law firm notes,

> In Morton v Canada (Fisheries and Oceans), 2015 FC 575, the Federal court put unusually strong reliance on the precautionary principle to strike down parts of an aquaculture licence granted by the Minister of Fisheries and Oceans (the "Minister") to Marine Harvest, a multinational seafood company. Marine Harvest operated a fish farm in Shelter Bay, BC, not far from the wild Pacific salmon migration route along the Fraser River. In March, 2013, the company transferred infected Atlantic salmon from one of its hatcheries to Shelter Bay. The Fisheries Act aquaculture licence allowed them to do it, because both the hatchery and the fish farm were within the same "Salmonid Transfer Zone".

> [...] [The court ruling noted,]

> [45] The evidence before the Court demonstrates that there is a body of credible scientific study, conducted by respected scientists in different countries, establishing a causal relationship between PRV [the virus] and HSMI [the disease]. The evidence also indicates that there are scientists who question the link – but concede that no other disease agent has been identified as the culprit for HSMI. ... Thus, although there is a healthy debate between respected scientists on the issue, the evidence suggests that the disease agent (PRV) may be harmful to the protection and conservation of fish, and therefore a "lack of full scientific certainty should not be used a reason for postponing measures to prevent environmental degradation."[34]

4.10　Endnotes

[1] Aesop. (2020). *Aesop's fables.* (G. F. Townsend, Trans.). Mint Editions. (Original work published 1484).

[2] Rackham, A. (1912). The fox and the lion [Illustration]. From *Aesop's* fables by Aesop (V. S. V. Jones, Trans.). Avenel Books. https://www.gutenberg.org/files/11339/11339-h/11339-h.htm#THE_FOX_AND_THE_LION

[3] Timmerman, P. (2009). The long haul: Ethics in the Canadian nuclear waste debate. In D. Durrant & G. Fuji-Johnson (Eds.), *Nuclear waste management in Canada: Critical issues, critical perspective.* UBC Press.

[4] Goldstein, B. D. (2001). The precautionary principle also applies to public health actions. *American Journal of Public Health, 91*(9), 1358-1361.

[5] Goldstein, B. D. (2001). The precautionary principle also applies to public health actions. *American Journal of Public Health, 91*(9), 1358-1361.

[6] Blaise Pascal, Wikipedia, https://simple.wikipedia.org/wiki/Blaise_Pascal#/media/File:Blaise_pascal.jpg

[7] Sachs, N. M. (2011). Rescuing the strong precautionary principle from its critics. *University of Illinois Law Review, 2011,* 1285-1338.

[8] U.S. Chamber of Commerce. (2010). *Precautionary principle*. https://www.uschamber.com/precautionary-principle

[9] U.S. Chamber of Commerce. (2010). *Precautionary principle*. https://www.uschamber.com/precautionary-principle

[10] Raul, F. R. (1927). Interior illustration to H. G. Wells' novel *The War of the Worlds* [Illustration]. From *Amazing Stories*, 1927, Experimenter Publishing. https://commons.wikimedia.org/wiki/File:War_of_the_Worlds_original_cover_bw.jpg

[11] (1900). Advertisement for Ogden's Guinea Gold cigarettes [Illustration]. Stanford University. http://tobacco.stanford.edu/tobacco_main/images.php?token2=fm_st023.php&token1=fm_img0499.php&theme_file=fm_mt012.php&theme_name=Targeting%20Women&subtheme_name=Early%20Years

[12] Tickner, J. A., Raffensperger, C., & Myers, N. (1999). *The precautionary principle in action: A handbook*. Science and Environmental Health Network.

[13] Whitmer, M., & Pacheco, W. (2020). *Asbestos facts & statistics*. The mesothelioma center. https://www.asbestos.com/asbestos/statistics-facts/

[14] Wikipedia (n.d.). Asbestos Mining in Quebec, https://en.wikipedia.org/wiki/File:Asbestos_mining_1876.jpg

[15] World Commission on the Ethics of Scientific Knowledge and Technology. (2005). *The precautionary principle*. UNESCO. http://unesdoc.unesco.org/images/0013/001395/139578e.pdf

[16] deFur, P. L., & Kaszuba, M. (2002). Implementing the precautionary principle. *The Science of the Total Environment, 288*(1-2), 155-165.

[17] United Nations. (1992). *Report of the United Nations conference on environment and development*. https://www.un.org/en/development/desa/population/migration/generalassembly/docs/globalcompact/A_CONF.151_26_Vol.I_Declaration.pdf

[18] Wingspread Conference Participants. (1998). *Wingspread conference on the precautionary principle*. Wingspread Conference. https://www.sehn.org/sehn/wingspread-conference-on-the-precautionary-principle

[19] Privy Council Office. (2003). *A framework for the application of precaution in science-based decision making about risk*. Government of Canada. https://www.who.int/ifcs/documents/forums/forum5/precaution_e.pdf

[20] Justice Laws Website, Federal Sustainable Development Act, S.C. 2008, c. 33, https://laws-lois.justice.gc.ca/eng/acts/f-8.6/page-1.html,

[21] University of Victoria. (2010). *The Precautionary principle in Canada*. Environmental Law Centre. http://www.elc.uvic.ca/wordpress/wp-content/uploads/2015/02/C2_PrecautionaryPrincipleBackgrounder-2010Jun14.pdf

[22] Weir, E., Schabas, R., Wilson, K., & Mackie, C. (2010). A Canadian framework for applying the precautionary principle to public health issues. *Canadian Journal of Public Health/Revue Canadienne de Sante Publique, 101*(5), 396-398.

[23] World Commission on the Ethics of Scientific Knowledge and Technology. (2005). *The precautionary principle*. UNESCO. http://unesdoc.unesco.org/images/0013/001395/139578e.pdf

[24] Martuzzi, M., & Tickner, J. A. (2004). *The precautionary principle: Protecting public health, the environment and the future of our children*. World Health Organization. http://www.euro.who.int/__data/assets/pdf_file/0003/91173/E83079.pdf

[25] Coyne, R. D. (2005). Wicked problems revisited. *Design Studies, 26*(1), 5-17.

[26] Perrow, C. (2011). *Normal accidents: Living with high risk technologies – Updated edition*. Princeton University Press.

[27] DeFries, R., & Nagendra, H. (2017). Ecosystem management as a wicked problem. *Science, 356*(6335), 265-270.

[28] Gardiner, S. M. (2006). A perfect moral storm: Climate change, intergenerational ethics and the problem of moral corruption. *Environmental Values, 15*(3), 397-413.

[29] Rawls, J. (2009). *A theory of justice*. Harvard University Press.

[30] United Nations. (1948). *Universal declaration of human rights*. http://www.un.org/en/documents/udhr/index.shtml

[31] Wingspread Conference Participants. (1998). *Wingspread conference on the precautionary principle*. Wingspread Conference. https://www.sehn.org/sehn/wingspread-conference-on-the-precautionary-principle

[32] Garnett, K., & Parsons, D. J. (2017). Multi-case review of the application of the precautionary principle in European Union law and case law. *Risk Analysis, 37*(3), 502-516.

[33] Hahn, A. (2015). *Precautionary principle and Canadian environmental law.* Dragun Corporation Environmental Advisors. https://www.dragun.ca/precautionary-principle-and-canadian-environmental-law/

[34] Siskinds LLP. (2015). *Precautionary principle stronger part of Canadian law.* https://www.siskinds.com/precautionary-principle-stronger-part-of-canadian-law/

CHAPTER 5 – VICTIM BLAMING

"Always the innocent are the first victims, so it has been for ages past, so it is now."

J.K. Rowling, *Harry Potter and the Sorcerer's Stone*

"When you blame and criticize others, you are avoiding some truth about yourself."

Deepak Chopra

Contents

5.1 Introduction

Blame is about assigning responsibility for wrongdoing and can be against an individual or an entity. The three players in the blame game are victims, harm-doers, and observers. Fundamental to assigning blame is the notion of responsibility, which depends upon agency, foreseeability, intent, ability to control outcomes, and of the presence of mitigating factors (e.g. provocation). Blaming someone or something can be a legitimate process, but can also be done maliciously.

From the perspective of actor-network theory, there are four basic models regarding responsibility, each of which has different social implications in terms of blame and liability:

- A moral model where actors are responsible for both problems and solutions.
- A compensatory model where actors are not responsible for a problem but are for a solution.
- A medical model where actors are not responsible for a problem or a solution.
- An enlightenment model were actors are responsible for problems but not for solutions.[1]

I suggest that victim blaming generally occurs within a moral model or an enlightenment model framework. This assumes that victims have agency, can foresee and control the outcomes of their actions, and have free will.

Moral responsibility can, within actor-network theory, be divided into four forms:

- *Role responsibility*, which is defined by social roles and normative behaviors.
- *Capacity responsibility,* which deals with a person's capacity to understand, reason, predict the future, and carry out behaviors.
- *Causal responsibility,* which refers to being a cause of an outcome (cause and effect).
- *Liability responsibility*, which generally deals with violations of law but can also be viewed morally.[2]

The medical model has many applications, one of which is socialized health care. Should people who smoke or behave in other ways that adversely affect their health pay a greater proportion of health care costs than those who live a healthier lifestyle? A person may use justice and equity arguments to defend this idea, but opposing arguments exist on this issue, as well. For instance, some people have addictions (such as smoking) that are beyond their control and may not have the ability to change their lifestyle. It also creates a double jeopardy situation since statistically smokers suffer more illnesses and therefore already pay a price for their addiction (as well as paying a high tax when they purchase cigarettes). Degrees of blame will depend upon justice principles such as proportionality, equality, need, duties and obligations, rights, and procedural justice. Another important practical question is: who would make the judgements of rewards and punishments for more or less healthy behaviors? Would it be doctors and the health care system? Do they have the training and moral authority to wield such power? Would the opportunity exist for smokers or those who do not exercise or eat a healthy diet to defend themselves in a hearing or trial? It is a principle of justice in most cultures that the accused be allowed a defence and to confront their accuser.[3]

Blaming serves the function of explaining why disasters happen. It is part of the sense-making process that people use to understand the world around them. As such, blame is an important disaster narrative. Where blame is assigned has important legal and social consequences, and is a mechanism for reinforcing and/or creating allegiances and power structures. Sometimes a "blame culture" exists in an organization where blame is used in lieu of problem solving and a culture of fear pervades.[4] A blame culture creates a reluctance or unwillingness to take risk or accept responsibility for mistakes due to the fear of criticisms or retaliation.[5] For example, within the medical profession in the U.S., fear of being sued or punished has created a blame culture and the practice of defensive medicine.[6]

Blame can be viewed as a causal explanation where there is no moral agent (e.g., the disaster was caused by the earthquake), or as a response to malfeasance. It can be directed at a set of actions (e.g., the plane crash was caused by the pilot doing the wrong action), an entity (e.g., Westray Mines is responsible for the disaster), or a belief structure (e.g., the disaster happened because a neoliberal economic structure results in the creation of vulnerable populations).[7, 8, 9]

We may blame a hurricane for the harm it causes, but because hurricanes are not moral agents that blame is impersonal and does not suggest a lack of morals or character on the part of the hurricane. Hurricanes also cannot be censured or sued. It is a common strategy for organizations to blame a "natural disaster"[i] on the physical event when they may have engaged in poor mitigation or prevention.

For example, after the Westray mine disaster in May of 1992 one narrative based upon the moral model put forth by the owners of the mine was that they were not responsible for the tragedy (neither the problem nor the solution), and therefore had no liability. In the words of their spokesperson, "Nature cannot always be predicted or controlled."[10] In an alternative blame narrative, an official enquiry in 1997 said that the disaster "was a complex mosaic of actions, omissions, mistakes, incompetence, apathy, cynicism, stupidity, and neglect."[11] In this competing narrative the moral model created blame in all four categories of role, capacity, causality and liability.

Blaming victims (one variant of this is self-blame) for their circumstances is a common theme, not just in disasters, but in life in general. In the mid-1970s an influential book written by William Ryan called *Blaming the Victim* explored the role played by society in creating victims.[12] To what extent are poor people (one of the groups most vulnerable to disasters) to blame for being poor, and to what extent do social processes beyond their control deny them opportunity, especially if they belong to a discriminated against minority?

---

[i] The phrase "natural disaster" is often called an oxymoron because the disaster results as much from human decision-making as from the natural hazard.

Certainly, there are times when blame seems like a reasonable attitude—after all, as the proverb says, "If you play with fire you will get burned." Are smokers to blame if they get lung cancer? Are people who do not have a healthy lifestyle to blame for having a heart attack? Taken to the extreme, anybody who does not live a "perfect" lifestyle could be assigned some level of blame for a wide range of problems or illnesses. Is that reasonable? Still, if someone lives recklessly (assuming that they have the capacity and ability to choose alternative lifestyles) isn't it their own fault if they come to harm? Who decides what is reasonable or not?

There are times when people are powerless (this is called lacking agency) and blaming them seems unjust (young children are a good example). When is blame justifiable and when is it misplaced? Should rape victims be blamed for their rape if they were scantily dressed, or is that kind of blame a form of immoral transference of responsibility from the perpetrator to the victim? Even if there are times when people are reaping the tragic rewards of their poor decision-making (such as not buying insurance when it was affordable), is it ethical to engage in the blame game?

This chapter will look at two kinds of situations where blame is assigned to the victims of disaster, that of divine justice and of social constructionism.

Blaming Victims:

Can you think of a time when you blamed victims for their tragic circumstances?

- Was it justified? If so, on what grounds?

- Was it helpful? If so, how?

- Was it harmful? If so, how?

5.2 Divine Justice

Historically, God is often thought to be the cause of disasters. According to Herodotus, Poseidon sent a tsunami in 479 BC to punish the Persians for their siege of Potidaea (see box below); such accounts are common in antiquity. It must also be acknowledged that God is given credit for saving people from disasters. This section is about divine command theory, the idea that goodness flows from God's commands. In other words, to be a moral person, one must follow the commands of God.

"Above all, we ought to submit to the Divine authority rather than to our own judgment even though the light of reason may seem to us to suggest, with the utmost clearness and evidence, something opposite."

Rene Descartes (1596–1650), mathematician and philosopher

On November 1, 1997, the Cook Islands (Figure 5.2) were hit by Tropical Cyclone Martin. Generating large waves and strong winds, it resulted in at least 11 deaths and widespread damage.[13] There were two diametrically opposing belief/value systems present in the affected communities in terms of understanding why this disaster happened. The first system, based upon the perspectives of many clergy of Christian churches in the islands, interpreted the event as punishment from an angry God because of the moral transgressions of their congregations. These transgressions included the failure to attend church, working on Sundays, and paying too much attention to a pearl-farm industry.[14] Accepting this worldview resulted in engaging in self-blame and guilt at a time when traumatized people were grieving and trying to recover. The alternate belief system was a non-judgmental therapeutic one, which viewed the people as victims and the disaster as a random act of nature that was not the result of improper or immoral behavior. From this perspective the clergy were harming their congregations instead of providing the encouragement and support they needed. (It should be noted that these same clergy were active in rescue and recovery operations.)

Excerpt from Book VIII, Chapter 129 of *The Histories* by Herodotus.

"But when Artabazus had besieged Potidaea for three months, there was a great ebb-tide in the sea, lasting for a long while, and when the foreigners saw that the sea was turned into a marsh they made to pass over it into Pallene. But when they had made their way over two fifths of it and three yet remained to cross ere they could be in Pallene, there came a great flood-tide, higher, as the people of the place say, than any one of the many that had been before; and some of them that knew not how to swim were drowned, and those that knew were slain by the Potidaeans, who came among them in boats. The Potidaeans say that the cause of the high sea and flood and the Persian disaster lay herein, that those same Persians who now perished in the sea had profaned the temple and the image of Poseidon that was in the suburb of the city; and I think that in saying that this was the cause they say rightly."

Figure 5.1: Herodotus[16]

Figure 5.2: Aerial photograph of Pukapuka Atoll in the Cook Islands.[17]

Role-playing Exercise:

- Have one student play the part of a clergy, speaking about the need to behave morally in order to avoid God's wrath, but also because it is the right way to be. Have two other students engage as parishioners, one who embraces the same worldview, and the other one who views the event as a random act of nature.

- Repeat the above exercise, except replace the role of the clergy with an agnostic family therapist.

- Following the exercise, have the parishioners describe their feelings. How would these feelings affect their recovery process?

The notion of disaster as God's punishment appears both historically (for example, in the biblical story of Sodom and Gomorrah) and currently in many societies, and is a persistent theme in some fundamentalist Christian and Islamic perspectives. Consider the following statement by Reverend Franklin Graham, son of Reverend Billy Graham, who suggested that New Orleans was targeted by Hurricane Katrina because of the city's sinful reputation. At a speech in Virginia, he said:

> This is one wicked city, OK? It's known for Mardi Gras, for Satan worship. It's known for sex perversion. It's known for every type of drugs and alcohol and the orgies and all of these things that go on down there in New Orleans. [...] There's been a black spiritual cloud over New Orleans for years. They believe God is going to use that storm to bring revival.[18]

Mike Pence, Vice President of the United States, expressed a similar worldview that blames victims for their suffering, as shown in the following blog post about the great biblical flood (Figure 5.3).

It's the one-time God actually wiped out the entirety of the human race save one family.

But why did he wipe them out? That's the part you need to focus on. The flood was in response to the wickedness of mankind. It was recorded that during this time men's thoughts focused on evil continually without relent. It's also says that fallen angels actually slept with women. Which polluted the human race resulting in the creation of giants.

It's believed that the human race became so corrupted that by this time Noah and his Family were the only pure humans left that were uncorrupted. Just as well, Noah and his family were the only ones left who followed the Lord. Could you imagine living in a world where your family are the only Believers left? Dang. Talk about a wakeup call.

So naturally, God poured out judgement and flooded the Earth enough to kill pretty much everybody save those who inhabited the Ark. There are people who call God a mass murderer for this... But honestly, I'd rather they all be dead. God wasn't killing innocence, he was killing animals. Because their minds had degenerated to a point that all they could do was wickedness continually. So, it was an act of cleansing if you ask me.[19]

Vice-President Mike Pence

The following quotation, referring to the cause of the 2010 earthquake in Iran, is an example of blame from an Islamic fundamentalist perspective:

Hojjat ol-eslam Kazem Sediqi, the acting Friday prayer leader in Tehran, said women should stick to strict codes of modesty to protect themselves. "Many women who do not dress modestly lead young men astray and spread adultery in society which increases earthquakes," he explained [...] "What can we do to avoid being buried under the rubble? There is no other solution but to take refuge in religion and to adapt our lives to Islam's moral codes."[20]

Figure 5.3: *Christ Stilleth the Tempest* by John Martin, 1852.[21]

From a divine justice perspective some disaster victims are innocents, such as children or the faithful. Why those are punished along with the "guilty" raises the difficult theological questions as to why a loving and just God punishes them. This is particularly important in Christian theology where God is all-good, all-loving and all-powerful, and became particularly important following the Lisbon disaster of 1755 when "Roman Catholic preachers said God was judging the sins of Lisbon, Protestants said he was judging the Catholic Inquisition, and supporters of the Inquisition said God was angry because the Inquisition had not gone far enough."[22] Following this disaster a debate raged in European society regarding the nature and existence of God. Though there are various arguments that have been developed to address this question, it is beyond the scope of this chapter. For faiths that do not believe in a personal God, this is less of an issue.

Blame Versus Therapy:

- When you consider the two very different positions, (1) the faith-based one that blames victims, and (2) the therapeutic ones that considers them blameless, how would you compare them from a moral and ethical perspective?

- Is one preferable to the other?

- What values underlie your choice?

The faith-based approach discussed above in this section (divine command) may not result in the greatest good, unless good is defined as obeying one particular perspective on God's law. Where good is defined as happiness or wealth, for example, this approach can fall short of maximization. Faith-based approaches rooted in obeying God's will are based in notions of right and wrong as defined in scripture and are therefore a deontological ethic. In contrast, the therapeutic approach is designed to maximize positive outcomes for traumatized victims and is therefore a consequentialist or utilitarian ethic. It could also be deontological, in part, if there is a belief of a duty to reduce suffering and that victims have the right to assistance. Both approaches would also be considered a virtuous act within their own moral framework, and a sinful one from the opposing framework.

There is much that is not known about the behavior and decision-making processes of the clergy of Cook Islands and others during and after the cyclone, but there are good arguments to suggest that both groups (clergy and therapists) recognized the issue as an ethical one and were explicit and transparent about their beliefs and values. Both groups, therefore, may be described as engaging in ethical behavior and decision-making, despite their very different approaches to dealing with the victims. Whether or not they acted morally depends upon your worldview and values.

From a deontological perspective Kant proposed two categorical imperatives that use reason to arrive at right action. The first is based upon the idea that actions are justified if they could be universalized. The second is that people should be treated as ends, not as means to an end. This views them as moral beings, as opposed to objects. How does blaming victims compare to a therapeutic approach, from this perspective?

Certainly, the therapeutic perspective treats people as ends, not as a means to an end. There is also a strong argument for universalizing supportive therapy for disaster victims. (Would you want to be offered supportive therapy if you were a victim?) It seems that this approach is well supported by Kant's two categorical imperatives.

Does blaming victims for a disaster treat them as an end, or as a means to an end? I argue that they are being treated as a means to an end (that being obedience to God's will). In terms of universality, the idea that all of society blames victims for their suffering (where it is perceived to be a result of the violation of divine command) would be acceptable to those who have that belief, but unacceptable to those who do not. This is, therefore, an example of circular reasoning. From Kant's perspective it is difficult to support blaming victims within a deontological argument. Kant's arguments are, however, based upon the notion that pure reason can be used to arrive at right action, which is a very different basis than using divine command.

An ethic based upon a feminist approach with an emphasis on caring, empathy, and compassion (such as Carol Gilligan's argument outlined in Chapter 3) would place more importance on relationships and the good health of the victims as opposed to more abstract issues such as their adherence to divine command. If society is composed of networks of social relationships between caregivers and care-receivers, then blaming by caregivers (in this case the clergy) is an immoral act. This approach replaces abstract issues of justice with tangible human caring relationships.

This discussion illustrates that while different people can engage in ethical decision-making and behave ethically, they can come to radically different decisions based upon different moral values and belief systems.

5.3 The Implications of Social Constructionism

Is it ethical to blame victims for their suffering? There is a long history of such blame. Often, however, blame is based upon the notion that people have not acted wisely and have either exposed themselves or made themselves vulnerable to some hazard, and are therefore responsible for their own suffering. One recent example of this occurred after Hurricane Maria devastated Puerto Rico in 2017. President Trump noted in some tweets (see below) that the people and government of Puerto Rico were largely to blame for the slow recovery. Ironically, some FEMA officials have subsequently been charged with corruption related this very disaster.[23]

President Trump tweeted:

> FEMA & the Military worked emergency miracles, but politicians like the crazed and incompetent Mayor of San Juan have done such a poor job of bringing the Island back to health. 91 Billion Dollars to Puerto Rico, and now the Dems want to give them more, taking dollars away from our Farmers and so many others. Disgraceful![24]

The trend in disaster research in recent decades towards vulnerability theory and social constructionism provide support for a blaming perspective.[25] The classic book by Dennis Mileti, *Disasters by Design*, is based upon the notion that we construct risk, and therefore design our own disasters.[26]

Depending upon your worldview you may or may not believe that victims are responsible for their suffering. Certainly, there are cases where this is demonstrably false,[ii] but even if it is considered true, is it moral to engage in the blame game? Consider the following questions:

- Is there a duty for stakeholders to blame victims?
- Do victims, who are already experiencing trauma, have the right not to be blamed?
- Does blaming victims contribute to the greater good?
- Does blaming victims demonstrate virtuous behavior?

There are both legal and psychological aspects that must be considered, as well as moral. If there is potential for legal liability then the causes of hazard, exposure and vulnerability should be clearly understood. If victims knowingly expose themselves to hazard or make themselves vulnerable beyond what is considered reasonable, then they have some level of responsibility for their suffering. There are, of course, many complicating factors related to social traps, powerlessness, and bounded rationality that limit people's responsibility for constructing their own risk.

From a psychological perspective victim blaming is a useful strategy for non-victims to feel safer.[27] This attitude is closely related to the just-world hypothesis.[28] This hypothesis proposes that people's need to believe in a just world requires them to rationalize blaming victims, no matter the circumstances. This has most often been explored around the issue of rape, but also applies to the victims of disaster. Janoff-Bulman[29] explores this in her book, *Shattered Assumptions*, and discusses how this cognitive strategy allows people to feel safer in an unsafe world. If people are to blame for their own misfortune, then that implies an ability to control outcomes; by not behaving in a particular way then one can feel safer.

So, let us consider the questions above. Is there a duty or obligation to blame victims? This is referred to as scapegoating when the motivation is vindictive.[30] Scapegoating is generally not considered a duty, but rather malfeasance. In some situations, one could argue there is a legal or institutional duty to

---

[ii] Some people, born into poverty and a culture of oppression, have no opportunity to escape their fate.

scapegoat due to the need to represent clients or protect institutions or employers. One example of this occurred after the Three Mile Island nuclear disaster, where Metropolitan Edison Company (Met-Ed), a subsidiary of GPU Inc. Energy division blamed the operators, while the operators blamed the company.[31]

Flood Plain Development:

- If people live in a known flood plain and then suffer a flood disaster, to what extent is there a duty or obligation in society to assist them in recovery? This obviously relates to moral hazard, as discussed in Chapter 3.

- What if an area was zoned for housing development by a municipal council 30 years before the flood, and new owners were not informed of flood risk?

- Should children, who were unable to participate in the decision-making suffer along with their parents?

"Province failed to control floodplain development, auditor general says"
Figure 5.4. Headline and photo from a story in the *Calgary Herald*[32]

Do victims have the right not to be blamed? There is no law prohibiting such and it is difficult to construct a deontological argument to support this as a general assertion. The ethics and morals of blaming are very situational.

When Blame is Necessary:

- Give an example where blaming in a post-disaster situation is important for legal or political purposes.

On utilitarian grounds it is easy to argue that in the response phase of a disaster, blaming victims will make it more difficult for them to deal with their trauma and will therefore be harmful. It would probably also reduce charitable donations. During the recovery/reconstruction stage of disaster, however, allocations of responsibility may be important so that exposure or vulnerability is not reproduced, reducing the chances of future disaster. Such allocations may also be important for legal, political, and psychological purposes.

From a virtue perspective, blaming victims appears cruel, particularly during response. It may demonstrate the virtues of honesty and courage (though this would be highly contextual; it might be deceptive and cowardly), but is certainly not compassionate. During the recovery/reconstruction stage it may be perceived as more virtuous, but during response I would judge it to be malignant.

In some cases, blaming victims may be an ethical choice if there are good arguments that the victim's decisions and behaviors played a significant role in creating exposure or vulnerability. The timing of such blame, however, is important and should contribute towards risk reduction activities or satisfy other duties.

We should note that there is also a reciprocal dynamic, that of victims blaming others. One example of this is the blame assigned to California Power Provider PG&E for wildfires that occurred in 2018 and 2019, and which resulted in the company filing for bankruptcy.[33] A parallel set of questions can then be raised.

- Do victims have a duty to blame other stakeholders?
- Do other stakeholders have the right not to be blamed?
- Does blaming other stakeholders contribute to the greater good?
- Does blaming other stakeholders demonstrate virtuous behavior?

There is an important contextual difference between this dynamic and the previous one, which is that non-victim stakeholders are likely not traumatized or working to recover from disaster. If there are good arguments that they share a significant portion of responsibility for creating exposure or vulnerability, then I would argue that the victims do indeed have a moral responsibility to blame perpetrators. The intent of this would be to encourage risk reduction activities and to create an environment where justice is more likely to occur, both of which would contribute toward the greater good.

An example of this is a recent lawsuit against General Electric over the Fukishima nuclear disaster. The plaintiffs claimed GE, who designed and primarily constructed the plant, was responsible for its upkeep and made decisions that resulted in the disaster. In response, "a spokesperson from GE emphasized past investigations that have concluded the tsunami catalyzed the nuclear disaster, not the reactor design."[34] Attribution of causation becomes critical in these kinds of cases.

The notion that stakeholders have the right not to be blamed if they are indeed responsible is at odds with a liberal, democratic society. When victims demand justice from stakeholders who have responsibility for disaster, then they may demonstrate virtues such as honesty and courage. If they are acting out of a need for revenge, then their actions are less virtuous.

5.4 Disaster Narratives as Moral Stances

5.4. Introducing Disaster Narratives

In a paper I am currently writing with Prof. Peter Timmerman at York University, we create a typology of disaster narratives, many of which have moral components. These narratives are based upon various worldviews that are heavily laden with moral assumptions and metaphors, as well as belief systems that may not be religious in nature, but that share with religions a faith-based understanding of the relationship between people, society and the world they inhabit.

This kind of narrative has at least two important sub-narratives. One is rooted in libertarian values – individualism, support of the free-market system and neo-liberal ideologies. Within this narrative individual freedom with minimal controls supposedly allows social systems to self-optimize. Wealth and power accumulate in the hands of the deserving few, but all benefit. In this view risk can be quantitatively calculated, strategies developed to reduce or optimize it, and human society marches onward towards an ever-increasing level of control and domination. The reoccurrence of disaster is seen as evidence of fixable flaws within the system or the cost of doing business, but do not challenge the fundamental paradigm of human supremacy and domination or the value of accumulating wealth (sometimes above all else).

Within the paradigm of "disasters are the cost of doing business", disasters are socially constructed events that serve the interests of hegemonies, intentionally or unintentionally. In this view they are not flaws in the machine but rather a part of a social/technological/economic machine that is needed (and used) by powerful elites to optimize and maintain the structures of power and wealth from which they benefit. Challenges to the moral rightness of this narrative are based upon social justice, environmental and egalitarian worldviews.

A fundamental difference between a social constructionist perspective of disasters and many historical ones is the issue of agency – historical narratives tend to imbue people and society with limited or no agency, whereas modern ones usually assume it. Disasters in modernity do not just happen, they happen because of human error, greed, corruption, evil, because it was too expensive to prevent them, or because of limits of the power and control human beings have over their environment. These narratives are often framed as dichotomies, for example as guilt/innocence, perpetrator/victim, or human/natural. Dichotomies are useful to simplify complexity or to serve vested interests but tend to obscure an understanding of events that requires a nuanced approach, and which should evaluate context and use system thinking. For example, the phrase "natural disasters" is something of an oxymoron, since by choice society builds communities, infrastructure and social systems that are exposed and vulnerable to hazards. Nevertheless, it is a commonly used phrase that represents a prevalent cultural narrative.

Some narratives occur at very deep cultural and moral levels that reflect fundamental worldviews and values. Layered on top of these deep narratives are metaphors and other strategic narratives that have explanatory power. One example of a deep narrative is the supremacy of man over nature (a kind of anti-environmentalist ethic), which has historical religious roots in the biblical story of creation. Strategic narratives that are derived from it would be ones of controlling natural hazards; war-like metaphors are commonly used to describe human-nature interactions, such as the "battle against the storm", or "flood defences". The UK, for example, often uses the phrase flood defences, such as shown in a story published in The Guardian about how more investment is needed in flood defences to protect against future flooding events[35]. There is a counter narrative; an alternative to battling nature is living with it. One example of this environmental narrative related to flooding has been adopted by the Netherlands, which they call "making room for the river" or "living with waters"[36]. This policy uses strategies of relocating dykes farther from riverbeds, the creation of side channels, lowering floodplain levels, having "green rivers", reducing the height of groynes, and removing obstacles to river flow. (This has however not precluded the Netherlands from being the world experts in building walls against floods.)

This layering of narratives can be analyzed in terms of kinds of disaster. Whether they are perceived as being natural, human, divine, or technological will shift narrative structures. For example, human agency may be viewed as low for natural disasters but high for human or technological ones -- though the underlying agency may still be human -- cumulative risk, or neglect, or other elements not immediately identifiable. Notions of confronting human evil are rare in natural disasters, but much more common in human caused events, and greatly affect how people respond to them[37].

5.4.1 Narrative Categories

We propose a categorization of disaster narratives as shown in Table 5.1, which can be used as a basis for further discussion and clarification. We note that the disaster types chosen are simplistic and problematical but are relevant because disasters are commonly perceived as belonging to these categories, and they are frequently used in disaster taxonomies and the media. For example, the World Health Organization says about disasters in Vietnam that "Disasters can be natural (e.g. typhoons or flooding) or man-made (e.g. chemical spills)"[38]. Note that in this categorization they merge man-made and technological events.

The narratives discussed below are not mutually exclusive as a way of understanding any particular event; a disaster will typically have multiple narratives, from which a dominant one typically emerges, and which may be a blend of more than one narrative. For each disaster type we suggest that there exists deep cultural narratives that profoundly influence how they are used in meaning-making, and what adaptive strategies are chosen.

	Perceived Disaster Type			
	Natural	**Technological**	**Human**	**The Divine**
Deep Cultural Narratives	N-1, N-2, N-3	T-1, T-2, T-3	H-1, H-2, H-3, H-4	D-1, D-2
Meaning Making				
Adaptive Strategies				

Narrative ("Natural"-1): Fatalism

The deep cultural narratives associated with N-1 are fatalism and lack of human agency. In some ways this is similar to Divine-1. The meaning derived from these are that there is nothing that can be done to prevent disasters; we are simply victims and results in a laissez-faire adaptive strategy.

Narrative ("Natural"-2): Human Supremacy over Nature

The deep cultural narratives associated with N-2 are human agency and human supremacy over nature. In this narrative nature is an enemy to be defeated. Meanings associated with this narrative are that humans have the knowledge and power to control nature and therefore prevent natural disasters (e.g. control flooding through infrastructure. Adaptive strategies associated with this narrative are social and physical engineering and risk management

Narrative ("Natural"-3): Living with Nature

The deep cultural narratives associated with N-3 is living with nature and that humans are part of the greater ecological whole. This means that disasters are part of the natural system and, to a degree, must be accepted. This aligns with Normal Accident Theory. Nature is not to be controlled, but to be lived with. Adaptive strategies include, as much as possible, let nature be, risk avoidance (e.g. don't live in floodplains), use of the precautionary principle, environmental protection and conservation.

Narrative (Technological-1): Technology will Solve Everything

The deep cultural narratives associated with T-1 are that humans in control (similar to N-2). Man's control and use of technology leads to the best possible outcomes but we must do it well, then disasters can be eliminated. This means that disasters happen because of incompetence, lack of investment or lack of training, but are preventable. Adaptive strategies are more and better standards, investment, education and training. High reliability theory is based upon this perspective.

Narrative (Technological-2): Technology will Solve Most Things

The deep cultural narratives associated with T-2 are that humans are mostly in control, and that man's control and use of technology leads to the best possible outcome. Unfortunately, disasters cannot all be prevented, and some suffer for the greater good. Disasters are unfortunate but the price we pay for the benefits of a technological society. The future can be predicted, but there are limits to what it is worth to prevent disasters. Adaptive strategies include risk analysis and cost-benefit analysis.

Narrative (Technological-3): Pandora's Box

The deep cultural narratives associated with T-3 are that human use of technology will result in catastrophe. Cultural metaphors include Frankenstein and Pandora's Box. This means that through technology we have unleashed uncontrollable forces that will eventually destroy us, and we suffer from the sin of hubris. The primary adaptive strategy is use of the precautionary principle to avoid ruinous outcomes.

Narrative (Human-1): The Hobbesian World

The deep cultural narratives associated with H-1 is that disasters happen because humans are fundamentally flawed - savage and selfish. This means that we must protect ourselves against the dangerous "other. Many conspiracy theories are rooted in this narrative. Adaptive strategies include an increased security state, isolationism, survivalism, and xenophobia.

Narrative (Human-2). Social Construction

There are two deep cultural narratives associated with N-1, which is that elites create disaster risk as they accumulate power and wealth at the expense of others. They are social Darwinism and social justice.

Type Human-2a: Social Darwinism.

In this narrative elites flourish because it is natural law that they should do so. This perspective is associated with libertarianism and neo-liberal economics. It assumes that the free market is the best solution to managing social-economic and political systems.

Type Human-2b: Social Justice.

In this narrative those in power unjustly choose to be selfish. The price for their elite status is paid by the vulnerable, who suffer disproportionately. Adaptive strategies are the socialization of risk, a welfare state and humanitarianism.

Narrative (Human-3): Disaster as Social Autopsy

In this narrative disasters are viewed as social autopsies that reveals the hidden underside of who we are (Klinenberg, 1999). They strip off concealing layers that prevent people from seeing the true nature of society, revealing otherwise hidden injustices and vulnerabilities. Adaptive strategies include the critical analysis of disasters using "root cause" theory. Disasters, therefore, are opportunities for social change and adaptive management.

Narrative (Human-4): Symbolism

In this narrative disasters become symbols that are used to mark meaningful events in our lives. They can represent the best or worst of human nature (heroism or villany) and are often turning points in people's lives. Adaptive strategies include commemorative books, statues and holidays.

Narrative (Divine-1): Punishment

The deep cultural narrative associated with D-1 is that disasters are punishments for our sins (e.g. Noah's flood). If people ignore God's laws disaster results, punishing us and reminding people to obey his strictures. The adaptive strategy is to obey God's laws.

Narrative (Divine-2).

This narrative is based upon the belief that suffering will be redeemed and is the price to be paid for a better future. Through suffering we can become more resilient and better people. In the extreme, the End of Times and Armageddon would fit into this narrative. The adaptive strategy is acceptance of God's plan.

Commonly there is a struggle within social space for one narrative to achieve dominance. Which narrative succeeds can have important consequences legally and in terms of disaster risk reduction policies and strategies. A number of the narratives explicitly address ethical/moral issues, including the assignment of blame. These are:

- N2 – Anti-Environmental ethics
- N3 – Environmental ethics
- T2 – Utilitarianism
- T3 – Precautionary Principle
- H1 – Human evil
- H2 – Libertarianism vs Social Justice
- D1, 2 – Divine Law

5.4.2 Case Study: The Westray Mine Disaster. Who is to Blame?

An explosion at the Westray Mine, Nova Scotia in May of 1992 caused the death of 26 miners. Outcomes of this disaster included: an official enquiry that stated the disaster *"was a complex mosaic of actions, omissions, mistakes, incompetence, apathy, cynicism, stupidity, and neglect"*[39]; legal actions (52 violations of the Health and Safety Act were filed, but later dropped in favor of a criminal prosecution that ended in a mistrial); several studies as to its causes; and the focus of a significant amount of media attention[40].

How this disaster was framed varied greatly depending upon the perspective of the viewer, and this event is a good example of how contrasting disaster narratives compete for dominance within the social sphere. In order to avoid legal liability and public censure the owners of the mine, Curragh Resources Incorporated (Curragh Inc.), needed to appear innocent of wrongdoing (narrative N-1); the miners saw themselves as victims and the mine company guilty of negligence or worse (narratives T-2, H-2 and H-3); and politicians wanted themselves to be seen as protecting the public good (narrative T-1).

The following statements appeared in July 1991, ten months before the mine exploded.

• In a letter to Labor Minister Leroy Legere, Liberal MLA Bernie Boudreau warns that the Westray coal mine "is potentially one of the most dangerous in the world."

• The minister responds: "I assume that my department and the mines safety people are doing as good a job at Westray as they are doing at all other mines in Nova Scotia."[41]

McMullan and McClung[42] discuss how this disaster was framed in terms of "Michel Foucault's concept of the 'politics of truth'[43] and Stanley Cohen's ideas about 'states of denial'"[44]. Within the notion of politics of truth, facts and truth are malleable, subject to interpretations. These interpretations are done within the context of vested interests, power structures and social values and determine what facts and issues receive attention. In the extreme they can also portray alternate realities and "fake news", a phrase much used in the U.S. during the Trump presidency. Denial can take four basic forms: (a) literal denial or the politics of lying (what you think is happening is actually not happening); (b) interpretive denial (reframing the event); (c) implicatory denial (justifying what happened) and (d) passive denial (silence – soon the media will move on to another story).

One narrative (N-1) put forth by Curragh Inc. was that they were not responsible for the tragedy, and therefore had no liability. In the words of their spokesperson, "Nature cannot always be predicted or controlled..."[45]. While literally true, as an explanation for the disaster it is inappropriate and misleading since the explosion was largely caused by human decisions - one miner commented (narrative H-2) that "the mine was "a disaster waiting to happen"[46]. It is revealing that the title of the Board of Inquiry report by Justice Richard is called a "Predictable Path to Disaster"[47]. The "nature as cause" state of denial used by the mining company is rooted in the notion of lack of human agency - that people are victims of forces outside of their control. This narrative is similar to narratives based upon disasters as being fated.

A counter narrative is rooted in the notion that risk is socially constructed, and there is strong empirical evidence to support this perspective both in general and for this disaster. Glasbeek and Tucker[48] describe in detail how numerous decisions made within the political and economic realms resulted in both exposure and vulnerability to mine hazards, and that a disaster was highly probable (if not inevitable) as a result. These decisions were molded by interests in obtaining and preserving power and wealth (narrative H-2). Within this narrative victims lack agency; those harmed by the disaster are innocent victims of perpetrators who knowingly and callously exposed others to harm through negligence or in order to serve their self-interests. And, these interests are supported by a dominant social-political hegemony that exists to maintain that structure at the expense of the less powerful.

One result of the counter narrative and the recommendations from the Board of Enquiry are the 2004 Nova Scotia Criminal Code amendments C-45, known as the Westray Law, which includes the following section; "S217.1 Every one who undertakes, or has the authority, to direct how another person does work or performs a task is under a legal duty to take reasonable steps to prevent bodily harm to that person, or any other person, arising from that work or task." Also added are Sections 22.1 and 22.2 to the Criminal Code imposing criminal liability on organizations and its representatives for negligence (22.1) and other offences (22.2)[49].

Narratives following a disaster can arise out of a need for meaning-making, to make sense of an event that has shattered people and communities, but they can also be powerful tools for the explicit or implicit exercise of power, by creating manufactured consent[50]. As noted above, the mining company engaged in various forms of denial and was ultimately successful in terms of avoiding legal liability, though the counter narrative of moral if not criminal accountability is still present in the media and various reports.

The numerous faults found by the Board of Enquiry as well as anecdotal reports by miners demonstrate a pattern of neglect, incompetence and possibly malfeasance (narratives H-1, H-2 and H-3) - "management at Westray displayed a certain disdain for safety and appeared to regard safety-conscious workers as the wimps in the organization."[51]. One argument presented in favor of the mining company is that the miners have free will and could choose to work or not to work in this particular mine (narrative T-2). This argument, however, does not account for lack of choice resulting from economic and job availability issues or differences in power between workers and management. Though some miners did quit, they were few in number and were the more experienced miners who had a better understanding of the risks that they were facing. Certainly, there were costs involved to Curragh Inc. to improve safety conditions, and the question "What acceptable level of risk should be planned for?" has relevance. Such determinations, however, should involve those at risk as a significant stakeholder in order to satisfy procedural justice standards, but this was not the case in Westray. By not following legal requirements or best practices, the argument can be made that they engaged in malfeasance (narrative H-2a).

The above narratives are rooted in dichotomies such as agency versus powerlessness, victim versus perpetrator, natural versus human, and guilt versus innocence. It might be considered a dialectic, where discourse from opposing perspectives is used to arrive at 'truth'. The dynamic, however, is more one of struggles to create a dominant narrative. The use of narratives as a tool to exert power is fundamental in understanding how different groups frame disaster to serve various ends, be it the maintenance of an existing hegemony, or the avoidance/pursuit of justice or affirmation.

5.5 Conclusions

Victim blaming is a common response to disaster. There are times when such blame is justified according to specific beliefs (such as divine retribution or social constructionism), but engaging in blame can be very destructive to disaster victims. However, in post-disaster times blaming can potentially serve useful legal, policy, or psychological purposes and result in better mitigation and prevention, which will reduce the chances of future disasters.

5.6 Endnotes

[1] Montada, L. (1991). Coping with life stress injustice and the question "Who is responsible? In H. Steensma & R. Vermunt (Ed.), *Social justice in human relations* (pp. 9-30). Springer.

[2] Buetow, S., & Elwyn, G. (2006). Are patients morally responsible for their errors? *Journal of Medical Ethics*, *32*(5), 260-262.

[3] Harris, J. (1995). Could we hold people responsible for their own adverse health? *Journal of Contemporary Health Law & Policy*, *12*(1), 147-153.

[4] Gorini, A., Miglioretti, M., & Pravettoni, G. (2012). A new perspective on blame culture: An experimental study. *Journal of Evaluation in Clinical Practice*, *18*(3), 671-675.

[5] Khatri, N., Brown, G. D., & Hicks, L. L. (2009) From a blame culture to a just culture in health care. *Health Care Management Review*, *34*(4), 312–322.

[6] Catino, M. (2009). Blame culture and defensive medicine. *Cognition, Technology & Work*, *11*(4), 245-253.

[7] Wallace, R. J. (1994). *Responsibility and the moral sentiments*. Harvard University Press.

[8] Wallace, R. J. (2011). Dispassionate opprobrium: On blame and the reactive sentiments. In R. J. Wallace, R. Kumar, & S. Freeman (Eds.), *Reasons and recognition: Essays on the philosophy of T. M. Scanlon* (pp. 348-372). Oxford University Press.

[9] Hieronymi, P. (2004). The force and fairness of blame. *Philosophical Perspectives*, *18*, 115–148.

[10] Glasbeek, H., & Tucker, E. (1994). Death by consensus: The Westray mine story. *NEW SOLUTIONS: A Journal of Environmental and Occupational Health Policy*, *3*(4), 14-41.

[11] Westray Response Committee. (1997). *Westray: A plan of action: Government's response to the report of the Westray Mine Public Inquiry*. Government of Nova Scotia.

[12] Ryan, W. (1976). *Blaming the victim*. Vintage Books.

[13] Taylor, A. J. W. (1998). Observations from a cyclone stress/trauma assignment in the Cook Islands. *Traumatology*, *4*(1), 30-40.

[14] Taylor, A. J. (1999). Value conflict arising from a disaster. *Australasian Journal of Disaster and Trauma Studies*, *3*(2).

[15] Herodotus. (1925). *The Persian Wars: Volume IV: Books 8-9* (A. D. Godley, Ed.). Loeb Classical Library. http://penelope.uchicago.edu/Thayer/E/Roman/Texts/Herodotus/8C*.html

[16] (2009). [Photograph of Herodotus sculpture] [Photograph] *Wikimedia Commons*. *https://commons.wikimedia.org/wiki/File:Wien-Parlament-Herodot.jpg*

[17] Smith, E. (1995). [Aerial photograph of Pukapuka Atoll in the Cook Islands] [Photograph]. https://commons.wikimedia.org/wiki/File:Pukapuka_Aerial_efs_1280.jpg

[18] Scarborough, J. (2005, October 5). Hurricane Katrina: Wrath of God? [Opinion television show]. *Scarborough Country*. http://www.nbcnews.com/id/9600878/ns/msnbc-morning_joe/t/hurricane-katrina-wrath-god/#.WwBOo-4vyHs

[19] Pence, M. (2015). Comment by Vice President Pence on Christians of Modbb, Jan 7, 2015, http://www.moddb.com/groups/christians-of-moddb/images/noahs-flood

[20] BBC News. (2010, April 20). *Iranian cleric blames quakes on promiscuous women*. http://news.bbc.co.uk/2/hi/middle_east/8631775.stm

[21] Martin, J. (1852). [Christ Stilleth the Tempest] [Oil on cardboard]. York Museums Trust. https://artuk.org/discover/artworks/christ-stilleth-the-tempest-8156

[22] Lutzer, E. W. (2011). *An act of God?: Answers to tough questions about God's role in natural disasters*. Tyndale House Publishers, Inc.

[23] Mazzei, P., & Robles, F. (2019, September 19). *Former FEMA official accused of taking bribes in Hurricane Maria recovery*. The New York Times. https://www.nytimes.com/2019/09/10/us/puerto-rico-fema-arrests-corruption.html

[24] Bort, R. (2019, April 2). *Trump claims he's the best thing that's ever happened to Puerto Rico*. Rolling Stone. https://www.rollingstone.com/politics/politics-news/trump-puerto-rico-funding-816453/

[25] Etkin, D. (2015). *Disaster theory: An interdisciplinary approach to concepts and causes*. Butterworth-Heinemann.

[26] Mileti, D. S. (1999). *Disasters by design: A reassessment of natural hazards in the United States*. Joseph Henry Press.

[27] Hayes, R. M., Lorenz, K., & Bell, K. A. (2013). Victim blaming others: Rape myth acceptance and the just world belief. *Feminist Criminology*, *8*(3), 202-220.

[28] Lerner, M., & Miller, D. (1978). Just world research and the attribution process: Looking back and ahead. *Psychological Bulletin, 85*(5), 1030-1051.

[29] Janoff-Bulman, R. (2010). *Shattered assumptions: Towards a new psychology of trauma*. Simon and Schuster.

[30] Drabek, T. E., & Quarantelli, E. L. (1967). Scapegoats, villains, and disasters. *Trans-action, 4*, 12-17.

[31] Perrow, C. (2011). *Normal accidents: Living with high risk technologies*. Princeton University Press.

[32] McClure, M. (2015, March 11). *Province failed to control floodplain development, auditor general says.* Calgary herald. https://calgaryherald.com/news/politics/province-failed-to-control-floodplain-development-auditor-general-says

[33] Westervelt, E., & Schwartz, M. S. (2019, January 29). *California power provider PG&E files for bankruptcy in wake of fire lawsuits*. NPR. https://www.npr.org/2019/01/29/689591066/california-power-provider-pg-e-files-for-bankruptcy-in-wake-of-fire-lawsuits

[34] Glatter, H. (2017, November 17). *General Electric sued for role in Fukushima nuclear disaster.* Boston magazine. https://www.bostonmagazine.com/news/2017/11/17/general-electric-fukushima-lawsuit/

[35] McKie, R. (2020). UK flood defence plans are inadequate, warn scientists. The Guardian, https://www.theguardian.com/environment/2020/feb/23/uk-flood-defence-plans-inadequate-warn-scientists, Feb. 23, 2020.

[36] Rijke, J., van Herk, S., Zevenbergen, C., & Ashley, R. (2012). Room for the River: delivering integrated river basin management in the Netherlands. *International journal of river basin management*, *10*(4), 369-382.

[37] Janoff-Bulman, R. (2010). *Shattered assumptions*. Simon and Schuster.

[38] WHO (n.d.). Disaster in Viet Nam, https://www.who.int/vietnam/health-topics/disasters

[39] Westray Mine Public Inquiry (N.S.), (1997). The Westray story: A predictable path to disaster: Report of the westray mine public inquiry. In K. Peter Richard (eds.)Commissioner. Halifax: Westray Mine Public Inquiry.

[40] *Boyle, Theresa (May 11, 1992). "Why did safety systems fail? Sad questions grow louder". The Toronto Star. Toronto. p. A10*

[41] Maclean's, v109 n29 p22, 15 July 1996, http://www.geocities.com/SouthBeach/Lights/6602/pics.html

[42] McMullan, J. L., & McClung, M. (2006). The media, the politics of truth, and the coverage of corporate violence: The Westray disaster and the public inquiry. *Critical Criminology*, *14*(1), 67-86.

[43] Foucault, M. (1991a). The discourse on power. In C. Kraus and S. Lotringer (eds.), *Michel Foucault: Remarks on Marx. Conversations with Duccio Trombadori*. New York: Semiotexte, pp. 147_187.

Foucault, M. (1991b). Politics and the study of discourse. In G. Burchell, C. Gordon and P. Miller (eds.), The Foucault Effect: Studies in Governmentality. Chicago: University of Chicago Press, pp. 53_72.

Foucault, M. (1991c). Questions of method. In G. Burchell, C. Gordon and P. Miller (eds.), The Foucault Effect: Studies in Governmentality. Chicago: University of Chicago Press, pp. 73-86.

[44] Cohen, S. (2001). *States of Denial: Knowing About Atrocities and Suffering*. Cambridge: Polity Press.

[45] Glasbeek, H., & Tucker, E. (1994). Death by consensus: the Westray mine story. *NEW SOLUTIONS: A Journal of Environmental and Occupational Health Policy*, *3*(4), 14-41.

[46] Glasbeek, H., & Tucker, E. (1994). Death by consensus: the Westray mine story. *NEW SOLUTIONS: A Journal of Environmental and Occupational Health Policy*, *3*(4), 14-41.

[47] Richard, K. P. (1997). *The Westray story: a predictable path to disaster*. Lieutenant Governor in Council.

[48] Glasbeek, H., & Tucker, E. (1994). Death by consensus: the Westray mine story. *NEW SOLUTIONS: A Journal of Environmental and Occupational Health Policy*, *3*(4), 14-41.

[49] Canadian Centre for Occupational Health and Safety, https://www.ccohs.ca/oshanswers/legisl/billc45.html

[50] Chomsky, N., & Herman, E. S. (2003). *Manufacturing consent: The political economy of the mass media*

[51] Richard, K. P. (1997). *The Westray story: a predictable path to disaster*. Lieutenant Governor in Council.

CHAPTER 6: DUTY TO RESPOND

"Knowing is not enough; we must apply.
Willing is not enough; we must do."
Goethe (1749–1832) German writer and statesman

Figure 6.1. Goethe in 1828, by Joseph Karl Stieler[1]

Contents

6.0 Introduction

As an emergency manager, under what conditions would you consider not responding to a disaster? Have your emergency plans considered the possibility that police, medical personnel or others involved in disaster response may not show up when they are activated? When might that occur, and are such actions morally defensible?

There are different kinds of duties and obligations. Some are legal requirements, such as the obligation to pay your taxes. Others are not bound by law but are normative expectations in society, such as helping family and friends. Caring ethics supports paying special attention to those with whom there are emotional relationships and responsibilities (such as towards family members). There are also special duties of care, such as parents have towards their children or caretakers towards their wards. Duty of care requires exercising the "care, diligence and skill a reasonably prudent person would exercise in comparable circumstances," and is enforceable by tort law, where negligence can be proven.[2] Many professions have duties and obligations specific to their job, and one of the obligations of first responders is to respond to emergencies. The list of duties for firefighters, for example, include driving firefighting and emergency vehicles, taking proper position and climbing ladders to rescue victims from upper levels of buildings, extinguishing fires, and rescuing those in danger.[3]

There are also duties that are not enforceable in law, such as the normative duty to help others in need. During Hurricane Sandy there was a tragic situation where two children died after they and their mother were denied refuge by a homeowner. However, "[l]egal experts consulted by CNN said that no crime would have been committed by a failure to render assistance."[4] Nevertheless, the public directed widespread anger and blame towards the homeowner who claimed, "It's unfortunate. She shouldn't have been out though. You know, it's one of those things," and "I'm not a rescue worker ... If I would have been outside, I would have been dead."[5]

This chapter focusses on situations where there are duties of care specific to job requirements, such as in the case of first responders. It is rare for those in response professions not to respond to an emergency, but research exists (Section 6.5) that suggests failure to respond could potentially be a serious problem in some disaster scenarios. Empirical research (Section 6.4) of actual disasters concludes that role abandonment as a serious problem is a myth; however, surveys of the ways first responders say they might respond in disaster scenarios paint a different picture, one where many responders might choose to abandon their professional roles in favor of other duties or obligations. What are the ethical dilemmas that must be addressed in terms of not responding to an emergency and how can they be resolved?

6.1 Case Study: The Fire in Makwa Sahgaiehcan First Nation Reserve in Saskatchewan, Canada

> ## Fire chief defends no response to fire that killed 2 toddlers
>
> While unknown whether firefighters could have prevented the children's deaths, the tragedy highlights gaps in fire protection on reserves

On February 2015 a house fire broke out in the Makwa Sahgaiehcan First Nation Reserve in Saskatchewan, Canada. Tragically, two children died. According to CTV News,

> The band had been paying the nearby village of Loon Lake for the services of its volunteer fire department. But in November the village decided to quit service to the reserve because it hadn't paid its fire bills since last spring.[6]

The mayor of the village stated that the reserve was notified of the service suspension, while the Chief of the reserve stated they were unaware of this and paid for services after they were rendered. Should the fire department have responded to the emergency alarm?

While there may not have been a legal obligation for the Loon Lake Fire Department to respond to the call, there are ethical arguments that they should have done so. One is based upon humanitarianism arguments related to the virtues of benevolence, charity, and the value of the sanctity of human life. It would be a virtuous act to respond.

A utilitarian perspective may argue that responding to fire alarms, no matter the circumstances, is in the interests of the greater good. One constraint on this argument relates to limited resources. As a small volunteer fire department, limited resources constrain their ability for unlimited response. This argument speaks to the Good Samaritan's Dilemma. When given aid, recipients can either use that aid to improve their situation or learn to rely upon it (a form of moral hazard). In the latter case, unless the capacity of the Good Samaritan is limitless, (s)he may be contributing to the creation of a culture of dependency that ultimately creates more harm than good. This is the basis of the argument Alex de Waal uses when discussing the failure of humanitarian aid in Africa in *Famine Crimes: Politics and the Disaster Relief Industry in Africa*.[7]

Clearly the band has an obligation to pay their bills and the fire department has a valid ethical argument in stating that they had no obligation to respond. If nobody had been hurt or killed it would not have become a media issue. No doubt the fire department would have responded if they had known that children would die as a result of their inaction, but that knowledge exists only in hindsight. An important context is that the Fire Chief has an obligation to be financially prudent in terms of how he uses the resources the city has allocated to him. For how long should they provide services to communities that do not provide compensation?

This case study is an example of an ethical dilemma, which is a choice between two rights or two wrongs. When ethical arguments and values provide support for both action and inaction, then there is no clear-cut answer of how to act.

Decision matrices or trees can be a useful tool to assist with decision-making; Table 6.1 is an example of a very simple one.

It is worth noting that society has very different values associated with acts of commission as opposed to acts of omission. The latter are much more forgivable, except in special circumstances where there is a normative duty of care (such as parents have towards their children, or the staff of an old age home have towards their residents). People are more likely to be pilloried for that which they do than for that which they do not do. It is for this reason that Good Samaritan laws exist. These laws apply to situations where a voluntary good-faith effort was made to render aid or assistance.

Ontario's Good Samaritan Act, 2001, S.O. 2001, c. 2[8]

Protection from liability
2. (1) Despite the rules of common law, a person [...] who voluntarily and without reasonable expectation of compensation or reward provides the services described in that subsection is not liable for damages that result from the person's negligence in acting or failing to act while providing the services, unless it is established that the damages were caused by the gross negligence of the person. 2001, c. 2, s. 2 (1).

Figure 6.2: *The Good Samaritan* by Jacob Jordaens, ca. 1616.[9]

	Harm Occurs	No Harm Occurs
Benevolent Action Taken	Ethically and morally defensible (though there are arguments against such action), even though harm was not averted. If the benevolent action increases the amount of harm, then ethical justification is more difficult, though in many places Good Samaritan laws protect you.	Ethically and morally defensible (though there are arguments against such action), and you are now a hero.
No Benevolent Action Taken	Ethically and morally debatable, and you are now subject to public and potential legal scrutiny. In the court of public opinion, you may be perceived as a villain.	Ethically and morally debatable. You are neither hero, nor villain.

Table 6.1: Decision-Making Matrix for Benevolent Action versus Inaction. In this example, without knowledge of the probability of harm, the benevolent row leads to outcomes that are preferable.

6.3 Historical Note: Cicero's Dissertation on Duty

One of the earliest surviving discussions about public duty was written by the Roman statesman and philosopher Cicero in 44 BCE. He lived during the time of Julius Caesar and opposed the transformation of the Roman Republic into a dictatorship. After the assassination of Caesar, he became the enemy of Mark Antony and was executed in 43 BCE.

"Justice consists of doing our fellow humans no injury, and decency of giving them no offense."

Cicero, Roman Statesman (106 BC- 46 BCE)

Figure 6.3: Bust of Marcus Tullius Cicero[10]

Cicero argued for public service rooted in sacrifice and service, not in right and privilege. His discussion of duty, entitled *De Officiis*, addresses what is honorable (virtuous) and useful in life, and endures as an important contribution to ethical thinking. According to Cicero virtue consists of prudence, justice, fortitude, and temperance.[i, 11, 12]

6.4 Empirical Evidence from Historical Disasters (Behavioral Studies)

Jane Kushma in her article, "Role Abandonment in Disaster: Should We Leave This Myth Behind?" points out the lack of evidence for significant role abandonment during disasters in the United States, though the myth persists.[13] Trainor and Barsky reviewed research on role abandonment, and in a meta-analysis of historical disasters found that "the problem of role abandonment will be minimal except under very specific conditions, such as those that were present in the case of the New Orleans Police Department during Hurricane Katrina."[14] There are also examples of role abandonment by care givers in nursing homes during the COVID-19 pandemic of 2020 (Chapter 10.4). These abandonments may be caused by first responders or care givers being at high risk or by other duties that make demands upon them (such as family), and are exacerbated by low wages and organizational cultures that do not provide enough support to their staff during emergency situations.

It does not necessarily follow, however, that because role abandonment has not been a serious problem thus far that it will not be in the future. Empirical evidence is limited by the disasters studied and may say little about future disasters that have not yet occurred within a social context that is different than those in present empirical studies. For this reason, research is done that is based upon surveys that ask people how they may behave in a variety of scenarios

6.5 Evidence from Surveys (Perception Studies)

There have been a number of studies that surveyed people on how they would address their professional duties in a disaster situation.[15, 16] These studies generally indicate larger role abandonment issues than empirical behavioral studies have shown. In one survey of health care personnel, reasons identified for possible abandonment include concern for family, loved ones, pets, and personal obligations. Other factors influencing this issue are perceived value in the response, level of belief in duty to care, the availability of personal protective equipment, length of the response, and the degree to which the basic needs of the responders could be met.[17] In one pandemic flu outbreak scenario only 11% of home health workers and 37% of registered nurses indicated that they would be willing to provide care for patients.[18] The results of surveys are highly variable; others have positive response rates of up to 95%.[19] MedPage reported that, during the COVID-19 pandemic, "[p]hysicians across the

---

[i] Cicero states,

> Virtue is a disposition [habitus] of spirit [animus] in harmony with the measure of nature and of reason. So when we know all its parts, we will have considered all the force of simple honor. It has four parts: prudence, justice, fortitude, temperance.

country are having to close their clinics and transition to remote patient visits when possible to stop the spread of COVID-19."[20] There are many variables at play that affect people's decisions to respond.

A study by the National Registry of Emergency Medical Technicians (NREMT) found the following for EMS professionals in the U.S.:

- 93% of EMS workers would report to work if required, but only 88% would report to work if asked but not required.
- Response willingness dropped to 48% if there were a chance that influenza could be transmitted to EMS workers' families.
- 80% of EMS workers would volunteer in a neighboring community experiencing an influenza outbreak if the chance of becoming ill were low. However, only 37% would volunteer in a neighboring community if the chance of becoming ill were high.
- In general, members of the local public health workforce in rural communities had higher levels of response willingness than individuals living in more urban areas.
- Response willingness was typically lower for man-made disasters (i.e., "dirty" bomb; inhalational anthrax) than for natural disasters (i.e., weather-related; pandemic influenza).[21]

The cause of the disaster matters. For example, Landahl and Cox found that the number of employees who were willing to report varied by disaster type: during SARS (48.4%), radiation (57.3%), smallpox (61.1%), a chemical event (67.7%), a snow storm (80.4%), an environmental disaster (84.2%), and a mass casualty incident (85.7%).[22] Familiarity and fear of the disaster type certainly plays a factor in the varying response rates.

6.6 Case Study: Hurricane Katrina and Police Officers

When Hurricane Katrina devastated the City of New Orleans in August of 2005 there were widespread media reports of New Orleans City police officers deserting their posts. Trainer and Barsky found that "240 of 1,450 officers on the force reportedly never showed up for work. Of those, 51 officers were fired for 'abandoning their posts.'"[23] Another 15 officers resigned after being placed under investigation.[24] Trainer and Barsky note that "[d]epending on which number one uses, that means between 3% and 16% abandoned their posts."[25] Superintendent Warren Riley commented to the press that the officers were "terminated due to them abandoning the department prior to the storm [...] They either left before the hurricane or 10 to 12 days after the storm and we have never heard from them."[26] According to Anderson and Farber, 60 officers resigned, 45 were fired, and two committed suicide. "Nearly 70% of the police force lost their homes. All together the NOPD lost approximately 7% of its officers."[27]

> # Police Chief: 249 New Orleans Officers Left Posts Without Permission During Katrina
>
>
>
> **(NEW ORLEANS)** -- Nearly 250 police officers -- roughly 15 percent of the force -- could face a special tribunal because they left their posts without permission during Hurricane Katrina and the storm's chaotic aftermath, the police chief said.

Figure 6.4: Newspaper headline about police officers deserting during Hurricane Katrina.[28]

The number of officers not reporting for duty in the Katrina disaster is an anomaly in U.S. disaster response statistics. This is thought to be largely due to a variety of institutional and cultural contexts, including high levels of corruption, low morale, low pay, and a response that was

> undermined by catastrophic communications failure. With the breakdown of communications came a loss of centralized command, which created innumerable problems, including the public perception of lawlessness, the failure of normal police procedures, and overall inefficiency of response. As the chain-of-command was reconstituted ad hoc, insufficient emergency planning, training, and equipment further hampered the department's ability to respond.[29]

According to the *New York Times*,

> W.J. Riley, the assistant superintendent of police, said there were about 1,200 officers on duty on Saturday. He said the department was not sure how many officers had decided to abandon their posts and how many simply could not get to work. [...] [S]ome of the officers who left the force "couldn't handle the pressure" and were "certainly not the people we need in this department." He said, "The others are not here because they lost a spouse, or their family or their home was destroyed."[30]

Some officers may have abandoned their roles because of fear or difficult working conditions, while others may have had to deal with an ethical dilemma—the obligation to fulfill their role as a police officer or focus on other duties related to family, friends, or community.

The Oath of Office sworn by police officers in New Orleans is as follows:

> I, (member's name), do solemnly swear (or affirm) that I will support the Constitution and laws of the United States; the Constitution and laws of this State and the Charter and Ordinances of this City; and I will faithfully and impartially discharge and perform all the duties incumbent upon me as (job title), according to the best of my ability and understanding.[31]

The phrase "according to the best of my ability" may allow room for officers to argue that their ability was compromised by their being victims of the storm and/or the needs of their family. What are the ethical arguments for and against role abandonment in a disaster of this magnitude?

6.7 Ethical Arguments for Role Abandonment

It is important to state at the beginning of this section that each disaster and each individual's situation in it is unique and contextual. There are many factors that determine levels of duties and obligations, capacity to respond, probable contribution, and people's needs, all of which would have to be considered in any ethical analysis.

In terms of duties and obligations, there are certainly potential conflicts (ethical dilemmas) in disaster situations. Professional responders have an obligation to fulfill their roles and to serve the public good. At the same time, they have a duty to protect their family and the right to protect themselves from unreasonable risks. This conflict is a deontological one. Balancing these conflicts is difficult and depends greatly on individual circumstances.

From a utilitarian perspective, responders reduce harm and save lives. The good that they do for society at large likely outweighs the good they might do for a few as they abandon their roles, and therefore utilitarian arguments would probably weigh against role abandonment.

What would a virtuous person do? People should be loyal to their employer, but also to their families. It could take courage to respond in the face of adversity, but also courage to abandon official roles for other duties.

The case of SARS or a pandemic exemplifies some of these issues. In SARS, about 30% of the reported cases of abandonment were from health care providers, and epidemics expose not just health care workers to infection but also their families. Early data from the COVID-19 pandemic suggest that health care providers have high rates of infection compared to the general populations; in Italy it has been reported as 9% of COVID cases.[32] It can be argued that health care workers have assumed a duty of care by entering their profession, and that they have also accepted a degree of risk that is associated with it. It does not follow, however, that they need to accept unreasonable degrees of risk. What constitutes "unreasonable" is obviously a contentious question. Clearly, it rose to that level for the staff of a nursing home in California in April 2020, where are majority of them failed to show up for work and abandoned the residents[33].

Role-playing Exercise:

Consider the scenario of a pandemic, where vaccines are not yet available. The disease appears to be highly contagious.

The exercise is a conversation between people assuming the two roles below, with the manager (role #1) instructing all paramedics to come to work on an overtime basis, and the paramedic (role #2) indicating that (s)he is very uncomfortable with the risk and prefers not to work until vaccines are available to paramedics and their families.

During this roleplay, think ethically. Analyze the situation from several ethical perspectives and identify

---

the values that underlie the differing perspectives. Be clear about what duties and obligations are relevant.

- Role #1 = You are a paramedic manager in a large city. There are numerous calls for ambulance and paramedic services, beyond the capacity of your organization to manage. You have been instructed by the city mayor to get "all hands on deck" and serve the public to the best of your ability, "or else…"

- Role #2 = You are a paramedic with a spouse and two small children. You are very concerned about getting the disease and infecting your family.

Thus far we have discussed issues related to individuals, but there are ethical implications that are organizational as well. Organizations have a duty to support their employees in extreme circumstances and if they have not performed adequately it can be argued that employees have a reduced obligation to their employer, though perhaps not to the public good. Trainor and Barsky recommend that EM organizations with the following characteristics are more likely to minimize role abandonment issues:

- Organizations and professions that instill a clear sense of purpose and value.
- Organizations with a cohesive culture and sense of obligation towards the group.
- Organizations that train and clearly establish employee expectations before and during an event.
- Organizations that honestly communicate with employees to help them understand why they are or are not taking risks.
- Organizations that provide meaningful support and protection for employees and their families.[34]

What is Your Organization Like?

- Consider the organization that you work for. To what extent does it support its employees in terms of role abandonment issues?

A number of years ago I was at a conference where a speaker (sadly, I can't remember who) discussed a flood disaster in India that he had studied. He interviewed the owner of the one company that did not go out of business in the flooded community and asked him how he survived. His answer was that he looked after the families of his employees. This created a loyalty and devotion to the company amongst his employees that prevented role abandonment, encouraged active problem solving, and ultimately allowed his company to survive the flood.

6.8 Conclusion

Experience has demonstrated that role abandonment is very unlikely, but does occur. Surveys, however, suggest that in some scenarios it may be more likely than historical rates suggest. Role abandonment may occur because of an ethical conflict experienced by responders, but organizations can take steps to minimize such occurrences.

6.9 Endnotes

[1] photograph by Joseph Karl Stieler, distributed under a CC-BY 2.0 license. Wikipedia, https://en.wikipedia.org/wiki/Johann_Wolfgang_von_Goethe#/media/File:Goethe_(Stieler_1828).jpg

[2] Thomson Reuters. (n.d.). *Duty of care.* Practical law. https://ca.practicallaw.thomsonreuters.com/1-569-0129?transitionType=Default&contextData=(sc.Default)&firstPage=true&bhcp=1

[3] Fire Science Degree Schools. (2020). *Types of firefighters and their job descriptions and duties.* https://www.firesciencedegreeschools.com/types-of-firefighters-and-their-job-descriptions-and-duties/

[4] Hume, T. (2012, November 4). *Young brothers, 'denied refuge,' swept to death by Sandy.* CNN. https://www.cnn.com/2012/11/02/world/americas/sandy-staten-island-brothers/index.html

[5] Hume, T. (2012, November 4). *Young brothers, 'denied refuge,' swept to death by Sandy.* CNN. https://www.cnn.com/2012/11/02/world/americas/sandy-staten-island-brothers/index.html

[6] Capiral, K. (2015, February 19). Saskatchewan village had working fire truck, but no crew to use it. *The Globe and Mail.* https://www.theglobeandmail.com/news/national/saskatchewan-village-had-working-fire-truck-but-no-crew-to-use-it/article23109565/

[7] De Waal, A. (1997). *Famine crimes: Politics & the disaster relief industry in Africa.* Indiana University Press.

[8] Good Samaritan Act, 2001, S.O. 2001, c. 2. https://www.ontario.ca/laws/statute/01g02

[9] Jordaens, J. (ca. 1616). [The Good Samaritan] [Oil on canvas]. Louvre Abu Dhabi. https://en.wikipedia.org/wiki/Parable_of_the_Good_Samaritan#/media/File:Jordaens_Podhorce.jpg

[10] Wikipedia (n.d.).Cicero, Kopiezeichnung einer Büste aus London (Herzog Wellington), https://en.wikipedia.org/wiki/Cicero

[11] Cicero, M. T. (1995). *Cicero on the genres of rhetoric* (J. F. Tinkler, Trans.). University of California, Davis. http://medieval.ucdavis.edu/20a/cicero.html

[12] Cicero, M. T. (1891). *De officiis* (Vol. 3). Teubner.

[13] Kushma, J. (2007). Role abandonment in disaster: Should we leave this myth behind? *Natural Hazards Observer,* XXXI(5).

[14] Trainor, J., & Barsky, L. (2011). *Reporting for duty? A synthesis of research on role conflict, strain, and abandonment among emergency responders during disasters and catastrophes.* Disaster Research Center. http://udspace.udel.edu/handle/19716/9885

[15] Trainor, J., & Barsky, L. (2011). *Reporting for duty? A synthesis of research on role conflict, strain, and abandonment among emergency responders during disasters and catastrophes.* Disaster Research Center. http://udspace.udel.edu/handle/19716/9885

[16] Chaffee, M. (2009). Willingness of health care personnel to work in a disaster: An integrative review of the literature. *Disaster Medicine and Public Health Preparedness*, 3(1), 42-56.

[17] Chaffee, M. (2009). Willingness of health care personnel to work in a disaster: An integrative review of the literature. *Disaster Medicine and Public Health Preparedness*, 3(1), 42-56.

[18] Gershon R. R. M., Qureshi K. A., Stone P. W., Pogorzelska, M., Silver, A., Damsky, M. R., Burdette, C., Gebbie, K. M., & Raveis, V. H. (2007). Home health care challenges and avian influenza. *Home Health Care Management & Practice*, 20, 58–69.

[19] DiGiovanni, Jr., C., Reynolds B., Harwell R., Stoneciper, E. B., & Burkle, Jr., F. M. (2003). Community reaction to bioterrorism: Prospective study of a simulated outbreak. *Emerging Infectious Diseases,* 9(6), 708–712.

[20] Hlavinka, E. (2020, March 27). *COVID-19 shutters some private practices.* MedPage Today. https://www.medpagetoday.com/infectiousdisease/covid19/85637

[21] Levine, R. (2016). Longitudinal emergency medical technician attributes and demographic study (LEADS) design and methodology. *Prehospital and Disaster Medicine, 31*(S1), S7-S17.

[22] Landahl, M., & Cox, C. (2009). Beyond the plan: Individual responder and family preparedness in the resilient organization. *Homeland Security Affairs,* 5(4).

[23] Trainor, J., & Barsky, L. (2011). *Reporting for duty? A synthesis of research on role conflict, strain, and abandonment among emergency responders during disasters and catastrophes.* Disaster Research Center. http://udspace.udel.edu/handle/19716/9885

[24] CBS News. (2005, October 28). *NOPD fires 51 for desertion.* https://www.cbsnews.com/news/nopd-fires-51-for-desertion

[25] Trainor, J., & Barsky, L. (2011). *Reporting for duty? A synthesis of research on role conflict, strain, and abandonment among emergency responders during disasters and catastrophes.* Disaster Research Center. http://udspace.udel.edu/handle/19716/9885

[26] CBS News. (2005, October 28). *NOPD fires 51 for desertion.* https://www.cbsnews.com/news/nopd-fires-51-for-desertion

[27] Anderson, W., & Farber, D. (2006). *"This isn't representative of our department": Lessons from Hurricane Katrina for police disaster response planning.* University of California Law School.

[28] Associated Press. (2005, September 27). *Police Chief: 249 New Orleans officers left posts without permission during Katrina.* https://www.wave3.com/story/3904630/police-chief-249-new-orleans-officers-left-posts-without-permission-during-katrina/

[29] Anderson, W., & Farber, D. (2006). *"This isn't representative of our department": Lessons from Hurricane Katrina for police disaster response planning.* University of California Law School.

[30] Treaster, J. B. (2005, September 4). *Law officers, overwhelmed, are quitting the force.* The New York times. https://www.nytimes.com/2005/09/04/us/nationalspecial/law-officers-overwhelmed-are-quitting-the-force.html

[31] New Orleans Police Department. (2017). *Title: Oath of office.* New Orleans police department operations manual. https://www.nola.gov/getattachment/NOPD/Policies/Chapter-1-1-1-Oath-of-Office-EFFECTIVE-10-22-17.pdf/

[32] International Council of Nurses. (2020, March 20). *High proportion of healthcare workers with COVID-19 in Italy is a stark warning to the world: protecting nurses and their colleagues must be the number one priority.* https://www.icn.ch/news/high-proportion-healthcare-workers-covid-19-italy-stark-warning-world-protecting-nurses-and

[33] Chiu, A. (2020). Coronavirus-wracked nursing home evacuated after most of staff failed to show for two days. Washington Post, April 9, 2020, https://www.washingtonpost.com/nation/2020/04/09/california-nursing-home-coronavirus/

[34] Trainor, J., & Barsky, L. (2011). *Reporting for duty? A synthesis of research on role conflict, strain, and abandonment among emergency responders during disasters and catastrophes.* Disaster Research Center. http://udspace.udel.edu/handle/19716/9885

CHAPTER 7: LAND USE PLANNING

"We abuse land because we regard it as a commodity belonging to us. When we see land as a community to which we belong, we may begin to use it with love and respect."

Aldo Leopold (1887-1948) conservationist, philosopher and author

"We have an arsenal of ideas about land use possibly as dangerous to human life on the planet as the use of nuclear arms."

Janet Kauffman (1945-), novelist and poet

Contents

7.1 Introduction

From an ethical EM perspective two issues related to land use are significant. The first is exposure to hazard, and the second is how we value the natural environment.

With respect to the first issue, though society often emphasizes response and recovery more than mitigation, the greatest gains in terms of cost-benefit for disaster risk reduction can be found within the mitigation and prevention pillars of the emergency management cycle. If possible, the best disaster management strategy is not to let disaster happen in the first place.

Land use planning may be the most important tool communities have to reduce some risks, primarily through minimizing exposure to hazards. Land use planning is most relevant to hazards that can be geographically delineated (such as flood plains), as opposed to ones that occur on very large spatial scales (such as drought).

The second issue addresses such problems as the overuse of the natural environment to feed the economy, and development and pollution that destroys ecosystems.

An example of a land use map for the city of Manila is shown in Figure 7.1.

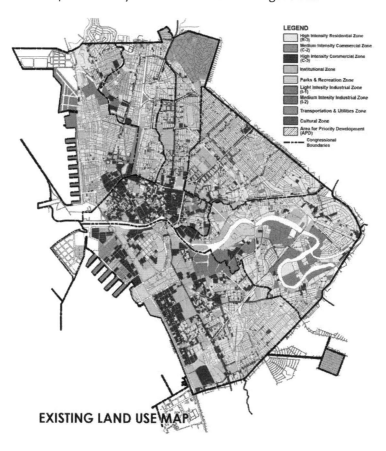

Figure 7.1: Land Use Map for Manila[1] To view the original figure in color go to
https://en.wikipedia.org/wiki/File:Existing_Land_Use_Map_of_Manila_2017.jpg

7.2 Paternalism Versus Libertarianism

A primary tension in land use planning related to hazard exposure is to what extent the state should limit the freedom of citizens in terms of building and living in risky locations. The social contract between citizens and the state varies from place to place in terms of how much individual freedom can be limited. A paternalistic approach emphasizes the state's power to make decisions that are perceived to benefit its citizens. The basis for this can be utilitarian. Though some individuals may have the knowledge and ability to make good decisions, that is not true of all, and the argument is that the greater good is served when the state intervenes. This is especially true when risks are poorly understood or knowledge about them is not widespread. For example, a legal requirement rarely exists for sellers to disclose whether or not a property is in a high-risk zone such as a flood zone or wildfire area. All of this contributes to bounded rationality, the idea that the ability of people to act rationally is limited by a number of factors such as emotion, limited knowledge, biases, and limited time to spend learning about and analyzing issues. This is an argument in support of paternalism.

The process by which land use planning occurs varies by country, state, and province, but generally involves a mix of public engagement and governmental planning. There are often special interests that wish to be served, such as developers who want to use land to pursue profit, citizen groups who desire more parkland, or NGOs wanting to protect cultural heritage. Some groups operate within civil society while others pursue their interests through lobbying or even corrupt practices. Central to this issue is the planning profession, which often functions at the boundaries between civil society and governmental institutions.

Glover et al. argue that a paternalistic culture within the planning profession has insufficiently engaged the public and led to planning philosophies that serve economic and political interests.[2, 3] They argue for a more community-based approach using participatory methods that emphasize civic engagement in a democratic manner. Fundamental to how land use planning occurs is who holds or does not hold power, and who is included and excluded from decision-making.

Gokcen et al. describe the tension between what institutions perceive as serving the public good and what individual professionals consider to be the public good as a classic dilemma that is found in any public service profession, including planning.[4] And, the actions of planners can never be value-free, so any approach or philosophy will serve specific interests that will always be at odds with somebody else. Hoekveld and Needham note that

> the effects of spatial planning are almost always discriminatory: the consequences benefit some more than others. Therefore, decisions about adopting and implementing spatial planning policies are inevitably political. As a result, they are affected by political world views about humanity, society and nature, and by the power structures at different spatial levels.[5]

Where neoliberal policies[i] are dominant, much of the critique points out the negative effects they have had on the disadvantaged or powerless.

Land use planning is central to many disaster risk reduction strategies. How land is developed will play a major role in exposure to many kinds of risks, particularly those that are geographically well-defined, such as flooding. Where exposure is high, communities may well be unsustainable in the long term.

7.3 Sustainable Development

The phrase sustainable development was made popular in the Brundtland Report (*Our Common Future*), which defined it as "development that meets the needs of the present without compromising the ability of future generations to meet their own needs."[6] To a large degree this addresses the use of resources, but also applies to the use of high-risk areas such as flood plains. Where there is excessive development in high-risk zones the stage is set for future disasters, which may well be unsustainable for communities in the long term. Sustainability requires balancing social, economic, and environmental stresses (Figure 7.2). Biodiversity is an important concept to environmental ethics, since it contributes towards a resilient and sustainable natural ecosystem. We should, therefore, from both a utilitarian and deontological perspective, value maintaining biodiversity, which is a great challenge in this time of species extinction.

There is an interesting ethical discourse on the rights of future generations and our duties towards them. An unsustainable overuse of resources (which is currently the case) provides the current generation with a relatively high standard of living that will be paid for by our children and future descendants, without their knowledge or permission. There are strong ethical arguments against this behavior in terms of intergenerational justice. The harm caused to the future in order to obtain (for many) a luxurious standard of living now is not justifiable on utilitarian grounds. There are also deontological arguments that such use of the world's resources violates duties we may owe to future generations.

---

[i] Neoliberal policies emphasize the free market system and minimizing government regulations and control over the economy.

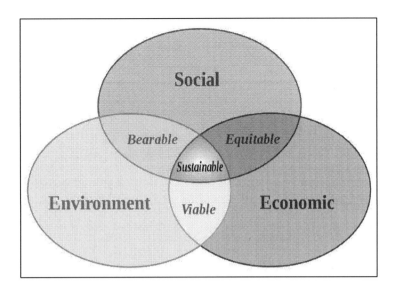

Figure 7.2: Sustainability occurs at the nexus of social, economic, and environmental stresses.

7.4 Principles of Land Use Planning:

Beatley describes traditional frameworks in planning as being narrowly economic and utilitarian.[7] He proposes the following framework for ethical land-use planning, which is rooted in Rawl's theory of justice (Chapter 1.4), but which also has a strong environmental bent:

- Land use decisions must strive to promote the interests of the least advantaged in society; land use decisions are influential in promoting a just society.
- Land use policy must protect the minimum environmental and other rights due to every individual irrespective of income or social position.
- Ethical land use policy sustains and protects natural ecosystems; ethics requires a small human 'footprint'.
- Ethical land use policy acknowledges that man is not the only species on the planet; non-human life has inherent worth as well.
- Ethical land use policy prevents or minimizes the imposition of harms; the principle of culpability holds those causing land use harms accountable for them.
- Ethical land use policy acknowledges important obligations to posterity and to peoples and generations yet to come.
- Ethical land use policy acknowledges that no political jurisdiction is freestanding; ethical obligations exist to other jurisdictions, particularly those which are adjacent or surrounding.
- Ethical land use allows individuals to pursue unique lifestyle choices; land use policy must assist individuals in pursuing their own fundamental life plans.
- Public land use authorities must keep the promises they make; land use ethics requires acknowledgment and respect for explicit and tacit promises made.
- Land use policy and decisions must be formulated through a fair and equitable political process; land use policy making must provide the opportunity for all interested and affected parties to participate.

- Land development must be viewed as a privilege, permissible at the discretion of the collective and subject to the conditions of the collective; landownership does not imply the right to radically change the environmental integrity of the land.

One of the main concepts used in debates about planning is social justice. For land use planning, the most important types are distributive justice and procedural justice. Distributive justice examines the fairness of how something is shared, but there are a number of metrics that can be used for this purpose. A good could be shared equally amongst all (equal shares), or people could be given equal opportunity to obtain the good (for example, a lottery). Or, sharing could be based upon need (equity), where those with greater needs are provided a larger share of good, in proportion to their need. Each of these approaches is rooted in a distributive justice ethic but leads to very different results. The approach chosen depends upon the normative values of society. Most people want a fair approach, but definitions of what is understood by the term "fair" vary considerably.

Procedural justice is about the process used to make ethical decisions. Is the process transparent, legitimate, and trustworthy? If the process is a legal one, has due process been followed? Have people's rights been respected, or has there been corruption in the form of bias or nepotism? Western democracies place a great deal of emphasis on procedural justice, both formally within the legal system and policy frameworks of government, and informally in terms of how the public and media perceive decision-making. Avoiding conflict of interest (or even the perception of this) is fundamental to procedural justice and is generally explicitly dealt with in codes of conduct. For example, the Professional Code of Practice for the Ontario Professional Planners Institute in Canada requires members to "ensure full disclosure to a client or employer of a possible conflict of interest arising from the Member's private or professional activities, in a timely manner."[8]

Hoekvled and Needham summarize an ethical planning process as follows:

- Make plans which respect and, if possible, improve the conditions under which humans and non-humans live. This principle is interpreted, effected and prioritized with the help of some sub-principles:
    - provide for the needs that are considered to be essential for human existence, such as for agriculture, for water and for housing;
    - ensure the safety and certainty necessary for maintenance and development of human life;
    - maintain an environment conducive to non-human life; and
    - respect the identities and specific needs of individuals, groups or areas, within publicly acknowledged limits (as set out in treaties, such as the UN or EU declarations of human rights).
- When making spatial plans and policies, explicitly take account of their possible consequences now and in the future, in particular how the benefits and harms are distributed between various groups and in the environment. When damage or loss is unavoidable, this should be justified and if necessary compensated and/or rectified. (Sometimes this principle comes down to making 'social justice' concrete.)

- Make spatial plans and policies in order to realize some conception of the 'common interest' or 'the public good'. When this concept is applied in a democratic society, that will normally be done in a utilitarian way: the effects for the majority weigh more heavily than the effects for the minority. Then this principle should be complemented with other principles (see above) which pay special attention to those who may be harmed, or passed over, by the action.
- Make the content of spatial plans and policies consistent with the ethical principles underlying, or inherent in, the relevant laws. When there are contradictions, the chosen solution should be explicitly explained.
- The way in which spatial plans and policies are made and implemented should follow general principles of responsible government. These include:
  - being honest and objective when representing the construction of spatial systems and processes therein (e.g. by framing and diagnosing problems, making cartographical illustrations, constructing categories or labels);
  - being open and transparent about the formal and moral responsibility for decisions and actions taken under the plan;
  - being open and transparent about the expected consequences and effects of the plan, and being able to justify them;
  - recognizing every person as a member of the community, especially with respect to basic rights and to participation in discussions which affect basic interests;
  - being impartial (bias and self-interest must be excluded from the processes) and treating like cases alike (the principle of equality); and
  - choosing measures that will inflict the least amount of damage necessary for achieving the selected goals (the principle of proportionality).[9]

Planners are subject to a number of constraints and influences, including legislation and policy, politics, ethics, and special interests. This reality can make it challenging for planners to act according to their best ethical analysis.

The Association of State Floodplain Managers advocates for a "No Adverse Impact" floodplain management approach.[10] This approach is justice-based, emphasizing procedural approaches that involve various stakeholders. The Association makes the following points about this approach:

- No Adverse Impact principles give communities a way to promote responsible floodplain development through community-based decision making.
- No Adverse Impact floodplain management takes place when the actions of one property owner are not allowed to adversely affect the rights of other property owners. The adverse effects or impacts can be measured in terms of increased flood peaks, increased flood stages, higher flood velocities, increased erosion and sedimentation, or other impacts the community considers important.
- The No Adverse impact philosophy can shape the default management criteria: a community develops and adopts a comprehensive plan to manage development that identifies acceptable levels of impact, specifies appropriate measures to mitigate those adverse impacts, and establishes a plan for implementation.[11]

7.5 Environmental Ethics and Land Use

Environmental ethics (Chapter 1.6) are concerned with the well-being of nature. A range of perspectives exist, from utilitarian approaches that view nature as a resource for humankind with no inherent value of its own, to deontological ones that imbue the natural world with rights and to whom people owe duties.

Utilitarian arguments lead to conservationism, the notion that we must conserve nature so that future generations continue to benefit from its resources. There is often a divergence of views, however, in terms of how land should be used. One method used to assist decision makers using a utilitarian perspective is cost-benefit analysis, though many ethicists are not comfortable with this commodification of nature. If everything is reduced to a monetary value, are important considerations being excluded? (The answer is yes.)

In order to do a cost-benefit analysis the value of natural spaces needs to be assessed. Because of this need, the notion of ecosystem services was developed. Ecosystem services (such as forests, grasslands, aquatic or agro systems) are about economically valuing ecosystems in terms of the services they provide to society—clearly a difficult task. These services include (1) provisioning services such as clean drinking water, soil formation, game and wild foods; (2) regulating services such as flood protection (e.g. mangrove areas), pollination, and carbon sequestration; and (3) cultural services such as parks and heritage sites. Land use planning will determine the degree to which areas will provide ecosystem services or will serve other functions such as housing.

One practice related to conservation and ecosystem services from a utilitarian perspective is biodiversity offsetting (Figure 7.3), which refers to allowing the degradation or destruction of biodiversity at one location that are compensated for at others. This practice is rooted in viewing nature as a tradable commodity and has become increasingly used over the past few decades.

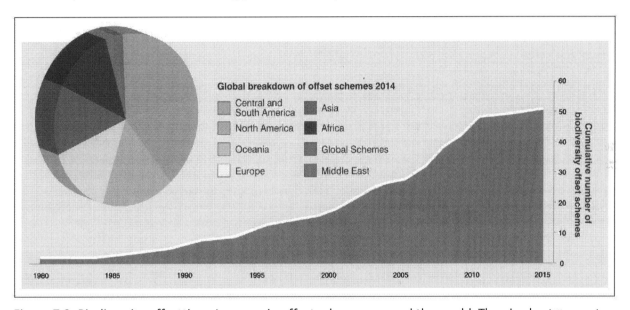

Figure 7.3: Biodiversity offsetting. Increase in offset schemes around the world. The pie chart presents a breakdown of these data by region. Of the approximately 51 operational schemes (including compulsory and voluntary schemes and those under trial), most have emerged since 2005. Data were collated via a review of academic and gray literature and consultation with academic experts on biodiversity offsetting. [13]

Perspectives that imbue the natural world with rights lead to protectionism, which is the idea that nature and biodiversity must be protected regardless of their benefit to people. This is different from conservationism in an important way, though protectionists would agree with conservation. Conservation views nature as a commodity that needs to be sustained for human use and is not rights-based.

The interesting idea of *moral community* is relevant to this discussion. To whom do emergency managers, and people in general, owe duties and obligations (to a greater or lesser degree)? This is our moral community. Clearly people who are citizens of the state fall into this category for an emergency manager in the public service, but beyond that perspectives vary. Some would say duties are owed to all people on the planet, though levels of duties tend to diminish as social and geographical distances increase. For non-humans, the situation is more complex. One argument for assigning rights to non-humans is based upon the notion of community. If a community is viewed as an interacting group of beings who are mutually interdependent, then non-humans are part of that community and it is reasonable to believe that they have rights. This point was argued by Aldo Leopold in his classic book *A Sand County Almanac*.[14]

Student Exercise:

As a city councilor, you have to evaluate competing plans for a forested area. A group of environmentalists advocate for protecting it in its current state. A second group of conservationists want to turn it into parkland, and a third group of developers want to build a condominium and townhouse development surrounded by commercial properties. This would provide much-needed tax revenue.

The area is home to old growth forest and some animal species that are on the endangered list of the World Wildlife Federation. First Nations peoples are actively advocating against the development, claiming the area is spiritually important to their culture.

- What are the competing values present in this discourse?

- What ethical theories are relevant?

- What procedure should be used in the decision-making process?

- What are you own biases, and how do they affect how you approach this issue?

How do the rights of people rank relative to the rights of nature? People can advocate for themselves, but the natural world is unable to do that, and unless advocates emerge from society it is a silent stakeholder. Because of that, I argue that people have a duty to speak for that which cannot speak for itself. Not all societies view land as a commodity. Omari when discussing land ethics in Africa notes that

> "[i]n traditional African societies land ownership rights resided with the larger social group, either the clan, kinship group or family. Land was considered a communal property belonging to both the living and the dead, and each individual had an obligation for its care and administration. No monetary transaction occurred between owner and occupiers, who held possession rights. Similarly, religious beliefs and values created a reverence for nature and natural places which meant that people and nature

interacted in such a way that harmony was maintained and a balanced ecosystem existed."[15]

This is similar to many other aboriginal cultures with animist worldviews[16].[ii] The importance of the difference between worldviews that place nature and the land alongside humankind as opposed to separate was emphasized by Beatley who said, "Of central importance is the replacement of paganism, which found spirits in nature objects and which as a result attached a certain reverence and seriousness to any action that might affect these spirits."[17]

In *Respect for Nature: A Theory of Environmental Ethics,* Paul Taylor identifies five principles that should be used with respect to the non-human world. These are: (1) the principle of self-defense, (2) the principle of proportionality, (3) the principle of minimum wrong, (4) the principle of distributive justice, and (5) the principle of restitutive justice. These principles are rooted in the acknowledgement that nature has rights and that people have duties towards nature.

Another approach to dealing with nature is that of deep ecology, which not only acknowledges the rights and duties discussed above, but which also embraces a spiritual relationship between man and nature. The Norwegian ecologist Arne Næss coined this phrase and argued that man and nature are integrated parts of the same system, rejecting the "us" and "it" perspective. He suggests that "the equal right to live and blossom is an intuitively clear and obvious value axiom. Its restriction to humans is an anthropocentrism with detrimental effects upon the life quality of humans themselves."[18]

From the perspective of virtue ethics, virtue language is common in environmental discourse.[19] Those with a strong environmental ethic view valuing nature for its own sake as a virtuous trait. Vices from an environmental ethic would include greed, apathy and wastefulness.

7.6 Conclusion

Land use planning plays a huge role in risk construction, especially within flood plains. The tension between paternalism (where the state controls where and how people can build) and individualism (where people make their own decisions) has important outcomes in terms of hazard exposure and vulnerability. Utilitarian arguments support a degree of paternalism, but conflict with the rights of individuals to accept risk. Environmental values are also important to land use planning, since it greatly impacts the natural world.

[ii] An animist worldview refers to a belief that all creatures, places and objects have a spiritual essence. i.e. the Living Waters

7.7 Endnotes

[1] Source: Wikipedia, https://upload.wikimedia.org/wikipedia/en/8/82/Existing_Land_Use_Map_of_Manila_2017.jpg

[2] Glover, T. D., Stewart, W. P., & Gladys, K. (2008). Social ethics of landscape change: Toward community-based land-use planning. *Qualitative Inquiry, 14*(3), 384-401.

[3] Glover, T. D., Stewart, W. P., & Gladdys, K. (2008). Social ethics of landscape change: Toward community-based land-use planning. *Qualitative Inquiry, 14*(3), 384-401.

[4] Kilinc, G., Ozgur, H., & Genc, F. N. (2009). Planning ethics at local level. In G. Keylan (Ed.), *Ethics for the prevention of corruption in Turkey: Academic research on public ethics* (pp. 174-291). Council of Europe Directorate General of Human Rights and Legal Affairs.

[5] Hoekveld, G., & Needham, B. (2013). Planning practice between ethics and the power game: Making and applying an ethical code for planning agencies. *International Journal of Urban and Regional Research, 37*(5), 1638-1653.

[6] World Commission on Environment and Development. (1987). *Our common future.* http://www.un-documents.net/our-common-future.pdf

[7] Beatley, T. (1989). Environmental ethics and planning theory. *Journal of Planning Literature, 4*(1), 1-32.

[8] Ontario Professional Planners Institute. (n.d.) *Professional code of practice.* https://ontarioplanners.ca/oppi/about-oppi/professional-code-of-practice-standards

[9] Hoekveld, G., & Needham, B. (2013). Planning practice between ethics and the power game: Making and applying an ethical code for planning agencies. *International Journal of Urban and Regional Research, 37*(5), 1638-1653.

[10] Association of State Floodplain Managers. (n.d.). *NAI—No adverse impact floodplain management.* https://www.floods.org/asfpm-nai-no-adverse-impact-floodplain-mgmt

[11] Association of State Floodplain Managers. (n.d.). *NAI—No adverse impact floodplain management.* https://www.floods.org/asfpm-nai-no-adverse-impact-floodplain-mgmt

[12] Association of State Floodplain Managers. (2015). *The code of ethics for certified floodplain managers.* https://www.floods.org/the-code-of-ethics-for-certified-floodplain-managers/

[13] Ives, C. D., & Bekessy, S. A. (2015). The ethics of offsetting nature. *Frontiers in Ecology and the Environment, 13*(10), 568-573.

[14] Leopold, A. (1989). *A Sand County almanac, and sketches here and there.* Oxford University Press.

[15] Omari, C. K. (1990). Traditional African land ethics. In J. R. Engel & J. G. Engel (Eds.), *Ethics of environment and development: Global challenge and international response* (pp. 167-175). Belhaven Press.

[16] Haudenosaunee Environmental Task Force. (1992). *Words that come before all else: Environmental philosophies of the Haudenosaunee.* Native North American Travelling College

[17] Beatley, T. (1989). Environmental ethics and planning theory. *Journal of Planning Literature, 4*(1), 1-32.

[18] Næss, A. (1973). The shallow and the deep, long-range ecology movement. A summary. *Inquiry, 16*, 95-100.

[19] van Wensveen, L. (2000). Dirty virtues: The emergence of ecological virtue ethics. Humanity Books.

CHAPTER 8: HUMANITARIANISM

"Life's most persistent and urgent question is, 'What are you doing for others?'"
Martin Luther King Jr., civil rights activist and clergyman. Winner of the Nobel Peace Prize 1964

Figure 8.1: Martin Luther King Jr.[1]

"If you can't feed a hundred people, feed just one."
Mother Teresa, founder of The Missionaries of Charity

Figure 8.2: Mother Teresa[2]

"Whatever you do will be insignificant, but it is very important that you do it."
Mahatma Gandhi, Indian nationalist and civil rights leader

Figure 8.3: Mahatma Gandhi[3]

"Overcoming poverty is not a task of charity, it is an act of justice."
Nelson Mandela, anti-apartheid activist and former president of South Africa

Figure 8.4: Nelson Mandela[4]

Contents

8.1 Introduction

Humanitarianism is about giving in order to reduce the suffering of others and to improve their lives. Its roots are ancient, going back to Aristotle in the Western philosophical tradition who emphasized various virtues such as compassion and the fundamental importance of politics to human nature.

Over the past decade there has been an increase in the numbers of people identified as being in need, with resultant increase in funding requirements (Figure 8.5). Humanitarian aid is, therefore, a topic of increasing importance.

Most religions (Eastern and Western) incorporate the notion of charity as a virtuous act. *Zakat* (which literally means "purification," because *zakat* is considered to purify one's heart of greed) is one of the pillars of Islam. According to one website about Islam, "[t]he whole concept of wealth is considered in Islam as a gift from God. God, who provided it to the person, made a portion of it for the poor, so the poor have a right over one's wealth."[5] From this perspective, giving is an obligation. In Judaism giving to the poor is an obligation that cannot be forsaken even by those who are themselves in need. According to Jewish law, Jews are required to give one-tenth of their income to the poor (just as Christians tithe to the church). Within the Christian tradition charity is considered to be the highest form of love, signifying the reciprocal love between God and man.[6] Charity is also fundamental to Buddhism, as demonstrated by the following quotation from a Buddhist monk, the Venerable V.Vajiramedhi:

> We as Buddhists believe in helping people as underlined in Lord Buddha's core teachings on the Principle of Giving, Five Precepts and Cultivating Four States of Mind [...] The Four States of Mind consist of 'Metta' for loving kindness to all fellow humans, 'Karuna' for compassion towards people in need without limits, 'Muditha' for sympathetic joy when other people are happy or safe from harm and 'Upekkha' for equanimity to see others without prejudice and bias.[7]

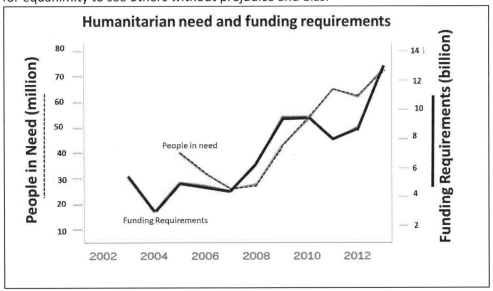

Figure 8.5: Humanitarian need and funding requirements.[8]

In terms of ethical theories, humanitarianism is based upon (1) the virtues of beneficence, compassion, charity and empathy; (2) the obligations to help those in need who cannot help themselves (deontology); (3) the greater good, to make the world a better place (utilitarianism); and (4) an egalitarian ethic of social justice. It is about helping others, but there are important ethical complexities that emerge as well, such as:

- What if help in the short-term causes harm in the long-term?
- Should all people be treated equally? What of those who have special needs, are family, are responsible for their own difficulties, or are perpetrators of harm?
- How should scarce resources be allocated, when they are insufficient to meet the needs of everyone?
- Do people who are suffering have rights to be helped (which makes helping a duty), or do they not (in which case helping is pure altruism)?

Some humanitarian organizations focus on short-term response while others have a developmental orientation. These two types of organizations have very different goals that can sometimes be complementary, but at other times are not. Developmental issues require an emphasis on strategic approaches, while response is more tactical.

In modern society there are many non-governmental organizations that are involved in humanitarian work (the Red Cross is one important example). Increasingly, various state institutions, including the military, are also engaging in humanitarian activities, though their motives may not always be unselfish (or even virtuous).

"Moreover, when policy was driven by moral motives it was often driven by narcissism. We intervened not only to save others, but to save ourselves, or rather an image of ourselves as defenders of universal decencies."[9]

Michael Ignatieff

(Leader of the Liberal Party of Canada and

Leader of the Official Opposition from 2008 until 2011)

This chapter reviews the ethics and ethical conflicts that are present in different humanitarian philosophies beginning with traditional humanitarian values and then contrasting them with the New Humanitarianism.

8.2 Traditional Humanitarian Values

"Did you feed us so we can die with a fat belly?" relief workers in Sarajevo were asked. What answer could they possibly give? Only, perhaps, that it was better than not feeding them at all.[10]

Though there is a long tradition of altruism and helping others in society, modern humanitarianism as an institution can arguably be said to begin with the formation of the Red Cross (page 8.6). Their statement of values is summarized in the bullets below (see Appendix 8.1 for more detail):

- *Humanity:* The International Red Cross and Red Crescent Movement ("the Movement"), born of a desire to bring assistance without discrimination to the wounded on the battlefield, endeavours, in its international and national capacity, to prevent and alleviate human suffering wherever it may be found. Its purpose is to protect life and health and to ensure respect for the human being. It promotes mutual understanding, friendship, cooperation and lasting peace amongst all peoples.

- *Impartiality:* It makes no discrimination as to nationality, race, religious beliefs, class or political opinions. It endeavours to relieve the suffering of individuals, being guided solely by their needs, and to give priority to the most urgent cases of distress.[i]

- *Neutrality:* In order to continue to enjoy the confidence of all, the Movement may not take sides in hostilities or engage at any time in controversies of a political, racial, religious or ideological nature.

- *Independence:* The Movement is independent. The National Societies, while auxiliaries in the humanitarian services of their governments and subject to the laws of their respective countries, must always maintain their autonomy so that they may be able at all times to act in accordance with the principles of the Movement.

- *Voluntary service:* It is a voluntary relief movement not prompted in any manner by desire for gain.

- *Unity:* There can be only one Red Cross or one Red Crescent Society in any one country. It must be open to all. It must carry on its humanitarian work throughout its territory.

---

[i] In a talk given by Prof. Hugo Slim on March 31, 2021 at York University, Prof. Slim notes that "impartiality is interesting as an ambition, but practically and experientially it operates as a myth because it doesn't really work. We don't work on the basis of greatest need, we work on different criteria."

- *Universality:* The International Red Cross and Red Crescent Movement, in which all Societies have equal status and share equal responsibilities and duties in helping each other, is worldwide.[11]

The standards of the Red Cross and many other humanitarian organizations are described in the following two documents, both of which are available on the internet:

- *The Humanitarian Charter and Minimum Standards in Disaster Response* of the Sphere Project,[12] and
- *The Code of Conduct for the International Red Cross and Red Crescent Movement and NGOs in Disaster Relief* of the International Federation of Red Cross and Red Crescent Societies.[13]

The Beginnings of the Red Cross.

The Red Cross idea was born in 1859, when Henry Dunant, a young Swiss man, came upon the scene of a bloody battle in Solferino, Italy, between the armies of imperial Austria and the Franco-Sardinian alliance. Some 40,000 men lay dead or dying on the battlefield and the wounded were lacking medical attention.

Dunant organized local people to bind the soldiers' wounds and to feed and comfort them. On his return, he called for the creation of national relief societies to assist those wounded in war, and pointed the way to the future Geneva Conventions.

"Would there not be some means, during a period of peace and calm, of forming relief societies whose object would be to have the wounded cared for in time of war by enthusiastic, devoted volunteers, fully qualified for the task?" he wrote.

The Red Cross was born in 1863 when five Geneva men, including Dunant, set up the International Committee for Relief to the Wounded, later to become the International Committee of the Red Cross. Its emblem was a red cross on a white background: the inverse of the Swiss flag. The following year, 12 governments adopted the first Geneva Convention; a milestone in the history of humanity, offering care for the wounded, and defining medical services as "neutral" on the battlefield.[14]

Figure 8.6: Henry Durant (1828-1910), winner of the Nobel Peace Prize[15]

Arguments for these principles exist in utilitarian, deontological and virtue ethics. They are all underlain by valuing human life, no matter whose. They are also supported by feminist approaches rooted in the ethics of care. By being non-political and independent, the Red Cross aims to maximize their access and ability to serve those in need, thereby adhering to a utilitarian argument. By many cultural and faith-based normative standards helping others is a "right" action, and therefore they are serving an obligation or duty that is commonly accepted and, at times, revered. One exemplar of this is Mother Teresa, who was given a number of honours including the 1962 Ramon Magsaysay Peace Prize, the 1979 Nobel Peace Prize, and was made a saint by the Catholic Church. Humanitarianism is a virtuous act, displaying the traits of compassion, caring, and beneficence. At times it also requires courage and dedication. There are, therefore, strong ethical arguments for humanitarian actions.

One important question that must be asked is what are our duties and obligations to the "distant other"? Depending upon one's values there is a wide range of answers, all of which largely depend upon your conception of your moral community. The phrase "moral community" refers to that group of beings to whom duties or obligations are owed, and who have rights to make a claim upon you. Certainly, one's moral community includes family, but as people (or beings, since some would argue that non-human life is part of our moral community) become more distant it can be argued that they become peripheral to our moral community, or even not within that sphere at all. In this case, giving becomes increasingly an act of charity as opposed to a duty.

Critique of traditional humanitarian principles and practice:

There have been a number of critiques of the traditional humanitarian approach. Some of these are empirical in nature, pointing out its numerous failures in terms of providing relief or of solving long-term problems that result in the need for humanitarian action.

Dale Jameson[16] and Nicholas Leader[17] summarize problems related to aid as follows:

- Funds are often spent inefficiently, in ways that do not benefit the poor but rather help special interests. Where aid occurs in conflict zones, it can be and often is used in ways that support and extend the conflict.
- There is little evidence from empirical studies that developmental assistance does actually contribute to development.
- There are theoretical arguments supporting the notion that development occurs because of complex cultural and historical reasons and is not strongly linked to humanitarian assistance.
- Developmental aid from states is often "tied" to donor countries (this is called tied aid) and is primarily intended to benefit the donors and not the recipients of aid.
- The existence of humanitarian aid creates moral hazard, which undermines the social contracts needed to prevent the need for aid in the first place.
- State-supported humanitarian aid can mask inaction of other kinds, such as political or military intervention that may be required to support justice.
- Humanitarian aid is largely market driven, is of variable quality and lacks accountability.
- Traditional humanitarian aid downplays the rights and protection of the vulnerable.

Richard Fanthorpe in a study of humanitarian aid during the civil war in Sierra Leone, found that:

- There was evidence to support the hypothesis that humanitarian aid can encourage violence; for example, he notes, "During the civil war in Sierra Leone, the Revolutionary United Front (RUF) repeatedly attacked refugee camps along the Guinean border, killing and abducting inhabitants and looting supplies."[18]
- Humanitarian agencies cannot avoid influencing politics, and that this interaction inevitably creates moral conflicts and dilemmas.
- Humanitarian actors, though they consult with local agencies, maintain control of their resources and decisions made regarding aid allocations. The justification of this is to ensure that the most vulnerable are helped, but it is also based upon values that are external to the people receiving aid and are made from "positions of power."[19]

One study of aid following the 2004 tsunami found that one of the primary factors that determined where aid was delivered was the presence of media. Humanitarian organizations needed to be seen in order to justify their work to their donors, and therefore a complex relationship evolved between the media and humanitarian objectives.[20] The ethics of this are debatable. Certainly, if aid organizations receive more funding then they will be better able to serve their purposes, but such an approach may also create mission drift that is counterproductive.

Is there evidence to support the hypothesis that humanitarian aid can increase violence? Wood and Sullivan examined this issue with respect to the Sudan and found that in this conflict zone there was "strong support for the argument that humanitarian aid is associated with increased rebel violence but less support for the relationship between aid and state violence."[21] Of course, this does not mean that it is true in every conflict situation, but does demonstrate that it can happen and is a valid concern. If humanitarian aid feeds into maintaining the conflict that created the need for humanitarian aid in the first place, is it moral to provide it?

The above critiques are serious, but does that mean that traditional humanitarianism should be abandoned?

Joanna Macrae, in a defence of traditional humanitarian values, grouped the critics into the following camps: anti-imperialists, realpolitikers, orthodox developmentalists, and neo-peaceniks.[22] The arguments put forward by these groups are, according to her, fallacious in that:

- Cultures and disasters are often very complex. To suggest that reducing aid will address the causes of disaster risk is simplistic and perhaps dangerous.
- It is problematical whether relief aid could or should serve a political function.
- The causes of conflict or vulnerability are often not internal but are rather driven by forces external to a country. Taking a rights-based approach absolves the international community of its role and responsibility.

Certainly, there are serious issues with traditional humanitarianism from a conceptual perspective, but also from the way that it has been practiced. The response of some parts of the humanitarian community to its real and perceived failures was to create a different set of principles, called the New Humanitarianism.

8.3 The New Humanitarianism

The New Humanitarianism addresses issues of social justice and is committed to speaking out against wrongdoing. It can be argued that its birth began during the Biafran famine of 1968, which largely resulted from conflict between Biafra and the Nigerian government. One strong critic of the non-interventionist approach was French doctor Bernard Kouchner, who resigned from the International Committee of the Red Cross (ICRC) and noted that their silence over Biafra made its workers "accomplices in the systematic massacre of a population."[23] Subsequently, in 1971 Bernard Kouchner created Médecins sans Frontières (MSF), which adopted a rights-based approach to delivering humanitarian aid.

Question to ponder:

Is Dr. Kouchner correct? If one is silent in the face of atrocities in order to help victims, does one become complicit?

One of the principles of MSF (see box on page 8.12) is to bear witness and speak publically about abuses of power. In part, the New Humanitarianism is a tool to promote human rights and political goals. It views the more traditional humanitarian approach as politically naïve and possibly immoral. Examples of organizations that have adopted this view are Oxfam, ActionAid and MSF. This approach has a strong utilitarian flavor since it argues that adopting the new humanitarianism approach makes the world is made a better place in the long term. It is also deontological in that it believes that people have a duty to speak out and act against wrongdoing.

As noted by Barfod[24], the New Humanitarianism is characterized by:

- "the integration of human rights and peace building into the humanitarian orbit;
- the ending of the distinction between development and humanitarian relief; and
- the rejection of the principle of neutrality."

Critiques of the New Humanitarianism:

There are critiques of the new approach, and these critiques are significant. They are:

- It creates classes of victims, where some are more deserving than others.

- The practice of humanitarian aid reproduces many of the attitudes of colonialism and paternalism, denying the voice and agency of those receiving that aid.
  - In an article about MSF winning the Nobel Peace Prize, Kirsten Sellars had the following to say about the operation of NGOs:

    Heeding the impulse to take up the latter-day 'White Man's Burden', battalions of NGOs marched into Mogadishu, Sarajevo and Goma armed with land cruisers, satellite phones and the latest liberal imperialist orthodoxies. Local governments retreated in their path, and soon many areas in these countries became de facto zones of occupation under the control of the humanitarian armies.[25]
  - US President Nixon stated in 1968: "[T]he main purpose of American aid is not to help other nations but to help ourselves."[26]

- Aid workers and those who run NGO aid organizations may not be appropriate people to make important political judgements. They are unelected and unaccountable to the public of either the state where they originate or the state where they operate.

- Access to those in need will be curtailed in some situations. The argument is that this is a price worth paying but there is little, if any, evidence that withholding support from aid organizations affects the behavior of abusive governments.

- As aid organizations take on politically active roles, they become more involved with and dependent upon state funding and lose much of their independence. State funding will inevitably be biased towards state goals which are in the national interest (as noted by President Nixon above) and not strictly oriented towards humanitarian goals. Rights-based humanitarian aid offers a moral justification for powerful governments to justify and engage in paternalistic and/or colonial activities. As well, abusive governments can always rationalize their behaviors to suit their needs. For example:
  - Benito Mussolini made social Darwinist claims about Fascist Italy bringing "modern civilization" to Africa. Renato Micheli's famous 1935 propaganda poem "Little Black Face" describes a young Ethiopian girl as "a slave among slaves" and an Italian soldier as her liberator.[27]
  - Japan claimed that it was invading Manchuria in self-defense, from the threat of Chinese bandits.[28]
  - Adolf Hitler claimed that he was putting an end to ethnic strife when he invaded the Sudetenland. In *Mein Kampf, Volume 1*, he said, "I believe today that my conduct is in accordance with the will of the Almighty Creator."[29]
  - The U.S. invaded Iraq in 2001 because it was "a regime that developed and used weapons of mass destruction, that harbored and supported terrorists, committed

outrageous human rights abuses, and defied the just demands of the United Nations and the world."[30]

- The New Humanitarianism prioritizes strengthening institutional processes above saving lives, at least in some cases.

Jonathon Benthall has described the New Humanitarianism as a moral "fairy story" with the following three elements, as summarized by David Chandler:

> The first component is the hapless victim in distress. In the famine "fairy story," this victim was always portrayed through film of the worst cases of child malnutrition in the worst feeding centers. In cases of civil conflict, the victims are often war refugees who have been "ethnically cleansed." The second component was the villain, the non-Western government or state authorities that caused famine and poverty through personal corruption or wrong spending policies or that consciously embarked on a policy of genocide or mass repression. The third component in the humanitarian "fairy tale" was the savior—the external aid agency, the international institution, or even the journalists covering the story whose interests were seen to be inseparable from those of the deserving victim.[31]

As an exercise, find a news story that illustrates the "fairy story" described by Chandler. Describe how it incorporates each of the three components.

Principles of Médecins sans Frontières (as quoted from their website).[32]

MSF's actions are guided by medical ethics and the principles of independence and impartiality.

- **Medical ethics**: MSF's actions are first and foremost medical. We carry out our work with respect for the rules of medical ethics, in particular the duty to provide care without causing harm to individuals or groups. We respect patients' autonomy, patient confidentiality and their right to informed consent. We treat our patients with dignity, and with respect for their cultural and religious beliefs. In accordance with these principles, MSF endeavours to provide high-quality medical care to all patients.

- **Independence**: our decision to offer assistance in any country or crisis is based on an independent assessment of people's needs. We strive to ensure that we have the power to freely evaluate medical needs, to access populations without restriction and to directly control the aid we provide. Our independence is facilitated by our policy to allow only a marginal portion of our funds to come from governments and intergovernmental organisations.

- **Impartiality and neutrality**: MSF offers assistance to people based on need and irrespective of race, religion, gender or political affiliation. We give priority to those in the most serious and immediate danger. Our decisions are not based on political, economic or religious interests. MSF does not take sides or intervene according to the demands of governments or warring parties.

- **Bearing witness**: the principles of impartiality and neutrality are not synonymous with silence. When MSF witnesses extreme acts of violence against individuals or groups, the organisation may speak out publicly. We may seek to bring attention to extreme need and unacceptable suffering when access to lifesaving medical care is hindered, when medical facilities come under threat, when crises are neglected, or when the provision of aid is inadequate or abused.

- **Accountability**: MSF is committed to regularly evaluating the effects of its activities. We assume the responsibility of accounting for our actions to our patients and donors.

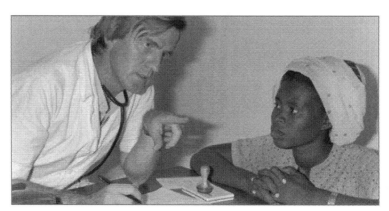

Figure 8.7: Bernard Kouchner, one of the founders of MSF[33]

One of the background papers I read while writing this chapter has the title "Choosing the Lesser Evil: Understanding Decision Making in Humanitarian Aid NGOs."[34] How to frame and deliver humanitarian aid can truly be described as a classical ethical dilemma, where the givers of aid are faced with choices between two wrongs and/or two rights. I do not believe that there is one universal approach that is best suited for all situations, and that having a heterogeneous blend of organizations which take a variety of philosophical and moral stances is the best approach.

8.4 Ethical Issues Faced by Health Care Workers During an Emergency Response

An interesting paper by Matthew Hunt described many of the difficulties faced by health care professionals during international disaster response, including:

- Tension between respecting local customs and values, and acting in ways that are consistent with one's core moral convictions,
- Barriers to the provision of adequate care,
- Divergent understandings and experiences of health and illness,
- Questions of identity as a professional, humanitarian and moral person, and
- Issues of trust and distrust.[35]

A narrative analysis of the stories of 20 Canadian health care professionals involved in disaster response had similar findings. In particular, they found that ethical challenges emerged from four main sources:

- Resource scarcity and the need to allocate them,
- Historical, political, social and commercial structures,
- Aid agency policies and agendas; and
- Perceived norms around health professionals' roles and interactions.[36]

Some of the conflicts related to (1) having to choose one patient over another (as a result of scarce resources), (2) the needs of current versus future patients (again, scarce resources), (3) not being allowed to treat patients of particular ethnic groups (particularly in conflict situations), (4) living in relative luxury while being surrounded by poverty, (5) not being allowed to treat people with specific diagnoses because of institutional policies (e.g., HIV and TB), (6) pressure to perform procedures without full consent, and (7) cultural pressures to not fully disclose illnesses to patients. In one case a women's consent for a C-section was insufficient (her husband's consent was needed; the patient died).

Health care professionals trained in Western countries are exposed to very different conditions and standards of care in other parts of the world, which creates difficult ethical dilemmas that are not easily resolved.

8.5 Moral Hazard (Yet Again)

One of the critiques of humanitarian and development programs is that they create moral hazard. Moral hazard occurs when expectations of payouts increase risky or fraudulent behavior. It is a huge problem for the insurance industry, and an interesting paper by Alan Kuperman looks at humanitarian ethics and moral hazard from an economic/insurance perspective.[37]

This hazard is very much related to the Good Samaritan's dilemma, where providing aid does not solve the cause of why aid is needed and can contribute to a culture of dependency. Kuperman, examining conflict situations, describes how expectations of military intervention encourage the creation of conflict by rebel groups. He notes,

> As subsequently revealed by the leaders of these rebellions—including in interviews that I conducted with the eventual presidents of Bosnia and Kosovo and with most of the senior civilian and military officials of each group—they rebelled because they expected that retaliation by the state would attract intervention sufficient for them to attain independence.[38]

He does not argue for the elimination of humanitarian aid or intervention, but rather for its reformation so that its tendency to promote risk taking is minimized. His proposed approach is to not intervene on behalf of rebels unless state retaliation is grossly disproportionate, to deliver purely humanitarian aid in ways that minimize benefit to rebels, to extend substantial resources to persuade states to address the legitimate grievances of nonviolent domestic groups, and not to coerce regime change or surrender sovereignty without robust preventative military intervention to protect against violent backlash.

8.6 Religion and Humanitarianism

A faith-based organization is

> characterized by having one or more of the following: affiliation with a religious body; a mission statement with explicit reference to religious values; financial support from religious sources; and/or a governance structure where selection of board members or staff is based on religious beliefs or affiliation and/or decision-making processes based on religious values.[39]

Examples include the Catholic Relief Services, Lutheran World Relief, United Methodist Committee on Relief, World Vision International, Samaritan's Purse, and Mercy Ships. The mission statement of Samaritan's Purse states,

> Samaritan's Purse is a nondenominational evangelical Christian organization providing spiritual and physical aid to hurting people around the world. Since 1970, Samaritan's Purse has helped meet needs of people who are victims of war, poverty, natural disasters, disease, and famine with the purpose of sharing God's love through His Son, Jesus Christ. The organization serves the church worldwide **to promote the Gospel of the Lord Jesus Christ** (emphasis added).[40]

Helping those in need, mercy, and charity are foundational to most religions, and humanitarianism is a natural route for them to take. Many faith-based groups therefore engage in humanitarian work, both at local and international levels. Over 300 of them have consultative status with the U.N. Economic and Social Council (Table 8.1).[41]

Religious affiliation	Number of organizations	Percentage of all religious NGOs
Christian	187	58 %
Muslim	52	16 %
Jewish	22	7 %
Buddhist	14	4 %
Hindu	3	1 %
Spiritual	25	8 %
Multireligious	11	4 %
Other religions	6	2 %

Table 8.1: Religious affiliation of 320 NGOs with the U.N. Economic and Social Council.[42]

Often, secular humanitarian organizations do not engage with local faith-based actors. This is an unfortunate gap that negatively impacts the effectiveness of both types of organizations. In many disasters, faith-based groups play a critical role both in terms of the practical side of response and recovery and on the psychological and spiritual side. Where communities are very religious their importance is crucial. However, an Oxfam report notes the following concerns about faith-based groups:

- They do not always adequately represent their entire communities, particularly the most vulnerable, and the people put forth as leaders often represent traditional hierarchies.
- They do not consistently embody and promote gender and lesbian, gay, bisexual, transgender, and queer (LGBTQ) equality.
- They do not consistently meet technical standards.
- They are not always able to scale up in times of crisis.
- They do not always subscribe or adhere to the humanitarian principles.[43]

The Nebraska Disaster Chaplain Network of Interchurch Ministries has developed a Code of Ethics and Guiding Principles for their chaplains, as follows:

- Disaster chaplains do not proselytize.
- Maintain confidentiality.
- You are a volunteer.
- Recognize your personal and professional limits.
- Know your boundaries.
- Remain flexible.
- Demonstrate sensitivity to all faith traditions.
- Avoid speculation.
- Be aware of all affected.
- Follow the incident command structure.[44]

The first of these principles, not to proselytize, contrasts with the mission of evangelical organizations. Many religions have, in scripture, an obligation to teach. For example, the Gospel of Matthew says,

> Go ye therefore, and teach all nations, baptizing them in the name of the Father, and of the Son, and of the Holy Spirit: Teaching them to observe all things whatsoever I have commanded you: and, lo, I am with you always, even unto the end of the world. Amen.[45]

When does teaching (a virtue) slide into the malfeasance of coercion?

There are examples of what are called "unethical conversations," where faith-based organizations have used their privileged position during and following a disaster, through coercion and bribery, for conversion purposes.[46] One example of this, or at least a perceived example, occurred in Sri Lanka after the 2004 tsunami. This catastrophe resulted in an influx of foreign NGOs into the country. Following this there were accusations of unethical conversations between some of the faith-based NGOs and victims, where conversions were attempted through the use of positions of power as opposed to a genuine change of belief. For example, in a New York Times article, David Rohde notes, "The Antioch Community Church is one of a growing number of evangelical groups that believe in mixing humanitarian aid with discussions of religion, an approach that older, more established Christian aid groups like Catholic Relief Services call unethical."[47] This resulted in a political response within Sri Lanka, a Private Member's Bill on

May 28, 2004 entitled "Prohibition of Forcible Conversion of Religion" (commonly referred to as the Anti-Conversion Bill), which was then challenged in court by a number of religious organizations. The counterargument, based upon divine command, is that conversion saves eternal souls and is therefore mandated by God.

8.7 Conclusion

Humanitarian aid represents what is best and most noble about human beings, by most moral standards. Yet it is a tool that can be used for Machiavellian purposes when used by states to promote national interests, or it can create opportunities for coercion practiced by evangelical organizations. Even when approached with altruistic motives it can create harm in the long term – hence the relevance of the Good Samaritan's dilemma. A debate exists as to whether humanitarian aid should promote a human rights agenda or be value free. Both approaches are fraught with ethical difficulties that have no easy solutions.

Appendix 8.1: International Red Cross Values

Humanity

The International Red Cross and Red Crescent Movement, born of a desire to bring assistance without discrimination to the wounded on the battlefield, endeavours, in its international and national capacity, to prevent and alleviate human suffering wherever it may be found. Its purpose is to protect life and health and to ensure respect for the human being. It promotes mutual understanding, friendship, cooperation and lasting peace amongst all peoples.

Analysis of the Fundamental Principle of Humanity
The fundamental principle of Humanity:
- recalls the <u>origins</u> of the Movement: "born of a desire to bring assistance without discrimination to the wounded on the battlefield."
- recalls the <u>double dimension</u> of the Movement: the national and the international.
- defines the <u>mission</u> of the Movement: "to prevent and alleviate human suffering wherever it may be found."

- defines the <u>purposes</u> of the Movement:
  - to protect life and health;
  - to ensure respect for the human being; and
  - to promote mutual understanding, friendship, cooperation and lasting peace amongst all peoples.

Consequences of the Fundamental Principle of Humanity

Unlike the other fundamental principles, the consequences of the principle of Humanity are not so much boundaries and guidelines for the Movement's action; the principle of Humanity is rather a constant reminder of what the objectives of the Movement are. The principle of Humanity expresses what the Movement places beyond anything else: the need to act in order to prevent and alleviate human suffering.

Impartiality

[The Movement] makes no discrimination as to nationality, race, religious beliefs, class or political opinions. It endeavours to relieve the suffering of individuals, being guided solely by their needs, and to give priority to the most urgent cases of distress.

Analysis of the Fundamental Principle of Impartiality

The fundamental principle of Impartiality includes two main elements. First, the Movement makes <u>no discrimination</u> (and this does not apply only to people it assists or protects). Non-discrimination is the refusal to apply distinctions of an adverse nature to human beings simply because they belong to a specific category. This does not exclude differences in the treatment given to people placed in different situations on the basis of, for example, sex or age. Five criteria which could lead to discrimination are mentioned: nationality, race, religious beliefs, class or political opinions. However, other factors which may lead to a discrimination are not mentioned. Depending on circumstances, a different treatment based on sex may or may not be discrimination.

Second, all those in need shall be helped, yet to treat everyone in the same way without taking into account how much they are suffering, or how urgent their needs are, would not be equitable. Impartiality means that, for the Movement, the <u>only priority</u> that can be set in dealing with those who require help must be <u>based on need</u>, and the order in which available aid is shared out must correspond to the urgency of the distress it is intended to relieve.

Consequences of the Fundamental principle of Impartiality

There are three primary consequences of the principle of Impartiality. First, this principle establishes one of the Movement's key values: non-discrimination. Non-discrimination is one of the most important elements of all aspects of the protection of the human being, as demonstrated through its importance in human rights law, humanitarian law, and refugee law.

Second, although the need to "enjoy the confidence of all" is mentioned in relation to the principle of Neutrality, this also applies to the principle of Impartiality. Only an impartial action can give the image of an organization that can be trusted by people to be assisted or protected. Therefore, systems have to be put in place to ensure that the people benefitting from the action of the Red Cross and Red Crescent are those whose vulnerability is the highest.

Impartiality in its true sense requires that subjective distinctions be set aside. To illustrate the difference between the two notions: a National Society that refuses to provide its services to a specific group of people because of their ethnic origin fails to observe the rule of non-discrimination, whereas a National Society staff member who, in the exercise of his functions, favors a friend by giving him better treatment than that given to others contravenes the principle of impartiality. Therefore, staff and volunteers should be trained to ensure that correct behavior becomes almost a reflex.

Neutrality

In order to continue to enjoy the confidence of all, the Movement may not take sides in hostilities or engage at any time in controversies of a political, racial, religious or ideological nature.

Analysis of the Fundamental Principle of Neutrality
The fundamental principle of Neutrality:
- enables the Movement to enjoy the confidence of all. Implicitly, this compliance with the principle of Neutrality is also a condition for operational efficiency, which requires confidence of all in many contexts (i.e., not only in armed conflicts contexts).
- prohibits a component of the Movement from taking part in hostilities.
- prohibits the Movement from engaging at any time in controversies of a political, racial, religious or ideological nature.

Consequences of the Fundamental Principle of Neutrality
Three main consequences of the principle of Neutrality exist. First, neutrality implies not acting in a way that could facilitate the conduct of hostilities by any of the parties involved. The role of National Societies as auxiliaries to public authorities in the humanitarian field when they assist medical services of armed forces (i.e., when they fulfill the initial function of National Societies) should not be seen as taking part in hostilities.

Second, neutrality includes many dimensions. Only the day-to-day acts and words of a National Society can constitute evidence of its respect of the principle of Neutrality. For instance, if a National Society branch expresses sympathy for a movement, a cause, or a political figure (for example, by permitting the latter to take advantage of Red Cross or Red Crescent membership for electoral purposes), many volunteers may cancel their membership. If a dispensary run by a National Society also displays a religious affiliation in a country in which there is tension between the members of different faiths, many patients will no longer wish or dare to come for treatment. In other words, neutrality is a state of mind, an attitude which must guide every step taken by the Movement's components.

Finally, due to the character of communication today, the violation of the principle of Neutrality by a component of the Movement can easily affect the image of other components and, thus, their ability to work in a given context. Therefore, the principle of Neutrality is to be seen in a global perspective.

Independence

The Movement is independent. The National Societies, while auxiliaries in the humanitarian services of their governments and subject to the laws of their respective countries, must always maintain their autonomy so that they may be able at all times to act in accordance with the principles of the Movement.

Analysis of the Fundamental Principle of Independence

The fundamental principle of Independence contains:

- a strong general statement that, as a matter of principle, the Movement is independent; and
- more detailed explanations on the specific case of National Societies regarding independence, putting the focus on the balance between, on the one hand, their status as auxiliary to public authorities in the humanitarian field and their submission to national law, and on the other hand, the need to maintain their autonomy.

Consequences of the Fundamental Principle of Independence

There are three consequences of the principle of Independence. First, Independence is one of the key elements that the Movement wants to maintain, despite the fact that no concrete consequences are explicitly defined by the principle itself. In its broadest sense, the principle of Independence is understood as meaning that the Red Cross and Red Crescent must resist any interference, whether political, ideological or economic, that is capable of diverting it from the course of action laid down by the requirements of humanity, impartiality and neutrality.

Second, there is a need for National Societies to enjoy a status allowing them to act at all times in accordance with the principles of the Movement. This has consequences on the legal status of National Societies in their country, their relations to public authorities, etc. The degree of autonomy necessary to a National Society cannot be defined uniformly and absolutely, since it depends partly on the political, economic and social conditions in the country. It must be free to relinquish certain tasks or to change its priorities in accordance with the material and human resources at its disposal. Its role as auxiliary to the public authorities does not in the least prevent a National Society from freely choosing the activities it carries out completely independently of the State.

Finally, the violation of the fundamental principle of Independence is often perceived as a serious threat to the integrity of a National Society. However, the debate on the independence of the Movement is broader than the question of the relationship between public authorities and a National Society, although that last aspect is a very important one.

Voluntary Service

It is a voluntary relief movement not prompted in any manner by desire for gain.

Analysis of the Fundamental Principle of Voluntary Service

The fundamental principle of Voluntary Service notes that the Movement is a voluntary relief movement and is not prompted in any manner by desire for gain.

Consequences of the Fundamental principle of Voluntary Service

There are three main consequences of the principle of Voluntary Service. First, the Movement is a volunteer-based organization. Second, if the Movement fails to recognize the value of voluntary service it is in danger of becoming bureaucratic, losing touch with a vital source of motivation, inspiration and initiative, and of cutting off the roots which maintain its contact with human needs and enable it to meet them. Finally, voluntary service is a source of economy. Imagine how much suffering would have to be neglected, for lack of means, if all the work done by volunteers had to be paid for. It is sometimes sufficient to have a relatively small but motivated support staff, with the necessary minimum of financial resources, to enable volunteers to render community services whose cost could never be borne either by the National Society or by the State.

Unity

There can be only one Red Cross or one Red Crescent Society in any one country. It must be open to all. It must carry on its humanitarian work throughout its territory.

Analysis of the Fundamental Principle of Unity

The fundamental principle of Unity notes that a country can only have one Red Cross or one Red Crescent Society. This National Society must be open to all and must carry on its humanitarian work throughout its territory. Each of these characteristics are also included in the conditions for recognition of National Societies by the ICRC.

Consequences of the Fundamental Principle of Unity

There are three consequences of the principle of Unity. First, a National Society could oppose the creation of another Red Cross or Red Crescent Society in its country. As States have agreed to the fundamental principles, they have an obligation to ensure that no other Society can be created on their territory if they have already recognized a National Society.

Second, a National Society has to open its membership to a broad base in the population. It has to recruit its members from all the ethnic, social and other groups in the country to ensure better efficiency of its action. In any case, any discrimination in the recruitment of members would be a violation of the principle of Unity.

Finally, a National Society has to be active in all parts of the country. This does not necessarily mean that the level of activities has to be the same country-wide; the principle of Impartiality may well justify that more activities are undertaken in the parts of a country where the needs are the largest. But what it prohibits is that a region is excluded from the activities of a National Society in a discriminatory manner (e.g., for reasons related with religion, ethnicity, etc.).

Universality

The International Red Cross and Red Crescent Movement, in which all Societies have equal status and share equal responsibilities and duties in helping each other, is worldwide.

Analysis of the Fundamental Principle of Universality
The fundamental principle of Universality notes that the Movement is worldwide, and that all Societies have equal status and share equal responsibilities and duties in helping each other.

Consequences of the Fundamental Principle of Universality
There are three consequences of the principle of Universality. First, one of the objectives of the Movement is to become universal, since it is one of the Movement's strengths that it has a National Society in almost every country of the world. There are a number of States which so far do not have a recognized National Society. However, this is to be seen as a temporary situation; once obstacles preventing Societies of those States to be recognized are lifted, the Movement will become truly global.

Next, solidarity between National Societies is the basis for cooperation between Societies. Finally, with regard to decision-making, all Societies carry one vote at the Federation's General Assembly, the Council of Delegates and the International Conference, irrelevant of their size or wealth.

8.8   Endnotes

[1] Martin Luther King Jr., Wikipedia (n.d.). https://commons.wikimedia.org/wiki/File:Martin_Luther_King,_Jr..jpg

[2] Mother Teresa, Wikipedia (1980). https://commons.wikimedia.org/wiki/File:Kay_Kelly_of_Liverpool_%26_Mother_Teresa_in_1980_(cropped).jpg

[3] Mahatma Gandhi, Wikipedia (n.d.). https://en.wikipedia.org/wiki/Mahatma_Gandhi

[4] Nelson Mandela, Wikipedia (n.d.). https://en.wikipedia.org/wiki/Presidency_of_Nelson_Mandela#/media/File:Mandela_1991.jpg

[5] Mufti, I. (2019, June 25). *The third pillar of Islam: Compulsory charity.* The religion of Islam. https://www.islamreligion.com/articles/46/third-pillar-of-islam/

[6] Encyclopaedia Britannica. (n.d.). *Charity: Christian concept.* https://www.britannica.com/topic/charity-Christian-concept

[7] The UN Refugee Agency (UNHCR). (2016, May 4). *"Humanitarianism and Buddhism" discussion.* https://www.unhcr.or.th/en/news/UNHCR_Buddhism_discussion

[8] Voutira, E., Einarsdottir, J., Baldursdottir, S., Hristova, P., Favoreu, E. K., Wood, T., Agapiou-Josephides K., & Hadjisavvas C. (2014). Emerging trends in humanitarian action and professionalization of humanitarian aid workers. *Dostupné dne.*

[9] Smith, D. (2006). *Ignatieff's World: A Liberal Leader for the 21st Century?.* James Lorimer & Company.

[10] Le Carre J. (2003). Foreword. In C. Bergman (Ed.), *Another day in paradise: International humanitarian workers tell their stories* (pp. 9-10). Orbis Books.

[11] International Federation of Red Cross and Red Crescent Societies. (2020). *The seven fundamental principles.* https://www.ifrc.org/en/who-we-are/vision-and-mission/the-seven-fundamental-principles/

[12] Sphere Project. (2004). *Humanitarian charter and minimum standards in disaster response.* https://ocw.jhsph.edu/courses/RefugeeHealthCare/PDFs/SphereProjectHandbook.pdf

[13] International Federation of Red Cross and Red Crescent Societies and the International Committee of the Red Cross. (1994). *Code of conduct for the International Red Cross and Red Crescent Movement and non-governmental organizations (NGOs) in disaster relief.* https://www.icrc.org/en/doc/assets/files/publications/icrc-002-1067.pdf

[14] International Committee of the Red Cross. (1998). *Henry Durant.* https://www.icrc.org/en/doc/resources/documents/misc/57jnvq.htm

[15] (ca. 1850-1860). [Henry Durant (1828–1910), Swiss philanthropist and co-founder of the International Committee of the Red Cross; Nobel Peace Prize laureate 1901] [Photograph]. Wikimedia Commons. https://en.wikipedia.org/wiki/Henry_Dunant

[16] Jamieson, D. (2005). Duties to the distant: Aid, assistance, and intervention in the developing world. *The Journal of Ethics, 9*(1), 151-170.

[17] Leader, N. (2000). *The politics of principle: The principles of humanitarian action in practice.* Overseas Development Institute. https://www.odi.org/sites/odi.org.uk/files/odi-assets/publications-opinion-files/311.pdf

[18] Fanthorpe, R. (2003). Humanitarian aid in post-war Sierra Leone: The politics of moral economy. In P. Collison (Ed.), *Power, livelihoods and conflict: Case studies in political economy analysis for humanitarian action.* Overseas Development Institute.

[19] Fanthorpe, R. (2003). Humanitarian aid in post-war Sierra Leone: The politics of moral economy. In P. Collison (Ed.), *Power, livelihoods and conflict: Case studies in political economy analysis for humanitarian action.* Overseas Development Institute.

[20] Korf, B. (2007). Antinomies of generosity: Moral geographies and post-tsunami aid in Southeast Asia. *Geoforum, 38*(2), 366-378.

[21] Wood, R. M., & Sullivan, C. (2015). Doing harm by doing good? The negative externalities of humanitarian aid provision during civil conflict. *The Journal of Politics, 77*(3), 736-748.

[22] Macrae, J. (2002). The death of humanitarianism?: An anatomy of the attack. *Disasters, 22*(4), 309-317

[23] Chandler, D. (2001). The road to military humanitarianism: How the human rights NGOs shaped a new humanitarian agenda. *Hum. Rts. Q., 23*, 678.

[24] Fox, F. (2001). New humanitarianism: Does it provide a moral banner for the 21st century? *Disasters*, *25*(4), 275-289.

[25] Sellars, K. (1999, October 23) *The New Imperialists.* The Spectator.

[26] Mbanda, G. (2018, August 2). *US loans to Africa have strings attached.* China daily. http://www.chinadaily.com.cn/a/201808/02/WS5b623d2ca31031a351e9189e.html

[27] LaMonica, J. (2017). Fascist ideology: The Italian case study by Jeffrey LaMonica. In J. LaMonica (Ed.), *Aspiration and dissonance: Readings in history, religion and global affairs* (pp. 16-24). Kendall Hunt Publishing.

[28] Chomsky, N. (1967). *On the backgrounds of the Pacific War.* Liberation. https://chomsky.info/196709   /

[29] Hitler, A. (1969). *Mein kampf.* Houghton Mifflin.

[30] Bureau of Public Affairs (2003). *Winning the war on terror.* U.S. Department of State. https://2001-2009.state.gov/documents/organization/24172.pdf

[31] Chandler, D. G. (2001). The road to military humanitarianism: How the human rights NGOs shaped a new humanitarian agenda. *Human Rights Quarterly*, 23(3), 678-700.

[32] Médecins Sans Frontières. (n.d.) *MSF charter and principles.* https://www.msf-azg.be/en/msf-charter-and-principles

[33] Gilbert, P. (2012, November 1). *Médecins sans frontières.* One quality, the finest. https://onequalitythefinest.com/2012/11/01/medecins-sans-frontieres/

[34] Heyse, L. (2016). *Choosing the lesser evil: Understanding decision making in humanitarian aid NGOs*. Routledge.

[35] Hunt, M. R. (2011). Establishing moral bearings: Ethics and expatriate health care professionals in humanitarian work. *Disasters*, *35*(3), 606-622.

[36] Schwartz, L., Sinding, C., Hunt, M., Elit, L., Redwood-Campbell, L., Adelson, N., Luther, L., Ranford, J., & DeLaat, S. (2010). Ethics in humanitarian aid work: Learning from the narratives of humanitarian health workers. *AJOB Primary Research*, *1*(3), 45-54.

[37] Kuperman, A. J. (2008). Mitigating the moral hazard of humanitarian intervention: Lessons from economics. *Global Governance*, *14*, 219-240.

[38] Kuperman, A. J. (2008). Mitigating the moral hazard of humanitarian intervention: Lessons from economics. *Global Governance*, *14*, 219-240.

[39] Ferris, E. (2005). Faith-based and secular humanitarian organizations. *International review of the Red Cross*, *87*(858), 311-325.

[40] Samaritan's Purse. (n.d.). *What is Samaritan's Purse?* https://www.samaritanspurse.ca/what-is-samaritans-purse/

[41] Petersen, M. J. (2010). International religious NGOs at the United Nations: A study of a group of religious organizations. *Journal of Humanitarian Assistance*, https://sites.tufts.edu/jha/archives/847

[42] Petersen, M. J. (2010). International religious NGOs at the United Nations: A study of a group of religious organizations. *Journal of Humanitarian Assistance*, https://sites.tufts.edu/jha/archives/847

[43] Gingerich, T. R., Moore, D. L., Brodrick, R., & Beriont, C. (2017). *Local humanitarian leadership and religious literacy: Engaging with religion, faith, and faith actors*. Oxfam International. https://www.oxfam.org/en/research/local-humanitarian-leadership-and-religious-literacy

[44] Nebraska Disaster Chaplain Network of Interchurch Ministries of Nebraska. (2006). *Disaster chaplain code of ethics and guiding principles.* http://cretscmhd.psych.ucla.edu/nola/Video/Clergy/Articles/Ecumenical/Disaster_Chaplain_Code_of_Ethics_and_Guiding_Principles.pdf

[45] Matthew 28:19-20, King James Version (n.d.). https://www.bible.com/bible/1/MAT.28.19-20.KJV

[46] Hertzberg, M. (2015). Waves of conversion? The tsunami, 'unethical conversions,' and political Buddhism in Sri Lanka. *International Journal of Mass Emergencies & Disasters*, *33*(1), 55-74.

[47] Rohde, D. (2005, January 22). *Mix of quake aid and preaching stirs concern*. The New York Times. https://www.nytimes.com/2005/01/22/world/worldspecial4/mix-of-quake-aid-and-preaching-stirs-concern.html?auth=login-email&login=email

CHAPTER 9: LIFEBOAT ETHICS AND THE VALUE OF LIFE

"Try not to become a man of success but rather try to become a man of value."

Albert Einstein (1879–1955), physicist and Nobel Prize winner

Figure 9.1. Albert Einstein

Contents

9.1 Introduction

Despite the difficulty of doing so, the question of how to value life is fundamental to the field of emergency management, as well as to many other disciplines. Society constantly struggles with this issue in terms of how to allocate limited and sometimes scarce resources, and this is the conundrum of lifeboat ethics. Its most obvious real-world application may be health care and triage, but valuing life is also a factor in risk assessment and all pillars of the emergency management cycle. In triage, the difficult question is who should be provided with health care when there are not enough resources for all. In risk assessment, the risks to life of different groups of people may have to be balanced against each other or valued relative to other considerations such as economic development. When allocating resources to mitigation, how much money should be spent to protect lives? If choices must be made between different programs, how should they be ethically decided upon?

This chapter will consider (1) the topic of lifeboat ethics, a rather extreme scenario where judgements must be made about who lives or dies, and (2) approaches that have been taken to financially value life.

9.2 The Lifeboat

Consider the scenario of being in a lifeboat where there is not enough food or water to save everybody. All cannot survive, and the only way for some to live is for others to die (a situation occasionally dramatically presented in movies – see Figure 9.2 for an example). Assuming you had the power to choose who lives and who dies, how would you go about making that decision?

Consider the following scenario:

You and nine other people are on a lifeboat but there is only enough food and water for seven to survive. Of the following list, who would you choose to sacrifice, if any?

- Yourself.
- An elderly man who donates large sums of money to humanitarian causes. He is a darling man and you like him very much. You wonder if he would be able to survive the rigors of the next few days until you are rescued.
- A 7-months pregnant 22-year-old woman. You do not know her at all, but she is terrified for herself and for her child.
- A billionaire who offers you ten million dollars if he can stay on the lifeboat. Everybody (including you) hates him. You could sure use that money... and think of all the good you could do with it!
- A family physician. He seems to be a good sort and might be helpful if there are injuries or sickness.
- A brilliant musician who is rather self-centered. He does have his instrument with him and offers to play for everybody. You are a fan and love his music.

- A shy 15-year-old girl. She is not saying a word.
- A 9-year-old boy who suffers from Down syndrome. You feel sorry for him, but he is rather whiney. He probably will not eat much though.
- A good friend of yours. He has helped you out many times.
- A sailor from the ship who claims to have good sailing and survival skills.

Figure 9.2: Scene from *Lifeboat*, a 1944 film about several survivors of a torpedoed ship who find themselves in the same boat with one of the men who sank it.[1]

An example of the lifeboat scenario played out in real life after the sinking of the SS William Brown in 1841. Details on this tragedy can be found at https://www.historicalcrimedetective.com/dying-for-survival-1841/, http://williambrownshipwreck.blogspot.com/, and in a book by Tom Koch called "The Wreck of the William Brown: A True Tale of Overcrowded Lifeboats and Murder at Sea".[2] He also has an excellent talk on YouTube called "The Failure of Lifeboat Ethics and of Scarcity as a Natural Condition". In this disaster the surviving sailors sacrificed many passengers in order to lighten the load on the lifeboat, that they might have a better chance of surviving. Koch argues in part that this occurred because the passengers were Irish Catholics, who at the time were a discriminated against group in Britain.

Scenarios such as this are useful pedagogical tools that can be used to clarify values and ethical thinking, even though they have been critiqued as being unrealistic. In humanitarian work (Chapter 8) and disaster situations, similar scenarios can and have occurred. For example, after Hurricane Katrina devastated New Orleans some hospitals found themselves having to make very difficult choices regarding patient care. In one extreme case, Dr. Anna Pou and two nurses from Memorial Hospital were charged with murder after providing euthanasia to four patients they believed were terminal and suffering. The charges were eventually dropped and the State of Louisiana paid Dr. Pou's legal fees, after which Dr. Pou "helped write and pass three laws in Louisiana offering immunity to health care workers from most civil lawsuits (except in cases of intentional misconduct) for their efforts in future mass casualty situations."[3] An analysis of Dr. Pou's legal liability according to the American Medical Association can be found in the article "The Case of Dr. Anna Pou: Physician Liability in Emergency Situations" by Ryan Bailey.[4]

Questions to Ponder:

With respect to your choices in the lifeboat scenario above:

- Would it make any difference if the problem were framed as (1) who you would allow on the boat (those whom you save), as compared to (2) who you would cast off the boat (those whom you sacrifice)?

- What ethical dilemmas do you face?

- Can you name specific values that determined your choice (e.g., duty to children, the lives of good people are worth more than the lives of bad people, loyalty to friends or family, etc.)?

- Would you consider a first-come-first-on or last-on-first-off approach as being a fair one?

- Did you consider ethical considerations such as:
  - Utilitarianism (greatest good for the greatest number);
  - Duty (do what is right, no matter the outcomes);
  - Justice (distributive or procedural);
  - Virtues (such as honesty, courage, empathy, beneficence, self-sacrifice);
  - Egoism (self-interest); and/or
  - Caring within personal relationships.

The COVID-19 pandemic created the need to triage patients in some hard-hit areas. According to a report in VOX, in Italy

> Doctors are reportedly weeping in the hallways as they decide which patients to save. "If you have a 99-year-old male or female patient who is a patient with a lot of diseases, and you have [a] young kid that need[s] to be intubated and you only have one ventilator, I mean, you're not going to … toss the coin," a surgeon and oncologist in Rome named Carlo Vitelli told NPR last week.[5]

Some people advocate that the lives of all people are of equal value, which is a normative value. In practice society seems to value the lives of some (particularly the wealthy and powerful) above others in terms of how resources are allocated. If you believe that all lives are of equal value then it becomes very challenging to make decisions regarding whose life to save, if all cannot be saved. Naomi Zack discusses this issue in her book *Ethics for Disaster*.[6] She concludes that we should "fairly save all who can be saved with the best preparation."[7]

If you believe that all lives are not of equal value, then they can be differentiated based on ethical theories. A utilitarian would consider who contributes and will contribute most to the greater good of all, and perhaps weigh accordingly the chances of those in the lifeboat surviving (if they were a physician or sailor, for example). Of course, this begs the thorny questions of what is "good," how to measure it, and what the future is likely to be. Who in society should, and would, make these decisions and what should the decision-making process look like? Power, wealth, and vested interests could bias or corrupt an otherwise fair procedural process, and different value systems would certainly rank people differently. An altruistic egalitarian would rank a humanitarian higher than a mafia criminal, but the "boss" of the mafia family would probably consider loyalty a priority and may well choose the criminal over the humanitarian. Ethnic cleansing applies very specific criterion for survival, which is widely considered malevolent by cultures other than the one doing it. Ranking based upon goodness is a thorny moral choice.

Virtue theory would require consideration of character. Those who display virtuous character traits such as beneficence, courage, honesty or patience would rate higher than those who do not. As well, duties and obligations could be assessed. For example, we could consider that we have duties to family members, friends or others who have helped us. From a professional point of view, as an emergency manager, there are obligations and duties to those who are part of our moral community, such as the residents of our city, state, province or country. There is also the issue of what is just and fair? Is it just to cast somebody off the boat because they were the last on it, or because they have poor health? If so, what do you mean by the term "justice"? The two types of justice most applicable to lifeboat ethics are procedural justice (which relates to using a fair process where decisions are as impartial and unbiased as possible) and distributive justice (which is about getting a fair share of something, such as wealth, opportunity, or risk). Procedural justice helps manage the fact that differing ethical systems clash in ways that can be irreconcilable. Distributive justice can be integrated into a procedural process, but still requires the application of values, in terms of what to distribute.

If justice is derived from divine law, then the commandment not to kill (present in the Judaic-Islamic-Christian tradition) must be followed. In this case one solution is not to sacrifice anybody and hope that all are saved by a good fortune or God's intervention. This would satisfy one distributive justice approach by treating all equally. In this case equity is served, though none may likely survive. Another distributive justice approach would be to give everybody an equal opportunity to survive (such as by drawing straws or some

"We must lighten the load ... you're a good company man, aren't you, Carruthers?"

other random process). This could also be seen as fair from a procedural justice perspective, but would not satisfy utilitarian, deontological, or virtue ethical approaches since goodness would not be maximized, rights and duties may be violated, and the character of people becomes irrelevant. A process of procedural fairness from an egalitarian perspective would give everybody a voice in terms of making the selection, though it seems unlikely that all would agree on the same solution. It might also be considered an abrogation of the duties of the commander of the boat (that is you) and a form of moral cowardice.

From a procedural perspective one approach would be to ask for volunteers. If three people volunteered then that would make life much easier for the decider (that is you), but it may well be that volunteers are the more virtuous of the group, in which case it could be viewed as an immoral selection. If the volunteers included those likely to help others survive (such as a doctor), then this process would not serve utilitarian maximization of the greater good. But, do you have the right to deny a person the right to sacrifice themselves? Is this a variant of the euthanasia problem?

Figure 9.3: *Allegory of Justice*.[8]

Lifeboat ethics creates a set of classical ethical dilemmas where one must decide between a set of "goods" or a set of "bads." There is no single solution that everybody can agree on and most people struggle with such choices. Such is the nature of ethical decision-making.

9.2.1 The Lifeboat Metaphor

In a well-known paper, "Living on a Lifeboat,"[9] written by Garrett Hardin in 1974 (also author of "The Tragedy of the Commons"[10]), Hardin uses the lifeboat scenario as a metaphor for how rich nations, especially the U.S., should deal with foreign aid and immigration. Metaphors are powerful, and he comments on their importance noting that "Susanne Langer [...] has shown that it is probably impossible to approach an unsolved problem save through the door of metaphor," and "'All of us,' said George Eliot in *Middlemarch*, 'get our thoughts entangled in metaphors, and act fatally on the strength of them.'"[11] In Chapter 2 on moral development I discussed the importance of framing. Choosing metaphors is one way of framing issues and can powerfully affect how decisions are made.

In the lifeboat metaphor Hardin claims,

> Metaphorically, each rich nation amounts to a lifeboat full of comparatively rich people. The poor of the world are in other, much more crowded lifeboats. Continuously, so to speak, the poor fall out of their lifeboats and swim for a while in the water outside, hoping to be admitted to a rich lifeboat, or in some other way to benefit from the "goodies" on board. What should the passengers on a rich lifeboat do? This is the central problem of "the ethics of a lifeboat."[12]

He goes on to argue against helping poor nations and against immigration through use of the lifeboat metaphor.

The main competing metaphor is Spaceship Earth where all of humanity and nature share a common space (this is like a single lifeboat for all humanity). There is truth in both metaphors, and both are flawed. We all share the same planet, but there are also political, geographical, cultural and other boundaries that separate us in various ways. A problem with the lifeboat metaphor as used by Hardin is that it ignores interdependence between nations, using a simple dualism that misrepresents the complexity of how the world works. For example, rich countries use most of the world's resources, much of which is imported from poorer countries. The lifeboat metaphor also conveniently justifies a sense of moral superiority for richer nations, much of whose wealth is derived from domination over developing nations.[13] This was especially true during times of colonial expansion by European nations. Ecofeminist approaches reject the validity of dualisms that are used to legitimate the dominance of one group over others and the dominance of man over nature, and view groups not in an oppositional relationship but rather in an interdependent ecological one; such an approach is very critical of Hardin's argument.

According to ecofeminists the creation of dualisms, such as those used by Hardin, are based upon five features:

- *Backgrounding*, which "involves an oppressor's attempt to use the oppressed, which creates a dependency on the oppressed, while simultaneously denying that dependency."[14]

- *Radical exclusion*, which "involves not merely recognizing some differences between dualized pairs, but seeing them as radically different."[15]

- *Incorporation*, which "involves constructing the identity of the devalued side of the dualized pair as lacking morally relevant features associated with the other side."[16]

- *Instrumentalism*. "Those groups deemed morally inferior are constructed as having no morally important independent interests. They are valuable, therefore, only instrumentally, in so far as they can be of use in promoting the interests of the morally relevant groups."[17]

- *Homogenization*, which "involves denying the differences between those on the underside of dualized pairs."[18] Thus, the less worthy other.

The idea that any country can be isolationist and manage to solve many of the serious problems that face humanity is a poor one, since problems such as climate change, terrorism, and ecological devastation require global solutions. My conclusion is that the lifeboat metaphor, though providing some useful insights, is inadequate to address issues of resource depletion, overpopulation, and immigration. On a more personal note I find the language used by Hardin in "Living on a Lifeboat" repugnant; for example, he disparages poorer countries having "slovenly rulers."[19] Equating wealth with moral superiority is an assumption and value that is highly debatable, at best. Nevertheless, it speaks powerfully to people with isolationist philosophies who fear that "the other" will endanger their wealth, safety or livelihoods, and has been used by many people in power to create political support.

9.2.2 Triage

The origin of the word triage is the French verb "trier," which means to separate, sort, sift or select. Originally used by the French as early as 1792, it has subsequently become a common ethical approach to providing care on the battlefield and is widely accepted as a rational procedure for medical care during disaster situations.[20]

The purpose of triage is to allocate limited medical resources as fairly and justly as possible, while minimizing the harm done to patients. It is based upon the utilitarian ethic of providing the greatest good for the greatest number. During crisis times the high standards normally expected from the medical community is not achievable and the standard of care during triage is diminished to "sufficiency of care."[21]

During triage, victims are generally divided into three categories that determine their level of treatment:

1. Those who are likely to live, regardless of what care they receive;
2. Those who are unlikely to live, regardless of what care they receive; and
3. Those for whom immediate care might make a positive difference in outcome.

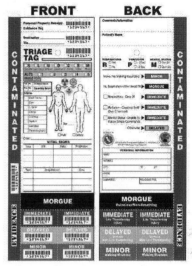

Figure 9.4: Example of a triage tag

Priority is given to the third category. This classification system can also be used for discharge (this is called reverse triage), as well as admittance. Interestingly, some research suggests that physicians find it more difficult to discharge existing patients using reverse triage, than to refuse admittance during triage.[22] Once a person has been admitted, a sense of duty to them is created that makes it difficult to make the decision to discharge them before they have recovered.

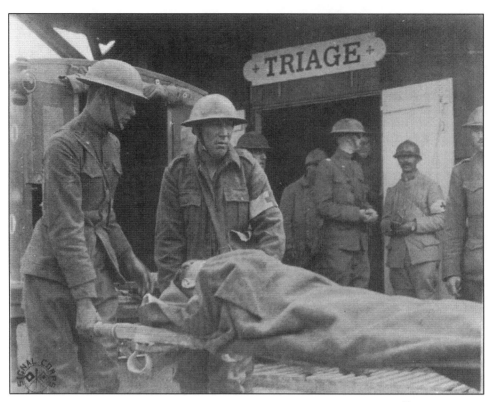

Figure 9.5: Triage station, Suippes, France, World War I.[23]

One area where the lifeboat metaphor works well is in triage situations. Traditional medical ethics in the west have been guided by the four principles of (1) autonomy (respecting the decision-making capacity of individual patients through informed consent), (2) beneficence (balancing risks and benefits of a given action), (3) nonmaleficence (avoiding the causation of harm), and (4) justice (distributing risks and benefits fairly). In a disaster, it is often not possible to follow all of these principles.

Triage is based upon rule utilitarianism. During battle situations it serves to maximize the ability of the military to put wounded soldiers back into action; it has also been applied to non-battle illnesses (see box below). During disasters where medical care is a scarce resource it is applied to incoming and outgoing hospital patients in order to maximize the number who survive. But how utilitarian is this, in terms of the common good? All people are treated as being equal, but in terms of their contribution to society people are clearly not equal from a number of perspectives, including financial (such as future costs or contributions to family and community) and moral (should we equate a humanitarian with a murderer?). Should quality of life years (QALY) be a factor? The common good of the community is hard to find in triage (though it does maximize population and not waste valuable medical resources); what it does do is avoid the tortuous issue of deciding whose life is more worthy, an issue for which it would be impossible to achieve a social consensus. From this viewpoint triage is utilitarian only in a very limited perspective. Triage as it is practiced within civil society may be as much a result of political expediency as it is utilitarian ethic.

If you were the commander of a military regiment during World War II with limited supplies of penicillin, would you give it to (a) wounded soldiers who would be a long time returning to active duty (if at all), or (b) to soldiers who had gotten a venereal disease by visiting brothels while on leave, but would be able to return to active duty quickly, if treated with penicillin? What is your ethical reasoning?

This situation did occur. Compare your reasoning to that of Dr. Beecher below.

Excerpt from *Research and the Individual* by Dr. Henry Beecher:

> When the wonders of penicillin were new, but recognized, and the supply heartbreakingly meager, a small shipment finally arrived in North Africa during World War II. The hospital beds were overflowing with wounded men. Many had been wounded in battles; many also had been wounded in brothels. Which group would get the penicillin? By all that is just, it would go to the heroes who had risked their lives, who were still in jeopardy, and some of whom were dying. They did not receive it, nor should they have; it was given to those infected in brothels. Before indignation takes over, let us examine the situation. First, there were desperate shortages of manpower at the front. Second, those with broken bodies and broken bones would not be swiftly restored to the battle line, even with penicillin, whereas those with venereal disease, on being treated with penicillin, would in a matter of days free the beds they were occupying and return to the front. Third, no one will catch osteomyelitis from his neighbor; the man with venereal disease remains, until he is cured, a reservoir of infection and constant threat. In terms of customary morality, a great in-justice was done; in view of the circumstances, I believe that the course chosen was the proper one.[24]

Can triage be justified on egalitarian principles? In their paper "Triage and Equality," Baker and Strosberg argue that triage is more strongly egalitarian than utilitarian, since egalitarian principles are based upon a social contract specifying (1) that powers of the state will not be used arbitrarily to constrain or terminate their lives, and (2) that all will be treated equally.[25] Triage satisfies both these egalitarian conditions and therefore is consistent with a social justice perspective.

9.3   Statistical People

Let me begin by saying that there are serious ethical problems with trying to value a life monetarily and I am in no way suggesting that economics is able to capture the worth of a person. Nevertheless, within some sectors of society there is a policy and legal need to do so. The policy need relates to some aspects of how much should be invested in risk reduction measures within a cost-benefit analysis. In this situation it would be more accurate to describe the calculation as the value of a "risk to life" as opposed to the value of life. The legal need resides in a tort system that awards financial compensation for wrongful death. In this case the value of life is being addressed. But how can one put a price on a life? Well, as it turns out, economists have developed a methodology for doing this by creating the "statistical person."

The statistical person is based on a collection of risks that result in a life expectancy for a population of persons. From this, the value of a statistical life (VSL) can be calculated when combined with surveys of willingness to pay for risk reduction measures. There are three kinds of willingness to pay studies: (1) contingent valuation surveys that obtain respondents' values directly; (2) wage-risk studies, which estimate the extra wages paid to induce workers to take risky jobs; and (3) consumer behavior studies, (e.g., the VSL implicit in decisions to buy smoke detectors).[26]

The value of a statistical life is lower for jobs that have higher risk and for jobs that have lower wages (Figure 9.6). Note that this is not a representation of the normative values of society (what lives should be worth), but rather reflects empirical or descriptive ethics (describing how society values lives in practice).

Though the statistical value of life is often presented in terms of averages or ranges, Figure 9.6 clearly shows the importance of mortality risk in calculating the VSL. In fact, the bottom curve on Figure 9.6 calculates a value of VSL near zero for the highest risk occupations. This (bizarre to me) analysis assigns a much higher value of life to a hedge fund manager than to a firefighter.

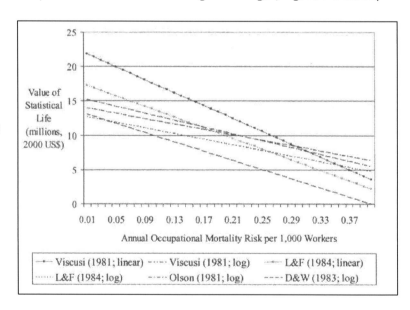

Figure 9.6: The value of a statistical life as a function of mortality risk.[27]

The value of a statistical life varies by country as well as by occupation (Tables 9.1 and 9.2). The reasons for this are that wages and levels of occupational safety vary by country. The highest values in Table 9.1 are from the U.S. because of relatively high wages and high occupational safety regulations. The value of statistical lives in the developing world are generally much lower.

As noted above and worth repeating, these studies are descriptive in nature, not normative. The question as to what the economic value of a life should be—if "cashing out" a human life is even a valid notion—is very different.

Values in the Value of a Statistical Life:

- What is your reaction to the VSL methodology?

- Explain your reaction in terms of the values you hold, considering utilitarian and deontological ethical theories.

Table 1
Labor Market Estimates of Value of Statistical Life Throughout the World

Study/Country	Value of Statistical Life ($ millions)[a]
Median value from 30 U.S. studies	7.0
Australia	4.2
Austria	3.9 – 6.5
Canada	3.9 – 4.7
Hong Kong	1.7
India	1.2 – 1.5
Japan	9.7
South Korea	0.8
Switzerland	6.3 - 8.6
Taiwan	0.2 – 0.9
United Kingdom	4.2

a. All estimates are in year 2000 U.S. dollars. See W. Kip Viscusi and Joseph E. Aldy, "The Value of a Statistical Life: A Critical Review of Market Estimates Throughout the World," *Journal of Risk and Uncertainty* 27, No. 1 (2003): 5-76. For concreteness single representative studies are drawn from their Table 4.

Table 9.1: Value of Statistical Lives in Different Countries.[28]

There are social and moral ramifications of these calculations. Given the inequities in society in terms of wages (Table 9.2), the value of the statistical lives of white men in the U.S. (and many other western countries) is higher than of women or non-white men. This is also generally true for those who are retired. Stay-at-home caregivers (usually women raising children) also have lower VSL. This methodology, therefore, reinforces existing inequalities in society, and can be arguably described as sexist and racist.

Table 1. Median Weekly Earnings and Gender Earnings Ratio for Full-Time Workers, 16 Years and Older by Race/Ethnic Background, 2017 and 2018

Racial/ Ethnic Background	2018				2017 (in 2018 dollars)			
	Women	Men	Female Earnings as % of Male Earnings of Same Group	Female Earnings as % of White Male Earnings	Women	Men	Female Earnings as % of Male Earnings of Same Group	Female Earnings as % of White Male Earnings
All Races/ Ethnicities	$789	$973	81.1%	N/A	$789	$964	81.8%	N/A
White	$817	$1,002	81.5%	81.5%	$814	$995	81.9%	81.9%
Black	$654	$735	89.0%	65.3%	$673	$727	92.5%	67.7%
Hispanic	$617	$720	85.7%	61.6%	$618	$707	87.4%	62.1%
Asian	$937	$1,241	75.5%	93.5%	$925	$1,236	74.8%	93.0%

Notes: Hispanic workers may be of any race. White, Black, and Asian workers include Hispanics. Annual averages of median weekly earnings.
Source: See Table 2.

Table 9.2: Gender Wage Gaps.[29]

Value of a Statistical Life:

- Given the need within the legal system to compensate people for wrongful death, how moral do you think it is to use the VSL methodology?

- If you disagree with its use, what would you use as an alternative?

Are all Lives of Equal Value?

From a secular perspective, using any of the ethical theories that have been discussed earlier (both normative and descriptive) differentiates people in terms of their moral contribution to others, both human and non-human. But according to the Bill and Melinda Gates Foundation and many faith-based organizations, all lives are of equal value.

Upon what basis is this true? Certainly, people do not contribute equal levels of good to society (in fact, some are evil and contribute to the detriment of others), so in that sense they are not equal. They are not equal in capacity, opportunity, or potential.

There is a faith-based belief held by many that all human life is sacred, holy and precious. In their statement on the sanctity of life, the Christian and Missionary Alliance note the following:

> Since all life exists for God's purposes and all human lives are equally sacred […] All human beings, regardless of race, gender, age, mental capacity or physical condition, born or unborn, rich or poor, educated or uneducated, young or old, reflect God's image. […] Men and women were created with imperishable souls to fellowship with God throughout eternity. The value of human life is infinitely greater than the relative worth currently ascribed to it by a secular society. Human life has intrinsic value because of its worth to God.[30]

In a Kantian system equality is based on the idea that everyone has their own ends, goals, and interests, and that makes them ends in themselves, and not means to someone else's ends.

What does it mean to say that all lives are of equal value, and what is the consequence of that belief? From a utilitarian perspective one would conclude that as many lives should be saved as possible, regardless of situation. On the other hand, a religious belief may not allow for the taking of life since that can only be done by God, and therefore from that perspective the captain of the lifeboat should not sacrifice others. Should some self-sacrifice in order that others may live? The Catechism of the Catholic Church states,

> Human life is sacred because from its beginning it involves the creative action of God and it remains forever in a special relationship with the Creator, Who is its sole end. God alone is the Lord of life from its beginning until its end: no one can under any circumstance claim for himself the right directly to destroy an innocent human being.[31]

Suicide is therefore not permitted though self-sacrifice is a virtue, and may be. On the lifeboat if some do not sacrifice, will not more sacred lives be lost?

In "Thinking the Unthinkable: Sacred Values and Taboo Cognitions," Philip Tetlock notes,

> Many people insist that their commitments to certain values (e.g. love, honor, justice) are absolute and inviolable – in effect, sacred. They treat the mere thought of trading off sacred values against secular ones (such as money) as transparently outrageous – in effect, taboo. Economists insist, however, that in a world of scarce resources, taboo trade-offs are unavoidable. Research shows that, although people do respond with moral outrage to taboo trade-offs, they often acquiesce when secular violations of sacred values are rhetorically reframed as routine or tragic trade-offs.

Those who hold all lives are sacred are faced with a terrible dilemma in the lifeboat scenario. It may be that some would consider that all lives are not equally sacred. Are there degrees of sacredness? Is the life of a holy person more sacred than the live of a murderer? Even if the answer is yes, that may not matter because of the prohibition of taking a life. The solution to this problem may be to switch how it is framed. Sacrifice nobody and let God's will be done. If God wishes for the people in the lifeboat to survive, then (s)he will provide a miracle.

9.3.1 Quality Adjusted Life Years (QALY)

Another approach to valuing life considers how many years a statistical person is likely to live, and the quality of that life. It is not uncommon for people, when considering medical treatment for example, to evaluate how it will affect their quality of life as well as life expectancy. To many people one good year may well be viewed as more valuable than two poor ones.

There are obvious problems in defining quality; it is a highly subjective exercise. A trap in assessing QALY is creating metrics or processes that empower particular agendas or groups while disadvantaging others. One theoretical issue with this approach is that it is easy to conceive of a negative number, where death is preferable to life. I have used this approach with pets, whose painful existence seemed to be worse than death and therefore decided to have them put down.

Some countries have enacted legislation allowing people the right to die. For example, the Criminal Code of Canada was modified in 2016 to allow for medical assistance in dying. It now states,

Exemption for medical assistance in dying

241 (2) No medical practitioner or nurse practitioner commits an offence under paragraph (1)(b) if they provide a person with medical assistance in dying in accordance with section 241.2.[32]

The basis of this law is deontological in that people have the right to die if they so wish (and to be assisted in doing so through euthanasia), but using QALY as a paradigm, it could also be argued (from at least one version of a utilitarian perspective) that beings with a negative quality of life should have their life terminated. This argument is similar to the ones used to justify the horrors of eugenics in Nazi Germany, which resulted in the massacre of millions of "undesirables".

QALY approaches have obvious relevance to lifeboat ethics. According to this metric a child with many years of life ahead of them would tend to rank much higher than an elderly person. There is an argument based upon justice and fairness that supports this approach. Such a metric has been shown to be abhorrent to many elderly people, and the Environmental Protection Agency had to back off of using such an approach in a cost-benefit analysis related to anti-pollution legislation in 2003.[33] John Harris argues that QALY is fatally flawed because it is inherently racist, sexist, and ageist.[34] By many metrics QALY would also preference people who are wealthy or privileged, and disadvantage victims of disaster. Like many moral choices it has both pros and cons. Where the process is transparent, rule-based, and avoids issues of personal bias (such as limiting the process to preferring the young over the old) it has benefits that are appealing. Those benefits include rapid decision-making and the avoidance of operational moral dilemmas. For example, "Doctors in Italy, Spain and Sweden have… been prioritizing younger over older patients" for access to ventilators during the 2020 COVID-19 pandemic.[35] Arguments for this approach are bolstered by statistics that show higher survival rates for younger patients. By this metric, women should also have preference over men, since they have a lower mortality rate in COVID-19; is the extension of this principle to gender one you are comfortable with? If not, why?

The reliance upon a single ethical approach has the potential to create outcomes that are morally repugnant because problems tend to be framed narrowly, which is why I argue for ethical pluralism. A pluralistic approach does not reject an emphasis upon one particular ethic but allows for the consideration of a wider group of choices. QALY can provide useful input into an ethical decision-making model, but must be balanced by other perspectives. Such a process is challenging indeed, and must include a diverse group of voices and values, a process that is transparent, and careful consideration of biases, prejudices, and power imbalances.

9.4 Conclusion

Lifeboat ethics presents extreme situations that are unlikely in non-emergency times but must be faced during disasters. It is important, therefore, to consider a range of scenarios, and the ethical and moral choices that must be faced. As a metaphor for how the world works, as used by Hardin, it fails to capture many of the important complexities that exist in a globalized and complex society.

At times there is a need to quantify the value of life, but there is no methodology that is morally and ethically satisfying to everybody (or perhaps even most people). We are left, therefore, in the uncomfortable position of having to make difficult choices that advantage some and disadvantage others. How we go about this reflects our fundamental values.

9.5 Endnotes

[1] Hitchcock, A. (1944). *Lifeboat* [Film]. Twentieth Century Fox. https://en.wikiquote.org/wiki/Lifeboat_(film)#/media/File:Lifeboat_(1944)_1.jpg
[2] Koch, T. (2005). *The Wreck of the William Brown: A True Tale of Overcrowded Lifeboats and Murder at Sea.* McGraw Hill Professional.

[3] Fink, S. (2009, August 25). *The deadly choices at Memorial.* The New York times. https://www.nytimes.com/2009/08/30/magazine/30doctors.html?pagewanted=all

[4] Bailey, R. (2010). The case of Dr. Anna Pou: Physician liability in emergency situations. *The Virtual Mentor, 12(9),* 726-730.

[5] Romeo, N. (2020, March 31). The grim ethical dilemma of rationing medical care, explained. Vox. https://www.vox.com/coronavirus-covid19/2020/3/31/21199721/coronavirus-covid-19-hospitals-triage-rationing-italy-new-york

[6] Zack, N. (2009). *Ethics for disaster.* Rowman & Littlefield Publishers Inc.

[7] Zack, N. (2009). *Ethics for disaster.* Rowman & Littlefield Publishers Inc.

[8] Cinganelli, M., Tarchiani, F., Rosselli, M., & Vannini, O. (1620-1625). [Allegory of Justice] [Painting]. Palazzo Pitti, Florence. [https://en.wikipedia.org/wiki/Justice#/media/File:Allegoria_della_Giustizia_-_galleria_del_Poccetti.jpg

[9] Hardin, G. (1974). Commentary: Living on a lifeboat. *BioScience, 24*(10), 561-568.

[10] Hardin, G. (1968). The tragedy of the commons. *Science, 162*(3859), 1243-1248.

[11] Hardin, G. (1974). Commentary: Living on a lifeboat. *BioScience, 24*(10), 561-568.

[12] Hardin, G. (1974). Commentary: Living on a lifeboat. *BioScience, 24*(10), 561-568.

[13] Davion, V. (2002). Ecofeminism, lifeboat ethics and illegal immigration. *Global Dialogue, 4*(1), 114-124.

[14] Davion, V. (2002). Ecofeminism, lifeboat ethics and illegal immigration. *Global Dialogue, 4*(1), 114-124.

[15] Davion, V. (2002). Ecofeminism, lifeboat ethics and illegal immigration. *Global Dialogue, 4*(1), 114-124.

[16] Davion, V. (2002). Ecofeminism, lifeboat ethics and illegal immigration. *Global Dialogue, 4*(1), 114-124.

[17] Davion, V. (2002). Ecofeminism, lifeboat ethics and illegal immigration. *Global Dialogue, 4*(1), 114-124.

[18] Davion, V. (2002). Ecofeminism, lifeboat ethics and illegal immigration. *Global Dialogue, 4*(1), 114-124.

[19] Hardin, G. (1974). Commentary: Living on a lifeboat. *BioScience, 24*(10), 561-568.

[20] Robertson-Steel, I. (2006). Evolution of triage systems. *Emergency Medicine Journal, 23*(2), 154-155.

[21] Kraus, C. K., Levy, F., & Kelen, G. D. (2007). Lifeboat ethics: Considerations in the discharge of inpatients for the creation of hospital surge capacity. *Disaster Medicine and Public Health Preparedness, 1*(1), 51-56.

[22] Tallgren M., Klepstad P., Petersson J., Skram U., & Hynninen M. (2005). Ethical issues in intensive care: A survey among Scandanavian intensivists. *Acta Anaesthesiol Scand, 49*(8), 1092–1100.

[23] National Museum of Health and Medicine. (ca. 1914-1918). [Wounded arriving at triage station in Suippes, France from sanitary train] [Photograph]. National Museum of Health and Medicine, Otis Historical Archives. https://www.flickr.com/photos/medicalmuseum/249929233/in/photolist-o5XfH-8H9pEe

[24] Beecher, H. K. (1970). *Research and the individual: Human studies.* Little, Brown.

[25] Baker, R., & Strosberg, M. (1992). Triage and equality: An historical reassessment of utilitarian analyses of triage. *Kennedy Institute of Ethics Journal, 2*(2), 103-123.

[26] Miller, T. R. (2000). Variations between countries in values of statistical life. *Journal of Transport Economics and Policy, 34*(2), 169-188.

[27] Viscusi, W. K. (2005). *The value of life: Discussion paper no. 517.* Harvard Law School John M. Olin Center for Law, Economics and Business.

[28] Viscusi, W. K., & Aldy, J. E. (2003). The value of a statistical life: a critical review of market estimates throughout the world. *Journal of risk and uncertainty, 27*(1), 5-76.

[29] Hegewisch, A., & Hartmann, H. (2019, March 7). *The gender wage gap: 2018 earnings differences by race and ethnicity.* Institute for women's policy research. https://iwpr.org/publications/gender-wage-gap-2018/

[30] The Christian and Missionary Alliance. (1981). *Sanctity of life.* https://www.cmalliance.org/about/beliefs/perspectives/sanctity-of-life

[31] The Holy See. (n.d.) *Catechism of the Catholic Church.* https://www.vatican.va/archive/ccc_css/archive/catechism/p3s2c2a5.htm

[32] Criminal Code (R.S.C., 1985, c. C-46). https://laws-lois.justice.gc.ca/eng/acts/c-46/page-53.html#h-119953

[33] Hahn, R., & Wallstein, S. (2003). Whose Life is Worth More? And Why Is It Horrible to Ask. *Washington Post*, B3.

[34] Harris, J. (1987). QALYfying the value of life. *Journal of Medical Ethics, 13*(3), 117-123.

[35] Popescu, D., & Marcoci, A. (2020, April 22). *Coronavirus: allocating ICU beds and ventilators based on age is discriminatory.* The conversation. https://theconversation.com/coronavirus-allocating-icu-beds-and-ventilators-based-on-age-is-discriminatory-136459

CHAPTER 10: SPECIAL TOPICS

Contents

10.1 Introduction

There are many ethical issues and dilemmas in the theory and practice of emergency management. This chapter considers four issues relevant to many of the topics previously discussed: (1) price gouging, (2) disaster financial assistance, and (3) pandemic planning.

10.2 Price Gouging

Before reading further, write down your initial thoughts in the table below:

Price Gouging	Disaster Financial Assistance (DFA)
Ethical arguments in favor of price gouging:	Ethical arguments in favor of DFA:
Ethical arguments against price gouging:	Ethical arguments against DFA:

In the wake of disaster, the prices of many goods and services increase. Price gouging refers to a significant increase in prices that do not reflect supplier costs or increased risk on the part of the vendor; rather, the increase is due to taking advantage of a temporary scarcity of supply.

According to the company AccuWeather:

- In the wake of [Hurricane] Katrina ... A hotel manager was sentenced to five years in prison for boosting prices.
- In Louisiana, the office of the Attorney General fielded hundreds of reports from renters complaining about heightened rents following the storm, as some landlords were reportedly trying to use the storm as an excuse to evict poorer tenants.
- After [Hurricane] Sandy, 185 residents received over $282,000 in reimbursements from hotels, gas stations and hardware stores for price gouging.
- [P]rice gouging claims only increased after [Hurricanes] Harvey and Irma. Reports of $20 per gallon of gas and $99 cases of water were cited in Texas, despite Attorney General Ken Paxton's warnings. Numerous hotels were cited as well, some of which tripled their nightly costs. In the end, 48 businesses paid over $166,000 in civil restitution to Texas residents.
- In Puerto Rico, the reports were even more rampant. Cases of water were again selling for $99 while other reports highlighted $3,200 plane tickets. Nearly 8,000 complaints were made following Hurricane Irma.[1]

Raising prices following disaster is often perceived as immoral by the public and elicits strong emotional reactions from consumers. In the U.S. many states have enacted legislation to prevent price gouging (Figure 10.1), though its definition is often not precise. Reasonable price increases are allowed, especially if they result from increased supplier costs or international market trends. But price increases that are "excessive," "unreasonable," "gross," or "unconscionable" are restricted. These restrictions can be applied to all goods and services, or only ones that are considered essential. Price gouging is particularly relevant to products that are considered to be inelastic, where demand does not depend (or depends very weakly) upon price. One example is insulin. Type 1 and many type 2 diabetics require insulin to live and will pay whatever price is required to purchase it (if they have the necessary financial resources).

Various authors have made supporting arguments in favor of allowing large price increases in disaster zones. Zwolinski, for example, argues that in some circumstances price gouging is praiseworthy because of its net positive effect on the economy and therefore society.[2] He notes that the exchange is voluntary and both parties benefit from it. Arguments in support of price gouging are mainly economic in nature, arguing that a free market system will maximize economic efficiency. Where prices increase (it is argued) there will be a greater influx of supplies into the disaster zone, thereby meeting the needs of victims and also pushing down prices. Without this effect, shortages might continue in the absence of governmental or NGO intervention.

Price gouging can also deter hoarding. For example, a news story from the Foundation for Economic Education reported that one man said, "I was grateful for Walmart because by raising its price for milk it thwarted the greedy customers who, without consideration for others, snatch up two and three gallons."[3] Hoarding favors the wealthy and greedy, and results in large inequities. However, beyond increasing prices, other methods exist to inhibit hoarding, such as caps on purchases.

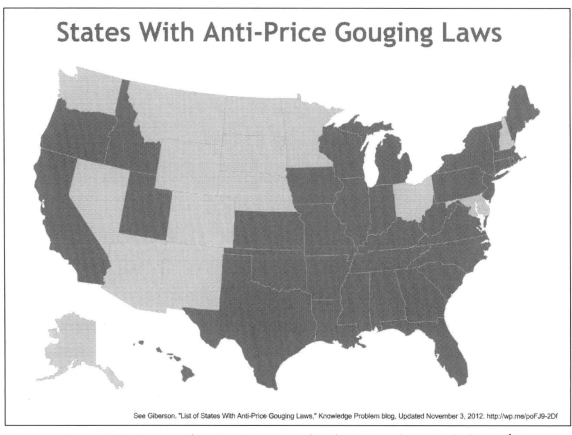

States With Anti-Price Gouging Laws

See Giberson, "List of States With Anti-Price Gouging Laws," Knowledge Problem blog, Updated November 3, 2012. http://wp.me/poFJ9-2Df

Figure 10.1: States with anti-price gouging legislation are shown in dark grey.[4]

Critics of price gouging comment that market efficiency is an insufficient argument for pricing during disasters, and that other factors such as social justice and equity must be considered.[5] Snyder acknowledges that in non-emergency situations the free market can create an optimum pricing structure, resulting in a net benefit to society. This happens when there are not monopolies on goods and services, and when both sellers and buyers have the freedom to refuse to sell or buy. But, one of the defining features of emergencies and disasters is that some goods and services that were previously unconstrained become a scarce resource. Multiple vendors may or may not exist or be accessible. Price gouging creates a situation where the wealthy have the resources to access expensive products while others do not. Should the distribution of essential goods during disasters be based upon wealth or some other method such as a lottery (one application of distributive justice) or need (that can be justified on utilitarian, social justice, or deontological grounds)?

Figure 10.2: Price Gouging at Walmart.[6]

An ethical analysis on price gouging will depend upon three main factors, (1) whether or not particular goods and services are essential (such as food and water), non-essential (such as replacing worn clothing), or luxury items (such as jewelry), (2) whether or not particular goods or services are a scarce resource, and (3) who is affected by the price gouging. From an ethical perspective, price gouging is mostly an issue for essential goods and services when they are scarce. If they are non-essential or luxury items then a choice can be made to wait to purchase them, without incurring hardship. Where scarcity is not an issue, unless a monopoly is present, vendor competitiveness is likely to prevent large price increases. The people most affected are vulnerable disaster victims, especially the poor, the elderly, children, or those who are unwell or suffer from disabilities. Below, this issue is examined from several ethical perspectives.

Utilitarian Perspective:

Consider the scenario of a vendor who has an essential supply that is a scarce resource, such as drinkable bottled water. Drinking water is normally a pure public good in most places, but during disasters this may not be the case – it can become impure or a private good. What is the effect of selling water for ten times the normal price compared to selling it at near normal prices, assuming that there is an existing inventory and no increased supplier costs or risk? Because people need drinking water to live, a vendor would be able to sell his inventory and make a large profit that benefits him financially (he may, however, suffer condemnation for his business practices). His customers would benefit from obtaining the water, albeit at a high price. Equity issues would certainly surface, however, as the wealthy would be able to purchase far more water than the less wealthy, and some might not be able to purchase any if they have no financial resources available. This would create hardship and the seller's increased profit would be insufficient to balance out the harm caused.

An economic perspective would argue that price gouging optimizes the economic system and results in increased resources becoming available to disaster victims. However, this argument hinges on context and the type of product or service. If the resource is hotel rooms, a temporary shortage will not result in an increase in supply, as it might for potable water. The greater good would be served by renting them out to those in greatest need, or equitably distributing them using a lottery system. Where there are available supplies that can be rapidly transported to the disaster area and where undue hardship will not occur until they arrive, then the argument for the free market system is stronger.

Virtue Ethics Perspective:

There are many virtues, including generosity, beneficence, empathy, and caring. Lusting after wealth is often included is a list of vices, but I have never seen it as a virtue. The decision to charge ten times the price for the water does not suggest a virtuous character and therefore virtue theory does not support price gouging.

Deontological Perspective:

Corporate social responsibility suggests that companies have a duty to society beyond the maximization of profits to shareholders. That duty would argue against price gouging, because of the inequitable social justice problems it creates.

I suggest that the reciprocal duties citizens owe to each other and to the community they live in are different during disasters. When in possession of a scarce resource, duties to oneself (egoism) is diminished relative to duty to others when the other is in greater need, and I therefore argue that during emergencies the free hand of the marketplace should receive a lesser emphasis relative to communitarian values, as compared to non-emergency times.

In Chapter 1.2 the ethics of Kant was introduced. Recall that his ethic is based upon the following principles:

- *Universalizability*: Act only according to that maxim by which you can also will that it would become a universal law. (Should everybody do it, or would that be self-defeating?)

- *Reversibility (Golden Rule):* Do unto others as you would have them do unto you.

- *Respect (no exploitation):* Act in such a way that you always treat humanity, whether in your own person or in the person of any other, never simply as a means, but always at the same time as an end. (The end does not justify the means.)

With respect to universalizability, would it be best if everybody engaged in price gouging, or if nobody did it? If the former, it would lead to significant social equity and justice problems as those with less resources would suffer. From an egalitarian viewpoint, it would be highly immoral and would certainly increase animosity and distrust within society. In terms of the Golden Rule, people would generally prefer not to be the subject of price gouging no matter what their wealth. With respect to the third principle of respect, price gouging treats people as a means to and end rather than an end in itself. Deontological ethics, therefore, appears to weigh in against price gouging.

Consider the approach taken by Zack (Chapter 1.2). Her principles are:

- "Human life has intrinsic worth.
- Everyone's life is equally valuable.
- Everyone has the same right to freedom from harm by others.
- Everyone is entitled to protection from harm by nonhuman forces."[7]

From these, a set of ethical principles follow:

- "We are obligated to care for ourselves and our dependents.
- We are obligated not to harm one another.
- We are obligated to care for strangers when it doesn't harm us to do so."[8]

Price gouging harms those who cannot afford to purchase scarce products or services. This would be a violation of Zack's ethical principles, though the free market economic approach argues that not allowing price gouging results in greater harm in the future.

Rawls' social justice approach (Chapter 1.3) is based upon "Two Principles of Justice," which determine how economic goods and civil liberties are distributed in society. The first principle maximizes the total amount of liberty, ensuring that they are granted to all (with the constraint that the liberties of people not infringe upon the liberties of others), while the second principle allows inequalities but requires that there be equal opportunity with the greatest benefit going to the least advantaged (with the proviso that some benefit is saved for future generations).

One liberty in western liberal democracies is the right of vendors to charge what they wish for products, though constraints exist in many places on public goods where prices are controlled by the state. In contrast, Article 25 of the Universal Declaration of Human Rights states that "Everyone has the right to a standard of living adequate for the health and well-being of himself and of his family, including food, clothing, housing and medical care."[9] This right can conflict with the freedom of vendors to charge exorbitant prices. With respect to the Rawls' second principle, price gouging does not provide the greatest benefit to the least advantaged; in fact, it does the opposite. It provides the greatest benefit to the wealthy and the least benefit to the disadvantaged.

The economic argument for price gouging is utilitarian, suggesting that the long-term positive effects of maintaining a free market system, even in exceptional circumstances, creates the greatest good through market efficiency. The assumption is that this good is greater than the short-term harm caused. But can this be assumed to be generally true?

It is not difficult to imagine a scenario where this assumption is violated. For example, suppose a widespread power blackout during a heat wave resulted in a loss of electricity for an extended period of time. Fuel for backup generators is in short supply. Price gouging results in it being purchased mainly by the rich who use it primarily for air conditioning, but also for refrigeration. At the same time hospitals, cooling centres, and people on home dialysis are running out of fuel, resulting in high mortality rates. It is difficult to imagine how marginal increases in economic efficiency in the disaster area offset the harms done by price gouging in this scenario. It seems that price gouging during emergencies and disasters can lead to the greater good in some situations but not others (i.e., it is situational and contextual), and if it causes immediate harm, then the burden of proof is on the proponents of price gouging to provide evidence for its benefit in any particular situation. This is an application of the precautionary principle (Chapter 4).

Student Exercise:

The following scenario is used by Dwight Lee in his argument against price gouging laws:

> Raleigh, North Carolina, lost electricity for several days in September 1996 from damage caused by Hurricane Fran. Ice was urgently needed to prevent items such as insulin and baby formula as well as other perishable food from spoiling. According to Michael Munger (2007),[10] ice was soon available temporarily because of the efforts of four young men from Goldsboro, about fifty miles away and bypassed by Fran. The four men rented two freezer trucks, filled them with ice bought for $1.70 a bag and drove them to downtown Raleigh, which required chain sawing and removing fallen trees that were blocking roads. They were soon selling ice in two locations for more than $8.00 a bag. Some residents complained about the price, but few refused to buy. After about an hour, two police cars arrived at one of the two locations (what happened at the other isn't mentioned), arrested the two men there for "price gouging," and impounded the truck and ice, preventing those still in line from buying ice they valued more than the price being charged. Yet those buying the ice applauded the men's arrest.[11]

1. Were the citizen of Raleigh better off or worse off before the men were arrested?
2. Were the four men better or worse off before they were arrested?
3. Analyze the scenario from a variety of ethical theories.
4. Evaluate the level of moral development of the four men, using the frameworks presented in Chapter 2.

In summary, there appears to be one utilitarian argument in favor of price gouging in emergency and disaster situations, which is that the free market system optimizes prices and encourages the supply of scarce resources. This is a very situational argument, however, that may be valid in some scenarios, but which cannot be generalized. Other ethical theories do not support price gouging. As such, it should be considered immoral unless demonstrated otherwise.

10.3   Disaster Financial Assistance (DFA)

10.3.1   Introduction

Following a disaster there are two sources of aid for affected communities. The first is governmental aid and the second is charitable donations. Payouts from private insurance are also important but are not considered aid since they were purchased prior to the disaster. Charitable donations are addressed in Chapter 8 on humanitarian aid. This chapter focusses on the ethics of disaster financial assistance from governmental sources.

10.3.2   Trends in Disaster Financial Assistance

Over time, social contracts regarding

> **Denial of Disaster Financial Assistance in the U.S. in 1887:**
>
> *"I feel obliged to withhold my approval of the plan, as proposed by this bill, to indulge a benevolent and charitable sentiment through the appropriation of public funds for that purpose.*
>
> *"I can find no warrant for such an appropriation in the Constitution, and I do not believe that the power and duty of the General Government ought to be extended to the relief of individual suffering which is in no manner properly related to the public service or benefit."*[12]
>
> President Grover Cleveland, 1887, in response to a bill to donate seed grain to farmers in Texas after a drought.

Figure 10.3: President Grover Cleveland.[13]

governmental disaster financial assistance have shifted. Previously, it was deemed not to be the role of government to assist in disaster relief (see side box for an example). However, in recent times, governments at provincial, state, and federal levels increasingly consider it as part of their mandate, and citizens have learned to expect such aid.

For example, in the U.S. the federal government provided 1.0% of disaster relief in 1953, but by the mid-1970s had increased that to over 70%. More recently those costs have continued to increase, as shown for flood insurance payouts in Figures 10.4 and 10.5.[14] Figure 10.5 shows a gradual increase in percentage payments, except during the Reagan presidency from 1981 to 1989 and under President Bush from 1989 to 1993.

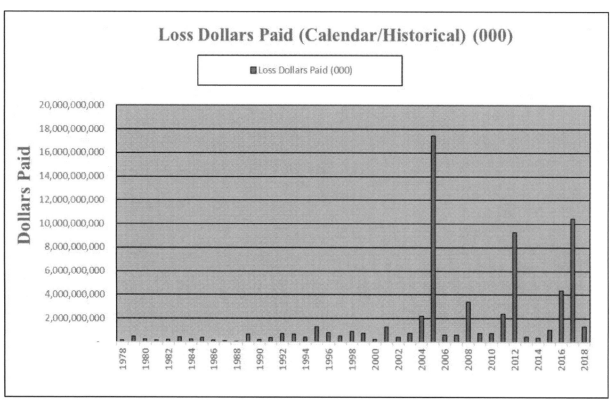

Figure 10.4: U.S. Flood Loss Dollars Paid by Calendar Year.[15]

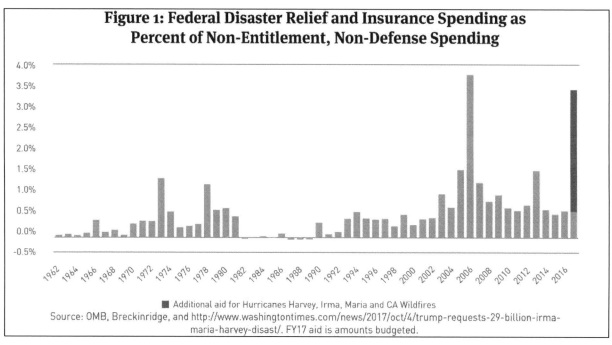

Figure 10.5: U.S. Disaster Relief and Insurance Spending as Percent of Non-Entitlement, Non-Defense Spending.[16] The data shown here includes direct grant aid from the Federal Emergency Management Agency (FEMA), as well as payouts from federal insurance programs such as the National Flood Insurance Program.

In Canada, "[t]he average annual federal share of response and recovery costs of natural disasters paid under the DFAA has increased from $10 million in 1970-1995, to $110 million in 1996-2010, to $360 million in 2011-2016."[17] These trends reflect changes in governmental policies and legislation, but also that exposure (such as development in flood plains) and vulnerability to many hazards has increased, resulting in an increase in the number and cost of natural disasters. It also seems probable that climate change is, and increasingly will, make some hazards more severe in terms of frequency and severity.[18]

As the public purse pays increasingly for the cost of disasters various ethical issues arise, especially as those costs become burdensome. In the U.S., the Government Accountability Office (GAO) found that the National Flood Insurance Program

> has had to borrow from the Department of the Treasury to pay claims from major natural disasters. As of September 2018, FEMA's debt stood at $20.5 billion despite Congress having canceled $16 billion in debt in October 2017. Without reforms, the financial condition of NFIP could continue to worsen.[19]

Questions that need to be addressed are:
- To what extent should the individual and different levels of government be responsible for disaster costs?
- What levels of prevention and mitigation should be required as a condition of being eligible for DFA?
- How does DFA contribute in the long term to hazard exposure, vulnerability, and resilience?

10.3.3   Private Insurance versus Disaster Financial Assistance

Private insurance requires the following seven characteristics to be viable:

1. There must be a large number of exposure units,
2. The loss must be accidental and unintentional,
3. The loss must be determinable and measurable,
4. The loss should not be catastrophic,
5. The chance of loss must be calculable,
6. The premium must be economically feasible, and
7. Losses should be random and uncorrelated.[20]

Of these seven conditions the last four are violated by disasters: the losses can be catastrophic (by definition), probabilities are very difficult to estimate, premiums need to be very high, and there is a high correlation between individual risks. For this reason, the private sector is unable to insure disasters effectively, and uptake even in wealthy countries is relatively low. As a result, in many countries the public sector has increasingly taken on responsibility for disaster recovery.

DFA can take various forms including loans (possibly at low interest) and grants to private individuals or governmental organizations. They can be ad hoc or from a catastrophe fund. These loans and grants can be subject to conditions such as the requirement to have purchased insurance if it were available, or of having undertaken mitigation measures to reduce hazard impact.

In the U.S., communities may voluntarily join the National Flood Insurance Program (NFIP) by agreeing to adopt minimal floodplain management regulations; in exchange, their residents become eligible to purchase flood insurance policies through the NFIP. FEMA offers "flood insurance policy premium discounts in communities that develop and execute extra measures beyond minimum floodplain management requirements to provide protection from flooding."[21] For properties that are substantially damaged from a flood, they will be "required to meet all local regulations for building in a floodplain."[22]

Examples of DFA:

- The U.S. Department of Agriculture (USDA) offers several permanently authorized programs to help farmers recover financially from a natural disaster, including federal crop insurance, the noninsured assistance program and emergency disaster loans.
- Nearly two-thirds of the current federal spending is used to subsidize producer premiums, and the balance primarily covers the government share of program losses and reimburses participating private insurance companies for their administrative and operating expenses.
- Producers who grow a crop that is currently ineligible for crop insurance may be eligible for a direct payment under USDA's noninsured assistance program (NAP).
- Low-interest emergency disaster (EM) loans available through USDA's Farm Service Agency.
- Various support and stimulus packages during the COVID-19 pandemic, such as the HEALS and Coronavirus Aid, Relief, and Economic Security Acts in the U.S. and Canada's COVID-19 Economic Response Plan.

Swiss Re, in cooperation with the Institute for Catastrophic Loss Reduction, examined various policy approaches to flood insurance in Canada.[23] They highlight the problem of adverse selection (which is the same as moral hazard) and note that bundling flood insurance with other perils can overcome this problem, that very high risk homeowners should be excluded, that deductibles should be risk-based to ensure economic viability and to reduce moral hazard, that flood insurance should not encourage development in flood prone areas or risky behavior, and that it would work best as a partnership between the public and private sectors.

Such an approach is a significant step towards the socialization of risk in society, where the costs of risks is shared by all instead of borne by individuals. Other examples of this are Medicare and social assistance programs. Such programs are based upon egalitarian/communitarian principles and are supported by a distributive justice approach. Libertarians would not be in favor of an insurance program supported by public funds.

10.3.4   DFA and Moral Hazard

Where there is an expectation of insurance or aid in the event of a disaster, the motivation to avoid risky behavior decreases. This is referred to as moral hazard or charity hazard. Risky behavior includes not purchasing insurance, but also the creation of exposure and vulnerability to hazard such as living in a flood plain. Kousky et al. found a "crowding out" effect, where "receiving individual assistance grants decreases the average quantity of insurance purchased the following year by between $4000 and $5000.[24] The reduction we find is roughly 3% of the mean insurance coverage." Within the insurance industry moral hazard can be minimized through the use of deductibles, coinsurance, or exclusion from coverage.

From an economic perspective based upon expected utility theory,[i] governmental DFA distorts the free market, resulting in opportunities for moral hazard that would not otherwise exist. However, the free market has been shown to be ineffective; estimates are that the demand for disaster insurance is very low (typically around 10-20%), much lower than would be expected from a mathematical analysis of risk. As noted by Raschky and Weck-Hannemann, economic critiques of DFA include:

- There are "costs on society emerging from the inefficient allocation of governmental disaster relief."[25]
- There is "underinsurance of individuals as a result of anticipated governmental assistance—charity hazard.
    - One major problem of governmental relief is the allocative failure that prevents the financial resources from reaching those who suffered the greatest damage
    - victims have no incentive to reveal their preferences for disaster assistance to governmental agents."[26]
- "[A]s federal disaster assistance is available for free there are no prices to guide its allocation. In addition, Governmental agents have weaker incentives to carefully deal with their resources and to search for information where the disaster assistance is needed the most."[27]
- "Governmental disaster relief can also be subject to political concerns."[28]

Governments can address moral hazard by either making disaster insurance mandatory (such as exists for car insurance) or by not providing any governmental aid. Some countries, such as Spain and Switzerland, mandate the purchase of insurance.

In the U.S. Republicans made the argument that the $600 weekly COVID-29 relief benefit had the effect of incentivizing people not to go back to work.[29] Senator McConnell is quoted as saying "Unemployment is extremely important. And we need to make sure, for those who are not able to recover their jobs, unemployment is adequate … That is a different issue from whether we ought to pay people a bonus not

---

[i] This is a normative theory (of how people should make decisions) based upon unbiased estimates of probabilities and outcomes.

to go back to work. And so I think that was a mistake." This comment likely results in part from "reports of some businesses unable to find employees because of the booster (i.e., potential hires were making more money on unemployment than they would working a particular job)".[30] However, one study by Scott et al.[31] found that "workers with higher post-CARES replacement rates did not experience larger declines in employment or hours of work when the benefits expansion went into effect. They have also returned to their previous jobs over time at similar rates as others."

There is a paradox in how we manage disasters, which is that many of the strategies used to manage disaster risk in the short term can potentially have the result of increasing it in the long term. Moral hazard is one of these. This should not be taken as an argument to refrain from disaster relief, but rather to do it in such a way that moral hazard is minimized and that long-term disaster risk reduction goals are served, as well as short-term goals.

10.3.5   Ethical Justifications for DFA

One argument for DFA is that since funds are being redistributed (via the taxation system) to those in need, that society is improved overall. This is a utilitarian argument. However, if this approach is being taken one could ask why that aid should not being given to the neediest in society (such as the homeless or those living in poverty), which would result in a greater net benefit. This may be a false dichotomy, though (why not say that funds given to the arts should go to the homeless?); the question could also be framed as "Since we provide aid to well-off disaster victims, why don't we also provide more assistance to the homeless?"

Helping people and communities to survive has a broad social benefit, since those communities will again contribute to the larger social good once they have recovered. A good example is farmers. If a disaster puts farmers out of business, then an important commodity needed by society suffers. There is, therefore, a selfish argument for disaster aid (this is an example of ethical egoism – the ethic of serving oneself). DFA contributes to the resilience of society. The more, and stronger links that exist between people and communities the greater the social resilience, which ultimately benefits all. There is a large literature on resilience, but little or nothing has been written on how ethics ties into the creation of a resilient society. (There is some literature on faith-based organizations and social resilience.) It seems likely that the wider the definition of moral community and the greater the degree to which society engages in DFA (which also does not too greatly diminish the need for people and communities to be responsible for risk creation), the more resilient a society will become overall.

Helping those in need is certainly virtuous by most normative standards but is more relevant to the provision of charity than DFA since the former is voluntary and the latter is mandatory. There are many charitable organizations such as the Red Cross or faith-based groups that raise funds to help people and communities recover from disaster.

Is there a duty or obligation on the part of governments to assist disaster victims? President Grover Cleveland thought not, and during the 2012 presidential campaign in the U.S. Republican candidate Mitt Romney described DFA as immoral (see box below). This libertarian approach restricts the role of the state far more than currently exists in the western liberal democratic tradition, viewing DFA as an unfair intrusion into the liberties of the individual.

Moral Position on DFA by Mitt Romney[32]

The following exchange took place during a debate in 2011 during the 2012 presidential campaign:

> "Every time you have an occasion to take something from the federal government and send it back to the states, that's the right direction," Romney told debate moderator John King. "And if you can go even further, and send it back to the private sector, that's even better. Instead of thinking, in the federal budget, what we should cut, we should ask the opposite question, what should we keep?"

> When John King interrupted to clarify, "Including disaster relief?" Romney continued, "We cannot afford to do those things without jeopardizing the future for our kids. It is simply immoral, in my view, for us to continue to rack up larger and larger debts and pass them on to our kids, knowing full well that we'll all be dead and gone before it's paid off. It makes no sense at all."

The current set of values that support DFA, as well as having a utilitarian aspect, are based upon the notion of fairness. Traditional views of disaster viewed them as resulting from what economists call an *externality*, which refers to an unusual event outside the control of society. Fairness would then dictate that people have suffered due to events beyond their control and should therefore be helped to be restored to their previous state.

Student Exercise:

- Find an example of a disaster where, in your opinion, the state clearly has obligations to assist with recovery, and one where they clearly do not.

- Explain why.

More recent approaches to understanding disaster based upon a social constructionism view most of them as being caused by internal forces. This leads to quite a different ethic. If people suffer because of their own poor decisions then that is a fair consequence, and the argument that society does not have a duty or obligation to assist them is stronger. The question of who suffers is critical though; if there is a lack of agency on the part of the vulnerable, then the moral landscape shifts.

Context becomes critical. Consider the case of a municipality that zoned a flood plain for development, did not maintain flood defenses adequately, and did not provide information about flood risk to purchasers. Should a flood disaster be viewed as an externality, or not? In terms of the level of duties and obligations that should be embedded into the social contract between the state and its citizens, a range of scenarios exist.

10.4 Ethical Considerations in Pandemic Planning

"There have been as many plagues as wars in history; yet always plagues and wars take people equally by surprise."
Albert Camus, *The Plague*, 1947[33]

"Nobody knew there'd be a pandemic or an epidemic of this proportion. Nobody had ever seen anything like this before."
President Donald Trump, March 19, 2020[34]

"[T]he news about Spain's nursing homes has come as a particular shock. Soldiers who were sent to disinfect nursing homes had found people "completely abandoned, or even dead, in their beds."
Spain's Defense Secretary, Margarita Robles, March, 2020[35]

As I write this section in May 2021, we are still in the midst of the COVID-19 pandemic, though the end is in sight in Canada due to progress in vaccinations. This is not true for much of the rest of the world. We are seeing a host of ethical issues and dilemmas play out in real time, but none of them are new. A literature survey creates a strong sense of déjà vu.

When browsing media discussions of the pandemic, one of the striking features I found (in the North American media at least) is the lack of an historical perspective. Aside from the occasional reference to the 1918 Spanish flu little is said, but plagues are part of recorded human history from its earliest times. People and institutions are often not good at learning from the past (except perhaps from the recent past, and then only sometimes), but there is an argument that we have a moral duty to do so.

The History of the Peloponnesian War by Thucydides, 431 BC.[36]

[A] pestilence of such extent and mortality was nowhere remembered. Neither were the physicians at first of any service, ignorant as they were of the proper way to treat it, but they died themselves the most thickly, as they visited the sick most often; nor did any human art succeed any better. Supplications in the temples, divinations, and so forth were found equally futile, till the overwhelming nature of the disaster at last put a stop to them altogether.

Figure 10.6: Destruction of the Athenian army at Syracuse.[37]

The Decameron, written in the 14th century by Giovanni Boccaccio following an outbreak of the plague in Florence that killed around 60% of the population, provides advice on how to deal with pandemics. André Spicer notes,

> Boccaccio suggested you could save yourself by fleeing towns, surrounding yourself with pleasant company and telling amusing stories to keep spirits up. Through a mixture of social isolation and pleasant activities, it was possible to survive the worst days of an epidemic.[38]

"[F]or towards the latter end men's hearts were hardened, and death was so always before their eyes, that they did not so much concern themselves for the loss of their friends, expecting that themselves should be summoned the next hour."
Daniel Defoe, *A Journal of the Plague Year (1722)*[39]

Figure 10.7: Portrait of Daniel Defoe[40]

One study of pandemic policies in 2009 found "no instance of any ethical term as a result of this search."[41] Another study of U.S. state pandemic plans done in 2007 noted "the most striking finding was an absence of ethical language. Although some states acknowledged the need for ethical decision-making, very few prescribed how it should happen."[42] The 2005 report "Stand on Guard for Thee: Ethical Considerations in Preparedness Planning for Pandemic Influenza" emphasizes the importance of ethical planning:

> [P]eople are more likely to accept such decisions if the decision-making processes are reasonable, open and transparent, inclusive, responsive and accountable, and if reciprocal obligations are respected. Although these principles can sometimes be difficult to implement during a crisis, SARS showed there are costs from not having an agreed-upon ethical framework, including loss of trust, low morale, fear and misinformation. SARS taught the world that if ethical frameworks had been more widely used to guide decision-making, this would have increased trust and solidarity within and between health care organizations.[43]

Historically there are three to four global pandemics per century, although there are many more epidemics. Recent pandemics include the Spanish flu (H1N1, 1918-1919), Asian flu (H2N2, 1957-1958), Hong Kong flu (H3N2, 1968-1970), HIV (1981-present), Swine flu (H1N1, 2009-2010), SARS (Coronavirus, 2002-2003), Ebola (2014-2016), MERS (Coronavirus, 2015-present) and COVID-19 (2019-present). Death tolls are as high as 40-50 million for the Spanish flu. Fatality estimates can vary widely, but Table 10.1 shows estimates for epidemic and pandemic events in the 20th and 21st centuries where the number of deaths exceeds 1,000 (with the exception of SARS, which was included although the number of deaths attributed to it were under 1,000). The data is dominated by smallpox and the 1918-19 Spanish flu, illustrating that like other disaster data, pandemics are a fat-tailed problem. This means that from a risk perspective, a large proportion of cumulative impacts occur from rare events as opposed to near the mean, and thinking in terms of an "average" pandemic is not helpful at best and likely misleading.[44]

Figure 10.8: The Great Plague of London in 1665. The last major outbreak of the bubonic plague in England.[45]

Table 10.1: Deaths over 1,000 During the 20th and 21st Century from Pandemics.[46]

Death toll (estimate)	Location	Date	Event	Disease
> 800,000	Europe, Asia, Africa	1899–1923	Sixth cholera pandemic	Cholera
40,000	China	1910–1912	1910 China plague	Bubonic plague
1,500,000	Worldwide	1915–1926	1915 Encephalitis lethargica pandemic	Encephalitis lethargica
> 7,000	United States of America	1916		Poliomyelitis and Influenza A H1N1
17,000,000-100,000,000	Worldwide	1918–1920	Spanish flu (pandemic)	Influenza A virus subtype H1N1
				Spanish Flu Virus
1,845	United States of America	1946		Poliomyelitis
2,720	United States of America	1949		Poliomyelitis
3,145	United States of America	1952		Poliomyelitis
2,000,000	Worldwide	1957–1958	Asian flu	Influenza A virus subtype H2N2
500,000,000	Worldwide	1877–1977		Smallpox
1,000,000	Worldwide	1968–1969	Hong Kong flu	Influenza A virus subtype H3N2
> 32,000,000	Worldwide	1960–present (as of 2010)	HIV/AIDS pandemic	HIV/AIDS
1,027	United States	1972–1973	London flu	Influenza A virus subtype H3N2
15,000	India	1974	1974 smallpox epidemic of India	Smallpox

Death toll (estimate)	Location	Date	Event	Disease
774	Worldwide	2002–2004	2002–2004 SARS outbreak	Severe acute respiratory syndrome (SARS)
4,293	Zimbabwe	2008–2009	2008–2009 Zimbabwean cholera outbreak	Cholera
10,075 (May 2017)	Hispaniola	2010–present	Haiti cholera outbreak	Cholera (strain serogroup O1, serotype Ogawa)
> 4,500 (February 2014)	Democratic Republic of the Congo	2011–present		Measles
>> 11,300	Worldwide, primarily concentrated in Guinea, Liberia, Sierra Leone	2013–2016	Ebola virus epidemic in West Africa	Ebola virus disease
				Ebola virus virion
2,035	India	2015	2015 Indian swine flu outbreak	Influenza A virus subtype H1N1
3,886 (as of 30 November 2019)	Yemen	2016–present	2016–20 Yemen cholera outbreak	Cholera
> 5,000 (as of November 2019)	Democratic Republic of the Congo	2019–present	2019 measles outbreak in the Democratic Republic of the Congo	Measles
83	Samoa	2019–present	2019 Samoa measles outbreak	Measles
> 2,000	Asia-Pacific, Latin America	2019–present	2019-20 dengue fever epidemic	Dengue fever

Pandemics are different from many other disasters in that they have the potential to be global. In this sense they require an approach that is more communitarian. Managing disease vectors require a cooperative approach.

The Centre for Disease Control identifies the following general ethical considerations during a pandemic:

- "Identification of clear planning goals
- Commitment to transparency
- Public engagement and involvement
- Maximizing of preparedness
- Sound guidelines based on best available scientific evidence
- Global involvement and cooperation
- Balancing of individual liberty and community interest
- Diversity in ethical decision making
- Fair process (procedural justice)"[47]

The main ethical issues/dilemmas in planning for and managing a pandemic, which will be discussed in this chapter, are as follows:

1. The duty or obligation of health care workers (HCW) to provide care during a communicable disease outbreak.
2. The degree to which individual liberties can or should be restricted in order to serve the greater good.
3. The way in which scarce resources should be allocated, both nationally and internationally.
4. Health impacts versus economic impacts.
5. Risk communication, including how much information should be made available to the public.

A summary of ethical considerations from the University of Toronto Joint Centre for Bioethics Pandemic Influenza Working Group and the Bellagio Statement of Principles on Social Justice and Influenza can be found in Appendix 10.2.

10.4.1   Duty of Health Care Workers to Provide Care

From a utilitarian perspective it makes sense for health care workers (HCW) to provide care, since the number of people they will help is large compared to the number of HCWs. This may, however, involve a significant degree of self-sacrifice since it exposes them and their families to infection. An example of this is that about 500 New York City Fire Department responders became infected with COVID-19 by early April 2020, around a quarter of their workforce.[48] There is also the issue that if they are ill, they cannot care for others. From a deontological ethic, HCWs owe an obligation to their clients and patients, but they also have a duty to their families. As well, they have the right not to take unreasonable risks with respect to their own health. What can be considered "unreasonable" in these circumstances?

Opinion 9.067 - Physician Obligation in Disaster Preparedness and Response of the American Medical Association Code of Medical Ethics' Opinion on Physician Duty to Treat, says:

> "National, regional, and local responses to epidemics, terrorist attacks, and other disasters require extensive involvement of physicians. Because of their commitment to care for the sick and injured, individual physicians have an obligation to provide urgent medical care during disasters. This ethical obligation holds even in the face of greater than usual risks to their own safety, health or life. The physician workforce, however, is not an unlimited resource; therefore, when participating in disaster responses, physicians should balance immediate benefits to individual patients with ability to care for patients in the future."[49]

Legislation exists in many places that can require HCW to perform their duties. Though in Canada "[t]here is limited case law, literature and legislation on a physician's legal duty of care during a pandemic," many provinces have enacted legislation that grants special powers during a disaster that "[a]uthorize or require any person to render assistance of a type that the person is qualified to provide or that otherwise is or may be required to prevent, respond to or alleviate the effects of an emergency or disaster."[50] In the U.S., recommendations of the Model State Emergency Health Powers Act grant similar powers and have been adopted by most states. Critiques of these Acts argue that they create the potential for abuse by overly restricting the rights of individuals.

One of the arguments for performance of duty during pandemics is that upon entering the health care profession, people knowingly and willingly undertook the risks associated with it, that they have special skills not present elsewhere that are critical and essential, and therefore a social contract exists that they should accept high risks. But is that true for all levels of risk, no matter how high? There are also arguments that requiring such care in very high-risk environments exceeds what is reasonable.[51]

One study of general practitioners (GP) in Australia found a general willingness to provide treatment during a pandemic, but that it depended in part upon "the need for timely communication, for greater training, for appropriate guidelines and protocols, for clear role delineation in outbreak response and provision of specialized equipment and vaccination."[52] Comments by those surveyed include:

- "I wouldn't be much of a human being if I closed up shop and headed for the hills." (GP 14)
- "Who would take care of my patients if I wasn't there for them?" (GP 1)
- "I will take care of patients because that is what I signed up to do." (GP 47)
- "I have kids and won't endanger myself otherwise who will take care of them. If there is no gear then I definitely won't work." (GP32)
- "I remember masks ran out with SARS where I worked. I kept working anyway." (GP 2)

During COVD-19 heroic efforts are being made by many HCWs, but there are anecdotal reports of role abandonment. In California "[m]ore than 80 patients were [...] evacuated from a nursing home in [Riverside ...] after employees of the facility 'did not show up to care for sick patients two days in a row.'"[53] Also, in Spain, "Spanish soldiers who were sent to disinfect nursing homes found people 'completely abandoned, or even dead, in their beds.'"[54] The COVID-19 pandemic creates high risk for caretakers that impacts their willingness to work. For example, in Pinecrest Nursing Home in Bobcaygeon, Ontario, Canada, as of April 9, 2020, not only had 30 residents died, but 28 staff had tested positive for COVID-19.[55] In Italy it has been reported that HCWs comprise 9% of COVID-19 cases, an extremely high percentage.[56] There are numerous anecdotal reports of general practitioners restricting their practice to phone and video interactions.

If there is a social contract between HCW (and the institutions that employ them) and society, then there is a reciprocal obligation to provide HCW with sufficient resources and the personal protective equipment (PPE) they need to do their job as safely as possible. The COVID-19 pandemic has clearly shown that this reciprocal obligation has generally not been met because of insufficient disaster preparedness on the part of governments and health care institutions. Stockpiles of basic PPE such as masks and gowns were insufficient to meet the short-term need in the early phases of the pandemic. This deficit weakens arguments related to the obligations of HCWs to perform their duties. That the vast majority of them continue to serve in high-risk environments speaks volumes to their character. It is in virtue ethics (e.g., beneficence, altruism, and empathy) and ethics of care that much of the motivation exists for HCW to continue to care for their patients.

10.4.2   Restriction of Individual Liberties

ORDERS CONCEIVED AND PUBLISHED BY THE LORD MAYOR AND ALDERMEN OF THE CITY OF LONDON CONCERNING THE INFECTION OF THE PLAGUE, 1665.

As soon as any man shall be found by this examiner, chirurgeon, or searcher to be sick of the plague, he shall the same night be sequestered in the same house; and in case he be so sequestered, then though he afterwards die not, the house wherein he sickened should be shut up for a month, after the use of the due preservatives taken by the rest.

If any person shall have visited any man known to be infected of the plague, or entered willingly into any known infected house, being not allowed, the house wherein he inhabiteth shall be shut up for certain days by the examiner's direction.

That all plays, bear-baitings, games, singing of ballads, buckler-play, or such-like causes of assemblies of people be utterly prohibited, and the parties offending severely punished by every alderman in his ward.

Daniel Defoe, *A Journal of a Plague Year*[57]

Many of the public health tools used to fight pandemics restrict personal liberties. One of Rawls' principles is that total liberty be maximized, with the constraint that the liberties of people not infringe upon the liberties of others. During a pandemic people have the right not to be infected by others due to negligent actions, and therefore this principle supports a shift towards less personal liberty for the greater good; thus, the justification for self-isolation, quarantine, social distancing, wearing face masks, and the closing of public spaces.

There are important ethical issues related to equity and the use of power. Where liberties are restricted it should be done as fairly as possible, and individual human rights need to be respected. Those rights, though, include the right not to be infected by carriers who roam freely. It is a balancing act.[58]

These policies are for the common good, but also are of benefit to those who are restricted. They are often done on a voluntary basis, but most states have the authority to mandate them under emergency management legislation. For example, upon the Declaration of a Public Welfare Emergency, the Government of Canada has the authority under the Emergencies Act to:

> [M]ake such orders or regulations with respect to the following matters as the Governor in Council believes, on reasonable grounds, are necessary for dealing with the emergency:
>
> > (a) the regulation or prohibition of travel to, from or within any specified area, where necessary for the protection of the health or safety of individuals;
> >
> > (b) the evacuation of persons and the removal of personal property from any specified area and the making of arrangements for the adequate care and protection of the persons and property;
> >
> > (c) the requisition, use or disposition of property;
> >
> > (d) the authorization of or direction to any person, or any person of a class of persons, to render essential services of a type that that person, or a person of that class, is competent to provide and the provision of reasonable compensation in respect of services so rendered;
> >
> > (e) the regulation of the distribution and availability of essential goods, services and resources;
> >
> > (f) the authorization and making of emergency payments;
> >
> > (g) the establishment of emergency shelters and hospitals;
> >
> > (h) the assessment of damage to any works or undertakings and the repair, replacement or restoration thereof;
> >
> > (i) the assessment of damage to the environment and the elimination or alleviation of the damage; and
> >
> > (j) the imposition:

(i) on summary conviction, of a fine not exceeding five hundred dollars or imprisonment not exceeding six months or both that fine and imprisonment, or

(ii) on indictment, of a fine not exceeding five thousand dollars or imprisonment not exceeding five years or both that fine and imprisonment, for contravention of any order or regulation made under this section.[59]

The argument for increased government control is that pandemics require a shift (depending upon the country and culture) from an individualist ethic to a communitarian ethic that emphasizes egalitarianism, equity and social justice, and a transfer of power to the state. Such measures should be used carefully so that they do not create unintended consequences. For example,

> extreme heavy-handed tactics, such as use of the military to enforce quarantine, are likely to destabilise a community by creating panic, causing people to flee and spread disease. This occurred in China where a rumour that all of Beijing would be quarantined during the SARS epidemic led to 250,000 people fleeing the city overnight.[60]

There is also a high economic and social price to be paid for the widespread use of self-isolation and the closing of public and private spaces that includes the loss of important personal, social and professional connections, and livelihoods. Different countries, provinces and states have taken different approaches to dealing with individual liberties. Sweden did not take the more extreme measures to limit social distancing that has happened in many other countries.[61] A comparison of the death rate per million people (Figure 10.9) shows worse outcomes than many other countries, especially the neighboring ones of Denmark, Finland and Norway. The data appears to indicate that stronger public health enforcement measures results in fewer fatalities.

Even within the U.S., various states have taken different approaches. "Arkansas Governor Asa Hutchinson said at a news conference on March 16, 2020 that restaurants can remain open 'on their own choosing and based upon market demand,'" while "Connecticut Governor Ned Lamont, in a joint statement with the governors of New York and New Jersey, announced that bars, restaurants and cinemas will close on March 16." [62] In Florida, "the stay-at-home executive order Florida Gov. Ron DeSantis issued... doesn't bar churches from holding services."[63]

Pandemics do not affect all equally. Some are more vulnerable to disease (usually including the elderly and those with underlying medical issues) or have lesser access to good levels of health care. The poor and disadvantaged always suffer more. Fatality rates from the 1918 Spanish Flu ranged from about 0.3% in Australia to over 4% in India. Even larger ranges are evident if smaller scales are looked at.[64] In the 2020/21 COVID-19 pandemic nursing homes in Canada were particularly hard hit, accounting for 69% of all COVID-19 related fatalities during the first 2 waves from March 1, 2020 to February 15, 2021.[65]

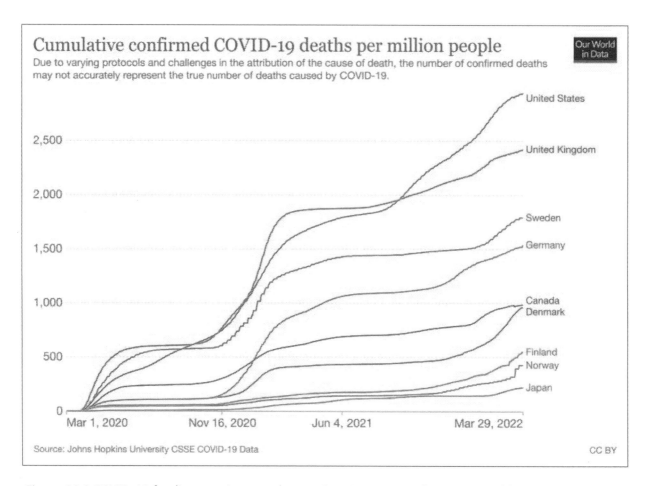

Figure 10.9 COVID-19 fatality rates in several countries. Countries with stronger public health measures tend to have fewer fatalities.

Many of those who accept liberty restrictions or economic hardship are not in the highly vulnerable group. Should they be compensated for their self-sacrifice? Reciprocity and compensatory justice principles suggest that they should be. In this light, but also because of a need to minimize economic impacts due to self-interest, many countries provide aid packages to people, companies and state entities during and following pandemics. In 2020/21, the aid packages being put together by various governments are substantial. As a share of GDP for G20 countries, as of March 31, 2021, the packages ranged from 1.9% for Mexico to 54.5% for Japan. Canada's package was 19% and the U.S. was 26%.[66]

It is clear that stronger public health measures result in fewer infections and fatalities (Figure 10.10). Those who refuse to follow them using an argument of individual rights and freedoms face a very strong counter argument in terms of how their behaviors impact others, who also have a right to not be infected.

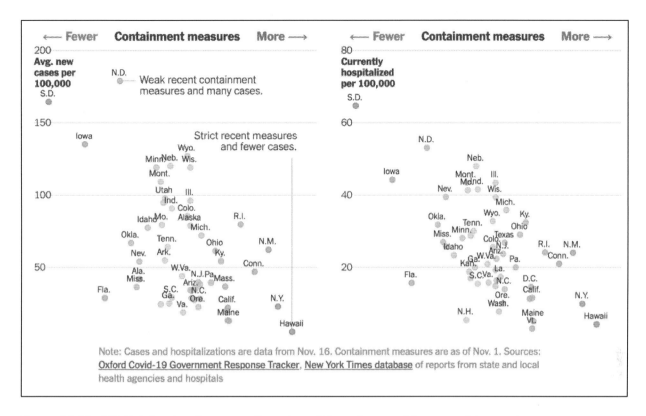

Figure 10.10. COVID Infection Rates as a Function of Containment Measures. More strict measures are highly correlated with lower infection rates and hospitalizations.

10.4.3 Allocation of Scarce Resources

In a pandemic it is likely that there will not be enough resources to meet the health needs of population or the professional needs of health care workers. This could include the number of beds in intensive care units (ICUs), personal protective equipment, and human resources. As well, developing a vaccine could take a year or longer and would initially be in short supply. This results in very difficult decisions: who should be a priority, and who should make the decisions regarding who gets what when? Lifeboat ethics (Chapter 9) is relevant to this discussion.

One set of arguments relates to health care workers and first responders being the first priority. From a utilitarian perspective they are needed to treat the sick, so keeping them healthy would benefit all of society. Since they are also the group that often suffers one of the highest rates of infections (e.g., during SARS and COVID-19) as a result of their working to save others, reciprocity suggests that they receive priority. Society has a duty to help those who self-sacrifice for the greater good. As well, if HCWs know that they are first in line for prevention, mitigation, and treatment, they may be less likely to abandon their roles because of fear of contracting the illness themselves or infecting their loved ones. Thus, there is an element of self-interest in prioritizing HCWs, as well as many other essential care workers.

Another approach to allocation is based upon equality, that all be given equal access to health care. But, should the more vulnerable be given priority over those more likely to recover? Giving the greatest benefit to the least advantaged (as per Rawls) may not result in saving as many lives as possible, especially when success rates for ventilation are low. According to one preliminary study, "[m]ortality could be as high as two thirds among patients with COVID-19 who require ventilation."[67] In some cases patients who are on ventilators will have a poorer chance of surviving than incoming patients who need them. Should they be taken off ventilators so that the machines can be reallocated to others that have a greater chance of success?

The strategy of "first come first served" can work well when there is not a shortage, but it is generally considered an immoral strategy when resources are scarce. Triage is fundamentally a utilitarian approach. In 2010 the European Society of Intensive Care Medicine's task force for ICU Triage during an Influenza Epidemic or Mass Disaster recommended that the triage process be "objective, ethical, transparent and equitably applied." but did not choose between "first come first served" or "greatest benefit."[68] I suggest that there are strong ethical arguments that triage should be used where those who are most likely to have the greatest benefit are given priority over others and that "first come first served" is not appropriate.

 Is it equitable for the elderly to have the same access to health care as children? A "fair innings" approach would use Quality Adjusted Life Years (Chapter 9) as a factor, giving priority to younger people. One can believe that all lives are of equal value but still differentiate between who to save based upon the potential benefit a patient would likely get from treatment (e.g., a longer life).

If one believes that some lives are more valuable than others (a humanitarian, for example, as compared to a murderer), then there is an ethical argument to save the more virtuous before the less virtuous. Who is more virtuous, however, will often be subject to contentious debate! The potential for abuse is enormous, and it is not clear (especially in an emergency situation) who should have the power to make such decisions. In my opinion saving lives based upon relative worth, though theoretically appealing to some, suffers from serious procedural issues that makes it unworkable.

Prioritization of Influenza Vaccine:

In terms of vaccination, the U.S. Department of Health and Services recommends the following for the prioritization of pandemic influenza vaccine:
   "Tier 1A: Health-care workers
- Health-care workers with direct patient contact and critical health-care support staff
- Vaccine and antiviral manufacturing personnel

Tier 1B: Highest-risk groups
- Patients 65 and older with at least one high-risk condition
- Patients 6 months to 64 years with at least two high-risk conditions
- Patients hospitalized in the past year because of pneumonia, influenza, or other high-risk condition

---

Tier 1C: Household contacts and pregnancy
- Household contacts of children under 6 months
- Household contacts of severely immunocompromised individuals
- Pregnant women

Tier 1D: Pandemic responders
- Key government leaders and critical pandemic public health responders

Tier 2A Other high-risk groups
- Patients 65 and older with no high-risk conditions
- Patients 6 months to 64 years with one high-risk condition
- Children 6 months to 23 months

Tier 2B: Critical infrastructure groups
- Other public health emergency responders, public safety workers, utility workers, critical transportation workers, and telecommunications workers

Tier 3:
- Other key government health-care decision makers
- Individuals providing mortuary services

Tier 4:
- Healthy patients 2 to 64 years without any high-risk conditions"[69]

Whatever process is used to allocate scarce resources it should be procedurally ethical. Standards and processes should reflect a broad social discourse that has transparency, be as objective as possible, and incorporates the views of all stakeholders. During a disaster is not the time for such discussions; they should take place during times of reflective quiet and become embedded into the emergency planning process.

10.4.4 Health Versus the Economy

"I had two important things before me: the one was the carrying on my business and shop, which was considerable, and in which was embarked all my effects in the world; and the other was the preservation of my life in so dismal a calamity as I saw apparently was coming upon the whole city, and which, however great it was, my fears perhaps, as well as other people's, represented to be much greater than it could be."[70]

Daniel Defoe, *A Journal of the Plague Year, 1665*

On April 15,2020 there was a rally in Michigan to protest the extended "stay at home" order by the state governor. Initially planned for a couple of hours with people staying in their cars, it lasted about eight hours and included a large number of people on foot in public spaces, many of whom were not wearing protective masks and did not maintain a social distance of two meters. One protester was quoted as saying, "This arbitrary blanket spread of shutting down businesses, about putting all of these workers out of business, is just a disaster. It's an economic disaster for Michigan [...] and people are sick and tired of it."[71] The "Freedom Convoys" in Canada and other countries were also a demonstration of libertarianism in opposition to public health measures.

Protests against public health measures to reduce the spread of the pandemic have continued, not just within civil society but also from mainly far right politicians.[72] There is a legitimate moral discussion to be had regarding the extent to which society closes down to reduce the spread of COVID, but partisan politics, tribalism and cultural wars have also led to Machiavellian framing in order to promote personal and special interests.[73]

The framing of this issue during the protest was one of protecting health versus protecting the economy. Both are crucial to people and therefore this is a classical ethical dilemma. And it is not just about wealth; people lose their livelihoods and their security.

It is also a question of degree. There are many levels of intervention available to the government in terms of mandating protective measures. As measures increasingly interfere with personal freedom and the ability of people to earn income, they become unpalatable, especially if the risk perception of a person is that they are relatively safe.

There is no question but that policies in place to combat the pandemic have serious economic impacts and taking away people's livelihoods. Some analyses suggest a slow recovery or an extended recession at a global level because of the reductions in production, trade, etc.[74]

A utilitarian analysis would have to balance the economy with people's health. To do this a value would have to be assigned to life (Chapter 9), a very difficult and complex task for which there would probably not be widespread agreement. An emphasis upon the economy does not benefit the most vulnerable to infection in society (in fact, it may do the opposite), so violates one of the principles of utilitarian ethical theory.

People have a right to life. They also have a right to have a livelihood.

Student Exercise:
- How would you balance right to life versus right to livelihoods?

However, the above may not be a valid frame. A pandemic without non-pharmaceutical interventions (NPI) also negatively affects the economy. According to one study of the 1918 pandemic looking at U.S. data,

> cities that intervened earlier and more aggressively do not perform worse and, if anything, grow faster after the pandemic is over. Our findings thus indicate that NPIs

not only lower mortality; they also mitigate the adverse economic consequences of a pandemic.[75]

The authors of this study suggest that these findings may be transferable to the COVID-19 pandemic, noting

> Anecdotal evidence suggests that our results have parallels in the COVID-19 outbreak. Countries that implemented early NPIs such as Taiwan and Singapore have not only limited infection growth. They also appear to have mitigated the worst economic disruption caused by the pandemic. Well-calibrated early and forceful NPIs should therefore not be seen as having major economic costs in a pandemic.[76]

Society makes many tradeoffs between the economy and health. Examples include the level of support for Medicare programs compared to economic incentives for the private sector. There are situations, however, where such a framing may be inappropriate and result in erroneous analyses. It is very possible that this is such a scenario.

10.4.5 Risk Communication

"Truth never damages a cause that is just."
Mahatma Gandhi

"In war, the first casualty is truth."
Terry Hayes, *I Am Pilgrim*

The main ethical issue in public risk communication is to what extent should governments and institutions be truthful. It has often been the case that the truth has been withheld because of a belief that the public would panic, or otherwise not respond well to accurately knowing their risks, and that they would be better served by withholding information. This is a utilitarian perspective. From a deontological perspective, lying is considered to be morally wrong and people have the right to hear the truth.

Eric Klinenberg refers to the initial tendency of institutions to be untruthful when faced with crisis as "deny, deflect, defend."[77] This pattern of behavior has been documented, for example, in the European and Chicago heat waves of 2003 and 1995. It also can be seen in the initial response of China and the U.S. to the COVID-19 pandemic.

We all lie at times, for a variety of reasons. Often it is because of self-interest, but it may also be for morally justifiable reasons such as to prevent harm. The question that needs to be addressed, with respect to pandemic risk communication, is whether withholding information from the public would result in a greater good. Given that the media and the public process such information in ways that can either diminish or exacerbate threats, this is a valid question. Below is an example of withholding information during the Spanish flu pandemic. Do you agree with this decision?

> Adviser Walter Lippman [...] sent President Woodrow Wilson a memo saying that most citizens were "mentally children" and advising that "self-determination" had to be subordinated to "order" and "prosperity". In 1917, the day after receiving Lippman's memo, Wilson issued an executive order to control all government communication strategy during the war that was premised on keeping up morale. As a result, when the full-blown and lethal pandemic wave arrived in the United States in September 1918, Wilson never made a single statement about it, and lesser public figures provided only reassurance.[78]

There is a larger issue of trust that is relevant. Trust is lost when people are lied to or misinformed, and without trust there is a loss of moral authority. When authorities cannot be trusted, people will not be compliant and will turn to other sources of information that may not be reliable. This makes voluntary public health measures far more difficult to be accepted and mandatory measures more likely to be violated.

The excerpt below,[79] from an article by Professor John Barry in the New York Times (based upon an article published in Nature[80]), emphasizes the benefits of truth-telling to the public.

Excerpt from The Single Most Important Lesson from the 1918 Influenza" by John Barry.[81]

"[T]he hope was that if most people followed most of the advice most of the time, the interventions could significantly reduce the spread of the disease, or 'flatten the curve,' a phrase now all too familiar.

[...]

Assuming suppression fails, we must initiate aggressive mitigation, where communities try to lessen the impact of the disease. The crucial statistic from China is that the case fatality rate inside Wuhan is 5.8 percent but only 0.7 percent in other areas in China, an eightfold difference — explained by an overwhelmed health care system. That illustrates why flattening the curve matters; lessening stress on the health care system, especially the availability of intensive care beds, saves lives.

Saying that is easier than doing it. The difficulties lie in timing and compliance. Analysis of when cities in 1918 closed schools, saloons and theaters; banned public events; urged social distancing and the like demonstrated that intervening early, before a virus spreads throughout the community, did flatten the curve.

[...]

But this raises another issue: compliance. [...] The Army surgeon general demanded 'influenza be kept out' of the basic-training camps, where new soldiers were being prepared to fight in World War I. [...] He barred civilians from the camps and ordered that soldiers entering them be quarantined, soldiers showing symptoms be isolated and whole units quarantined if several soldiers were ill. Of 120 camps, 99 imposed those measures.

But an Army study found no difference in morbidity and mortality between camps that did and did not follow orders, because over time most became sloppy. Further investigation found that only a tiny

---

number of camps rigidly enforced measures.

For interventions to work, people have to comply and they have to sustain that compliance; most of that depends on voluntary efforts and individual behavior. Army camps in wartime failed to sustain compliance, so it will be an enormous challenge for civilian communities in peacetime to do so. At the height of the H1N1 outbreak, Mexico City urged mask usage on public transit and distributed free masks. Usage peaked at 65 percent; 10 days later it was at 10 percent.

[…]

In 1918 many cities imposed restrictions, lifted them too soon, then reimposed them. […] [I]f the public is going to comply over time, they will have to be led, inspired or compelled.

That brings us back to the most important lesson of 1918, one that all the working groups on pandemic planning agreed upon: Tell the truth (emphasis added). That instruction is built into the federal pandemic preparedness plans and the plan for every state and territory.

In 1918, pressured to maintain wartime morale, neither national nor local government officials told the truth. The disease was called 'Spanish flu,' and one national public-health leader said, 'This is ordinary influenza by another name.' Most local health commissioners followed that lead. Newspapers echoed them. After Philadelphia began digging mass graves; closed schools, saloons and theaters; and banned public gatherings, one newspaper even wrote: 'This is not a public health measure. There is no cause for alarm.'

Trust in authority disintegrated, and at its core, society is based on trust. Not knowing whom or what to believe, people also lost trust in one another. They became alienated, isolated. Intimacy was destroyed. 'You had no school life, you had no church life, you had nothing,' a survivor recalled. 'People were afraid to kiss one another, people were afraid to eat with one another.' Some people actually starved to death because no one would deliver food to them.

[…]

The few places where leadership told the truth had a different experience. In San Francisco, the mayor and business, labor and medical leaders jointly signed a full-page ad that read in huge all-caps type, 'Wear a Mask and Save Your Life.' They didn't know that masks offered little protection, but they did know they trusted the public. The community feared but came together. "

Though there may be times when the public good is served by the withholding of information (such as due to security concerns during war), evidence suggests that during pandemics a policy of openness and honesty is the most effective one.

10.5   Further Reading

If you are interested in further reading, beyond what I can cover in this short review I recommend the following articles:

- Upshur, R., Faith, K., Gibson, J., Thompson, A., Tracy, C., Wilson, K., & Singer, P. (2005). Stand on guard for thee: Ethical considerations for preparedness planning for pandemic influenza. *A*

Report of the University of Toronto Joint Centre for Bioethics Pandemic Influenza Working Group. http://www.jcb.utoronto.ca/people/documents/upshur_stand_guard.pdf

- Mack, A., Choffnes, E. R., Sparling, P. F., Hamburg, M. A., & Lemon, S. M. (Eds.). (2007). *Ethical and legal considerations in mitigating pandemic disease: Workshop summary.* National Academies Press.

- Berkman, B. E. (2009). Incorporating explicit ethical reasoning into pandemic influenza policies. *The Journal of Contemporary Health Law and Policy, 26*(1), 1.

Appendix 10.1:   Summary of Ethical Considerations from the University of Toronto Joint Centre for Bioethics Pandemic Influenza Working Group[82]

Ten substantive values to guide ethical decision-making for a pandemic influenza outbreak

Substantive value	Description
Individual liberty	In a public health crisis, restrictions to individual liberty may be necessary to protect the public from serious harm. Restrictions to individual liberty should: • be proportional, necessary, and relevant; • employ the least restrictive means; and • be applied equitably.
Protection of the public from harm	To protect the public from harm, health care organizations and public health authorities may be required to take actions that impinge on individual liberty. Decision makers should: • weigh the imperative for compliance; • provide reasons for public health measures to encourage compliance; and • establish mechanisms to review decisions.
Proportionality	Proportionality requires that restrictions to individual liberty and measures taken to protect the public from harm should not exceed what is necessary to address the actual level of risk to or critical needs of the community.
Privacy	Individuals have a right to privacy in health care. In a public health crisis, it may be necessary to override this right to protect the public from

Substantive value	Description
	serious harm.
Duty to provide care	Inherent to all codes of ethics for health care professionals is the duty to provide care and to respond to suffering. Health care providers will have to weigh demands of their professional roles against other competing obligations to their own health, and to family and friends. Moreover, health care workers will face significant challenges related to resource allocation, scope of practice, professional liability, and workplace conditions.
Reciprocity	Reciprocity requires that society support those who face a disproportionate burden in protecting the public good, and take steps to minimize burdens as much as possible. Measures to protect the public good are likely to impose a disproportionate burden on health care workers, patients, and their families.
Equity	All patients have an equal claim to receive the health care they need under normal conditions. During a pandemic, difficult decisions will need to be made about which health services to maintain and which to defer. Depending on the severity of the health crisis, this could curtail not only elective surgeries, but could also limit the provision of emergency or necessary services.
Trust	Trust is an essential component of the relationships among clinicians and patients, staff and their organizations, the public and health care providers or organizations, and among organizations within a health system. Decision makers will be confronted with the challenge of maintaining stakeholder trust while simultaneously implementing various control measures during an evolving health crisis. Trust is enhanced by upholding such process values as transparency.
Solidarity	As the world learned from SARS, a pandemic influenza outbreak, will require a new vision of global solidarity and a vision of solidarity among nations. A pandemic can challenge conventional ideas of national sovereignty, security or territoriality. It also requires solidarity within and among health care institutions. It calls for collaborative approaches that set aside traditional values of self-interest or territoriality among health care professionals, services, or institutions.

Substantive value	Description
Stewardship	Those entrusted with governance roles should be guided by the notion of stewardship. Inherent in stewardship are the notions of trust, ethical behavior, and good decision-making. This implies that decisions regarding resources are intended to achieve the best patient health and public health outcomes given the unique circumstances of the influenza crisis.

Five procedural values to guide ethical decision-making for a pandemic influenza outbreak

Procedural value	Description
Reasonable	Decisions should be based on reasons (i.e., evidence, principles, and values) that stakeholders can agree are relevant to meeting health needs in a pandemic influenza crisis. The decisions should be made by people who are credible and accountable.
Open and transparent	The process by which decisions are made must be open to scrutiny, and the basis upon which decisions are made should be publicly accessible.
Inclusive	Decisions should be made explicitly with stakeholder views in mind, and there should be opportunities to engage stakeholders in the decision-making process.
Responsive	There should be opportunities to revisit and revise decisions as new information emerges throughout the crisis. There should be mechanisms to address disputes and complaints.
Accountable	There should be mechanisms in place to ensure that decision makers are answerable for their actions and inactions. Defense of actions and inactions should be grounded in the 14 other ethical values proposed above.

Appendix 10.2: Bellagio Statement of Principles on Social Justice and Influenza[83]

PREAMBLE

Socially and economically disadvantaged groups and individuals are almost always the worst affected by epidemics. Too often, they have little voice in making and implementing policy responses to health emergencies – responses which, in turn, commonly neglect the needs and rights of the disadvantaged.

Consideration for the interests of the disadvantaged is important for practical as well as ethical reasons: public health efforts are more likely to succeed in an atmosphere of social solidarity and public trust, including the trust of disadvantaged people. Avian and human pandemic influenza planning and response should therefore not only be based on sound science and public health principles, but should also respect and give particular attention to the needs and rights of the disadvantaged, and include processes through which their preferences and interests can be articulated and incorporated. The following principles aim to help governments and intergovernmental and nongovernmental organizations take account of the interests of the disadvantaged in avian and pandemic influenza planning and response. "Checklists" of the type attached to this statement provide a ready means of ensuring that this occurs. These principles do not exhaust all relevant technical and moral considerations but focus rather on those with the most salience for the needs and rights of disadvantaged peoples.

PRINCIPLES

I. All people should have ready access to accurate, up-to-date and easily understood information about avian and human pandemic influenza, public policy responses, and appropriate local and individual actions. Communications should be tailored to overcome obstacles that disadvantaged groups face in accessing such information.

II. Veterinary and public health strategies should foster wide engagement in planning for and responding to the avian and pandemic influenza threat. Civil society, religious groups and the private sector should be involved in helping to overcome barriers to effective engagement by disadvantaged groups.

III. Planning and response should facilitate public involvement in surveillance and reporting of possible cases without fear of discrimination, reprisal or uncompensated loss of livelihood. Recognizing their vulnerability, special efforts are needed to foster reporting by disadvantaged groups, as well as to protect them from negative impacts which could worsen their situation.

IV. The impact and effectiveness of interventions and policies need to be evaluated and monitored, especially with respect to prospects for providing fair benefits to, and avoiding undue burdens on, disadvantaged groups, so that corrective adjustments can be made in a timely manner.

V.	Developing as well as developed countries should have access to the best available scientific and socio-economic data and analyses to inform avian and pandemic influenza planning and response, including information on the particular burdens and secondary harms that a pandemic and pandemic responses may inflict on disadvantaged groups.

VI.	National and international efforts are needed to promote equitable access to vaccines, antivirals and other appropriate public health and social interventions, both between and within countries, so as to provide fair and non-discriminatory treatment for traditionally disadvantaged groups as well as those who are specially disadvantaged in the context of avian and human influenza.

10.6   Endnotes

[1] Puleo, M. (2018). *The history of price gouging amid US disasters and how different states fight against it*, Yahoo news, https://news.yahoo.com/history-price-gouging-amid-us-135800725.html

[2] Zwolinski, M. (2009). Dialogue on price gouging: Price gouging, non-worseness, and distributive justice. *Business Ethics Quarterly, 19*(2), 295-306.

[3] Steckbeck, M. (2017, September 6). *How price gouging helped my family during a storm.* FEE. https://fee.org/articles/how-price-gouging-helped-my-family-during-a-storm/

[4] Giberson, M. (2012). *List of State Anti-Price Gouging Laws*, Knowledge Problem, https://knowledgeproblem.com/2012/11/03/list-of-price-gouging-laws/

[5] Snyder, J. (2009). What's the matter with price gouging? *Business Ethics Quarterly, 19*(2), 275-293.

[6] Steckbeck, M. (2017). How Price Gouging Helped My Family during a Storm, Foundation for Economic Education https://fee.org/articles/how-price-gouging-helped-my-family-during-a-storm/

[7] Zack, N. (2009). *Ethics for disaster*. Rowman & Littlefield Publishers Inc.

[8] Zack, N. (2009). *Ethics for disaster*. Rowman & Littlefield Publishers Inc.

[9] United Nations. (1948). *Universal declaration of human rights.* http://www.un.org/en/documents/udhr/index.shtml

[10] Munger, M. (2007, January 8). They clapped: Can price gouging laws prohibit scarcity? *The Library of Economics and Liberty.* http://www.econlib.org/library/Columns/y2007/Mungergouging.html

[11] Lee, D. R. (2015). Making the case against "price gouging" laws: A challenge and an opportunity. *Independent Review, 19*(4), 583-598.

[12] United States. Congress. House, & John Davis Batchelder Collection (Library of Congress). (1898). *Journal of the House of Representatives of the United States* (Vol. 55, No. 2). US Government Printing Office.

[13] (ca. 1961-1986). [Portrait of Grover Cleveland] [Photograph]. U.S. National Archives and Record Administration. https://en.wikipedia.org/wiki/Grover_Cleveland#

[14] Federal Emergency Management Agency (FEMA). (2020). *Loss dollars paid by calendar year.* https://www.fema.gov/loss-dollars-paid-calendar-year

[15] FEMA. (n.d.) *FEMA.* www.fema.gov

[16] Stern, A. (2017, October 13). *Municipal credit and the path of federal natural disaster support.* Breckinridge Capital Advisors. https://www.breckinridge.com/insights/details/municipal-credit-and-the-path-of-federal-natural-disaster-support/

[17] Public Safety Canada. (2017). *2016-2017 Evaluation of the Disaster Financial Assistance Arrangements.* https://www.publicsafety.gc.ca/cnt/rsrcs/pblctns/vltn-dsstr-fnncl-ssstnc-2016-17/index-en.aspx

[18] Seneviratne, S. I., Nicholls, N., Easterling, D., Goodess, C. M., Kanae, S., Kossin, J., Luo, Y., Marengo, J. A., Mcinnes, K. L., Rahimi, M., Reichstein, M., Sorteberg, A., Vera, C., & Zhang, X. (2012). Changes in climate extremes and their impacts on the natural physical environment. In C. B. Field, V. Barros, T. F. Stocker, D. Qin, D. J. Dokken, K. L. Ebi, M. D. Mastrandrea, K. J. Mach, G.-K. Plattner, S. K. Allen, M. Tignor, and P.M. Midgley (Eds.), *Managing the risks of extreme events and disasters to advance climate change adaptation* (pp. 109-230). Cambridge University Press.

[19] U.S. Government Accountability Office. (2019). *National flood insurance program.* https://www.gao.gov/highrisk/national_flood_insurance/why_did_study#t=1

[20] Goes, A., & Skees, J. R. (2003). Financing natural disaster risk using charity contributions and ex ante index insurance. *2003 Annual Meeting, American Agricultural Economics Association.*

[21] FEMA. (2020). *National flood insurance program: Flood insurance manual.* https://www.fema.gov/media-library/assets/documents/186514

[22] FEMA. (2019). *"Substantial damage" triggers flood mitigation requirements.* https://www.fema.gov/news-release/2018/05/03/substantial-damage-triggers-flood-mitigation-requirements

[23]Sandink, D., Kovacs, P., Oulahen, G., & McGillivray, G. (2010). *Making flood insurable for Canadian homeowners: A discussion paper.* Institute for Catastrophic Loss Reduction and Swiss Reinsurance Company Ltd.

[24] Kousky, C., Michel-Kerjan, E. O., & Raschky, P. A. (2018). Does federal disaster assistance crowd out flood insurance? *Journal of Environmental Economics and Management, 87,* 150-164.

[25] Raschky, P. A., & Weck-Hannemann, H. (2007). Charity hazard—A real hazard to natural disaster insurance? *Environmental Hazards, 7*(4), 321-329

[26] Raschky, P. A., & Weck-Hannemann, H. (2007). Charity hazard—A real hazard to natural disaster insurance? *Environmental Hazards, 7*(4), 321-329

[27] Raschky, P. A., & Weck-Hannemann, H. (2007). Charity hazard—A real hazard to natural disaster insurance? *Environmental Hazards, 7*(4), 321-329

[28] Raschky, P. A., & Weck-Hannemann, H. (2007). Charity hazard—A real hazard to natural disaster insurance? *Environmental Hazards, 7*(4), 321-329

[29] Kapur, S. (2020). The $600 federal unemployment benefit ends this month. GOP senators say enough already. NBC News, https://www.nbcnews.com/politics/congress/600-federal-unemployment-benefit-ends-month-gop-senators-say-enough-n1232588

[30] Kapur, S. (2020). The $600 federal unemployment benefit ends this month. GOP senators say enough already. NBC News, https://www.nbcnews.com/politics/congress/600-federal-unemployment-benefit-ends-month-gop-senators-say-enough-n1232588

[31] Scott, D., & Finamor, L. (2020). Employment Effects of Unemployment Insurance Generosity During the Pandemic.

[32] Wyler, G. (2012, October 29). *Mitt Romney would make major changes to federal disaster relief aid.* Business Insider. https://www.businessinsider.com/romney-fema-cuts-hurricane-2012-10

[33] Camus, A. (1991). *The plague.* Penguin Random House.

[34] Rieder, R. (2020). *Contrary to Trump's Claim, A Pandemic Was Widely Expected at Some Point*, FactCheck.org, https://www.factcheck.org/2020/03/contrary-to-trumps-claim-a-pandemic-was-widely-expected-at-some-point/

[35] Minder, R., & Peltier, E. (2020, March 25). *A deluged system leaves some elderly to die, rocking Spain's self-image.* The New York Times. https://www.nytimes.com/2020/03/25/world/europe/Spain-coronavirus-nursing-homes.html

[36] Thucydides. (2009). *The history of the Peloponnesian War* (R. Crawley, Trans.). Project Gutenberg. (Original work published 431 BC).

[37] Davis, J. S. (1900). [Destruction of the Athenian army at Syracuse] [Illustration]. Wikimedia Commons. https://en.wikipedia.org/wiki/Sicilian_Expedition#/media/File:Destruction_of_the_Athenian_army_at_Syracuse.jpg

[38] Spicer, A. (2020, March 9). *The Decameron – the 14th-century Italian book that shows us how to survive coronavirus.* New Statesman. https://www.newstatesman.com/2020/03/coronavirus-survive-italy-wellbeing-stories-decameron

[39] Defoe, D. (1904). *A journal of the plague year.* D. Estes & Company.

[40] (ca. 17th-18th century). [Portrait of Daniel Defoe] [Oil on canvas]. National Maritime Museum, London. https://en.wikipedia.org/wiki/Daniel_Defoe#/media/File:Daniel_Defoe_Kneller_Style.jpg

[41] Berkman, B. E. (2009). Incorporating explicit ethical reasoning into pandemic influenza policies. *The Journal of contemporary health law and policy, 26*(1), 1-19.

[42] Thomas, J. C., Dasgupta, N., & Martinot, A. (2007). Ethics in a pandemic: A survey of the state pandemic influenza plans. *American Journal of Public Health, 97*(Supplement 1), S26-S31.

[43] Upshur, R., Faith, K., Gibson, J., Thompson, A., Tracy, C., Wilson, K., & Singer, P. (2005). Stand on guard for thee: Ethical considerations for preparedness planning for pandemic influenza. *A Report of the University of Toronto Joint Centre for Bioethics Pandemic Influenza Working Group.* http://www.jcb.utoronto.ca/people/documents/upshur_stand_guard.pdf

[44] Etkin, D., Mamuji, A. & Clarke, L. (2018). Disaster Risk Analysis Part 1: The Importance of Including Rare Events. *Journal of Homeland Security and Emergency Management, 15*(2).

[45] (n.d.). [The Great Plague of London in 1665] [Illustration]. Wikimedia Commons. https://en.wikipedia.org/wiki/Great_Plague_of_London#/media/File:Great_plague_of_london-1665.jpg

[46] List of Epidemics (n.d.). In Wikipedia, Retrieved June 9, 2020, https://en.wikipedia.org/wiki/List_of_epidemics

[47] Kinlaw, K., & Levine, R. (2007). *Ethical guidelines in pandemic influenza.* Centers for Disease Control and Prevention. https://www.cdc.gov/od/science/integrity/phethics/panFlu_Ethic_Guidelines.pdf

[48] Katersky, A., & Carrega, C. (2020, April 7). *1,300 NYC first responders back at work after recovering from coronavirus or its symptoms.* ABC News. https://abcnews.go.com/Health/1300-nyc-responders-back-work-recovering-coronavirus-symptoms/story?id=70024465

[49] American Medical Association Council on Ethical and Judicial Affairs. (2010). *Opinion 9.067 – Physician obligation in disaster preparedness and response.* AMA Code of Medical Ethics' Opinion on Physician Duty to Treat. https://journalofethics.ama-assn.org/article/ama-code-medical-ethics-opinion-physician-duty-treat/2010-06

[50] Davies, C. E., & Shaul, R. Z. (2010). Physicians' legal duty of care and legal right to refuse to work during a pandemic. *CMAJ, 182*(2), 167-170.

[51] Coleman, C. H. (2008). Beyond the call of duty: Compelling health care professionals to work during an influenza pandemic. *Iowa Law Review, 94*(1), 1-47.

[52] Shaw, K. A., Chilcott, A., Hansen, E., & Winzenberg, T. (2006). The GP's response to pandemic influenza: A qualitative study. *Family Practice, 23*(3), 267-272.

[53] ABC 30 Action News. (2020, April 9). *Coronavirus: 84 residents evacuated from SoCal nursing home after employees do not show up for work.* https://abc30.com/health/ca-nursing-home-resident-evacuated-after-employees-dont-show-up/6086964/

[54] Kaiser Health News (KHN). (2020, March 26). *Tragedy in Spain's nursing homes shocks nation that prides itself on taking care of elderly.* KHN morning briefing. https://khn.org/morning-breakout/tragedy-in-spains-nursing-homes-shocks-nation-that-prides-itself-on-taking-care-of-elderly/

[55] Davis, G. (2020, April 9). *Coronavirus outbreak at Bobcaygeon, Ont. nursing home claims 29th resident.* Global news. https://globalnews.ca/news/6799094/coronavirus-covid-19-outbreak-bobcaygeon-nursing-home-deaths/

[56] International Council of Nurses. (2020, March 20). *High proportion of healthcare workers with COVID-19 in Italy is a stark warning to the world: protecting nurses and their colleagues must be the number one priority.* https://www.icn.ch/news/high-proportion-healthcare-workers-covid-19-italy-stark-warning-world-protecting-nurses-and

[57] Defoe, D. (1904). *A journal of the plague year.* D. Estes & Company.

[58] Afolabi, M. O. (2018). Pandemic influenza: A comparative ethical approach. *Public Health Disasters: A Global Ethical Framework, 12*, 59-96.

[59] Emergencies Act R.S.C., 1985, c. 22 (4th Supp.). https://laws-lois.justice.gc.ca/eng/acts/e-4.5/page-1.html

[60] Letts, J. (2006). Ethical challenges in planning for an influenza pandemic. *New South Wales Public Health Bulletin, 17*(10), 131-134.

[61] Al Jazeera. (2020, April 6). *Sweden's liberal virus strategy questioned as death toll mounts.* https://www.aljazeera.com/news/2020/04/sweden-liberal-virus-strategy-questioned-death-toll-mounts-200406153834335.html

[62] Al Jazeera. (2020, April 14). *Lockdowns, closures: How is each US state handling coronavirus?* https://www.aljazeera.com/news/2020/03/emergencies-closures-states-handling-coronavirus-200317213356419.html

[63] Siemaszko, C. (2020, April 7). *Florida's coronavirus stay-at-home order doesn't bar churches from holding services.* NBC news. https://www.nbcnews.com/news/us-news/church-vs-state-desantis-stay-home-executive-order-doesn-t-n1177876

[64] Murray, C. J., Lopez, A. D., Chin, B., Feehan, D., & Hill, K. H. (2006). Estimation of potential global pandemic influenza mortality on the basis of vital registry data from the 1918–20 pandemic: A quantitative analysis. *The Lancet, 368*(9554), 2211-2218.

[65] Canadian Institute for Health Information. *The Impact of COVID-19 on Long-Term Care in Canada: Focus on the First 6 Months.* Ottawa, ON: CIHI; 2021.

[66] Statista. Retrieved April 26, 2021, https://www.statista.com/statistics/1107572/covid-19-value-g20-stimulus-packages-share-gdp/.

[67] Swift, D. (2020). *Higher mortality rate in ventilated COVID-19 patients in large sample.* Medscape Medical News. https://www.medscape.com/viewarticle/928605

[68] Sprung, C. L., Zimmerman, J. L., Christian, M. D., Joynt, G. M., Hick, J. L., Taylor, B., Richards, G. A., Sandrock, C., Cohen, R., & Adini, B. (2010). Recommendations for intensive care unit and hospital preparations for an influenza epidemic or mass disaster: Summary report of the European Society of Intensive Care Medicine's task force for intensive care unit triage during an influenza epidemic or mass disaster. *Intensive Care Medicine, 36*(3), 428-443.

[69] U.S. Department of Health and Human Services (HHS). (2005). *HHS pandemic influenza plan.* http://www.hhs.gov/pandemicflu/plan/appendixd.html

[70] Defoe, D. (1904). *A journal of the plague year.* D. Estes & Company.

[71] Householder, M., & White, E. (2020). *Hundreds protest Michigan Governor's social distancing order by rallying at the State Capitol.* Time. https://time.com/5821873/michigan-protest-governor-social-distance-coronavirus/

[72] Silverstein, J. (2021). "He's dead wrong": Dr. Fauci clashes with Senator Rand Paul about wearing masks after vaccination, CBS News, https://www.cbsnews.com/news/anthony-fauci-rand-paul-masks-covid-vaccine/

[73] Biddlestone, M., Green, R., & Douglas, K. M. (2020). Cultural orientation, power, belief in conspiracy theories, and intentions to reduce the spread of COVID-19. *British Journal of Social Psychology, 59*(3), 663-673.

[74] Maital, S., & Barzani, E. (2020). The global economic impact of COVID-19: A summary of research. *Samuel Neaman Institute for National Policy Research.*

[75] Correia, S., Luck, S., & Verner, E. (2020). Pandemics depress the economy, public health interventions do not: Evidence from the 1918 flu. *SSRN.*

[76] Correia, S., Luck, S., & Verner, E. (2020). Pandemics depress the economy, public health interventions do not: Evidence from the 1918 flu. *SSRN.*

[77] Klinenberg, E. (2015). *Heat wave: A social autopsy of disaster in Chicago.* University of Chicago Press.

[78] Barry, J. M. (2009). Pandemics: Avoiding the mistakes of 1918. *Nature, 459*(7245), 324-325.

[79] Barry, J. M. (2020). *Opinion: The single most important lesson from the 1918 influenza.* The New York Times. https://www.nytimes.com/2020/03/17/opinion/coronavirus-1918-spanish-flu.html

[80] Barry, J. M. (2009). Pandemics: Avoiding the mistakes of 1918. *Nature, 459*(7245), 324-325.

[81] Barry, J. M. (2020). *Opinion: The single most important lesson from the 1918 influenza.* The New York Times. https://www.nytimes.com/2020/03/17/opinion/coronavirus-1918-spanish-flu.html

[82] Upshur, R., Faith, K., Gibson, J., Thompson, A., Tracy, C., Wilson, K., & Singer, P. (2005). Stand on guard for thee: Ethical considerations for preparedness planning for pandemic influenza. *A Report of the University of Toronto Joint Centre for Bioethics Pandemic Influenza Working Group.* http://www.jcb.utoronto.ca/people/documents/upshur_stand_guard.pdf

[83] Amon, J., Bond, K. C., Brahmbhatt, M., Buchanan, A., Capron, A. M., Cummings, D. A. T., Duggan, P. S., Faden, R. R., Gellin, B. G., Gust, I., Karron, R. A., Khan, K. S., Mfutso-Bengo, J., Nabarro, D., Nasidi, A., Nguyen, T. D., Otte, J.,

Silbergeld, E., Sinho, S., ... Zeng, G. (2006). *Bellagio statement of principles.* The Bellagio Meeting on Social Justice and Influenza. http://www.bioethicsinstitute.org/research/global-bioethics/flu-pandemic-the-bellagio-meeting

CHAPTER 11: A CODE OF ETHICS FOR EMERGENCY MANAGERS

"A code of ethics cannot be developed overnight by edict or official pronouncement. It is developed by years of practice and performance of duty according to high ethical standards. It must be self-policing. Without such a code… a group soon loses identity and effectiveness. Once we know our job, have a genuine code of ethics, and maintain unquestioned personal integrity, we have met the first and most demanding challenge of leadership."

Silas L. Copeland

"Live one day at a time emphasizing ethics rather than rules."

Wayne Dyer

Contents

11.1   Introduction

A number of years ago when I first began to get really interested in ethics, I thought back to my time as a federal civil servant in Canada and wondered if we had a code of ethics to guide our behavior and decision making. I didn't even know! With a little research I found it[i] and after looking it over did recall having to read it (or something like it) when I first entered public service. It was not a topic that came up again in my next 28 years of service, though I must say that, in general, the public servants I have worked with have a strong social conscience and pay attention to issues of right and wrong in their work and dealings with the public.

To me one of the interesting aspects about a Code of Ethics for Emergency Management is the relative lack of research or reports dealing with this issue compared to many other fields. Why does it not garner more attention? Is it not perceived to be important enough?

Codes can serve several purposes. They can be:

- A fundamental declaration that state who we are, what we believe in, and why these beliefs should be defended, such as the Declaration of the Rights of Man and of the Citizen, a human rights document written in 1789 following the French revolution;
- A document setting the foundation of future behaviors, such as the Rio Declaration;
- A charter that people pledge to in order to become part of a community, such as the Boy Scouts; or
- An enforceable code, such as a fire code.

A code of ethics is a set of principles and guidelines designed to guide decision-making and behavior within organizations. They can include:

- Statements of mission and values;
- Codes of organizational ethics that govern decision-making;
- Codes of conduct that govern personal behavior; and/or
- Codes of professional practice that govern behaviors related to job functions.

Codes provide guidance for how people and institutions should make decisions, act, and provide support for those who are seeking to act ethically.

The International Association of Emergency Managers (IAEM) has a Code of Ethics published on their web site (see Appendix 11.1).[1] It was a good exercise for the IAEM to develop this code and an important step forward. Compared to the codes of many other professions, however, it is not yet well developed. To put this in context, I would argue that most of the more developed codes would greatly benefit from a greater depth of analysis and discussion. More is needed, and towards that end the

---

[i] Government of Canada. (2011). *Values and ethics code for the public sector.* https://www.tbs-sct.gc.ca/pol/doc-eng.aspx?id=25049

Special Interest Groups (SIG) on ethics has been working on created a Code of Ethics for the Emergency Management Community. As of June, 2022 a draft code has been developed (Appendix 11.2).

A great deal of background thought needs to go into the development of a code of ethics and there are traps that need to be avoided. The process to create a Code of Ethics for Emergency Management should be transparent, inclusive, comprehensive, have significant consultation within the emergency management community, and involve professional ethicists as well as the emergency management community.

11.2   About Codes of Ethics

Why is it important to have a code of ethics? Basically, it is to help make that sure we do the right things (as much as possible). Codes of ethics:

- Provide guidance for behaviors;
- Protect employees from retaliation;
- Act as a legal resort to justify problematical decisions, especially ones that result from ethical dilemmas;
- Set standards and benchmarks;
- Help to create occupational identity;
- Contribute to the consistency of policy and procedures;
- Help avoid mission drift and maintain integrity;
- Minimize ad hoc decision-making; and
- Encourage and protect ethical decision-making.

Codes (or their elements) can be of two kinds, (1) prescriptive (Figure 11.1) or (2) aspirational (e.g. living for others, as noted by Albert Schweitzer – Figure 11.2). Prescriptive codes delineate minimal standards and generally tell people what they cannot do, but say little about what they should do. In this sense they are legalistic. Prescriptive codes:

- Include rules of conduct;
- Include prohibitions;
- Are enforceable; and
- Define minimal standards.

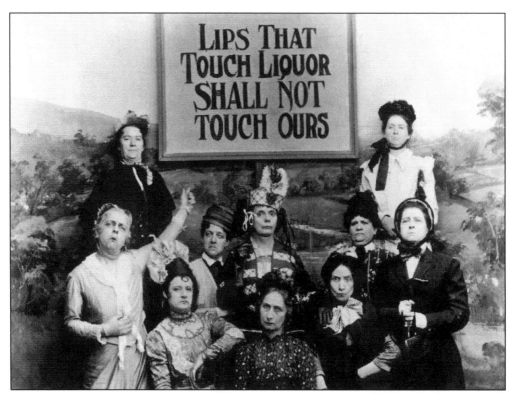

Figure 11.1: An example of a prescriptive code.[2]

Aspirational codes tend to be more general and abstract, and may be hard to interpret, but provide an ethical context that is important. Aspirational codes:

- Contain ethical or moral goals;
- Are not enforceable; and
- Outline standards to strive for.

Life becomes harder for us when we live for others, but it also becomes richer and happier.

Albert Schweitzer (1875–1965), winner of the Nobel Peace Prize, humanitarian, theologian, philosopher, and physician

Figure 11.2: Albert Schweitzer[3]

Codes of ethics have a long history. Examples are the Ten Commandments from the Old Testament (Figure 11.3), the Pirate Code of Conduct during the 18th century (box on page 11.6), the Athenian Oath of the Ephebes (box on page 11.8) and the ancient Greek Hippocratic Oath for physicians (box on page 11.10).

The Ten Commandments is an example of a code that includes elements that are both aspirational and prescriptive.

Figure 11.3: The second of two parchment sheets making up 4Q41 or 4QDeuteronomyn, also known as the "All Souls Deuteronomy," one of the Dead Sea Scrolls, dated to the first century BC. This second sheet contains Deuteronomy 5:1-6:1, and thus preserves one of the oldest extant copies of the Ten Commandments.[4]

Prescriptive Commandments:

- You shall have no other gods before Me.
- You shall not make idols.
- You shall not take the name of the Lord your God in vain.
- You shall not murder.
- You shall not commit adultery.
- You shall not steal.
- You shall not bear false witness against your neighbor.
- You shall not covet thy neighbor's wife.

Aspirational Commandments:

- Remember the Sabbath day, to keep it holy.
- Honor your father and your mother.

- "ARTICLE I - Every man shall have an equal vote in affairs of moment. He shall have an equal title to the fresh provisions or strong liquors at any time seized and shall use them at pleasure unless a scarcity may make it necessary for the common good that a retrenchment may be voted.
- ARTICLE II - Every man shall be called fairly in turn by the list on board of prizes, because over and above their proper share, they are allowed a shift of clothes. But if they defraud the company to the value of even one dollar in plate, jewels or money, they shall be marooned. If any man rob another he shall have his nose and ears slit, and be put ashore where he shall be sure to encounter hardships.
- ARTICLE III - None shall game for money either with dice or cards.
- ARTICLE IV - The lights and candles should be put out at eight at night, and if any of the crew desire to drink after that hour they shall sit upon the open deck without lights.
- ARTICLE V - Each man shall keep his piece, cutlass and pistols at all times clean and ready for action.
- ARTICLE VI - No boy or woman to be allowed amongst them. If any man shall be found seducing any of the latter sex and carrying her to sea in disguise, he shall suffer death.
- ARTICLE VII - He that shall desert the ship or his quarters in time of battle shall be punished by death or marooning.
- ARTICLE VIII - None shall strike another on board the ship, but every man's quarrel shall be ended on shore by sword or pistol in this manner. At the word of command from the quartermaster, each man being previously placed back to back, shall turn and fire immediately. If any man do not, the quartermaster shall knock the piece out of his hand. If both miss their aim they shall take to their cutlasses, and he that draweth first blood shall be declared the victor.
- ARTICLE IX - No man shall talk of breaking up their way of living till each has a share of 1,000. Every man who shall become a cripple or lose a limb in the service shall have 800 pieces of eight from the common stock and for lesser hurts proportionately.
- ARTICLE X - The captain and the quartermaster shall each receive two shares of a prize, the master gunner and boatswain, one- and one-half shares, all other officers one and one quarter, and private gentlemen of fortune one share each."[5]

Figure 11.4: Black Barty.[6]

The "FEMA Ethics Guide" for its employees begins with the following statements:

BASIC OBLIGATIONS OF PUBLIC SERVICE: EXECUTIVE ORDER 12674:

The Foundation for Ethical Behavior

To ensure public confidence in the integrity of the Federal Government, Executive Order 12674 (as amended) forms the framework for the ethical behavior required and expected of all Federal employees. As a condition of public service, you are expected to adhere to these fundamental principles of ethical behavior:

1. Public service is public trust, requiring you to place loyalty to the Constitution, the laws, and ethical principles above private gain.
2. You shall not hold financial interests that conflict with the conscientious performance of duty.
3. You shall not engage in financial transactions using non-public Government information or allow improper use of such information to further any private interest.
4. You shall not, except pursuant to such reasonable exceptions as are provided by regulation, solicit or accept any gift or other item of monetary value from any person or entity seeking official action from, doing business with, or conducting activities regulated by your agency, or whose interests may be substantially affected by the performance or nonperformance of your duties.
5. You shall make no unauthorized commitments or promise of any kind purported to bind the Government.
6. You shall put forth honest effort in the performance of your duties.
7. You shall not engage in outside employment or activities, including seeking or negotiating for employment, that conflict with your official Government duties and responsibilities.
8. You shall disclose waste, fraud, abuse, and corruption to appropriate authorities.
9. You shall satisfy in good faith your obligations as citizens, including all just financial obligations, especially those such as Federal, state, or local taxes that are imposed by law.
10. You shall adhere to all laws and regulations that provide equal opportunities for all Americans regardless of race, color, religion, gender, sexual orientation, age, or disability.
11. You shall not use your public office for private gain.
12. You shall act impartially and not give preferential treatment to any private organization or individual.

13. You shall protect and conserve Federal property and shall not use it for other than authorized activity.

14. You shall endeavor to avoid any actions creating the appearance that you are violating the law, the Standards of Ethical Conduct for Employees of the Executive Branch (5 C.F.R. Part 2635), any DHS supplemental ethics regulations, or Executive Order 12674.

With the possible exception of principle #6 and that part of #13 which addresses protecting and conserving federal property, this code is prescriptive in nature. I see little here to inspire emergency managers; it is oriented towards protecting the government against malfeasance from its employees. There is nothing wrong with that, but it is primarily a limiting Code of Professional Practice and does not include other important elements.

The Athenian Oath of the Ephebes (possibly around 330 BCE)[7]

- I will not bring disgrace upon my shield-and-the-rest-of-my-gear [*hopla*], which are sacred [*hiera*] [for me], and I will not abandon the fighter-who-stands-next [to me], no matter where I am stationed-in-the-battle-line.
- I will protect all things that are sacred [*hiera*] and all things that are divinely-sanctioned-for-human-use [*hosia*].
- The land-of-my-ancestors [*patris*] I will leave [to the next generation] in a condition that is not diminished but instead greater and better than it had been before.
- And I will do so both by myself and together with everyone else.
- And I will really listen to those who are authorized-, year after year, -to-bring-things-to-completion [*krainein*] with sound mind [*en-phronōs*], and I will also listen to the laws [*thesmoi*] that have been set and to whatever laws will be set with sound mind [*en-phronōs*] for the rest of time.
- If anyone tries to destroy them, I will prevent it both by myself and together with everyone else.
- And I will honor [*tīmân*] the sacred-things [*hiera*] of-the-ancestors [*patria*]. Witnesses [*histores*] [to the oath] are: [the] gods [*theoi*] Aglauros, Hestiā, Enuō, Arēs and Athena Areiā, Zeus, Thallō, Hēgemonē, Hēraklēs; [also] [the] boundaries [*horoi*] of the land-of-my-ancestors [*patris*]; [also] [the] wheat, barley, grapevines, olive-trees, fig-trees.

There are many codes of ethics or conduct that exist within the public and private spheres, and within NGOs. In a review by Jean Pettifor it was noted that there are three main problem areas with ethical codes that can create difficulties:

1) A lack of moral and philosophical foundations;
2) A specific cultural grounding that can result in unintentional discrimination; and
3) Multicultural issues are trivialized.[8]

To that list of three, for the profession of emergency management, I add a fourth:

> (4) a lack of reciprocal obligations between individual emergency managers and the organizations for whom they work.

There is no one right way to write a code of ethics; "however the absolutely wrong way is to produce a code of conduct with no institutional fabric. Codes as mere pieces of paper posted on a wall can actually do more mischief than having no code at all."[9]

How rigid should codes be? Cultural traits can affect how codes are written. For example, some cultures emphasize individual responsibility while others emphasize family and community interdependence. Pettifor also comments that "[a]bsolutist concepts of the use of power, definitions of professional identity, training, scope of practice, concepts of the nature of mental health and illness, and prohibition of dual relationships and batter may all be culturally insensitive and discriminatory."[10] Culture and context are important and codes that are rigidly rule-based will have difficulty respecting cultural diversity and individual circumstances.

Pettifor notes that "American codes tend to be more legalistic and rule oriented. Canadian codes tend to articulate the ethical principles or moral foundation on which rules and standards are based."[11] Certainly, the current FEMA code for emergency managers is very legalistic (as noted above). Both types of codes (aspirational and prescriptive) are needed.

The Hippocratic Oath (Translated by Michael North)[12]

The Hippocratic Oath (Ορκος) is perhaps the most widely known of Greek medical texts. It requires a new physician to swear upon a number of healing gods that he will uphold a number of professional ethical standards. It also strongly binds the student to his teacher and the greater community of physicians with responsibilities similar to that of a family member...

Over the centuries, it has been rewritten often in order to suit the values of different cultures influenced by Greek medicine. Contrary to popular belief, the Hippocratic Oath is not required by most modern medical schools, although some have adopted modern versions that suit many in the profession in the 21st century. It also does not explicitly contain the phrase, "First, do no harm," which is commonly attributed to it.

Hippocratic Oath

I swear by Apollo the physician, and Asclepius, and Hygieia and Panacea and all the gods and goddesses as my witnesses, that, according to my ability and judgement, I will keep this Oath and this contract:

- To hold him who taught me this art equally dear to me as my parents, to be a partner in life with him, and to fulfill his needs when required; to look upon his offspring as equals to my own siblings, and to teach them this art, if they shall wish to learn it, without fee or contract; and that by the set rules, lectures, and

---

every other mode of instruction, I will impart a knowledge of the art to my own sons, and those of my teachers, and to students bound by this contract and having sworn this Oath to the law of medicine, but to no others.

- I will use those dietary regimens which will benefit my patients according to my greatest ability and judgement, and I will do no harm or injustice to them.

- I will not give a lethal drug to anyone if I am asked, nor will I advise such a plan; and similarly I will not give a woman a pessary to cause an abortion.

- In purity and according to divine law will I carry out my life and my art.

- I will not use the knife, even upon those suffering from stones, but I will leave this to those who are trained in this craft.

- Into whatever homes I go, I will enter them for the benefit of the sick, avoiding any voluntary act of impropriety or corruption, including the seduction of women or men, whether they are free men or slaves.

- Whatever I see or hear in the lives of my patients, whether in connection with my professional practice or not, which ought not to be spoken of outside, I will keep secret, as considering all such things to be private.

- So long as I maintain this Oath faithfully and without corruption, may it be granted to me to partake of life fully and the practice of my art, gaining the respect of all men for all time. However, should I transgress this Oath and violate it, may the opposite be my fate.

Figure 11.5: Engraving of Hippocrates.[13]

How much does having a code of ethics affect conduct in organizations? That depends greatly upon organizational culture, and how it is created and implemented. Like an emergency plan it can be subject to the "paper plan syndrome," where it exists in paper form but not in terms of practice. As a result, there has been a change in focus "from writing a comprehensive code of rules to regulate conduct to leveraging a values-based code that inspires principled performance among employees, management and executives." [14]

One survey of corporations illustrates that it can have a significant impact (Figures 11.6 and 11.7).[15] The level of impact depends upon leadership and the corporate culture, which can support or undermine ethical behavior. There are a variety of tools that can be used to assess how effective a code of ethics is, including employee surveys, independent audits, helpline analyses, targeted feedback, and informal feedback.

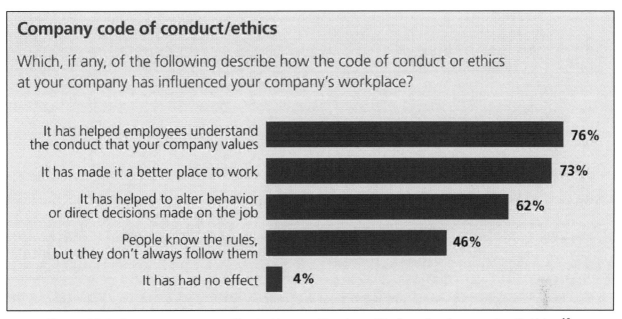

Figure 11.6: A corporate survey illustrating positive benefits from having a code of ethics.[16]

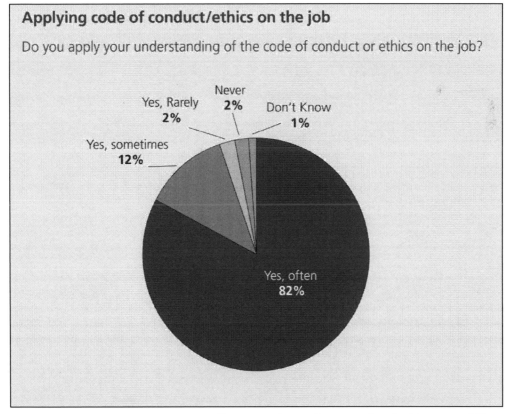

Figure 11.7: A corporate survey illustrating how often a code of ethics is used.[17]

11.3　Suggested Principles for a Code of Ethics for Emergency Management in the Public Sector

In this section I suggest a set of principles that could form the basis of a Code of Ethics for Emergency Managers and Emergency Management Organizations.[18] It would apply to cultures that have the following characteristics:

- Democratic political system;
- History of public service for the common good;
- Strong public service institutions; and
- Low corruption.

Suggested Principles:

1. Two Codes are Needed: The first and perhaps most important principle is that a Code of Ethics for Emergency Managers must be accompanied by a Code of Ethics for Emergency Management organizations. They need to be mutually supportive. Without this interplay between individuals and the organizations that they work for, it is extremely challenging for emergency managers to act in ways they consider to be ethical, but that might conflict with competing organizational goals or priorities, or because of corruption.

2. Ethical Plurality: More than one ethical theory is relevant to determining ethical decision making and behavior. At a minimum, consequentialist, deontological, environmental and virtue theories should be considered.

3. Cultural Relevance: The application of ethical theory varies according to cultural norms, in order to reflect differences in values between different cultures. Codes of Ethics, therefore, should reflect cultural diversity. However, this does not mean that some values may not be considered absolute, such as prohibitions against murder.

4. Moral Being and Moral Community:

    a. Emergency managers are moral beings who shall endeavor to act in ways that reflect ethical reasoning. Emergency management organizations shall endeavor to be moral organizations that incorporate and promote ethical reasoning in the development and application of policies and procedures in an ongoing process; these policies and procedures must be an integral component of organizational culture and encourage employees to act in moral ways.

    b. The moral community served by emergency managers and emergency management organizations must, at a minimum, include all citizens. People, particularly the victims of disaster, shall not be placed in the category of things but must be considered as beings imbued with rights and duties.

5. Utilitarian Ethics:

   a. Where utilitarian ethics are used, careful consideration must be given to whose good is being evaluated and how it is measured. The good of victims will generally have priority over the good of non-victims. The lives of the "least advantaged" should receive special attention.

   b. Where utilitarian ethics are used, disadvantaged individuals and groups who sacrifice for the greater good are entitled to reasonable compensation.

6. Deontological Ethics:

   a. Where deontological ethics are used, they shall reflect the normative values of society. This can be challenging in a multicultural society and requires a broad social discourse.

7. Duty of Care: Governments owe a special duty of care to some vulnerable populations.

   a. This is particularly true for wards of the state, such as hospital patients and retirement home residents.

   b. A greater duty of care exists for especially vulnerable people, which justifies some level of paternalism.

   c. Governments have a duty of care to their employees.

   d. A duty of care exists for disaster victims that is greater than for citizens who have not suffered in a disaster, all other things being equal. This justifies the allocation of resources to victims as compared to non-victims who may be in greater need.

      i. This duty is diminished when victims knowingly engaged in risky actions, where they had the choice of less risky options. Care must be taken to avoid the trap of "blaming the victim."

      ii. This duty may also be diminished where relief may result in the creation of a culture of dependency. This risk must be balanced against the urgent needs of victims who are in need of help for recovery.

8. Ethical Dilemmas: Where ethical dilemmas exist, an open, transparent, and fair system will be used to resolve differences (procedural justice), based upon ethical reasoning.

9. Socialization of Risk: Various ethical theories can support the socialization of risk (e.g., Disaster Financial Assistance) and this can result in increased moral hazard. Moral hazard can be justified on the basis of ethical reasoning where the greater good is served or rights are maintained.

However, such programs should be used with care to avoid, as much as possible, social traps such as the creation of cultures of dependency, and to encourage resilience.

10. <u>Good Samaritan Behavior and Rule-Based Utilitarianism</u>: No bureaucracy can anticipate all possible situations. A result of this is that the applications of policies will, in some cases, be perceived as being unfair.

    a. Emergency managers shall use moral reasoning to resolve such situations, in favor of rigidly following rules.

    b. As a corollary, emergency management organizations shall have a Good Samaritan Policy, recognizing the overarching duty of their employees to act in ethical ways.

    c. It is recognized that the rejection of rules because of moral reasoning should be exceptional events.

11. <u>Virtues</u>: The behavior of emergency managers and emergency management organizations shall reflect the following virtues: honesty, caring, compassion, generosity, empathy, impartiality, integrity (which refers to acting consistently according to one's stated values or principles), diligence, kindness, openness, reliability, resoluteness, respectfulness, sensitivity, tolerance, toughness, trustworthiness, and truthfulness.

12. <u>Social Contract Ethics</u>: The policies and procedures of emergency management organizations shall reflect the formal and informal social contract that exists between government and its citizens.

    a. Crisis situations shall not be used as opportunities to further special interests that are not supported by the normative values of society.

13. <u>Environmental Ethics:</u> Citizens have a right to a healthy natural environment, which also enhances sustainability and disaster resilience.

    a. Emergency management organizations shall endeavor to protect and nurture the natural environment, particularly where it mitigates disaster risk.

11.4   Proposed Content

What should a Code of Ethics look like? There are many examples from other professions, and a perusal of them suggests inclusion of the following sections:

Possible Table of Contents:

- Preamble
- Introduction
- Mandate and Limitations

- Summary of Ethical Theories
  - Relevance of Theory to Emergency Management
- Core Values
- Principles
  - Critical Ethical Issues
  - Special Obligations[ii, 19] in Emergency Management
  - Ethics of Competence
- The Process of Ethical Decision Making
  - How to Resolve Ethical Dilemmas
- Conclusion
- Resources
- Case Studies

Many of the codes from other professions include lists of values, principles, etc., which are good, but lack depth, and because of that, they are of limited usefulness in practice. For example, core values typically include:

- Social justice
- Integrity
- Respect
- Impartiality
- Objectivity
- Honor diversity
- Competence and excellence
- Do no harm.

Consider the first category of social justice, which is subject to a variety of interpretations from both a theoretical and cultural perspective. There are several categories of social justice, including distributive justice, corrective justice, and procedural justice. Different cultures and legal systems approach them quite differently depending upon the social contract that exists. For example, distributive justice can consider fair distributions of opportunity, wealth, risk, welfare, etc. (Chapter 1). In a multicultural society such complexities are far from trivial and should be discussed in a code. "Do no harm" is a particularly difficult statement since ethical dilemmas frequently involve harming somebody (perhaps through omission). A more useful statement might be "Do as little harm as possible," which is a utilitarian approach.

Case studies are particularly important. A code of ethics needs to go beyond broad statements. It should also include a set of scenarios with examples of applied ethical reasoning and the identification and analysis of ethical dilemmas specific to emergency management. Such case studies can provide a template for ethical reasoning that professional emergency managers could use in their practice.

[ii] Obligations exist to self, employers, clients, institutions, partners and the moral community. Special obligations may exist to wards of the state, disabled or especially vulnerable people, volunteers and employees.

11.5   Conclusion

It is important for the field of emergency management to develop a sophisticated code of ethics. If it is to become a recognized profession this must be part of the process. Codes should be developed for both individual emergency managers and emergency management organizations, if they are to be effective. Aspects of the codes should be aspirational as well as prescriptive and should include statements of mission and values, a code of organizational ethics, a code of conduct, and a code of professional practice.

11.6   Further Reading

- Feldmann-Jensen, S., Smith, S., Etkin, D., & Jensen, S. (2016). Toward a substantive dialogue: The case for an ethical framework in emergency management, Part 1. *The Australasian Journal of Disaster and Trauma Studies, 20*(1), 45-47. http://www.massey.ac.nz/~trauma/issues/2016-1/AJDTS_20_1_Feldmann-Jensen.pdf

- Etkin, D., Feldmann-Jensen, S., Smith, S., & Jensen, S. (2016). Toward A substantive dialogue: The case for an ethical framework in emergency management, Part 2. *The Australasian Journal of Disaster and Trauma Studies, 20*(1), 49-53. http://www.massey.ac.nz/~trauma/issues/2016-1/AJDTS_20_1_Etkin.pdf

- Etkin, D. (2015). *Disaster Theory: An interdisciplinary approach to concepts and causes*. Butterworth-Heineman. http://store.elsevier.com/Disaster-Theory/David-Etkin/isbn-9780128002278/

- Etkin, D. & Timmerman, P. (2013). Emergency management and ethics. *International Journal of Emergency Management, 9*(4), 277-297. https://www.researchgate.net/profile/David_Etkin/publication/264812137_Emergency_management_and_ethics/links/569cf37008ae8f8ddc711cdf.pdf

- Etkin, D. & Stefanovic, I. L. (2005). Mitigating natural disasters: The role of eco-ethics. *Mitigation and Adaptation Strategies for Global Change. 10*, 469-490.

Appendix 11.1: IAEM Code of Ethics and Professional Conduct

IAEM Code of Ethics and Professional Conduct[20]

The International Association of Emergency Managers (IAEM) is an international organization dedicated to promoting the goals of saving lives and protecting property by mitigating, preparing for, responding to, and recovering from disasters/emergencies. IAEM sponsors the Associate Emergency Manager (AEM) and Certified Emergency Manager (CEM) Program to maintain professionalism through the certification process.

The Code of Ethics and Professional Conduct must be embraced and upheld by all individuals who are awarded the AEM/CEM designation. The promise to uphold the Code signifies the assumption that the emergency manager will act prudently and responsibly beyond the requirements of law and codes. The Code of Ethics and Professional Conduct embodies the certification program philosophy and objectives. Each AEM/CEM promises to adhere to the Code.

Preamble

IAEM has a Code of Professional Conduct that seeks to address a range of issues that impact the emergency management professional on their day-to-day work. Maintenance of public trust and confidence is central to the effectiveness of the Emergency Management Profession. This Code aims to ensure and justify public trust and confidence in the services provided by members of the International Associations of Emergency Managers (IAEM).

It seeks to ensure that high levels of competence and professional conduct are maintained. The members of the International Association of Emergency Managers (IAEM) adhere to the highest standards of ethical and professional conduct. The Code of Professional Conduct for the IAEM members and AEMs/CEMs (whether or not they are IAEM members) reflects the spirit and proper conduct dictated by the conscience of society and commitment to the well-being of all.

Principles

The members of the Association agree to conduct themselves in accordance with the basic principles of RESPECT, COMMITMENT, and PROFESSIONALISM.

Respect

- Respect for supervising officials, colleagues, associates, and most importantly, for the people we serve is the standard for IAEM members. We comply with all laws and regulations applicable to our purpose and position, and responsibly and impartially apply them to all concerned. We respect fiscal resources by evaluating organizational decisions to provide the best service or product at a minimal cost without sacrificing quality.

Commitment

- IAEM members commit themselves to promoting decisions that engender trust and those we serve. We commit to continuous improvement by fairly administering the affairs of our positions, by fostering honest and trustworthy relationships, and by striving for impeccable accuracy and clarity in what we say or write. We commit to enhancing stewardship of resources and the caliber of service we deliver while striving to improve the quality of life in the community we serve.

Professionalism

- IAEM is an organization that actively promotes professionalism to ensure public confidence in Emergency Management. Our reputations are built on the faithful discharge of our duties. Our professionalism is founded on Education, Safety and Protection of Life and Property.

Code

- *Quality*: Members shall aim to maintain high quality work at all times and apply the Principles of Emergency Management in their professional undertakings. Quality may be assessed by audits, monitoring, quality processes, or other appropriate means.

- *Professional Independence*: IAEM Members, however employed, owe a primary loyalty to the people in the community they serve and the environment they affect. Their practice should be performed according to high standards and ethical principles, maintaining respect for human dignity. Emergency management practitioners shall seek to ensure professional independence in the execution of their functions. The term professional independence relates to the function of the practitioners within the organization in which they practice. Their role may be advisory or executive.

- *Legal Requirements:* Members must abide by the legal requirements relating to their practice, and practitioners have a duty to make themselves aware of the appropriate legal requirements for the territory in which they practice.

- *Objectivity:* Members called to give an opinion in their professional capacity shall be honest and, to the best of their ability, objective and reliable. Objectivity and reliability is based on the best current available knowledge, or in the absence of such knowledge, reference to appropriate emergency planning and management principles.

- *Competence:* Members shall not undertake responsibilities as emergency management practitioners if they do not believe themselves competent to discharge them. Members shall acknowledge any limitations in their own competence. In pursuit of this members shall take all reasonable steps to obtain, maintain and develop their professional competence by attention to new developments and shall encourage others working under their supervision to do so. Competence is defined as 'the possession of sufficient knowledge, experience and skill to enable a person to know what he or she is doing and to be able to carry out a task in the way in which a person competent in the activity would expect it to be done and to have an appreciation of one's own limitations'. Competence is maintained by undertaking continuing professional development and certification (CEM®) and may be supplemented at appropriate levels by membership of other specialist bodies.

- *Abuse of Membership:* Members shall not improperly use their membership of IAEM for commercial or personal gain.

- *Conflict of Interest*: Members shall avoid their professional judgment being influenced by any conflict of interest and shall inform their employer, or client, of any conflict between their own personal interest and service to the relevant party. For example, a consultant may be aware that his/her recommendations are not being implemented, but continues to advise the organization in order to avoid losing the revenue associated with the contract. The members, officers and agents of the Association shall act in the best interest of the Association at all times and shall avoid activities resulting in actual or implied personal gain in keeping with the highest standards of ethics and professionalism.

- *Confidentiality*: Members shall not improperly disclose any information which may reasonably be considered to be prejudicial to the business of any present or past employer or client.

- *Professional Responsibility*: Members shall accept professional responsibility for all their work and shall take all reasonable steps to ensure that persons working under their authority or supervision are competent to carry out the tasks assigned to them; are treated with fairness and equal opportunity; and accept responsibility for the work done on the authority delegated by them. Where members have good reason to believe that their professional advice is not being followed, they shall take all reasonable steps to ensure that persons overruling or neglecting their advice are made aware of the potential adverse consequences which may result. In such instances it is advisable that such actions are recorded in writing.

- *Upholding the Aims and Objectives:* Members shall have regard to the reputation and good standing of The Society, other members' professional practice and standards, and shall not knowingly bring them into disrepute. Disrepute amounts to the loss of a previously good reputation. It may arise from the conduct of a member who by act or omission lowers the professional reputation of The Association and its members in the view of right-thinking members of The Association generally. At all times members shall seek to uphold the bylaws and APPs of the IAEM.

- *Professional Reputation*: Members shall not in the course of their practice recklessly or maliciously injure, or attempt to injure, whether directly or indirectly, the professional reputation, prospects or business of another.

- *Members Relations Inter Se*: Members shall at all times treat other members of the Association with the utmost respect and fairness, and at no time undermine their integrity and dignity. Members will at all times seek to work in a cooperative and productive way with each other. Elected representatives have a particular responsibility in this regard; to ensure that all members and their views are heard, valued, and respected.

- *Financial Propriety*: Members shall maintain financial propriety in all their professional dealings with employers and clients. Any inducements which may be seen as prejudicial to professional independence or in breach of contractual or moral obligations should be discouraged.

- *IAEM Member Conduct:* All members of IAEM, including those holding IAEM certifications, are expected to at all times while participating in IAEM events, conferences, conventions, or activities treat their fellow members and professionals within the emergency management community with the utmost dignity and respect and to adhere to the policies of IAEM as adopted by its Board of Directors from time to time, including, but not limited to, the IAEM Non-Discrimination and Anti-Harassment Policy.

Appendix 11.2 Draft Code of Ethics: FEMA SIG Ethics Committee

Code of Ethics and Professional Standards of Conduct
for Emergency Management Professionals

Introduction

Emergency management is a managerial function charged with creating the framework within which communities reduce vulnerability to hazards and cope with disasters. Emergency management professionals seek to promote safer, less vulnerable communities with the capacity to cope with hazards and disasters. Communities in this context are broadly defined to include humans, organizations, the environment, and government.

Emergency management professionals work with a diverse group of stakeholders in a wide variety of businesses and industry sectors, in non-profit organizations, and in all levels of government. Emergency management professionals are relied upon for their subject matter expertise and support in managing a diverse, complex risk portfolio for the communities they serve. Emergency management professionals recognize the value of, and are committed to, developing and promoting in themselves and their organizations the following competencies: disaster risk management; community engagement; governance and civics; leadership; scientific, geographic, sociocultural, technological, and systems literacy; operations consistent with the emergency management framework, principles, and body of knowledge; critical thinking; continual learning; and, compliance with professional ethics.

Inherent in the practice of emergency management is a series of duties and responsibilities to affected populations, partners, stakeholders, the public, the environment, colleagues, employers, the profession, and self. These duties and responsibilities were examined in concert with established competency behavioral anchors related to professional ethics (see Appendix B) and foundational ethical tenets to develop expected professional conduct standards. In its totality, the Code of Ethics and Professional Conduct for Emergency Management Professionals delineates an ethical framework to guide practice in both known and uncertain environments.

Code of Ethics
The Code of Ethics provides emergency management professionals with a set of foundational tenets that guide ethical practice and decision-making. These tenets emphasize the need to think and act ethically. Emergency management professionals have a duty of care that requires a careful, critical decision-making process grounded in ethical deliberation.

This Code of Ethics is intended to help frame ethical thinking about behaviors and decisions in conjunction with the Code of Professional Conduct. Emergency management professionals can utilize this Code of Ethics to ensure a more careful and critical process regarding behaviors or decisions that are morally or ethically challenging. The foundational tenets, both aspirational and prescriptive, capture the essence of effective and just emergency management practice.

Foundational Tenets

(1) <u>Think ethically, act morally.</u>

Sometimes it is clear what the right thing to do is, but often it can be difficult to sort out, especially if there are conflicting ethical arguments (see Appendix C). It is not enough to be able to ethically analyze situations or to know what the right thing to do is; emergency management professionals must act morally. To act morally, emergency management professionals' actions should evidence moral courage, integrity, honesty, respect, kindness, professionalism, competence, impartiality, and objectivity. These actions delineate the requisite moral character for professional emergency management practice. Ethical decision-making is strongest when the knowledge and skills to analyze
the ethics of complicated situations and the moral character to act in the best way possible are both present.

(2) <u>Obey the law.</u>

A social contract exists between citizens and their governments, with duties and obligations on both sides. As citizens and as emergency management professionals, there is an obligation to obey the law, except in very rare cases where a law is immoral. But there is an important distinction between what is legal and what is moral. The law is prescriptive, not aspirational, and represents minimal standards of morality. There are times when it is sufficient to simply obey

the law, and there are other times when obeying the law is not enough to satisfy moral imperatives. For example, the law does not require
emergency management professionals to treat victims with kindness, but it is moral to do so.

(3) <u>Maximize the good done for people and society, taking into consideration the needs of the most vulnerable.</u>

A basic principle of ethics is to do the greatest good for the greatest number, as long as the most vulnerable are not disadvantaged. This principle is important and must be tempered in two ways. First, what is good and how is it measured must be debated and agreed upon (e.g., political parties often disagree on what is good, as do environmentalists compared to real estate developers). It is not solely up to emergency management professionals to decide what is good – these decisions are best made by engaging stakeholders to derive public values. Second, people and institutions have rights that should not be needlessly or thoughtlessly trampled over in the pursuit of a greater good.

(4) <u>Respect the rights of people and organizations; fulfill duties and obligations to those served.</u>

One of the problems with maximizing good is that it can be used to justify bad actions if the needs of many are served. As a society, we agree that some actions that serve the greater good are immoral (e.g., we do not harvest organs from people without their consent, even if doing so would save several lives). We need to be aware of, and respect, the rights of others whether they are constitutionally based, defined by laws, or accepted as cultural norms. There are also times when the perceived rights of some conflict with the common good, or the rights of others (e.g., choosing not to wear a face mask during a pandemic may conflict with the rights of others not to get infected, or the health of the public at large).

Emergency management professionals have duties and obligations to employers, clients, and stakeholders, which must be fulfilled. While many of these duties and obligations are defined by job descriptions, some are a result of societal expectations (which though unwritten, are important and can be powerful). Emergency management professionals must act ethically and professionally in the execution of their duties and obligations.

(5) <u>Build trusting relationships.</u>

Trust is an asymmetrical relationship, which means that it is hard to gain and easy to lose. Trusting relationships are essential to effective emergency management practice. Trust is gained by having a virtuous character (particularly fidelity), being competent, following the law, and avoiding conflicts of interest.

A conflict of interest is a situation in which an emergency management professional has a private or personal interest sufficient to influence (or even have the appearance to influence) the objective exercise of his or her official duties. Emergency management professionals must avoid their judgment being influenced by any conflict of interest and shall inform their employer, or client, of any conflict between their own personal interest and service to the relevant party.

(6) <u>When faced with an ethical dilemma, use an ethical decision-making process.</u>

Ethical dilemmas (having to choose between two rights or two wrongs) present difficult choices between competing ethical principles. Ethical dilemmas occur either because different ethical perspectives (such as the greater good versus individual rights) lead to different decisions, or because of varying underlying values (such as defining good as economic development versus environmental protection). Ethical dilemmas can be extremely difficult and contentious to manage. When faced with an ethical dilemma there is generally no one correct answer. In addressing these dilemmas, a transparent, inclusive and effective decision-making process should be used to arrive at an equitable outcome based on ethical reasoning (see Appendix C).

Code of Professional Conduct
These standards present ethical expectations for all emergency management professionals and extend across all areas of practice as well as individuals' representation of the profession of emergency management. These standards focus heavily on the duty of care inherent in the practice of emergency management and seek to clearly delineate expected professional behaviors. These standards may reach beyond organizational or jurisdictional policies, requirements, or laws; conversely, organizational or jurisdictional policies, requirements, or laws may issue more stringent standards. These standards
should be viewed as universal baseline expectations for all emergency management professionals.

<u>Responsibility to Affected Populations</u>
- STANDARD 1: Emergency management professionals recognize that diversity in needs exist and work to provide services without discrimination or preference.
- STANDARD 2: Emergency management use their expertise to communicate clearly, effectively, and appropriately regarding risks.
- STANDARD 3: Emergency management professionals collaborate with stakeholders to understand vulnerabilities, exposures, threats, and the unique characteristics of communities in determining risk reduction measures.
- STANDARD 4: Emergency management professionals advance the development and implementation of programs, plans, strategies, and initiatives to support life safety, reduce or eliminate damage to property and the environment, and support quality of life.

<u>Responsibility to the Partners, Stakeholders, and Public</u>
- STANDARD 5: Emergency management professionals create and maintain robust, effective relationships with a wide variety of partners.
- STANDARD 6: Emergency management professionals are aware of and operate within applicable laws and regulations.

- STANDARD 7: Emergency management professionals educate, inform, and promote change in programs, policies, regulations, and laws that conflict with the professional and effective practice of emergency management.
- STANDARD 8: Emergency management professionals accurately represent their qualifications.
- STANDARD 9: Emergency management professionals support and guide evidence-based choices and actions by clearly communicating the adverse impacts of hazards and threats based on scientific evidence.
- STANDARD 10: Emergency management professionals stay informed about new research, practice standards, relevant tools, and technologies.
- STANDARD 11: Emergency management professionals remain current on issues that affect public risk.
- STANDARD 12: Emergency management professionals do not engage in or endorse abusive, harassing, or hostile professional relationships.
- STANDARD 13: Emergency management professionals make sound fiscal decisions that support effective practice and the stewardship of resources.

Responsibility to the Environment
- STANDARD 14: Emergency management professionals understand the interconnectedness, interdependence, and sensitivities between the human, built, cyber, and natural environments.
- STANDARD 15: Emergency management professionals seek to protect the natural environment from harm and, where practical, nurture its recovery.

Responsibility to Colleagues
- STANDARD 16: Emergency management professionals support and assist other professionals in meeting and elevating emergency management practice.
- STANDARD 17: Emergency management professionals respond appropriately to unethical and problematic behavior of their colleagues.

Responsibility to Employers
- STANDARD 18: Emergency management professionals take direction from employers without deviating from ethical standards.
- STANDARD 19: Emergency management professionals have a duty to provide employers with all available relevant facts, data, and resources so that they are able make informed decisions.
- STANDARD 20: Emergency management professionals, whether in formal or informal leadership roles, have an obligation to model and support ethical decision-making and

to help create an organizational culture that promotes and encourages professional behavior.

Responsibility to the Profession
- STANDARD 21: Emergency management professionals have a duty to further the standing of the profession through their words, behaviors, and actions.
- STANDARD 22: Emergency management professionals have an obligation to advocate for a representative and diverse profession.
- STANDARD 23: Emergency management professionals promote the continuing development and improvement of their profession.
- STANDARD 24: Emergency management professionals support and assist emergency management students in their learning and career development, including opportunities to engage in relevant internships and practicums, participate in training and practice activities, and contribute to meaningful work projects and initiatives.

Responsibility to Self
- STANDARD 25: Emergency management professionals have a commitment to lifelong learning and to continually advance their knowledge and skills to serve their community and the profession.
- STANDARD 26: Emergency management professionals recognize how their own cultural and social backgrounds, beliefs, values, and biases may affect competent and just service, and strive to make proactive positive changes for the benefit of their constituents.
- STANDARD 27: Emergency management professionals are mindful of the ways in which stress can affect their health and well-being and take appropriate self-care measures.
- STANDARD 28: Emergency management professionals practice continual self-reflection focused on professional growth and development.

Appendices
- Appendix A: Definitional Framing of Select Terms
- Appendix B: Behavioral Anchors
- Appendix C: Ethics in Action
- Appendix D: Ethical Decision-making Process

Appendix A: Definitional Framing of Select Terms (under revision)

- *Discrimination*: The practice of unfairly treating a person or group differently from other people or groups of people.
- *Diversity:* The practice or quality of including or involving people from a range of different social and ethnic backgrounds and of different genders, sexual orientations, etc. Duty: A moral or legal obligation.
- *Emergency management (discipline):* The study of how human beings interact and cope with hazards, vulnerabilities, and associated events. The discipline focusses its study on how humans cope with hazard events through disaster risk reduction and the functional areas of preparedness, response, recovery, and mitigation.
- *Emergency management (profession):* Emergency management is the managerial function charged with creating the framework within which communities reduce vulnerability to hazards and cope with disasters (FEMA, Principles of Emergency Management, 2007).
- *Emergency management professionals:* Those engaged in the professional practice of emergency management.
- *Employer:* A person, company, or organization that employs people.
- *Equity:* Recognition that each person has different circumstances and allocating the exact resources and opportunities needed to reach an equal outcome.
- *Equitable:* Fair and just treatment of all concerned.
- Public risk: Possible loss, damage, or threat from hazards that affect the public.
- *Qualifications:* Special skills, knowledge, or abilities that make someone suitable for emergency
- management practice.
- *Quality of life:* Maintaining a standard of health, comfort, and access to services and resources by individuals or groups.
- *Risk reduction:* Reduction of the likelihood that a hazard will occur or the extent of its impact.
- *Scientific evidence:* Information gathered from scientific research.
- *Stakeholder:* Any individual, group, or government entity that has something to gain or lose from the creation of, interaction with, or coping with hazards, risks, vulnerabilities, and associated events.

Appendix B: Behavioral Anchors

Excerpted from: The Next Generation Core Competencies for Emergency Management Professionals: Handbook of Behavioral Anchors and Key Actions for Measurement, August 2017

- Behavioral Anchor 1. Respect: Actualizes honoring of individuals and groups of people by promoting dignity, diversity, and the rights of others; recognizes and respects the weight of their own actions as they work in communities.
- Behavioral Anchor 2. Veracity: Demonstrates truthfulness and accuracy of facts, and abstains from misrepresentation in all situations.
- Behavioral Anchor 3. Justice: Embodies a sense of obligation to the common good and treats others equitably and fairly; honors the rights of all species (present and future) when making decisions regarding the distribution of resources.
- Behavioral Anchor 4. Integrity: Displays consistency between belief and action in all arenas of life.
- Behavioral Anchor 5. Service: Acts to help others; is altruistically motivated. Puts others first, operating beyond the ego.
- Behavioral Anchor 6. Duty to protect: Considers the moral obligation to avert harm (both present and future) and works toward a common good; facilitates community building, cognizant that all actions have consequences affecting people and performance.
- Behavioral Anchor 7. Integrates ethical principles within stakeholder discourse: Guides ethical decision making across multiple stakeholders, who have varying interests, to derive public value.

Appendix C: Ethics in Action
(Under development)

Appendix D: Ethical Decision-Making Process

When faced with an ethical dilemma there is generally no one correct answer. In addressing these dilemmas, a transparent, inclusive, and effective decision-making process should be used to arrive at an equitable outcome based on ethical reasoning.

Decision-making Process for Ethical Dilemmas	
Context	<ul><li>Know the facts of the case and antecedents.</li><li>Know the expectations of those involved.</li><li>Be aware of social and political pressures on decision-makers and stakeholders.</li></ul>
Nature of the decision-maker	<ul><li>What are the biases and values of the decision-maker?</li><li>What knowledge do they have of ethics and relevant codes?</li><li>What relevant experience do they have?</li><li>What is their character like?</li></ul>
Recognition of the problem as ethical	<ul><li>To what extent does the situation evoke ethical concerns?</li><li>To what extent does the situation evoke personal and cultural values?</li><li>Apply the following three intuitive tests:<ul><li>The pillow test - would your decision allow you to sleep at night?</li><li>The child test - what would you tell your child to do?</li><li>The media test – would you want your decision to be in the public view?</li></ul></li></ul>
Problem clarification	<ul><li>Identify relevant rights, duties, responsibilities, and cultural norms/values.</li><li>Identify pressures on decision-makers and stakeholders.</li><li>Identify other relevant information needed to clarify the situation and possible actions.</li></ul>
Action identification and evaluation	<ul><li>Generate action possibilities<ul><li>Determine the consequences of the various actions.</li><li>Examine the rights, duties, norms, and values associated with the various actions.</li><li>Develop an initial justification for each possibility.</li></ul></li><li>Assess the justifications<ul><li>Is the approach being used in a comprehensive and logical way?</li><li>Is the argument consistent?</li><li>Are all ethical concerns identified?</li><li>Is there moral self-awareness?</li></ul></li></ul>
Choice of actions and implantation	<ul><li>Consider which action choice or combination of choices is best defended by ethical arguments.</li><li>Identify factors that might impede a chosen ethical action.</li><li>Consider how those impediments might be overcome.</li><li>Eliminate impediments where possible and implement ethical actions.</li></ul>

11.7　Endnotes

[1] International Association of Emergency Managers (IAEM). (2020). *IAEM code of ethics and professional conduct.* http://www.iaem.com/page.cfm?p=about/code-of-ethics

[2] Porter, E. S. (1901). *Kansas Saloon Smashers* [Film]. Black Maria. https://commons.wikimedia.org/wiki/File:Kansas_Saloon_Smashers.jpg

[3] (Albert Schweitzer, n.d.), in Wikipedia, https://en.wikiquote.org/wiki/Albert_Schweitzer#/media/File:Portrait_of_A._Schweitzer_Wellcome_L0004769.jpg

[4] Halevi, S. (2012). [Image of two fragments of the Dead Sea Scrolls] [Photograph]. Israel Antiques Authority. https://www.deadseascrolls.org.il/explore-the-archive/image/B-298337

[5] (Pirate Code of Conduct, n.d.). http://www.elizabethan-era.org.uk/pirate-code-conduct.htm

[6] (Bartholomew Roberts n.d.), in Wikipedia, https://en.wikipedia.org/wiki/Bartholomew_Roberts#/media/File:Bartholomew_Roberts.jpg

[7] Nagy, G. (2018). The Oath of the Ephebes as a symbol of democracy—and of environmentalism, Classical Inquiries, https://classical-inquiries.chs.harvard.edu/the-oath-of-the-ephebes-as-a-symbol-of-democracy-and-of-environmentalism/

[8] Pettifor, J. L. (2007). Are professional codes of ethics relevant for multicultural counselling? *Canadian Journal of Counselling and Psychotherapy/Revue canadienne de counseling et de psychothérapie, 35*(1), 26-35.

[9] Widen, W. H. (2003). Enron at the Margin. *The Business Lawyer*, 961-1002.

[10] Widen, W. H. (2003). Enron at the Margin. *The Business Lawyer*, 961-1002

[11] Widen, W. H. (2003). Enron at the Margin. *The Business Lawyer*, 961-1002

[12] Hippocrates. (2002). *The Hippocratic Oath* (M. North, Trans,). National Library of Medicine, 2002. (Original work published 5th century BC)

[13] Pontius, P. (1638). [Portrait of Hippocrates, sculpted bust] [Engraving]. Wellcome Collection. https://wellcomecollection.org/works/vmwkbj7u

[14] LRN. (2006). *The impact of codes of conduct on corporate culture: Measuring the immeasurable.* https://assets.hcca-info.org/Portals/0/PDFs/Resources/library/ImpactCodesConduct_LRN.pdf

[15] LRN. (2006). *The impact of codes of conduct on corporate culture: Measuring the immeasurable.* https://assets.hcca-info.org/Portals/0/PDFs/Resources/library/ImpactCodesConduct_LRN.pdf

[16] LRN. (2006). *The impact of codes of conduct on corporate culture: Measuring the immeasurable.* https://assets.hcca-info.org/Portals/0/PDFs/Resources/library/ImpactCodesConduct_LRN.pdf

[17] LRN. (2006). *The impact of codes of conduct on corporate culture: Measuring the immeasurable.* https://assets.hcca-info.org/Portals/0/PDFs/Resources/library/ImpactCodesConduct_LRN.pdf

[18] Gilman, S. C. (2005). *Ethics codes and codes of conduct as tools for promoting an ethical and professional public service: Comparative successes and lessons.* PREM, the World Bank. https://www.oecd.org/mena/governance/35521418.pdf

[19] Gilman, S. C. (2005). *Ethics codes and codes of conduct as tools for promoting an ethical and professional public service: Comparative successes and lessons.* PREM, the World Bank. https://www.oecd.org/mena/governance/35521418.pdf

[20] International Association of Emergency Managers (IAEM). (2020). *IAEM code of ethics and professional conduct.* Code of Ethics. Source: https://www.iaem.org/About/Code-of-Ethics

CHAPTER 12: EASTERN APPROACHES TO ETHICS

Peter Timmerman, June 2020

"Disaster could be called a crash course in Buddhist principles of compassion for all beings, of non-attachment, of abandoning the illusion of one's sense of separateness, of being fully present, of awareness of ephemerality, and of fearlessness or at least aplomb in the face of uncertainty."
- Rebecca Solnit, A Paradise Built in Hell, p. 118.

"A Zen master's life could be said to be so many years of one wrong thing after another, one continuous mistake (shoshaku jushaku)."
- Shunryu Suzuki, Zen Mind, Beginner's Mind, p.39.

Contents

12.1 Introduction

There is no universal "non-Western" culture covering both pre-literate cultures and the "high civilizations", so this chapter selectively addresses some general themes that appear in various significant places, and primarily draws on traditional "high civilization" articulations from Japan, China, and India. It is important to recognize, however, that in much of South, East, and Southeast Asia, there is a diverse and complex weave of multiple forms of religious belief and practice, including traditional folk religions, local customs, plus historic waves of Buddhism, Islam, and Christianity, as well as the increasing spread of modern/capitalist influences.

Until very recently, three central structural devices of Western culture were missing from other world cultures: Monotheism; goal-directed history; and a primarily justice-based sense of natural law. All three of these were shaped or influenced by the central roles played by Judaism and Christianity in the rise towards the modern world. Not only does the absence of these narrative touchstones underscore the vast diversity of Eastern religious traditions (internally and externally), but they allowed for different responses to the natural world, and by extension to the etiology of disasters. Explanations of the dynamics of the world and humanity's place in it generate responses that are sometimes very similar to Western approaches — all human beings face similar vulnerabilities — but often stress quite different facets of experience and "meaning making". "Meaning making" is one of the signal roles that religions play before, during, and after disasters, though in the contemporary world their role and influence can be hard to tease out or measure.[i]

12.2 Buddhist Ethics: Impermanence

One example for many. Schoolchildren in Japan are required to read <u>Hojoki</u> (Hermit's hut) a famous 13th century meditation on disasters.[ii] The hermit, a Buddhist monk, meditates on a wide range of catastrophes, characteristic of Japan's notorious vulnerability to earthquakes, tsunamis, and devastating fires. His overarching theme is of the evanescence of all things, of how everything and all of our selves are temporary. To learn to live with that, with wisdom and compassion, is essential in a world without a fixed essential of anything. Ours is a transient, fragile "bubble" life.[iii]

This characterizes one major ethical framework in Eastern thought, Buddhist ethics. Buddhist ethics derive from the teachings of the Buddha, who lived in the 5-6 century B.C.E. in northern India, and whose teachings spread through South and SouthEast Asia, and eventually migrated to China, Korea, and Japan. Central to his teaching is the discovery he made through deep meditation, that, contrary to the core belief of other available world views, there is no such thing as a permanent self, no fixed soul, and by extension, no permanence anywhere. There are no permanent selves, worlds or gods. If so, then how is one to live?

Human beings are taught in Buddhism, by various practices, to develop a deep perception of how things are, and to consider what ethics follow from them — more or less generating an ethic on how to live from the experience of being inside phenomena, not as if experiencing life from the outside, or being ruled by an external god. Among the then internally generated explanations for the human world we see around us is the notion of **karma** — that our current existence depends on our previous actions in this and in other lifetimes (if we can penetrate back to those other lifetimes) that leave influential traces (pollutions), on what seems to be our being. Again, this is different than the belief that an outside god or gods is punishing or rewarding us.

Figure 12.1: Buddha's statue near Belum Caves, Andhra Pradesh India.[iv]

In sometimes confusing contrast to this approach, early Hinduism — against which the Buddha proclaimed his teachings — believed in a strong self (an **atman**), at least one supreme god (**Brahman**), and a deterministic karmic system.[v] The early Hindu version of things promoted as its major ethical framework (slightly more akin to familiar Western themes), the deep search for an ensouled self that ultimately embraces the great Self of the universe. The difference (as mentioned at the outset) is that Hinduism is a very baggy religious tradition, and there are endless Hindu versions of this search, with endless variations on who or what is worshipped as the supreme god or goddess or spiritual principle. Hinduism is thus a very centrifugal religion — the sacred may be diversely embodied or enshrined. The most famous Hindu ethicist of modern times, Mahatma Gandhi, was influenced at various times in his life by Jain teachings, a deep love of Krishna, the teachings of the Buddha, the Bengali worship of the goddess Kali, and even elements of Christianity.

12.3 Karma and Justice

A brief digression on karma at this point is important, since it opens up the discussion towards a very significant difference between the ethical realm of East and West. A central (often underplayed) element of attempting to understand and respond to disasters is the need for an explanation of "Why me?" or "Why this or that?" This involves (potentially) both attempts at physical explanations, and/or spiritual explanations so as to enable a sense of meaning to emerge in our lives. The Western tradition, as mentioned, is strongly influenced by a monotheistic frame, and is further influenced by a particular kind of judicial analysis derived from the Romans. Together they have created, in the Western tradition, a deep sense of concern over justice — Who is to blame, Whom do I prosecute, Who do I go to (which High Court) for wrong to be made right, When is the Last Judgement going to come to sort the sheep from the goats? This can be characterised as a search for an external judge or set of fixed laws to which one can appeal.

Karma is one of the ways in which Indian traditions have attempted something different: as already mentioned, it is an internal explanation — without appeal to a God — for the injustices of the world. **Karma** originally derives (in very early Hinduism, i.e. 1000 B.C.E. or earlier) from the concept of mistakes made in public sacrifices. In tribal India — as elsewhere — mass public religious rituals (e.g. sacrifices) were designed to influence the gods by mimicking and matching the patterns of the cosmos.[vi] These fundamental patterns are the cosmic **dharma** or rules of the game (A different example might be the rituals the Navaho use in the American Southwest to bring rain, or to ensure that the sun comes up every morning). If the ritual is performed wrongly, for instance if the priest trips and falls during the service, then **karma** is generated, a trace or smear of pollution. In later Hinduism, Jainism, and Buddhism, as urban life developed and public rituals became private, this public **karma** became associated with personal **karma** — my mistakes pollute and influence my subsequent behaviour. My personal **dharma**, my own microcosmic path through life, is karmically influenced, and as a miniature version of the previous public ritual, it participates in the cosmic **dharma**, influencing its path. One's personal **dharma** — in Hinduism — is reciprocally influenced by where one is in the social order (traditionally, one's caste). Without going into details about caste, a man who was born into the caste of warriors (a **kshatriya**) fulfills his **dharma** by following the warrior path; as in their separate castes does a priest, a merchant, and a manual laborer. This stratified social system is still widely influential in India (though officially banned).

12.4 Sewa, Sarvodaya, Tzu Chi

On the other hand, and on a more positive note, "selfless service" (**sewa**) is a widespread Hindu teaching, deriving ultimately from the scriptural <u>Bhagavad-Gita</u>, which proclaims such service as part of "**karma yoga**" — the selfless practice of one's **dharma** on behalf of the world (Patton, 2008). This ancient teaching has contemporary practical significance in disaster management. SEWA INTERNATIONAL is perhaps the most famous Hindu NGO, and it is based on this principle of selfless service. It has a worldwide network of volunteers engaged in everything from education, digital literacy campaigns, women's vocational work, support for tribal peoples, to (now) covid-19 relief. It began in 1993 as a disaster and humanitarian relief organization, networking among the globally widespread Indian Hindu community, and now has over a hundred thousand members. It has been prominent as a local relief agency in every major South Asian disaster over the last twenty years (but has also been involved in assisting in floods in places like Houston, Texas (<u>https://sewainternational.org/About-Us</u>).

A similarly spiritually based NGO, primarily Buddhist, blending Gandhian teachings with Buddhist precepts, is SARVODAYA SHRAMADANA ("The awakening of all"). Begun in 1957 by Dr. A. T. Ariyaratne at the village level in Sri Lanka, and devoted to the giving of work — irrigation, latrine building, school construction — as a practical, but still spiritual "gift" (**dana** in Buddhism has traditionally meant the gift of alms), it rapidly expanded and evolved, and became internationally prominent in peace work across the Buddhist/Tamil divide during the country's bitter Civil War. Since the 2004 tsunami, Sarvodaya has been a major actor in relief and rebuilding work throughout the affected areas in Sri Lanka (Macintosh, 2009); as well as the 2016 floods, the Easter Sunday 2019 Bombing, and now covid-19 responses (<u>https://www.sarvodaya.org/disaster-management-unit</u>).

An equally prominent Buddhist disaster relief organization is the Tzu Chi Foundation in Taiwan, begun by a nun in 1966, based on Buddhist precepts (slightly modified), originally funded with pennies donated from housewives, the funds going to medical clinics and the building of hospitals. It now has a membership of over 10 million people with chapters in 47 countries[vii]. It is most famous for being one of the few organizations based in Taiwan that has been able to bridge into Mainland China, due to its non-proselytizing stance, and a variety of its working principles, including what it calls "direct giving" — with no strings attached — in a number of disasters, including floods and earthquakes. Tzu Chi now works around the world (for example, it was strongly mobilized during Katrina, involving the contributing of millions of dollars and extensive volunteer assistance).[viii] Tzu Chi has, nevertheless, at its a core, Buddhist nuns and monks, surrounded by its global ring of thousands of volunteers.

12.5 The Laws of Dharma and The Tao

Returning to foundational theory, we come upon another great difference, already alluded to, between Western and Eastern approaches; that is, different ways of conceiving of "law" in the context of nature. One core aspect of modernity has been the gradual loss of belief in a moral law woven through the universe. This is due primarily to the ebbing of Christianity. The version of moral law that was prevalent for 1000 years in the West was like a moral law of gravity — the physical world (like the moral world) followed moral principles derived from God's designs. Failure to follow them entailed punishment (often institutional). We know that there is a strong tendency in traditional cultures to assign blame for disasters to transgressions on earth that have caused the gods to punish: in the Western context this tendency became codified and crystallized into the commandments, the ultimate judgement of God, and assignment to heaven or hell in an afterlife.

Figure 12.2: Chinese character for the word Tao

In Eastern traditions, the core idea of "natural law" was different (though many of its mythologies certainly pictured afterlives in various heavens and hells). Laws were not judicial but constitutive. That is, unlike laws in a courtroom — if we think of the universe as a courtroom — these other traditions see laws as being like the rules of basketball or chess. You needed to learn the rules in order to play the game, and to excel in a sport or craft. You need to get a "feel" for things.

This alternative approach has many names, including (as already discussed) **dharma;** and, in China, it is called the **Tao**. This is "a Way" model. You learn the Way by "getting that feel" for how things work, especially things that work well. To achieve this "feel for things" requires great discipline, and is not just "letting it all hang out". We can experience a taste of this when, in a sport or craft, we have become so practiced that sometimes things beyond our expected self-capacity take over and produce special outcomes. Often this is described as our unconscious taking over from our more limited conscious mind — for Taoists, what takes over is more cosmic. It is the Way, the **Tao**.[ix]

What all this means for disaster ethics is that if we can imagine a disaster manager following the Way, she would thus enter into a disaster seeking or being already aware of an initial frame of how things ordinarily "go", and how they have become disrupted, and through her skills and understanding she eventually may come to a sense of what will restore the proper flow of things (sometimes called **ch'i** — the natural energy that, if unblocked, courses through everything). This process is what the Chinese call **wu wei** or "non-action" — a watching to understand before (and during) the heading out into activity. Precipitous activity is assumed to be more than likely a problem, rather than a solution. So it is not an advocacy of not doing anything, but more of a careful wariness before possibly interfering foolishly. Alternatively, a Taoist approach is one in which we are familiar with our own failings and limitations — we get in our own way — and we need to eliminate or minimize them if we are to act appropriately.

Three examples of Eastern approaches follow: a Chinese philosophical theory; a Japanese response to the Fukushima event in 2012; and a folk case from Indonesia.

12.6 Chinese Ethics

A different concept from the **Tao** was also present in China, which involved an equally influential frame, that of Confucianism— Confucian ethics (derived from the Analects, a collection of sayings from the master) depends on an obedience to a set of rules of common conduct, ranging all the way from the emperor to the ordinary person[x,xi] Corruption of these rules — which include performance of rituals, appropriate language, and familial (and ancestral) forms of respect — at any level is dangerous, and may threaten the whole cultural apparatus. It is very akin to "virtue ethics" — sometimes referred to as **shengsheng** 生生 (life generation), a kind of self-responsibility in all beings, and thus tends to result in an ethic that is private and day-to-day, rather than hierarchical. It is worth noting that in a comparative study of disaster response to the Padang City earthquake in Indonesia in 2009, the Muslim and Christian organizations, nationally and internationally, strongly supported their members, while the local

Confucian Chinese fended for themselves, their families, and their near neighbours. But, on the other hand, a study of the influence of Confucianism on South Korea's emergency response stressed that on a national scale a strong command-and-control theme can emerge that weaves together paternalism, family ties, and forms of ritual.[xii] Context is everything.

Figure 12.3: Portrait of Confucius, giving a Lecture, 8th Century.[xiii]

A famous version of a Confucian ethic on a national (or global) scale is the historical so-called "Mandate of Heaven" which supports or overthrows the legitimacy of an emperor or a government. In the Han Dynasty (roughly 200 B.C.E. to 200 A.D.), an intellectual named Dong Zhongshu proposed a theory called "Tien Ren Gan Ying" which attributed natural disasters to the cultural failings of the emperor and other incompetents — from whom the "mandate" would be withdrawn. He states:

> Among substances between the heaven and the earth, there are abnormal changes, which are considered to be anomalies. In contrast to anomalies, the lesser ones are recognized as disasters. It is disasters that regularly occur first, followed by anomalies. Disasters are reprimands from Heaven while anomalies are Heaven's intimidation. If the sovereign still had not realized his faults after Heaven reprimanded him, Heaven would frighten him with awe. This is what the poem says: "to regard Heaven with reverence for its prestige." The misgovernment of the state is utterly at the root of disasters and anomalies. When the signs of misgovernment begin to appear, Heaven would warn, as well as reprimand, the sovereign through disasters and calamities...."[xiv]

This claim has haunted Chinese governments ever since. In particular, the prestige of dam building goes even further back, to the ideal emperor Yu, who founded the Xia dynasty (2123-2025 B.C.E.) when he himself earned the kingdom from his beginnings as a lowly working dam and flood-control builder. The much later Communist regime of Mao Tse-Tung (1949-1976 A.D.) prided itself as well on its dam building as a symbol of its contemporary power and prestige, but hearkening back to the ancient cultural roots. After swimming across the Yangtze River in 1958, Mao penned a poem about the regime's obsession with dams: *Great plans are being made/ Walls of stone will stand upstream to the* west *...The mountain goddess if she is still there/ Will marvel at a world so changed.*" While the prevention of flooding has saved many lives, the cost in lives from forced dam building has also been tremendous (and often hushed up).[xv] Certainly, the mass restructuring of the Chinese environment, and the impacts on its up- and downstream neighbours cast a big question mark over any current claims concerning a special Chinese reverence for nature.

12.7 Japan: Buddhism and Fukushima

On March 11, 2011, an earthquake off the northeast coast of Japan set in motion a massive tsunami that inundated a nuclear power plant in Fukushima. Overall, at least 16,000 people were killed, and the uncertain status of the consequences of the failed nuclear plant meant that at least 100,000 people were dislocated, many permanently.[xvi,xvii] The northeast area, Tohoku region, somewhat built up, but mostly rural in character, was devastated.

The main religious tradition of the area, Buddhism, was initially crippled — many temples were inundated and citizens missing — but then rose to the occasion.[xviii] The Buddhist monks and priests housed and fed refugees, comforted survivors, and organized document centres. In Japan, the Buddhist tradition is strongly centred around the rituals of death and dying, and in the Fukushima situation many bodies and cemeteries were swept away. Cremation is a standard practice, and mass cremations were undertaken — so many in fact that, because the harbours were clogged, the lack of available fuel for cremations became an issue.[xix]

Various Buddhist figures have spoken of their experiences of, and reflections on the response to the disaster, stressing a reverence for life, a recognition that the disaster is a powerful example of the passing of life, and their own role in the situation. Rev. Toku-un Tanaka (from a temple 17 kilometers from the nuclear reactors) reported:

> "I knew what was right in my mind, but when you actually go there, you can't do such things. When I would visit with parishioners, they would serve me tea and say, 'Reverend, do come by more often,'; 'Sure,' I said, while in my mind I was thinking: 'This water is probably contaminated.' But I am a Buddhist priest, so I should drink it.'.[xx]

Reverend Masazumi Shojun Okano said:

> 'In Buddhist-based activities of helping others, we can certainly discover the spiritual meaning of generosity or giving (***dana/fuse***). Giving is the practice of refining one's own mind and it is done for one's own spiritual benefit. The attempt to help others may end up in failure, or others may not appreciate what you have done and may even criticize you. These are the times when we must remember that we are engaged in refining our mind. At the same time, however, we must not forget that the final goal is to help the disaster victims become re-energised, self-reliant, and happy.'.[xxi]

In contrast to familiar official Western disaster responses, the Soto Zen sect of Buddhism developed an alternative model of the famous traditional formal tea ceremony, **gyocha** — a very private, elite, meeting of priest and practitioner. The new adopted practice was sparked by a comment from a parishioner during a 2004 earthquake, who said to a priest, "We are thankful to receive the hot meal, but as you are a Buddhist priest, we victims would like you to listen deeply to our stories." This idea of deep listening has been transformed into tea sessions at places like evacuation centres, where priests can sit down with ordinary people in a mixture of formal and informal practice, listen and respond. **Gyocha** has been expanded and developed, and has become widespread over the past few years as an example of a new form of Buddhist practice in support of its underlying ethics.[xxii]

12.8 Indonesian Approaches

As noted above, there can be multiple layers at work in religious responses to disaster, and a still strong layer (or foundation) found all over the world is folk religion and folk practice. To tackle this in any responsible way is the provenance of anthropology, so only a brief reference is made here to two examples from Indonesia. Though Indonesia is now mostly Muslim, with a substantial Christian and smaller Buddhist populations, there are islands and pockets of folk religions throughout the region.

For example, there was a vast mudflow volcano (dubbed Lapindo) on the island of East Java after the gas drilling company (Lapindo Brantas) that was suspected as having triggered the slow eruption (there was also an earthquake at the time the mudflow began in 2006 which may have been the actual cause). There were dozens of deaths, many related illnesses, and the displacement of many thousands of people. The response was complicated by the inability to assign absolute final responsibility for the ongoing catastrophe.[xxiii]

In November 2006, a goat (and cows and chickens) were sacrificed to the volcano by Sumatran mystics who had gathered to consider what to do as their disaster response. In his extensive discussion of this disaster, Philip Drake cites various signs that people used to try and understand what was going on, both mystical and pragmatic. Perhaps the most ironic in this context was the general view that "the higher the position of officials at the site, the higher the explosions of mud."[xxiv]

In May 2006, an earthquake struck elsewhere on Java, killing at least 6,000 people. To quote Judith Schlele, an anthropologist who conducted extensive research before and after the event:

> "Although everybody knows that the disaster was the result of tectonic activity, this knowledge co-exists with religious beliefs in manifold ways....The spirits are said to have sent the disaster to remind the Javanese — and most importantly the Sultan and other people in power — of their traditions.".[xxv]

The religious beliefs centred around the goddess of the South Sea (Ratu Kidul) and her role in binding together the rulers and the ruled in the community. The thrust of concern was the commitment of the current Sultan to modernity — he ignored the myths of the region — and the general complementary loss of traditional practices. The linking of the loss of traditional values has become a standard alternative explanation throughout Indonesia for the sequence of earthquakes, tsunamis, and volcanos. Schelele reports on a national event during the Islamic New Year of 2008, where government officials, mystics, "and royal families from 104 kingdoms across the archipelago" gathered together in a series of rituals to protect the country against future disasters. She cites the Chair of the Indonesia Royal Palace Forum, the King of Badung in Bali, who said in the Jakarta Post, "The recent spree of natural disasters is the result of our collective wrongdoings. This very moment is the right time to look back and make promises not to repeat what we have done.".[xxvi]

Figure 12.4. An artwork depicting Kanjeng Ratu Kidul by Gunawan Kartapranata[xxvii]

This kind of explanation, from the Indonesia context, could be repeated in other places and other times worldwide.

12.9 Conclusion

This chapter has barely scratched the surface of the complexity of the diverse array of ethical themes and practices of a particular part of the non-Western world; especially when these are now strongly affected by the waves of Western modernization that have also inundated the region and are prominent in all official government and responsible emergency management systems. Nevertheless, the local and traditional ways of life still persist and colour and shape response and relief efforts.

Beyond the well-known ethical teachings discussed in this chapter, it is worth closing by pointing out that unmentioned here are the beliefs and practices of many tribal and marginalized peoples found all over Asia. They, like indigenous peoples all over the world, are under massive pressure from a myriad of encroaching threats — multiple disasters to whole ways of life. The term "ways of life" signifies that there may be no single ethic or list of values that can be extracted from the rich lives, different languages, and community experiences of a tribe or people — what is right is what they do in their own way. This is one reason why the expropriation or other forced removal of tribes and peoples from their lands can be so devastating, not just in terms of lives lost or maimed, but because for many of these tribes and peoples, their ways of life are also rooted in the specific places where they live. The places can be where the ways of life are learned and listened to. To uproot them is literally to uproot them, multiplying the potential vulnerabilities of displacement. The Eastern world is not exempt from the phenomenon of expropriation, mass migration, and the plight of refugees.

12.10 Endnotes

[i] Park, C. L. (2015). "Meaning Making in the Context of Disasters", *Journal of Clinical Psychology,* Vol. 72(12), pp. 1234-1246.

[ii] No Chomei, K. (2013). Hojoki (trans. M. Stavros) Toronto: Penguin Classics.

[iii] Chomei (1998). *Hojoki: Visions of a Torn World.* (trans. Hoffmann, M.). Berkeley, Calf.: Stone Bridge Press.

[iv] Purshi (2008). Wikipedia, Creative Commons Attribution-Share Alike 3.0 Unported license. https://en.wikipedia.org/wiki/List_of_writers_on_Buddhism#/media/File:Buddha's_statue_near_Belum_Caves_Andhra_Pradesh_India.jpg

[v] Adamson, P.and Jonardon, G. (2020). *Classical Indian Philosophy.* Oxford: University Press

[vi] Adamson, P.and Jonardon, G. (2020). *Classical Indian Philosophy.* Oxford: University Press

[vii] Wikipedia (n.d.). Tzu Chi, https://en.wikipedia.org/wiki/Tzu_Chi

[viii] Relief Web/Tzu Chi Foundation. (2005). *"Tzu Chi volunteers assist Katrina evacuees in Houston"*, (Sept).

https://reliefweb.int/report/united-states-america/usa-tzu-chi-volunteers-assist-katrina-evacuees-houston

[ix] Wei-Ming, Tu. (1985). *Confucian Thought: Selfhood as Creative Transformation.* Albany: NY: SUNY Press.

[x] Wei-Ming, Tu. (1985). *Confucian Thought: Selfhood as Creative Transformation.* Albany: NY: SUNY Press.

[xi] Ames, R.T. and Rosemont, H.Jr. (trans.) (1998). *The Analects of Confucius.* New York, NY: Random House/Ballantine Books.

[xii] Ha, Kyoo-Man (2018). "The Role of Confucianism in South Korea's Emergency Management System," Disasters, Vol. 42 (4), pp. 804-822.

[xiii] Wikipedia (n.d.). https://simple.wikipedia.org/wiki/Confucianism#/media/File:Confucius_02.png

[xiv] Yang, X. (2016). *"The Principle of Dong Zhongshu's Omen Discourse and Wang Chong's Criticism of Heaven's Reprimand in the Chapter 'Qian Gao' 譴告"*. Masters thesis. Fayetteville, Arkansas, USA: University of Arkansas

[xv] Higginbottom, J. (2019). *"230,000 died in a dam collapse that China kept secret for years."* https://www.ozy.com/true-and-stories/230000-died-in-a-dam-collapse-that-china-kept-secret-for-years/91699/.

[xvi] Graf, T. and Jakob, M. (2012). "Souls of Zen," (documentary). https://www.youtube.com/watch?v=x3oAY5bher0&feature=emb_logo

[xvii] Lochbaum, D.A. et al. (2014). Fukushima: The Story of a Nuclear Disaster. New York, NY: New Press/Union of Concerned Scientists.

[xviii] Graf, T. and Montrasio, J. (2012). "Souls of Zen," (documentary). https://www.youtube.com/watch?v=x3oAY5bher0&feature=emb_logo

[xix] Graf, T. and Montrasio, J. (2012). "Souls of Zen," (documentary). https://www.youtube.com/watch?v=x3oAY5bher0&feature=emb_logo

[xx] Tanaka, T. (2012). *"My Struggle to Revive the Cultural and Natural Heritage of Soma in Fukushima"*, in Graf and Montrasio, pp. 19-25.

[xxi] Okano, M.S. (2012). *"Considering the Relation between Restoration and Co-Existence"*, in Graf and Montrasio, pp. 55-60.

[xxii] Kyuma, T. (2012). "The Deep Listening *Gyocha* Volunteer Activities of the Soto Zen Youth Association", in Graf and Montrasio, pp. 67-73.

[xxiii] Drake, P. (2017). *Indonesia and the Politics of Disaster: Power and Representation in Indonesia's Mud Volcano.* New York, NY: Routledge.

[xxiv] Drake, P. (2017). *Indonesia and the Politics of Disaster: Power and Representation in Indonesia's Mud Volcano.* New York, NY: Routledge.

[xxv] Schlele, J. (2010). "Anthropology of Religion: Disasters and the representations of traditions and modernity", *Religion, Vol. 40*, pp. 112-120.

[xxvi] Schlele, J. (2010). "Anthropology of Religion: Disasters and the representations of traditions and modernity", *Religion, Vol. 40*, pp. 112-120.

[xxvii] Wikipedia. https://commons.wikimedia.org/wiki/File:Kanjeng_Ratu_Kidul.jpg

CHAPTER 13: CONCLUDING THOUGHTS

"Compassion is the basis of morality."

Figure 13.1. Arthur Schopenhauer (1788–1860), philosopher

"Here is your country. Cherish these natural wonders, cherish the natural resources, cherish the history and romance as a sacred heritage, for your children and your children's children. Do not let selfish men or greedy interests skin your country of its beauty, its riches or its romance."

Figure 13.2. Theodore Roosevelt (1858–1919), conservationist, naturalist, and writer who served as the 26th president of the United States

"I believe this will be the central challenge—as ingenuity gaps widen the gulfs of wealth and power among us, we need imagination, metaphor and empathy more than ever, to help us remember each other's essential humanity."
Thomas Homer Dixon (1956-), professor and author

This book begins with the argument that ethics and morals are fundamentally important to the field of emergency management and the question "What is the right thing to do?" There is often no easy answer to this question, or even one answer that is clearly better than others. Ethical thinking is not about finding one correct answer, but about an inclusive, transparent decision-making process that incorporates ethical analysis along with explicit statements of assumptions and values.

The purpose of this book is to introduce students and practitioners of emergency management to the topic of ethics, and to provide a framework with which to use ethics in their profession. To accomplish this I included an overview of the primary ethical theories relevant to emergency management and addressed a number of relevant topics, including moral development, ethical risk assessment, the precautionary principle, blaming victims, duty to respond, land use planning, humanitarianism, lifeboat ethics, and a code of ethics for emergency management. This list is not exhaustive, but hopefully creates a base that students and professionals will be able to use in their decision-making.

In Chapter 1 several ethical theories were presented, each of which provides an important perspective. No one theory is sufficient to address all possible ethical and moral concerns, and therefore the notion of ethical plurality (using all the theories as they are relevant to the issue under consideration) is proposed, in order to balance virtues with duties and obligations, the greater good and other ethical perspectives. There is no objective formula that can be used to do this – context and subjective judgements are inevitable.

Chapter 2 on moral development looks at different stages or schema of development beginning with rudimentary ones related to the self and obeying rules, to post-conventional levels that incorporate abstract ethical principles in a broad social context. Moral foundations theory illustrates how different social groups, such as the political left and right, emphasize different moral foundations, suggesting that one group is not necessarily more moral than the other (in spite of how people feel) but rather gives different levels of importance to ingroup loyalty, purity and authority. Moral traps exist, which we should be aware of and avoid when possible, and ethics is an important component of leadership.

Chapter 3 takes a very critical view of the practice of risk assessment, noting that ethical analysis is largely absent. There is a long history of research on ethical decision-making, but very little of it has been incorporated into the theory and practice of risk assessment. This must change and a process for doing so is outlined in Chapter 3.3.

Chapter 4 on the precautionary principle shows how traditional risk analysis fails in situations where ambiguity is high, outcomes uncertain, cost-benefit analyses are problematical, causal chains are unclear, and outcomes are irreversible. These situations can lead to ruin, but do not lend themselves to quantitative analysis. A different philosophical approach is needed, which emphasizes wherein lies the burden of proof, who is vulnerable, and imbalances in power. The precautionary principle fills this gap and has the potential to prevent great harm. It must be used carefully and cautiously, however, since it is only valid under a particular set of conditions.

In Chapter 5 the issue of victim blaming is addressed. There may be times when victim blaming is valid, but it often serves dysfunctional or inimical purposes. It may be most harmful when used to shift responsibility from those who construct risk to victims. Generally, it should be avoided during and just following a disaster but may be constructive if it leads to the avoidance of risk creation during reconstruction (such as not living in high-risk zones). Blaming lies at the foundation of many disaster narratives and thus plays an important role in how we understand these kinds of events.

Chapter 6 on duty to respond notes that with very few exceptions (notably Hurricane Katrina in New Orleans) role abandonment has not been an issue. Surveys about how people might respond in scenarios that have not yet occurred, however, suggest that it could be a problem. Responders may be caught in an ethical dilemma with respect to duty to family versus obligations to their employer or the public. Emergency management organizations can mitigate this potential, and I argue have an obligation to do so.

Chapter 7 looks at the important topic of land use planning, one of the most important tools that can be used to reduce exposure to hazard. There is a strong tension between paternalism and libertarianism in this area, and different countries have taken very different approaches that greatly influence disaster impacts. Libertarian approaches result in greater exposure that inevitably creates wider social costs through the socialization of risk, but these costs must be balanced against the rights of individuals. Environmental ethics are relevant to land use planning and the rights of non-humans should factor into decision-making. For this to happen, since nature cannot advocate for itself, we must advocate for it. This will benefit the natural environment and ourselves since we are dependent upon it.

Chapter 8 addressed humanitarianism. There is empirical evidence that traditional humanitarian approaches that emphasize impartiality, neutrality, and short-term response have done little good in the long run in terms of preventing future disasters, thus not satisfying utilitarian ethical goals. A new humanitarianism approach has arisen that emphasizes social justice, which hopes to address the root causes of many disasters but that also creates new moral dilemmas. There are strong ethical arguments both for and against the two approaches and I conclude that context is critical; neither approach by themselves is sufficient.

Chapter 9 on lifeboat ethics forces us to think about who to save, when all cannot be saved. Questions such as "Are all lives of equal value?" or "How can one value a life?" are addressed and force emergency managers to confront their most basic values. These questions are important in disaster situations where capacity is overwhelmed. Lifeboat ethics is also an important metaphor for larger social issues such as those discussed by Garret Hardin. When applied to global issues the lifeboat metaphor has important limitations and other metaphors such as Spaceship Earth provide useful alternative perspectives.

Chapter 10 looks at three ethical issues – price gouging, disaster financial assistance (DFA), and pandemic planning. I conclude that arguments in favor of price gouging are weak and might only be valid in unusual circumstances where the greater good might be served by the free market approach. Disaster financial assistance from public funds is supported by utilitarian, deontological and virtue ethics approaches, but also creates moral hazard, which should be minimized to the degree that it does not sabotage DFA public policy. Pandemic planning is rife with moral dilemmas, and ethical considerations should be included in planning documents to a much greater degree than they have in the past.

Chapter 11 discussed what a Code of Ethics for emergency managers and emergency management organizations might look like. Codes should have elements that are both prescriptive and aspirational, and it is important that an EM Code of Ethics have both elements. There should be two intertwined codes, one for individual emergency managers and another for the organizations that employ them. If the field of emergency management is to become professionalized in ways that others have, then having a well-developed Code of Ethics is mandatory. This process is underway, being led by a FEMA SIG group, and a draft code has been developed.

Chapter 12 was written so that those of us growing up in Western cultures could be exposed to ethical perspectives based on Eastern cultures. It provides an opportunity to examine our taken-for-granted assumptions.

It is easy to fall into the habit of not thinking ethically, but rather rely upon intuition and the "way things are done" (both of which are very important, of course). This is especially true when the institutions people work for do not reinforce ethical thinking practices amongst their staff. Unfortunately, this can result in reproducing analyses and strategies that are biased and sometimes inadequate. I believe that far too often this is how we behave.

My sense is that the importance of ethics within the emergency management field is becoming increasingly recognized as being fundamental to our way of doing business, and that in the future ethical thinking will weave its way throughout our profession in a much more explicit fashion. Society is facing numerous difficult challenges, some of which are likely to greatly alter the world that we live in. Population growth, technological change, environmental degradation, emergent diseases, species extinction and climate change all create serious threats, some of which may be existential to our way of life. Any solution to these problems must incorporate an ethical and moral component if it is to be successful.

One way of thinking about the future is to look at the present state of the world and current trends and try to predict what will happen. In the long term (and perhaps even in the short term) this is an impossible task given the complex, chaotic nature of human society and its interrelationships with the natural world (for those who consider society-nature a false dichotomy, please forgive me). Another way of looking at this issue is to imagine a future that you want and recognize what pathways will lead to that outcome. This is a far more straightforward process. If you imagine a just world, then we must act justly. If you imagine a world that is environmentally healthy, then we must nurture and protect the environment. If you imagine a world where our children and children's children will thrive, then we must not act selfishly but rather accept that we have obligations towards them, and act upon those obligations. If you imagine a profession of emergency management that is trusted and respected, and that is effective in meeting the needs of society, then ethical thinking and moral actions must form the base of our professional practice.

The Starfish Thrower (Adapted from *The Star Thrower*[1])

One day, as was his habit, a wise old man was walking along his favorite beach, contemplating the mysteries of the universe. He noticed that the beach was littered with thousands of starfish that had been washed ashore by the previous night's storm surge. Saddened by the starfish tragedy, he thought deeply about the vagaries and impermanence of life. Before long he came across a child who was eagerly throwing the starfish back into the ocean, one by one.

The wise old man watched the child for a while and then said to him, "Child, there are thousands and thousands of starfish on this beach and only one of you. What difference can you really make?"

The child paused, picked up a starfish, gently tossed it back into the sea and said to the wise old man, "Sir, I made a difference to that one!"

The wise old man took a moment to reflect upon the value of ethical plurality, and then joined the child as they both tossed starfish back into the sea.

The future is uncertain, the problems our profession faces are complex, and our ability to prevent disasters challenging. And yet, we can throw starfish back into the sea.

Endnotes:

---

[1] Eiseley, L. C. (1979). *The star thrower*. Houghton Mifflin Harcourt.

Made in the USA
Monee, IL
03 August 2022

fa7992c4-2315-4859-bad4-c87a34f7406bR01